Understanding
Korean Christianity

Understanding Korean Christianity

Grassroot Perspectives on
Causes, Culture, and Responses

K. KALE YU

PICKWICK *Publications* · Eugene, Oregon

UNDERSTANDING KOREAN CHRISTIANITY
Grassroot Perspectives on Causes, Culture, and Responses

Pickwick Publications
An Imprint of Wipf and Stock Publishers
199 W. 8th Ave., Suite 3
Eugene, OR 97401

www.wipfandstock.com

PAPERBACK ISBN: 978-1-5326-9253-6
HARDCOVER ISBN: 978-1-5326-9254-3
EBOOK ISBN: 978-1-5326-9255-0

Cataloguing-in-Publication data:

Names: Yu, K. Kale, author.

Title: Understanding Korean Christianity : grassroots perspectives on causes, culture, and responses / K. Kale Yu.

Description: Eugene, OR: Pickwick Publications, 2019 | Includes bibliographical references and index.

Identifiers: ISBN 978-1-5326-9253-6 (paperback) | ISBN 978-1-5326-9254-3 (hardcover) | ISBN 978-1-5326-9255-0 (ebook)

Subjects: LCSH: Christianity—Korea—History | Korea—Religion | Protestant churches—Korea—History

Classification: BR1328 K9 2019 (print) | BR1328 (ebook)

Manufactured in the U.S.A.   OCTOBER 9, 2019

To
Julia

"I know. I was there. I saw the great void in your soul, and you saw mine."

—SEBASTIAN FAULKS IN *BIRDSONG*

Contents

List of Photos and Photo Acknowledgements

On the Cover (from the top):

1937, Sungjin Central Church in Central Hamkyung

1920-1929, Second Presbyterian Church in Sinuiju where Kyung Chik Han was removed as pastor in 1941 and imprisoned by the Japanese colonial government for refusing to worship the Japanese emperor

Billygraham.org: p.1; Korean Methodist Church and Institute: p.1; Openendedsocialstudies.com: p.1; University of Southern California (Korean Digital Archive): p.1; Princeton Theological Seminary (Samuel H. Moffett Korea Collection): p.1.

Acknowledgements

IN THE COURSE OF writing this book, the traditional Korean saying that "it is even easier for two people to move one sheet of paper [백지장도 맞들면 낫다]" has become particularly meaningful. The meaning of the saying is universal: many hands make light work and it aptly describes my experience. This book has been made possible thanks to the support, encouragement, and feedback I have received from many people, but most especially from my wife, Julia, who has been with me through all the ups and downs and encouraged me to press on. My special thanks are due to five mentors who guided and pushed me at different points in the process: Samuel H. Moffett, Andrew Walls, Douglas Sloan, Robbie McClintock, and Wm. Theodore de Bary. Warmest thanks are extended to the following for reading all or parts of this book and providing helpful commentary: Tom Hastings, Luther Oconer, Amos Yong, Jane Naomi Iwamura, Hyung-Jin Park, Peter Phan, Rebecca Kim, Daniel Shin, and anonymous readers. It goes without saying that the responsibility for any errors and shortcomings remains mine alone.

Grateful acknowledgement is also due to the helpfulness, good humor, and patience of archivists, librarians, and staff at the Methodist Archives at Drew University, Burke Missionary Research Archives and CV Starr Library at Columbia University, Samuel H. Moffett Collection at Princeton Theological Seminary, and Day Missions Library at Yale Divinity School. My continuing appreciation to numerous institutions while working on this book: Department of East Asian Languages and Cultures at Columbia University, Summer Wesley Seminar at Duke Divinity School, Princeton Theological Seminary, Nyack College, and High Point University. To my family, I can never adequately thank you enough for your patience and understanding of my self-imposed isolation to complete this book. Thanks finally to God for what has been a long journey.

Notes on Romanization and Translation

Korean words are rendered according to the Revised Romanization of Korea (RRK), the romanization system introduced by the South Korean government in July 2000. The RRK has become the romanization system used by the South Korean government in all official documents and translations, e.g. 2018 Pyeongchang Winter Olympics and 2018 Incheon World Tour Grand Finals. The RRK has many advantages such as the elimination of all diacritic signs, such as breve or acute marks over letters. For the general reader, the removal of diacritic signs enhances the reading experience and facilitates computer typing.

The Korean names of individuals have been transliterated according to the RRK system unless their names have their own unique or divergent orthography, such as Syngman Rhee. To maintain consistency in a book that covers Koreans and Korean Americans, Korean names are transliterated with last names last except for those names that are well-established with last names first, such as Kim Il-sung and Kim Gu.

Pyeongyang, 1900s. "Rally." Photo credit: Moffett Korea Collection.
Princeton Theological Seminary.

Pyeongyang, 1928. "Women's Bible Class." On the back of the photo: "800 country women—walked 5 to 50 mi to attend. Each paid own way. 12 days. 400 city women attended a similar class in Feb. 1300 men came to 6-day class in bitter cold weather after Christmas 1927. Every one & 300 local churches of the province has a similar class in the winter, and another in the slack farming time in Aug. just after the first weeding. Over ½ of total enrolled adherent age of the Church each year attends."

Photo credit: Moffett Collection. Princeton Theological Seminary.

Introduction

APPOINTED AS THE FOREIGN mission agent of the Presbyterian Church of Australia from 1902 to 1925, Frank H. L. Paton (1870–1938) traveled abroad to mission fields to facilitate the work of the missionaries as well as to report the progress. Prior to his appointment, Paton was a missionary and administrator in the New Hebrides, the group of islands in the South Pacific known as Vanuatu today.[1] Although Paton, in his role as a foreign mission agent, was concerned with missionaries affiliated with the Presbyterian Church of Australia, he was also well-versed with the development of missions in the region. Paton surveyed many locations in Oceania and Asia and understood, as an insider, the difficulties of planting Christian missions in the Asian context but Paton reported in the 1912 issue of *The Missionary Review of the World* that nations are "looking to [Korea] for spiritual inspiration and leadership."[2] Paton was surprised how Korea quickly transformed its reputation since Korea only five years earlier was according to Paton "a byword in the East for helplessness."[3]

When Frank Paton arrived in Korea to take stock of the Christian community in the early twentieth century, the news of the surprising growth of Christianity had already become well-known but he was unprepared for the unusual lengths Koreans took to Christianity. In a tour of the Christian community in Pyeongyang, Paton encountered a thriving church that outgrew its facilities. The church accommodated 2,000 people but over 3,500 clamored to fill the space. Paton asked a Korean "why they did not build a second church and divide"—a reference to the ecclesial practice of dividing

1. "Rev. F. H. L. Paton," 13. While as a foreign mission agent, Paton also served as the moderator of the Presbyterian Church of Victoria.

2. Paton, "Picture of Korean Christianity," 615.

3. Paton, "Picture of Korean Christianity," 615. The image of Korea as "helpless" stems in a large part to the country's inability to prevent the loss of sovereignty at the hands of imperialist foreign powers. In 1905, Korea became a protectorate of Japan. In 1910, Japan colonized Korea.

a segment from a large, thriving church in order to start a second congregation. The Korean replied that it had been divided already 39 times and the
current situation was the latest overcrowding.[4]

In the report, Paton shared other remarkable stories of Koreans' en-
thusiasm for Christianity but he was careful to avoid creating an impression
that Koreans are "easy to win for Christ." The abundance of evidence on the
Korean mission field point to an extraordinary affinity to Christianity but
Paton was not satisfied with casual observations or anecdotal encounters.
Paton spent time in Korea in order to gain "a deeper knowledge" of the way
Koreans made sense of the foreign religion. At first, Paton expected to find
affinity or complementary features between Korean culture and Christianity but he was surprised at what he discovered. With "conviction," Paton
concluded that Koreans were in fact "hard to win" for Christianity.[5]

Such dichotomy not only attests to the unique development of Christianity in the Korean context, but it also underscores the tensions and con-
tradictions that fueled its growth. For one, Koreans overcame formidable
social and familial barriers in order to convert to Christianity. It meant de-
nouncing sacred elements of Korean culture and time-honored traditions.
In particular, the rejection of ancestral rituals was uniquely difficult.

When a young Christian man in 1912, out of his Christian convictions, refused to bury his dead father in the traditional Confucian ritual, he
unleashed a furious "storm." His action was shocking to a culture that prized
filiality. It was tantamount to one of the worst things a Korean could do in
pre-modern Korea. His angry relatives punished him and he "suffered the
loss of home, fields, and livelihood."[6] Abandoned, homeless, and impoverished but "still he remained faithful to Christ." The punishment inflicted on
the young man by his family was meant to turn him from the error of his
ways. Not only did he remain a Christian, but he returned kindness to his
oppressors. He went to his family preaching God's redemptive love and the
love that he demonstrated was more than what they could bear. Sixty of his
relatives became Christians as a result. That was not the end as "a year ago
[in 1911] he experienced the joy of seeing the last home in his village turn
Christian!"[7]

The Methodist missionary Lulu Miller recounted in 1913 the persecution a Christian couple received from their villagers and family members:

---

4. Paton, "Picture of Korean Christianity," 615.

5. Paton, "Picture of Korean Christianity," 615.

6. "Fruit of Fidelity," 554.

7. "Fruit of Fidelity," 554.

For three years my husband and I alone of all our family believed in Jesus, and during those three years we were greatly persecuted. During harvest we could get no one to help us. From the tide grounds we were not allowed to gather clams—an occupation by which we had formerly made a living. Our neighbors would not come near our house and the children of the village cried, "Dirty place! Dirty place!" Our courtyard fence was broken down and we were refused the use of the water from the village well. My sons would not buy shoes for me, that I might not be able to walk the twenty *li* into Chemulpo city [Incheon] to attend divine service, so I went barefooted until I reached the edge of the city, where I would sit down and put on my shoes and stockings. I had to start from home long before daylight on Sunday morning in order to reach the church in time for Sunday school; and my feet were constantly bruised from walking over the stony paths.

In the inside room of my home my sister scolded, while in the guest room my sons wept, because I refused to discontinue the Christian worship. My nephew said to me, "Hurry up and die. We will bury you in a warm place." It was three years ago that I was so persecuted, but now my whole family believes in Jesus Christ and six families in the neighborhood have also become Christians.[8]

These stories testified to the extraordinary and unusual reactions to Christianity. When Paton toured Korea, he witnessed churches filled to the brim. For those unable to crowd inside the church, they sat outside but close enough to the windows and doorways to listen to the messages and participate in the services. When Paton visited a weekday prayer meeting on a cold winter night with the temperature six below zero, a Korean elder of the church, prior to the meeting, told Paton to keep his expectations down. He "expressed regret" that the attendance "was so thin owing to an epidemic of influenza."[9] Expecting few in attendance, Paton entered the building and "found a company of 950 people gathered for their week-night prayer-meeting!" How did Paton reconcile the unremitting attraction for Christianity with the finding that Koreans were in fact resistant to the faith?

Paton did not have clear answers. The phenomenon puzzled scores of other missionaries and observers that witnessed the growth of Christianity in Korea. The pioneer missionary Samuel A. Moffett, who entered Korea in 1889 and settled in Pyeongyang, the largest city in northern Korea, witnessed

8. Miller, "Over Charcoal Fire," 173.
9. Miller, "Over Charcoal Fire," 173.

first-hand the explosive growth of Christianity including the Great Revival of 1907 that experienced the greatest outburst in Pyeongyang. Moffett was asked "time and again by word and by letter" of why Christianity grew so much in Korea. Moffett answered, "I do not know that anyone can answer that question further than to say that according to His own wise plans and purposes God has been pleased to pour forth His Spirit upon the Korean people, and to call out a Church of great spiritual power and evangelistic zeal in which to manifest His grace and His power, to the accomplishment of what as yet is not fully revealed."[10]

When Paton visited Korea in 1912, the number of Protestants exceeded 30,000.[11] By 1940, Protestants reached over half a million; by 1995, close to nine million Protestants were in South Korea.[12] Paton would be surprised to learn that in a hundred years since his visit that the single largest congregation in the world would be in Korea, the Yoido Full Gospel Church with over half a million members and over 180,000 in Sunday attendance.[13] In comparison, Joel Osteen's Lakewood Church in Houston, Texas was in 2016 the largest church in the United States with 52,000 in average Sunday attendance.[14] In addition to Yoido, South Korea has some of the largest megachurches in the world including Onnuri Community Church in Seoul with 75,000 in weekly attendance and Pyungkang Cheil Presbyterian Church in Seoul with 60,000.

KOREAN CHRISTIANITY: A PUZZLE

The surprising growth of Christianity in Korea raises the question of the forces and influences that bear on the formation of Christian character in

10. Moffett, "Native Church," 235.

11. 21,136 (1900); 323,574 (1920); 507,922 (1940); 623,072 (1960); 7,180,627 (1980); 8,765,000 (1995). Figures up to 1940 refer to the whole of Korea; figures from 1960 only refer to South Korea (Hong, "Nominalism in Korean Protestantism," 136).

12. Hong, "Nominalism in Korean Protestantism," 136.

13. "Under [David Yonggi Cho's] charismatic leadership there are now 633 pastors, 400 elders, and 50,000 deacons or deaconesses shepherding this burgeoning flock. The church operates a Sunday School program with an enrollment of more than 26,000, a ten-week training course for home-cell leaders, a sixteen-week training course for church officers and lay leaders, and a three-year Bible Institute for training pastors. . . . It is probably most accurate to view Yoido Full Gospel Church as a distinct denomination since it includes nine satellite churches, affiliated churches, educational institutions, and has sent more than 250 missionaries overseas" (Mullins, "Empire Strikes Back," 89–90).

14. Zaimov, "Joel Osteen's Lakewood Church." Also see Vaughan, "1.6 Million People."

a land where religious institutions appeared to be conspicuously absent—a confounding revelation for missionaries and observers. In 1892 missionaries commented on the "strange lack in Korea of any religion commanding respect or even attention from the people."[15] In a joint letter written by Bishop Scott of North China and Bishop Bickersteth of Japan, they reported to the Archbishop of Canterbury that "Koreans are the least religious of all these Eastern [Asian] nations."[16] Beyond superstitious beliefs and marginal adherence to Buddhism, missionaries noted that "there was no trace of any religious feeling having any hold upon the people."[17] After Hendrik Hamel and his Dutch crew on the *Sparrow Hawk* were shipwrecked on Jeju Island on 1653, captured by the Korean government, and later escaped, Hamel wrote *An Account of the Shipwreck of a Dutch Vessel on the Coast of the Isle of Quelpaert* [Jeju], *Together with the Description of the Kingdom of Corea* (published in Amsterdam and Rotterdam in 1668) that included a description of the religious life of Koreans. Hamel wrote, "As for Religion, the *Coresians* [i.e., Koreans] have scarce any."[18]

In 1908, William Ellis, an American observer in Korea, noted how the attraction of Christianity among Koreans surprised missionaries and left them without a plausible explanation. Ellis wrote, "These Koreans seem to have a genius for Christianity. They grasp it with a comprehension, and a comprehensiveness, that amazes the missionary."[19] From early on, it became clear to the missionaries that the experience on the Korean mission field was highly unorthodox, considering the conventions of missionary progress. In 1909, a missionary in Korea exclaimed, "In no pagan country have we had the same success in the same length of time as in Korea, and perhaps there is no pagan country in the world that is so ripe for Christian evangelization. The growth of the work has been phenomenal."[20]

WORLD CHRISTIANITY AND METHODOLOGY

The surprising progress of Christianity in Korea produced many questions. The situation was an anomaly in the annals of the history of missions. Clues abound but few answers were forthcoming. Where did this extraordinary response to Christianity come from? What led Koreans to embrace

15. "What is the Religion of Korea?," 138.

16. "What is the Religion of Korea?," 138.

17. D. Lee, "Effective Internet Ministry Strategy," 138.

18. Hamel in Ledyard, *Dutch Come to Korea*, 214.

19. Ellis, "Korea," 96

20. "Methodist Missions in Korea," 143.

Christianity in such fashion? Did Christianity stir something dormant in Korean culture?

The unexpected way Christianity sprouted on the Korean mission field confounded even the leading missionaries of the day. The fact that Christianity in Korea developed in many ways outside the purview of foreign intervention muddles the picture further. The mystery derives in large part to the fact that the development departs from the expected linear progression from one point to another as a series of planned steps on the mission field.

Contemporary and historical accounts agree that the development of Christianity in Korea was a momentous movement in Christian missions not only in Asia but in modern history. Indeed, the success of missions in Korea merits close attention, especially since neighboring countries with similar traditions and civilizations in contrast experienced only minimal growth. Unfortunately, however, attempts to explain Korean's surprising development of Christianity must confront the fact that the explanations originate overwhelmingly from Western interpretations that exclude native interpretations from the narrative. The acceptance of Western interpretations for the growth of Korean Christianity has left indigenous contributions, such as the Korean Bible Women, underrepresented in the missional narrative. This book attempts to address the imbalance by identifying formative local factors as loci of Christian growth and development.

The methodological turn toward native perspectives for understanding the transmission of Christianity has already taken place within the field of World Christianity that has shifted the focus away from exclusively external factors in explaining the development of Christianity in the Global South.[21] The case in Korea, as well as others around the world, suggests other dynamic forces at work in a culture's response to the Christian message. Andrew Walls makes the provocative claim that Christianity in Africa and parts of Asia showed significant growth once Western missionaries left. The growth of Christianity in the absence of foreign missionaries indicates that

---

21. In his influential book, *Whose Religion is Christianity?*, Lamin Sanneh distinguished "world Christianity" from "global Christianity." Born from Christendom, the latter retains the forms and patterns of European Christianity, while "world Christianity" legitimizes the unique rootedness of Christianity in the diverse contexts around the world. It acknowledges the indigenization of Christianity to the local context without all the trappings of Western Christianity. See Sanneh, *Whose Religion is Christianity?*, 22–23. Peter Phan wrote of the "myth of Christianity as a Western religion." Critiquing the Western-centric interpretation of the expansion of Christianity, "a different narrative of the Christian movement must be fashioned," Phan wrote, "other than the one peddled by standard textbooks of church history" (Phan, "World Christianity and Christian Mission," 194).

they, according to Walls, "have not been the sole agency."[22] Other factors are at work and play significant roles from the beginning but they, especially indigenous considerations, Walls adds, have "been little studied."[23]

A part of the problem is the focus on "sending churches" and their strategies and accomplishments rather than on the "receiving churches." Although the objective, of course, was delivering the gospel to non-Western settings, the historical narrative often documented what the "sending churches" have done in the respective countries where missionaries worked. Using commercial terms to describe the relationship between Western missions and Asian countries, the Vietnamese-American theologian Peter Phan wrote, "The emphasis is laid on the 'exporters' rather on than on the 'importers,' and on the exported merchandise rather than on how the imported merchandise is bought and put to use by the locals."[24]

This study partly answers Andrew Walls's call for scholars to "discuss how far missions were a lay movement, developing in spite of church structures rather than because of them, and constantly subversive of church order and diversionary to concerns that seemed consumingly important at home."[25] By situating this study within the growing field of World Christianity, this book inverts the 'sending church' approach, offering a 'receiving church' focus, using participant production as the grounding perspective.[26]

The methodological shift was necessitated by the reality that the picture of the church worldwide has been inverted. In 1900, Christianity was distinctly an extension of Western civilization as 66 percent of all Christians lived in Europe according to the Pew Study on Christianity in Global Context.[27] Counting North America with Europe, 80 percent of *all* Christians in 1900 lived in the Global North. In over a hundred years, Christianity underwent a seismic shift of global proportions. By 2010, Europe's share of all Christians dropped to 25.6 percent. In 1900, Africa had less than 2 percent of all Christians; in 2010, it jumped to 22 percent and the numbers are still growing. In all, the Global North's Christian population had less than 40 percent in 2010 and is expected to fall below 30 percent before 2050. By 2050, it is estimated that Africa, Asia, and Latin America combined will account for 71 percent of the world's Christian population while Europe

22. Walls, *Cross-Cultural Process*, 65.

23. Walls, *Cross-Cultural Process*, 65.

24. Phan, "World Christianity and Christian Mission," 194.

25. Walls, *Cross-Cultural Process*, 65.

26. For a discussion of Andrew Walls's pioneering role in the field of World Christianity, see Burrows et al., *Understanding World Christianity*.

27. Johnson, "Christianity in Global Context."

and Northern America will be reduced to 28 percent.[28] The Global South or the so-called Two-Thirds World which was the recipient of the missionary movement a hundred years ago is experiencing the most dynamic growth of Christianity today.

The texture of Christianity in the Global South stands in sharp contrast with Western Christianity which has its foundations in Christendom and Enlightenment. Cultural and political Christianity had deep roots in Western Europe as far back as the fourth century when Constantine, by signing the Edict of Milan (313 AD), proclaimed toleration for Christianity in the Roman Empire. The eventual convergence of Christianity and the state in Western Europe created Christendom that reinforced a monocentric and monocultural framework over the centuries. The intertwined relationship between church and state nurtured cultural self-identification through the church and the close association served as a marker of social acceptability and assimiliability. However, the understanding of God in Asia, as Peter Phan noted, "is not monochromatic, nor even polychromatic, if by color is meant only race, even if race is an important individual and social identity marker, in Asia as well as elsewhere."[29]

The context in the Global South where Christianity took root often resembles the church of the New Testament where Christians endured in places that were at times hostile to what Christianity represented. In *The Next Christendom*, Global Christianity, according to Philip Jenkins, grows from a markedly different soil than from its Western cousin. Many Christians in non-Western regions confront daily suspicion, discrimination, persecution, or violence as a minority religion.[30] In most of those communities, Christians are disenfranchised from the loci of power, status, and wealth. They cautiously tread under the gaze of a dominant religion or ideology suspicious of Christianity and co-exist in precarious situations unlike anything Western Christianity experienced since the pre-Constantinian persecutions. Today, the movement of Christianity is multi-directional and polycentric where mission sending is "from everywhere to everywhere," an indication of how its development is emerging outside of established Christian centers.

---

28. By 2050, Africa is estimated to have 29 percent, Asia 20 percent, and Latin America 22 percent of the world's Christian population—with Europe at 16 percent and Northern America at 12 percent (Johnson, "Christianity in Global Context").

29. Phan, *Being Religious Interreligiously*, 117.

30. "Next Christendom" is the title of Philip Jenkins's book (see Jenkins, *Next Christendom*). Over the last century, "the center of gravity in the Christian world has shifted inexorably away from Europe, southward, to Africa and Latin America, and eastward, toward Asia. Today, the largest Christian communities on the planet are to be found in those regions" (Jenkins, *Next Christendom*, 1).

Polycentric Christianity, according to Tite Tiénou, frees Christianity from the trappings of "any single culture" and promotes the indigenization of Christianity from the local context.[31]

The receiving church as the point of analysis defines the methodological turn in World Christianity in which scholars consider the merits of the multi-directional pivot as a way to address the increasing diversification of the church. On reflecting on the missiological framework for the future, Steven Bevans asks the question, 'What has contextual theology to offer the church of the twenty-first century?' Recognizing the significance of the polycentric growth of the worldwide church, Bevans responds, "Theology should only be done from local experience and local context."[32] For such a development to take place, Bevans argues that contextual theologizing should "not [be] tied to Western ways, themes, and methods of theology."[33] However, the actualization of those goals proves more elusive.

Despite the emphasis on the importance of validating local theologies, Asian theologians lament how Western theology and Enlightenment perspectives cast a long shadow over Asian Christianity. The 1982 conference that assembled 82 delegates from Asia, Africa, Latin America, the Caribbean and the Pacific Islands produced "The Seoul Declaration" that acknowledged how the Western approach to theology has "a number of pitfalls," especially for the Global South.[34] The preoccupations of Western theology remains profoundly influential in the Global South, yet "hardly addresses the questions of people living in situations characterized by religious pluralism, secularism, resurgent Islam or Marxist totalitarianism," or, in other words, the context of the Global South.[35]

During the Age of Missions, the theological foundation for the interpretation of Christianity was established by missionaries and church leaders from the West and, in the process, de-legitimized the development of a theology nurtured from an Asian perspective and experience by asserting the supremacy of Western epistemology that elevates rationalism and positivism above the philosophical inclinations of the local environment. More often than not, Christian scholars in Asia are trained in the West and in

---

31. Tiénou continues: "The good news, in this case, is that since people of color now represent the majority of Christians in the world, the perception of Christianity as a Western religion can be corrected" (Tiénou, "Christian Theology," 41). For an overview of the five missions conferences and their contribution to World Christianity, see Yeh, *Polycentric Missiology*.

32. Bevans, "What Has Contextual Theology," 11.

33. Bevans, "What Has Contextual Theology," 11.

34. "Seoul Declaration," 491.

35. "Seoul Declaration," 491.

the theologico-political discourse of the West. Academically detached from the concerns of the local communities from which they commenced, they become the gatekeepers of theological education. The missiologist Moon-jang Lee writes, "Indigenous but foreign-educated theologians have formed a theological hierarchy within theological institutions and helped Western theology to maintain its dominant influence in Asia."[36]

As Simon Chan and others have noted, the problematic relationship Asian theologians have with Western theological frameworks reinforces an elitist discourse that not only perpetuates the uncritical assimilation of Western theological parameters but also neglects to acknowledge and support indigenous Christian movements. The resulting effect continues to complicate the work of Asian theology and according to Simon Chan, "what passes as Asian theology tends to be confined to a limited number of themes and theologians."[37] The unfortunate tendency has been the cloning or replication of Western models on Asian soils without the unique qualities of the local environment. The Westernization of Korean Christianity has transpired "to such a degree," according to the anthropologist Charles Kraft, "that one worshipping in any of the churches of Seoul could easily imagine him/herself in America, except for the language."[38]

In his examination of indigenous Asian theology, Hwa Yung, Bishop emeritus of the Malaysian Methodist Church, asks if Asian Christianity on the inside is mango (Asian) or banana (Western) in his book, *Mangoes or Bananas? The Quest for an Authentic Asian Christian Theology* (2004).[39] Yung recognizes the progress made in the development of Asian theology since the Seoul Declaration but he is disappointed that much of the material remains "superficially contextual."[40] They, Yung continues, "often failed to really address the questions that the Asian church at the grass-roots was wrestling with."[41] Peter Phan critiques the notion that Christianity is a Western religion when it took root in Asia before being "clothed in Greek, Latin, and Teutonic categories." Phan writes, "In fact, in the first four centuries, the most successful fields of mission were not Europe but (West) Asia and Africa, with Syria as the center of gravity of Christianity before 500."[42]

36. M. Lee, "Identifying an Asian Theology," 264.

37. Simon Chan writes: "Although there are some refreshing exceptions in recent years, the old perception of Asian theology is so deeply entrenched that it has become virtually the received view in the West" (Chan, *Grassroots Asian Theology*, 23).

38. Kraft, *Appropriate Christianity*, 265.

39. See Yung, *Mangoes or Bananas?*

40. Yung, *Mangoes or Bananas?*, xi.

41. Yung, *Mangoes or Bananas?*, xi.

42. Phan, "World Christianity and Christian Mission," 16. "The most vibrant and

TERRACULTURALISM

In shifting the center of the meaning-making process to the receiving church as the focal point of analysis, this book uses what I term terraculture as an approach to analyze local circumstances and patterns that create distinctive responses from the transmission of Christianity. The word terraculture is a combination of the Latin words *terra* (earth) and *cultura* (to till, cultivate). By turning the focus of cross-cultural engagement to the landscape, we may gain greater insight into the workings of the native mind that influenced Christianity's traction at the local setting. The dictionary definition of terraculture is "cultivation of the earth" and the term aptly describes the breaking and turning over earth that happens on the local scene with the plowing of the fields by sowers but the process is hardly linear as it produces a dynamic interaction with local religion(s), cultural self-understanding, and socio-political consciousness.

Used in the academic field of World Christianity, terraculture focuses on the hybridization of Christianity at the local level. The annals of mission history are filled with disappointed missionaries whose expectations on the mission field have not been met. Terraculture however is interested in examining the Christian domestication of the landscape by local agents, conditions, and forces, such as the dominant values of a local culture that shape the moral promptings or the latent value systems that govern social norms. Terraculture furthermore analyzes how these formative cultural systems and socio-political climates interact and react with the Christian witness.

Conscious of the need to examine the ways a culture's religio-philosophical foundations influence people's responses to their interaction with Christianity, terraculture repositions the methodological focus to identify a culture's highest ideals and to correlate how the process of domestication shapes the evolving receptivity to the Christian message. Terraculture asks two main questions: what are the key cultural values that determine a society's highest ideals that not only normalizes one's understanding of self but also marks and regulates moral boundaries and, secondly, what are the resulting complications and unanticipated effects that arise from the hybridization of Christianity to these larger religio-social forces.

Terraculture begins by positioning the receiving church as an active participant in the transmission of Christianity. For too long, the over-emphasis

---

influential Christian centers were found not in any city of the western part of the Roman empire but in Asian and African cities" (Phan, "World Christianity and Christian Mission," 16). For an extensive examination of the various manifestations of Christianity in Asia, see Phan, *Christianities in Asia*.

on external forces and causality dominated the missiological narrative and terraculture balances the Christian analysis of the landscape transformation in the Global South. Terraculture rejects the Lockean perspective that human nature is a blank canvas and that a person's knowledge is gained mostly through the direct imprint of experience. If the Lockean model is applied on the mission field, the missionary becomes the sole agent of transformation while the receiving culture is viewed as a blank slate (tabula rasa), ready to be inscribed by the impressions gained from religious experience and teachings. The problematic aspects of this model on the mission field are many and it disfigures, at the very least, the relationship with the receiving culture. The distorted view nullifies the possibility that the receiving culture has complementary aspects to Christianity since the view presumes that the receiving culture is without any ideas relatable to Christianity.

Terraculture partly rectifies the situation by validating the receiving culture as a creative participant in the transmission of Christianity. Christianization takes place on the ground and the interactions between the gospel and receiving culture produces, at many times in the history of missions, unexpected results—for good or ill. The process of a receiving culture constructing for itself a Christian identity is a dynamic process that brings to surface the most pressing concerns of a particular community. For example, Albert Raboteau, in his seminal book *Slave Religion*, noted how the binary Christian themes of present circumstance vs. future glory, suffering vs. freedom, distress vs. relief, injustice vs. heavenly redemption, and despair vs. spiritual joy interacted and interwove with the culture of American slaves to spontaneously produce a distinctive African-American Christian culture that addressed their particular condition.[43]

Terraculture presumes that the transmission of Christianity tests and unsettles the boundaries of the pre-existing religious establishment and challenges cultural frameworks of the local landscape. God in Christ, according to Andrew Walls, takes people "as they are" in order to "transform them into what He wants them to be."[44] The receiving culture undergoes a kind of religious meld with the interaction but the process often produces unexpected results. Terraculture analyzes and reflects upon what Andrew Walls calls the "points at which cultural specificities change, that the distinctive nature of the Christian faith becomes manifest in its developing dialogue with culture."[45] As each culture's response with Christianity is

43. Raboteau, *Slave Religion*. Not all slaves were Christian but "by the eve of the Civil War, Christianity had pervaded the slave community" (Raboteau, *Slave Religion*, 212).

44. Walls, *Missionary Movement in Christian History*, 8.

45. Walls, *Missionary Movement in Christian History*, xvi.

shaped by their socio-political context, terraculture examines the "serial progression" of its interaction with Christianity, a development that may help lead the church toward the missional engagement with cultures.

A culture's interaction with Christianity often brings unpredictable results and it stems in part from the fact that new concepts are created in the translation of Christianity and few can predict a recognizable trajectory of its development. As Walls indicated, the transmission of Christianity to a foreign culture must coopt words and concepts from the native culture to explain the Christian message and people in the Global South will no doubt interpret Christianity through their existing cultural and religious orientation. However, the process is a messy one due to the challenges inherent in translating new terms and concepts to a different culture. The dissonance created by the introduction of new concepts, especially religious ones, often causes unpredictable results and at times friction.

For example, one of the first challenges when local cultures encounter Christianity is the problem of translating Christian concepts when the meaning of such words never neatly match up in different languages. Often there are words that are similar but they are not the exact fit of the original meaning or, more problematically, rooted in local paganistic traditions. In *The Making of Korean Christianity*, Sung-Deuk Oak examines the difficulty among Korean Christians in the late nineteenth century of choosing the word for God as Protestantism began to make inroads into Korea.[46] Historically, animistic beliefs were widespread in Korea and the usage of any of the commonly known words for god or gods would have brought paganistic associations if coopted by Christians—a fact that brought consternation and opposition to many Korean Christians in the late nineteenth century. Eventually, despite reservations, they chose to coopt the vernacular Korean word *hananim* (the conjunction of *hanuel* [Heaven] with *nim* [honorific suffix] to form 'the Heavenly One') as the word for the Christian God.

At first, terraculturalism may sound similar to contextualization. While both models recognize culture as the canvas on which the missional enterprise takes place, there are significant distinctions between the two. Contextualization or models that approximate its meaning such as incarnation, indigenization, or inculturation affirm the theological necessity for the Christian transmission to take a fresh shape in each culture, since the gospel

46. Oak devotes chapter 1 ("God: Search for the Korean Name for God, *Hanănim*) to the problem of finding the right word for the Christian God (Oak, *Making of Korean Christianity*, 33–84). Oaks writes: "This assimilative method entailed the problem of syncretism with the existing religions, provoking the opposition of those religious groups that claimed that missionaries had stolen their indigenous god and that Christians had no right to call on their god" (Oak, *Making of Korean Christianity*, 35).

takes unique root to each situation. Prior to the popular usage of contextualization, 'indigenization' was the widely used term in modern missions that identified most closely with the self-governing, self-supporting, and self-propagating formula, which in the Korean context was better known as the Nevius method.[47]

Contextualization, as a concept, began to be used more widely after the 1972 publication of the Theological Education Fund report entitled *Ministry in Context*. The authors of *Ministry in Context* acknowledged the missional interaction with traditional cultures which defines the process of indigenization but contextualization aims to go beyond. The authors write, "Contextualization has to do with how we assess the peculiarity of Third World contexts. . . . [It] takes into account the process of secularity, technology, and the struggle for human justice, which characterize the historical moment of nations in the Third World."[48] Contextualization affirms the incarnational implantation of the gospel to particular cultures or specific historical-cultural situations in the pursuit of context specific theology. In the end, contextualization facilitates those who are receiving the gospel to see it as their own. As the gospel becomes rooted in a particular culture, contextualization according to Darrell Whiteman is "concerned with how the Gospel and culture relate to one another across geographic space and down through time."[49]

At the same time, scholars point to syncretism as a possible outcome in the work of contextualization, a theologizing process that integrates the local systems of culture and thought in the formation of its missional approach. In the process of incorporating elements of local culture, some wonder how far should the gospel be contextualized? Scholars question if Christian unity will be compromised in the affirmation of local theologies. Will the recognition of variant forms of Christianity lead to divisions within the universal Church? Paul Hiebert, for one, warns of "uncritical contextualization" based on undiscerning acceptance of preexisting native religious

47. The three-self movement (self-governing, self-supporting, and self-propagating) or the Nevius method is a controversial topic in Korean Christianity. Yoo discusses the tension in his book *American Missionaries*. Many American missionaries credited the growth of Korean Christianity to the Nevius method but Korean Christian scholars denied that such process even took place. Yoo writes: "In 1931, K. S. Yum sharply criticized Charles Allen Clark's book, in which the missionary argued the Nevius method was the primary reason for Korean church growth, for advancing 'superficial' interpretation that overlooked the political and social movements in the country and oversimplified the ministries of the Korean Presbyterians themselves" (Yoo, *American Missionaries*, 211–12).

48. *Ministry in Context*, 20.

49. Whiteman, "Contextualization," 2.

elements that leads to syncretism.[50] Then, there are others like D. A. Carson who argued that it is an impossible task to neatly determine what is the core or the essence of the gospel message and the unessential, expendable husk.[51] Despite concerns, most missiologists agree with Wilbert Shenk who advocates for the formation of a dynamic theology through a "vigorous engagement of culture by the Gospel, accompanied by critical reflection on that process."[52]

Contextualization takes into account the cultural forms and categories of a local culture for the purpose of developing a theological articulation befitting the particular setting. Contextualization grapples with the integration of the gospel to the culture in a way that serves ultimately the production of a missional praxis. For terraculturalism, the historiographical study of the Christian interaction with a culture becomes the primary task. Contextualization is a theological process that seeks to discover how the church may engage more fully in various contexts. Terraculturalism, as a perspective that considers missional relationships from the viewpoint of the receiving church, is less of a prescriptive approach than an articulation of the lived experience. The conclusions from a terracultural research may be applied to missional activities but terraculture views the study of the landscape as intellectually necessary and instructive to the discussion about effects, implications, and consequences.

Terraculturalism does this by examining the points of interaction and integration, especially the underlying forces of native systems that lay at the root of local adaptation to Christian ideals. Today, Christianity in the Global South is growing at a rate far faster than at any other time and it is taking place, in a large part, independent of external missionary guidance. A terracultural analysis would provide understanding from the ground since terraculturalism is a particularistic, historically orientated perspective

---

50. Hiebert, "Critical Contextualization," 287–96. To avoid "uncritical contextualization," Hiebert suggests "critical contextualization." For a further discussion of the contextualization model in Korea, see Hong, "Toward Korean Contextualization," 18–28.

51. See Carson, *Biblical Interpretation and the Church*, 11–29. Grenz also expresses this viewpoint: "The commitment to contextualization entails an implicit rejection of the older evangelical conception of theology as the construction of truth on the basis of the Bible alone. No longer can the theologian focus merely on Scripture as the one complete theological norm. Instead, the process of contextualization requires a movement between two poles—the Bible as the source of truth and the culture as the source of the categories through which the theologian expresses biblical truth" (Grenz, *Revisioning Evangelical Theology*, 30).

52. Shenk, "Recasting Theology of Mission," 98.

based on the premise that landscape changes need to be understood in light of the social and cultural forces within which they were produced.

In addition, the speed with which cultures change today makes the task of contextualization all the more challenging. Today, cultures shift at a rate faster than ever before, enabled by digital, scientific, and technological advancements that evolve quicker than we can determine their implications, and theologizing a missional approach to the shifting context may be rendered noncurrent in the face of rapid cultural changes. The elusive task of contextualization is exemplified when examining Korean Christianity. In the late nineteenth century when Protestant missionaries entered Korea, Korea was still ruled by a monarchal dynasty that was founded in 1392. The outbreak of Christianity in Korea in the early twentieth century took place while imperialistic powers were overpowering the country's rulers and Western culture was displacing traditional Korean culture.

The priorities of Korean Christianity shifted dramatically shortly thereafter when Japan colonized Korea from 1910 to 1945. Christians in particular suffered greatly at the hands of their colonial rulers that enforced the view that the Japanese emperor was a deity deserving of worship and obedience. The end of World War II liberated Korea in 1945 but in five years Korea underwent a devastating Korean War (1950–1953) that pitted Koreans against Koreans and impoverished the country. The Korean Christians who experienced the horrors of communism, especially those who fled from northern Korea, theologized a staunch anti-communist position and embraced the ushering of an industrialized-capitalistic society in a war-torn, poverty-stricken Korea. Contemporary Korean Christianity grapples with first-world problems: saturation in materialism, Westernized culture, and technology.

While terraculturalism, like contextualization, examines the local setting, terraculturalism does not seek to contextualize Christianity to a particular cultural form but instead identifies the culture's moral framework for the purpose of examining points of interaction. Understanding a culture's underlying value system reveals the deepest aspects of their self-understanding through what they perceive as sacred and highest ideals. Terraculture fosters critical reflection and debates the culture's moral framework for the purpose of understanding the outcome of interaction with Christianity. In doing so, the study yields meaningful, substantial methodological discussions about the points of contact.

TERRACULTURALISM AND CHAPTER SUMMARY

In using terraculture with which to understand Koreans' interactions with Christianity, this book begins with Confucianism, in particular the Korean version of Neo-Confucianism, as the most influential moral prompting in Korean society. Confucianism was introduced to Korea in the ancient period, mainly as a source of bureaucratic and administrative expertise. However over the centuries Confucian literati argued for a greater role in the body politic.

During Goryeo dynasty (918–1392), Buddhism and Confucianism served as Korea's twin pillars: Buddhism as the state religion and Confucianism as the bureaucratic backbone. However the Confucian literati, deeply dissatisfied over the state of affairs, agitated for governmental reform. As tensions with China's Ming dynasty mounted, the Confucian literati conspired against Goryeo and helped to successfully topple the government in favor of establishing Joseon dynasty (1392–1910). With the Confucian literati firmly entrenched in power, they introduced sweeping reforms to usher in the "Confucian transformation of Korea."[53]

By locating Confucianism as Korea's most significant ideology for over half a millennium, the first few chapters of the manuscript examine how Confucianism shaped the development of Korean Christianity at various historical periods under distinctly different challenges. Chapter 1 examines how the growth of Christianity in Korea cannot be understood without paying attention to Neo-Confucianism as a category of analysis. Centuries of Confucian ideology reinforced a preoccupation with ethical ideals and the pursuit of moral perfection as an individual and collective vision. Korean Confucianism became the touchstone of social authenticity that exacted heavy moral and cultural burdens. From the individual commitment to its uncompromising pursuit, Confucianism provided fertile soil in which to sow seeds of Christian principles such gaining eternal redemption and salvation from moral shortcomings.

Chapter 2 analyzes two characteristics of Confucianism that are unique to Korean Confucianism: orthodoxy and moral perfection. The Korean Confucian literati during the Joseon period developed an interpretative authority over Neo-Confucianism that surpassed China. As the keepers of orthodoxy, Koreans embraced orthodoxy, or the sense that they acquired "right learning," as the mark that separated them from all other civilizations. Coupled with orthodoxy was the relentless pursuit of

---

53. "The Confucian Transformation of Korea" was the title Deuchler's seminal book. Deuchler was one of the preeminent scholars of pre-modern Korea. See Deuchler, *Confucian Transformation of Korea.*

moral perfection, which was the goal for every Confucian. The path toward moral perfection, from the Korean perspective, was a taxing journey that demanded sacrifice and discipline. The no-compromise demeanor pushed Koreans beyond what Westerners would consider unreasonable and excessive. Yet, when Koreans converted to Christianity, they demonstrated a level of enthusiasm not found even among missionaries. Christianity's exclusivist claims appealed to the Korean mind that elevated enthusiastic commitment to the Confucian Way above all else.

Starting with the Catholic experience of the eighteenth century, chapter 3 examines persecution as a major theme of Korean Christianity since the eighteenth century. Like the Confucian forebearers who adamantly stood their ideological ground to the point of death, Korean Catholics who converted to Christianity on their own remained remarkably resilient. The persecution of Korean Christians at various periods of history resembles the experience of many Christians in the Global South who must endure suspicion, discrimination, or persecution as a daily part of their Christian existence. This chapter explores how conversion and maintaining Christian faith in a society adverse to Christianity shaped believers' self-understanding of the breadth of faith and acceptance of its mortal implications. Focusing on the Catholic and Protestant experience in Korea, Christian believers rigorously tested the country's attitudes against Christianity. In so doing, their experience provokes a critical reflection on the profoundness of the missionary mandate and illuminates the complexity with which their faith is forged as they must confront the brutal reality that they may be, at the very least, acting against established social and political norms. For many Korean Christians during Joseon dynasty and the Japanese colonial period (1910–1945), conversion of Christianity was part of the process that transformed for believers a religious identity that was understood to be profoundly detrimental to their relationship with the state.

Continuing the theme of the complementary aspects of Confucianism with Christianity, chapter 4 examines how the Protestant missionaries' dependence upon literature, in particular sacred scripture and literacy, complemented Korean Confucianism. From their entry into Korea in the late nineteenth century, Protestant missionaries placed a great deal of effort into creating a Christian identity using literacy and literature as cornerstones of missional strategy. The relationship between the Protestant missions' emphasis on reading and Korea's Confucian culture of learning is of particular importance for an understanding of the growth of Christianity in Korea because Christianity's close association with literacy and sacred writings energized Korean culture's Confucian imagination. Perceiving the reading of Christian literature, including the Bible, as a salient way to salvation,

Koreans turned to reading and memorizing the Scriptures to experience the manifestation of God's revelation. The high respect afforded to education and learning as a dominant cultural value constitutes an important, if overlooked, element in the replication of faith in Korean society that reproduced the gospel under their own familiar terms.

Chapter 5 considers the widespread belief in folk religion as an important factor in the conversion of many Koreans. The fear of demons, gods, and goblins dominated the minds of many Koreans. Sickness and diseases were attributed to demons. Demon possession was an accepted reality. When the missionaries started working in Korea in the late nineteenth century, they reacted as if they stepped into an imaginary world that they only read about in fairy tales. As the Koreans were subjected to substantial spiritual oppression, the demonstration of the superiority of the Christian God over their spirits proved instrumental in converting to Christianity. Exorcising demonic spirits was not part of the missionaries' training but encountering the spirit realm became an important part of the mission work. Korean church workers, who were versed in native practices and belief-systems, were particularly effective in waging a war against spirit forces.

Chapter 6 explores outliers on the mission field: Korean Bible Women. The early Bible Women were marginalized figures: they were illiterate, widows, older in age, and from the lower classes, and yet these Bible Women who in many ways stand in contrast to the ideal Christian leader with the proper education and training were indispensable in the early decades of frontier evangelism as they traveled to remote locations and unreached regions. The Korean Bible Women possessed unique attributes and characteristics that enabled them to negotiate complex gendered terrain and to traverse a pathway that was uniquely suited for them.

The political crisis at the turn of the twentieth century fueled nationalism across Korea. When Japan eventually gained colonial control over Korea, they noticed that a significant number of nationalists were Christians. The missionaries disavowed any influence that encouraged political activity and, yet, Korean Christians were on the frontlines of nationalistic engagement. Chapter 7 examines the connections between Christianity and nationalism. The identification of Christianity with nationalism was so strong that many Koreans became attracted to Christianity as a result. The development of nationalism among Korean Christians reinforces the fluidity and unpredictability of mission work as missionaries' ideological presuppositions produce unintended consequences.

The end of World War II (1945) brought liberation to Korea but the turmoil in the years that followed plunged the country into the Korean War that ultimately divided Korea into two, North and South Korea. Chapter 8 focuses on the chaotic turn of events, borne in the twentieth century, that continues to confront the Korean church today. The communists' reign of terror upon Christians left an indelible mark on South Korean Christianity, especially from those from the north who fled to the south as refugees. The Korean Protestant church in the South emerged from the War as ever vigilant against the communist North, unbending in its support of American military presence, and endorsing economic development and prosperity.

In the Conclusion, Korean Christianity in diaspora is examined, first, with the migration of Korean laborers to Hawaii from 1903 to 1905, and secondly, the large wave of Korean immigration in the post-1965 era. Both periods of Korean migration took place in very different conditions. The Koreans who migrated to Hawaii left right before Korea was colonized by Japan and as a result Korean Christians in Hawaii were preoccupied with the independence movement. The Korean immigrants of the post-1965 era moved to the United States while Korea was ruled by authoritarian rulers. Despite the varying circumstances, both periods of transnational communities reveals a collective consciousness that was fostered in the ethnic church. As Koreans immigrants encountered a racialized hierarchy in American society, the ethnic church became an essential part of their American experience.

Seodang (Village Academy). Confucian scholar with his pupils.

（金俗108）　Teacher and puplies　弟師の濟畫　（俗風鮮朝）

Confucian Teacher and Pupils. Photo credit: Moffett Korea Collection.
Princeton Theological Seminary.

1

Confucian Origins

ANNIE BAIRD, A MISSIONARY who entered Korea in 1891 and died in Pyeongyang in 1916, recalled in *Daybreak in Korea* (1909) a conversation in which an old Korean woman asked a Korean Christian why foreigners [i.e., missionaries] came to Korea. The Korean Christian replied that "they are here to teach a new doctrine."[1] Shocked and amazed by the answer, the old woman retorted, "A new doctrine! What doctrine have they got that is any better than the ones we have?"[2]

Her response reveals the mindset of Koreans on the nature of ideological orthodoxy—specifically the ways in which the notion of doctrinal allegiances shaped the Korean mind. Her reaction signaled the presumptive canons of Korea's Confucianism which served, throughout Joseon dynasty (1392–1910), as the benchmark by which all other ideologies were measured. Scholars in East Asian Studies have long recognized the unquestioned predominance of Confucianism in Korean society.

In church history and missiology, however, the link between Korean Confucianism and Christianity remains little more than the outline of Korea's historical past, partly because of the view of Confucianism subscribed by the missionaries in Korea.[3] Confucianism was widely viewed by mis-

1. Baird, *Daybreak in Korea*, 66.

2. Baird, *Daybreak in Korea*, 66.

3. There have been a few studies that intersect Korean Christianity with Confucianism. Grayson called the relationship between Confucianism and Christianity as "dynamic complementarity" in the context of facilitating South Korea's economic growth and modernization. "Modernization and industrialization in the Republic of Korea grew from a spiritual and cultural ground in which Confucianism and Protestantism

sionaries as an obstruction in the way of their Christian work. Missionaries encountered over and over again Koreans' unswerving allegiance to Confucian rites, traditions, and doctrines and viewed them as a roadblock to Christian work.

Unable to circumvent the Confucian edifice in Korea, many missionaries gave wide currency to the version that Confucianism no longer warranted such confidence among the people. The easy condemnation of Confucianism was so common among missionaries that the editors of *The Korean Repository* in 1898 criticized fellow missionaries who harbored a "'Confucius-is-in-Hell' spirit" that lent to "cheap abuse of smug, self-satisfied phariseeism."[4] Instead of writing off Confucianism as an ideological failure, the editors encouraged a "careful and prolonged examination" of Confucianism "with appreciation and respect."[5]

In *The History of Protestant Missions in Korea*, L. George Paik, the distinguished Korean church historian and former president of Yonsei University in Seoul, bemoaned the "superficial judgment" made by foreigners. Paik wrote, "In estimating the character of the Korean Christian we cannot depend on the superficial judgment of travelers who never have taken the trouble to concern themselves with the spiritual life of the Korean people."[6] In *Protestantism and Politics in Korea*, the historian Chung-shin Park wrote that Protestant missionaries "made no attempt to arrive at a compromise with the Confucian tradition. . . . They taught Korean converts that Confucian society was 'evil' or 'heathen' and that it should be Christianized."[7] "Aggressively denounced" as a form of paganism, Confucianism became an easy target for all the social evils that missionaries encountered in Korea.[8]

---

have reacted together in conditions of mutuality" (Grayson, "Dynamic Complementarity," 76). In fact, the linkage between Confucianism and rapid industrialization in East Asia has been well documented. See Tu, *Triadic Chord*; Vogel, *Four Little Dragons*; Berger and Hsiao, *In Search of East Asian Development*; Tai, *Confucianism and Economic Development*.

    4. "Christian Missions and Social Progress," 65.

    5. "Christian Missions and Social Progress," 65.

    6. Paik, *Protestant Missions in Korea*, 423.

    7. C. Park, *Protestantism and Politics in Korea*, 120. "Early missionaries instructed Koreans in Christian ideas: their teaching was not abstract theology, but rather dealt with specific matters of daily life. . . . They insisted on the abolition of the practices of ancestor worship, such as revering ancestors at the grave site on special occasions, holding memorial services on the anniversary of the ancestor's death, and paying frequent homage to the ancestral tablet enshrined at home. The Protestants' demand that members discontinue these Confucian rites was a direct challenge to the basic beliefs of Chosŏn society" (C. Park, *Protestantism and Politics in Korea*, 120).

    8. C. Park, *Protestantism and Politics in Korea*, 120. The uncompromising position of Protestants contrasted sharply with Jesuit missionaries centuries earlier. At the end

In East Asian Studies, Confucianism has long been viewed as a vigorous creative force in East Asian civilizations but within mission studies, Korean Christianity, and church history, Confucianism continues to struggle to find a voice as a contributing factor. In the absence of a Confucian narrative in the development of Korean Christianity, scholars espouse a sociohistorical analysis that focuses on the destabilizing loss of nationhood in the early twentieth century as creating a religious openness. Scholars also cite Korea's shamanistic beliefs as having a certain primitive strength of religious character that transferred to Christianity. Perhaps the most common explanation for the unexpected growth of Christianity in Korea is the "Nevius method" named for John Nevius, a missionary in China who advised missionaries in Korea.

While these explanations reflect aspects of Korean religion and society, this study considers Confucianism, specifically the unique Korean version of Confucianism, known in the scholarly literature as the Ch'eng-Chu School of orthodox Neo-Confucianism, as the primary cause for the Koreans' arousal of religious and moral passion and for the considerable lengths to which they went to practice the new doctrine found in Christianity.[9]

More than any other ideology or religion, Confucianism shaped Korea's moral and cultural landscape. A closer examination of the moral impulses

---

of the sixteenth century, Matteo Ricci in China "portrayed Catholicism as complementing rather than challenging Confucianism, by citing passages from the ancient Confucian classics to support an argument that Confucians had once believed in God. Ricci claimed that Neo-Confucianism, with its denial of the existence of a personal deity, had betrayed the beliefs, values, and teachings of the earliest Confucians and that Catholicism, which was founded on the principle of reverence for such a deity, represented a return to the spirit of original Confucianism" (P. Lee and de Bary, *Sources of Korean Tradition*, 268).

9. "Orthodox" Neo-Confucianism is distinguished from the broader "Neo-Confucian" movement. "There were, too, different forms of orthodoxy, but in the period treated here it was the local Chinese academies that first established Chu Hsi's teaching as 'orthodox' and it was only at the turn of the thirteenth to the fourteenth century that the Yuan dynasty adopted it officially for educational and examination purposes" (de Bary, *Neo-Confucian Education*, 2). "There is common agreement that, if nothing else, Chu Hsi was certainly the Great Synthesizer of Chinese thought, consciously employing and adopting numerous early Confucian terms and ideas and integrating them, not always very consciously, with ingrained Taoist notions and adaptable Buddhist concepts, concepts that were themselves influences from or results of stimula by indigenous Chinese beliefs. But synthesis need not mean lack of originality or creativity, for Chu Hsi so perfected previous undeveloped ideas to new levels of understanding that they acquired a completely new meaning and assumed far greater significance" (Wittenborn, *Further Reflections*, 12). For an overview of Chu Hsi's philosophy, see de Bary, *Neo-Confucian Orthodoxy*; de Bary and Bloom, *Principle and Practicality*; Ching, *Religious Thought of Chu Hsi*; Chan, *Chu Hsi and Neo-Confucianism*; Chan, *Sourcebook in Chinese Philosophy*, 588–646.

instilled by Korea's Confucianism reveals the extent to which Koreans not only adopted Christianity but also took self-initiative to disseminate it to their family, neighbors, and even around the country.

HISTORICAL CIRCUMSTANCES

A number of historians and political scientists have suggested that the growth of Korean Christianity was the response to the loss of faith in the Korean political establishment in the late nineteenth century that eventually resulted in the colonization of Korea in 1910 by Japan. Faith in the dynastic kingdom suffered a series of blows as domestic and foreign pressures debilitated the Korean government.

When Protestant missionaries first entered Korea in 1885 as permanent resident missionaries, the American minister to Korea warned them about the political turmoil brewing in the country. The country was still reeling from the effects of a failed coup a year earlier when a pro-West faction in the palace attempted to replace conservative senior officials of the government with reformers who favored modernization in an event known as the 1884 Gapsin Coup. The increasing presence of foreign powers in Korean affairs and the government's inability to fend off imperialist encroachment fueled, in part, internal unrest that set the stage for the Donghak Uprising (1894–1895), "the largest scale peasant insurrection in Korean history," that weakened the government even further.[10]

Sparked by corruption and mismanagement in the government, the Donghak Uprising started in southwest Korea that grew and expanded in strength and numbers. The uprising spread to different parts of the country as peasant joined the movement. They formed into militias and, as a shocking turn of events, they managed to not only defeat the government's military forces but they also overthrew local governments and held rebel-controlled areas. Unable to quell the expanding peasant rebellion, the Korean government called upon their strongest ally Qing China for military assistance. Responding to the influx of Chinese troops in Korea, Japan also sent its army into Korea and clashed with Chinese forces. Very quickly, the situation descended into chaos and China and Japan engaged in the Sino-Japanese War of 1894–1895, which was fought mostly on Korean soil.

The drama of Korea's collapse unfolded in a series of political violence, wars, and treaties that eventually culminated in the Japanese colonization of Korea in 1910. As a result of the national downfall, scholars contend that the tenuous circumstances created an opportunity for Koreans to break from

10. For an overview of the uprising, see Eckert et al., *Korea Old and New*, 214–22.

the past and to adhere to a new religion or doctrine. The unstable social and political conditions acted as a catalyst destabilizing the status quo as well as prompting greater openness to new ideas.[11]

Documents show that many Koreans were drawn to Christianity as part of a larger interest in Westernization but the same progression toward Westernization took place in many Asian countries without the development of a Christian movement like the one manifested in Korea. While Koreans of the late nineteenth and early twentieth centuries took greater interest in Christianity, socio-political conditions do not adequately explain the enthusiastic-type of Christianity embraced by Koreans. In addition, the similar phenomenon of the self-driven Christian movement occurred in Korea over a hundred years earlier at a time when no external threat to the Korean kingdom existed and the government was firmly entrenched in power.

SHAMANISM

Among scholars of religion, many point to shamanistic influences as a major contributing factor in the rise of Christianity in Korea. Throughout Korean history, shamanism existed without institutional support and yet persisted as a grassroots religion in Korea (and East Asia) for thousands of years. Shamanism's ability to operate in informal social networks allowed participation in the population without raising alarms from the dominant religion or ideology.

In examining the appearance of Korean Christianity, the argument that Christianity in Korea assimilated with shamanism has gained traction among scholars, with a few, like the sociologist of religion Andrew Kim,

---

11. "Structural strains, such as political instability, widespread poverty and the rigid class stratification, had been most significant, for they constituted fertile ground in which the imported faith flourished" (A. Kim, "Political Insecurity," 268). Chung-shin Park point to the "unique historical context" from which Protestant Christianity developed and the undeniable impact of the national trauma experienced by Koreans. See C. Park, *Protestantism and Politics in Korea*. Danielle Kane and June Mee Park argue that "geopolitical networks provoke nationalist rituals that alter the stakes of conversion at the microlevel" (Kane and Park, "Puzzle of Korean Christianity," 366). Jung Han Kim wrote, "In my view the success of Christianity in Korea is caused by Christianity's going hand in hand with nationalism, becoming an instrument of modernization" (J. Kim, "Christianity and Korean Culture," 137). In *Born Again*, Lee argues three interwoven reasons for the development of Christianity in Korea: the salvific quality of Christianity that attracted Koreans during a time of national crisis; Christianity fusing with the burgeoning nationalistic and anti-communist sentiment; and the "relentless proselytization efforts" that fueled evangelistic campaigns (T. Lee, *Born Again*, xiv–xv).

likening the process as the "shamanization" of Christianity.[12] In addition to scholars of religion, academics focusing on Korean Christianity have also drawn attention to the ways in which shamanism shaped Korean Christianity. According to the church historian Sung-Deuk Oak, a "syncretistic fusion" between Christianity and shamanism occurred whereby a "covert Christianity-indigenization process" took place.[13] The theologian David Kwang-sun Suh wrote, "Korean Protestantism has almost been reduced to a Christianized *mudang* [a female shaman] religion. That is, the form and language of the worship service are Christian, but the content and structure of what Korean Christians adhere to are basically *mudang* religion."[14] Shamanism, according to the sociologist of religion Mark Mullins, "has been the central force shaping the development of Korean Pentecostalism."[15]

The rationale for the collaboration between shamanism and Christianity is the assumption that shamanistic influence on Korean culture became part of the Christian experience. In other words, converts adopted Christian doctrines and practices but, scholars claim, a shamanistic interiority remained and was incorporated into Korean Christianity.[16] In the search for the causes of Christianity's growth in Korea, shamanism represents for many scholars the presence of a fluid folk religion that transitioned from one religious form to another. Shamanism's "influence was so profound," argues Andrew Kim, that Korean Christianity absorbed "elements of Shamanism."[17]

As a folk religion, Koreans have turned to shamans and shamanistic beliefs for prosperity, fortune-telling, healing of illnesses and diseases, and the casting out of malevolent spirits. Proponents of the shamanization theory also refer to how both shamanism and Christianity reflect a this-worldly outlook that reinforces a "blessing-orientation."[18] From this perspective, Christianity, or at least the attraction to Christianity, is viewed fundamentally as a "principal agent of economic, political and social modernization."[19]

12. A. Kim, "Christianity, Shamanism, and Modernization," 115.

13. Oak, *Making of Korean Christianity*, 143.

14. Suh, *Korean Minjung in Christ*, 116.

15. Mullins, "Empire Strikes Back," 92.

16. At a national level, the mythic legend of Dangun, the shaman-progenitor of Korea, became a thorn in the side of Korean evangelicals as Dangun is both regarded as founder of Korea as well as worshipped as a great shamanistic god. See T. Lee, "What Should Christians Do," 66–98.

17. A. Kim, "Christianity, Shamanism, and Modernization," 116. Chung wrote that Korean society is "fundamentally shamanistic" (Chung, *Syncretism*, xi).

18. A. Kim, "Christianity and Korean Culture," 132–52.

19. "Because the Church provided the basic tools of modernization and assumed a

Korean shamanism, according to the sociologist of religion Byong-suh Kim, "is the belief system of this-worldly blessing—material world, good health, and other personal and familial well-being."[20] As a result, "most of the Korean Protestant churches," Kim wrote, "have had a shamanistic tendency."[21] The acceptance of Christianity by Koreans represented, according to scholars, similar materialistic aspirations that were previously observed in shamanism. In other words, Christianity was the new religious form that preserved many elements of the old form.

Shamanism has indeed played a formidable role in Korean culture but the argument that the "emphasis on the fulfilment of material wishes" was the main motivating factor for conversion to Christianity overlooks the fact that other cultures that exhibit materialistic expectations have not turned to Christianity in the way Koreans did.[22] Even in other cultures with shamanistic roots, such as Mongolian, Siberian, or Japanese, Christianity remains marginal. While shamanism's "singular emphasis" may be "material success as the supreme goal," it is not alone.[23] For example, in Japan, people visit Shinto shrines primarily to pay respect to kami [spirits] and/or to pray for good fortune.[24]

Contemporary Taiwan, "an island full of folk religion," has seen the flourishing of popular religious activities, rooted in Daoist and sometime Buddhist religions that are "focused on rituals for bringing personal good fortune and a happy afterlife, not on organized efforts to improve one's moral life and change society."[25] The religious renaissance of Taiwanese folk

---

central role in the economic, political, and social modernization of South Korea, many Koreans viewed the acceptance of the Gospel not only as a means of entry into modern society but also as an access to what is believed to be a more advanced civilization" (A. Kim, "Christianity, Shamanism, and Modernization," 114).

20. "This emphasis on worldly personal blessing became a significant part of congregational life, especially in sectarian groups" (B. Kim, "Modernization and the Explosive Growth," 324).

21. B. Kim, "Modernization and the Explosive Growth," 324.

22. Andrew Kim continues, "In fact, the fundamental purpose of Shamanism is to fulfill practical needs: People solicit the service of a shaman in hopes of realizing their material wishes, such as longevity, health, male births, and wealth. With its emphasis on the existence of spirits, particularly those of ancestors, that are believed to wield power on shifting fortunes of each individual, Shamanism has thus catered to this-worldly, materialistic, fatalistic, magical, and even utilitarian tendencies of Koreans" (A. Kim, "Korean Religious Culture," 119).

23. A. Kim, "Christianity, Shamanism, and Modernization," 118.

24. In Japanese Shintoism, which is rooted in shamanism, has over eight million kami (i.e, spirits and/or forces). Kami, which can be good or evil, have power to influence natural forces or human events.

25. Madsen, "Religious Renaissance," 295.

religions continues to increase "despite the considerable efforts of foreign missionaries" who "saw themselves, with some degree of accuracy, as Taiwan's modernizers."[26] The Catholic and Protestant population in Taiwan never went beyond 7 percent and has been in decline.

NEVIUS METHOD

Among missionaries and church historians, the Nevius method is often cited as the reason for the success of Protestant Christianity in Korea, especially to the Presbyterian mission.[27] The Nevius method is often credited with "the rapid growth of the church in Korea."[28] According to the advocates of the approach, the benefits of the Nevius method "were clearly seen even at the beginning."[29] The adoption of the Nevius plan in Korea resulted in a "remarkable growth as they consistently applied his method. . . . Furthermore, the Nevius method, it is argued, nurtured the growth of the Korean church after World War II and the Korean War as evidenced by the emphasis on "personal evangelism, financial giving, planting churches, stalwart denominations, and purposeful Bible study and prayer."[30] The Nevius method became "so wildly successful that it has become known as *the* representative missionary policy in Korea."[31]

John L. Nevius (1829–1893) was a missionary in Shantung, China when he visited Korea in 1890. During his two-week visit, Nevius explained to the missionary community the "three-self" strategy: self-propagation, self-support, and self-governance.[32] The method aimed to develop churches

26. Madsen, "Religious Renaissance," 295.

27. "The Northern Presbyterians in Korea embraced the 'Nevius Plan,' as it came to be called, and church historians believe that it was the key to the institutional growth that made the Presbyterian denomination the largest Christian body in Korea from the beginning of the century" (Clark, *Living Dangerously in Korea*, 127). For an overview of the Nevius Method, see Oak, *Sources of Korean Christianity*.

28. Tucker, *From Jerusalem to Irian Jaya*, 264.

29. Y. Kim, "Re-evaluation," 77.

30. Gallagher, "John L. Nevius," 1616.

31. Cha, "Unequal Partners, Contested Relations," 6.

32. Contrary to the popular view that Nevius's self-propagating, self-governing, and self-supporting theory was original, Nevius borrowed the "three-self" theory from the missiologists Henry Venn of England and Rufus Anderson of the US. By the mid-1800s, Venn and Anderson independently "proposed a 'three-self' formula for establishing new churches." See Shenk, "Rufus Anderson and Henry Venn," 168–72. Venn and Anderson "established the 'three-self' goals that have served as the guiding principles of those determined to indigenize the gospel in local cultures" (Jacobs, "Contextualization in Mission," 238). Horace G. Underwood also said, "Dr. Nevius, although

work of training for the ministry and the preparing of books for a Christian reading public."[52]

As Korean churches increased in number and Korean Christians performed much of the work on the field, missionaries according to L. George Paik focused for the most part on the management of the Korean church. According to Paik, the Korean church in 1910 fell short of being a self-supporting, self-propagating, and self-governing church when he wrote, "It is true that by 1910 the [Korean] Christian community has not developed to such a stage of self-support, self-extension, and self-propagation that the [mission] agencies at the home bases could entirely cease the sending of missionaries, nor has it yet."[53]

Paik lamented at the lack of Korean participation in the governing mission board, which the missionary community exercised decision-making powers over the Korean church. Paik wrote, "In the case of Presbyterian missions in Korea, until 1901 the Korean Christians had no voice in the Council [of Missions Holding] meetings."[54] Paik called the absence of Korean self-governance "the theory of deferred organization"[55] and the dominance of missionaries in Korean church administration and government resulted, according to Paik, in the creation of "a foreign institution rather than a national [Korean] church."[56] Confirming Paik's observation, Kwang-soo Yi in 1918 noted the "ecclesiastical supremacy" the missionaries exercised over the Korean church. Yi wrote, "The Missionaries preached the form of Christianity which prevailed in the age of Puritanism, namely the Christianity of ecclesiastical supremacy. According to their doctrine, without faith in Christianity, neither morality nor knowledge is of any use."[57] In the end, the Korean church, according to Paik, suffered "from the weakness of the early missionary endeavors."[58]

52. Scranton, "Extracts," 132.

53. Paik, *Protestant Missions in Korea*, 424.

54. Paik, *Protestant Missions in Korea*, 307. "Even then, participation was in the form of conference for instruction of the Korean helpers in ecclesiastical matters, rather than the assemblage of a church court. There were two Council sessions, one in English and the other in Korean. The missionaries attended both, while the Koreans participated in the latter only" (Paik, *Protestant Missions in Korea*, 307).

55. "The theory of deferred organization evidently was adopted in order to train the Korean Christians to maturity in the faith, so that when an organization was formed, it should be composed of a Korean ministry" (Paik, *Protestant Missions in Korea*, 307).

56. Paik, *Protestant Missions in Korea*, 307.

57. Yi, "Defects of the Korean Church," 254.

58. Paik, *Protestant Missions in Korea*, 308.

According to a 1914 article in the *Korea Mission Field,* all mission schools (not including the private schools started by Koreans) had missionaries as the principles with the exception of Pai Chai Academy.[59] Eight years later, the conditions remained the same as an internal questionnaire taken within the missionary community regarding mission schools in 1922 confirmed that "not more than two or three schools [of all mission schools] have any Korean official supervision, by way of representation on governing school boards, etc., and these two or three have it to no large degree."[60]

Arthur Judson Brown, the influential missionary stateman who served on many ecumenical and global mission boards, including the Presbyterian Board of Missions, observed in 1912 unusual patterns in the ecclesiastical relationship between the native church and missionary community. In particular, Brown reported an "anomaly" from the standpoint of standard missionary procedure regarding the transference of ecclesiastical authority over to the native church. In other words, the Korean church failed to develop as a self-governing organization. Brown wrote, "In some other fields churches have been formally organized as soon as there were a very few Christians. Sometimes, indeed, churches and even Presbyteries were constituted before there were native Christians or ministers at all. . . . In Korea, on the contrary, ecclesiastical organization has been placed last. Not only is there no Presbytery, the missionaries all retaining their membership in their home Presbyteries, but there is not an ordained native Protestant minister in all Korea."[61]

Voices from the Korean church community echoed what they felt was excessive recognition of missionaries' contribution that stymied the development of indigenous theological maturity. By praising the Nevius method as the key to success in Korea, the attention shifted away from the challenges and struggles of the native church and toward the strategies and outcome of the mission work.[62] In attributing the superiority of the Nevius method in triggering the religious phenomenon, K. S. Yum in 1931 felt the native church received little consideration in the process of the transmission, as

59. "Statistics of Mission Schools in Korea," 359–63.

60. Coen, "Diagnosing Our Mission Schools," 116.

61. Brown, *Report of a Visitation*, 13.

62. While the Nevius method is the most recognized strategy of missionaries, scholars have also credited other approaches or contributions of missionaries as the source of Christianity's growth in Korea. Dae Young Ryu argues that missionaries planted in Korea an "evangelical-revivalistic" religion. "The discussions below will attempt to demonstrate that the American missionaries endeavored to transplant the evangelical-revivalistic version of American Protestantism in fertile Korean soil at the dawn of the twentieth century" (Ryu, "Origin and Characteristics," 372).

In China, Wang Yangming had great influence and his interpretation became mainstream in the Confucian nexus. In Korea, however, Wang's views were regarded as heresy or *idan* [Korean: heterodox teaching]. Yi Hwang (or Yi Toegye, 1501–1570), one of the greatest Korean Neo-Confucian scholars, whose face today is on the South Korean 1,000 won note (or the equivalent to an American dollar in terms being the most commonly used paper currency), aggressively denounced Wang's theories. In turn, Yi's philosophical critique of Wang became the orthodox position in Korea.[71] Following Yi's lead, Korea's scholars created a Neo-Confucian bulwark against Wang's heresy and initiated an intense effort to combat what they viewed as a heterodox teaching that was gaining popularity in China.[72]

Chu Hsi's interpretation had become so entrenched in Korea that Koreans, according to Wm. Theodore de Bary, the pre-eminent scholar of Neo-Confucianism, concluded that the "Chinese had gone out of their minds."[73] The turn away from Neo-Confucian orthodoxy, according to de Bary, convinced Koreans that China had declined into "a fatal decadence," leaving Korea as the "last bastion of orthodoxy."[74]

As a result, Koreans saw themselves as "the last custodians of civilization."[75] The outstanding historian of pre-modern Korea JaHyun Kim Haboush wrote, "It was not long before Koreans regarded themselves as more faithful to the Confucian tradition than the Chinese."[76] Over time, Koreans came to view themselves "superior to the Chinese because they were more faithful to Neo-Confucian orthodoxy."[77] Not surprisingly, missionaries observed the East Asian world-order based on Confucian civilization. James S. Gale, a Canadian missionary and keen observer of Korean society, wrote that Koreans believed "any nation exemplifying it [i.e., Confucian principles] is civilized and any failing to observe it is barbarous."[78]

71. "Yi [Hwang]'s critique of Wang became the orthodox interpretation, as Korean Neo-Confucians by and large remained faithful to Zhu Xi (Chu Hsi)" (de Bary, *Sources of East Asian Tradition*, 2:466).

72. Chung, *Korean Neo-Confucianism*, 34.

73. de Bary, *East Asian Civilizations*, 64. In the sixteenth century, "Wang Yangming offered a new interpretation of the mind-and-heart, emphasizing its essentially intuitive and affective, rather than intellective, character. Wang's teaching proved to be extremely appealing and indeed widely popular" (de Bary, *East Asian Civilizations*, 63).

74. de Bary, *Message of the Mind*, 80.

75. Haboush, "Confucianization of Korean Society," 86.

76. Haboush, "Confucianization of Korean Society," 85.

77. de Bary, *East Asian Civilizations*, 63.

78. Gale, *Korea in Transition*, 96.

The Confucian transformation of Korea began in 1392, when the Confucian literati saw an opportunity to overthrow the Goryeo dynasty (918–1392). They collaborated with General Yi Seonggye to stage a military coup against Goryeo, ushering a new dynasty with its foundations built on Confucian tenets. Buddhism, which was Goryeo's state religion, became the target of Confucian persecution as Buddhism was deemed "destructive of family mores and ruinous to the state."[79]

As the ideological transition was underway, the victors championed the immediate implementation of Neo-Confucianism as a national priority. The Korean literati viewed Neo-Confucianism, according to Haboush, "as the font of truth from which all civilized peoples should draw sustenance."[80] In the process of elevating Confucianism above all else, Buddhism was displaced from its position as the state religion. As part of the purge, Buddhism was banned from the capital and their holdings in Korea were stripped.[81] The new Confucian leaders filled the gaps by creating a Confucian state, a place where nearly every area of society was interpreted and reformed under Confucian orthodox beliefs. Laws that governed family rituals and relations were now based on Confucian ideals.[82]

79. Eckert et al., *Korea Old and New*, 102–3. Furthermore, Buddhism was criticized for eroding "the primary controls of society; social status had become meaningless because of social mobility; human relationships had collapsed because of detrimental customs; and correct social behavior (*ye*) clearly had disappeared" (Deuchler, *Confucian Transformation of Korea*, 103).

80. Haboush, "Confucianization of Korean Society," 85.

81. "Hundreds of [Buddhist] monasteries were disestablished (the number of temples dropping to 242 during the reign of T'aejong [r. 1401–1418]), and new construction was forbidden in the cities and villages of Korea. Monastic land holdings and temple slaves were confiscated by the government in 1406, undermining the economic viability of many monasteries. The vast power that Buddhists had wielded ruing the Silla and Koryŏ dynasties was not exerted by Confucians. Buddhism was kept virtually quarantined in the countryside, isolated from the intellectual debates of the times. Its lay adherents were more commonly the illiterate peasants of the countryside and women, rather than the educated male elites of the cities, as had been the case in ages past. Buddhism had become insular, and ineffective in generating creative responses to this Confucian challenge" (Buswell, *Zen Monastic Experience*, 23).

82. According to Deuchler, "Koryŏ [or Goryeo] society, however, was not prudish, and the generally free and easy contact between the sexes amazed the Chinese observers" (Deuchler, *Confucian Transformation of Korea*, 72). "Marriage in Koryŏ [or Goryeo] seems to have been a rather loose institution which was not restricted by a multitude of rules and regulations. This at least was the impression of contemporary Chinese observers received. Was this an accurate impression? The most persuasive evidence for its accuracy is the strong economic position married women enjoyed. Whether the residential arrangement was virilocal or uxorilocal, the wife retained her rights as heir in her natal family, a fact which gave her the liberty to leave an incompatible husband without jeopardizing her livelihood. But the same was true for the

The most strident faction within Korea's Neo-Confucianism was the *sarim* ("righteous oppressed"), a "new breed of scholar officials" of the sixteen century that proved more idealistic and confrontational than the established Confucian peerage.[91] Like the Puritans in sixteenth-century England, the *sarim* were deeply discontent with the pace of reform and directly challenged the crown and officialdom to enact a more systematic and thorough Confucian transformation of Korea. The *sarim* demanded a total and unwavering dedication to moral perfection not only of themselves but also of their king and peers. The *sarim* aimed to extol the virtues of Neo-Confucian principles by roundly criticizing the king and high officials whenever they fell short of a higher benchmark for Neo-Confucianism.

The heaviest burden rested on the Korean king who was expected to rule as a sage-king while representing Korea as the Confucian civilization. The king's mandate to rule rested on his ability to conduct virtuous governance. According to Haboush, the moral burden on the king "was an exceeding demanding one."[92] The Korean king was carefully monitored under a moral microscope in which his words and behavior "were recorded exactly by an official court historian in order to be later judged according to Confucian morality by future readers."[93] The sage-king was the centerpiece of the harmonious order of the universe in bringing and reinforcing the moral order in the kingdom. Understandably, many Joseon kings did not live up to the high moral standards but others however proved to be exemplary Confucian rulers.[94]

---

eliminate its Westerner rivals, and they in turn were removed by the coup d'etat led by the Westerners, who deposed Kwanghaegun and placed Injo on the throne in 1623. After a hiatus of relative quiescence, factional rivalry emerged once again after 1659 in a dispute ostensibly over the mourning ritual for a deceased king" (Palais, *Confucian Statecraft and Korean Institutions*, 63).

91. Lee and de Bary, *Sources of Korean Tradition*, 268.

92. Haboush, *Confucian Kingship in Korea*, 25.

93. C. Kim, *History of Korea*, 74. "The king was forbidden to read what the historian had written about him. The articles were only available for others to read after the king had passed on. These records were compiled in the *Annals of the Chŏson Dynasty (Chŏson wangjo sillok)*" (C. Kim, *History of Korea*, 74).

94. Haboush, *Confucian Kingship in Korea*, 9. In her close examination of King Yŏngjo's reign, Haboush wrote that he fulfill the demand for sage kingship. "Yŏngjo's pursuit of sage kingship was predicated on his belief that the rhetoric and ideas of the sage king would render him with effective means with which to deal with the demands of his court and society. The effectiveness of his pursuit, first of all, depended on whether he could persuade his bureaucrats and subjects of the seriousness of his intent. In this respect, Yŏngjo seems to have succeeded. He pursued his ideal with single-minded commitment. His relentless construction of an image as a sage king during his fifty-two-year reign, the longest Yi reign, led to bureaucratic capitulation to his moral

The *sarim's* brand of ideological purity led to a zealous moralistic crusade that enabled them to pursue their demands with unbending resolve, even in the face of intense persecution. The *sarim's* criticism often targeted the entrenched political establishment that had reached political rank through favor and lineage. "Speaking with the voice of unimpeachable moral authority, they became," according to Michael Kalton, an expert on Korean Neo-Confucianism as a philosophy, "increasingly dogmatic and inflexible."[95] The *sarim's* incessant demands unleashed a furious backlash that resulted in a series of bloody persecutions known as the "literati purges" of the sixteenth century.[96]

In the bloody aftermath of the purges, the *sarim* reaped the rewards of their persistence as their brand of idealistic moralism gradually became the prevailing worldview in Confucian Korea. The prominence of benchmarks raised by the *sarim* established the heightened pursuit of moral perfection as the fundamental idiom of national and personal identity. While Korean Neo-Confucianism emphasized the seriousness with which Koreans regard the personal pursuit of moral cultivation, the Neo-Confucian culture simultaneously expanded the sensibilities of didactic arousal as part of a larger endeavor aimed at the reshaping the moral contours.

CONCLUSION

At the turn of the twentieth century, the missionaries in Korea (as well as other missionaries serving around the world) were viewed as the vanguard of American civilization and democracy. In 1910, Charles Warren Fairbanks, the Vice-President under Theodore Roosevelt, wrote, "I was greatly impressed with the work accomplished by Christian missions in Korea. The progress they are making in the conversion of the Koreans to Christianity easily surpassed my expectations. . . . It may be said, in a word, that the good which the missionaries are doing in Korea is widespread and of inestimable value. There is no movement of the day which appeals more strongly to the Christians of the world than that which is made in behalf of the missionary cause of Korea."[97] George Scidmore, the US Consul-General to Korea, noted

---

superiority. His continued display of concern for his people seems to have earned gratitude and appreciation. His excursions into the streets in the later years of his life were greeted with spontaneous cheers, a rare phenomenon in Yi Korea" (Haboush, *Confucian Kingship in Korea*, 2).

95. Kalton, *To Become a Sage*, 11.

96. The *sahwa* or "literati purges" took place in 1498, 1504, 1519, and 1545. See Eckert et al., *Korea Old and New*, 136.

97. Fairbanks, "Korea's Redemption," 1677.

in 1910: "One striking feature of Korea's present condition is the magnificent work which is being done by the American missionaries."[98] In 1910, the US President William Howard Taft wrote, "The mission stations are the outposts of Christian civilization. Each missionary with his house and his staff forms a nucleus about which gathers an influence far in excess of the numerical list of converts."[99] Taft continued, "The lives the missionaries lead, the good they do, and the character of representatives they are, of the highest in our civilization, is what makes it so important that they should be sent, and be sent with all the instruments of usefulness possible into those far-distant lands."[100]

It goes without saying that many missionaries, especially in the early years of Protestant missions, exemplified America's Christian civilization and demonstrated extraordinary qualities that left a deep impression upon the Korean people. Many suffered persecution for the faith and others died on the Korean mission field, such as Henry G. Appenzeller (1858–1902) who drowned in Mokpo while attempting to save a Korean girl and Dr. William James Hall (1860–1894), a medical missionary who died when he contracted typhus fever while treating the wounded in Pyeongyang during the Sino-Japanese War (1894–1895).

As Taft and others have noted, the work of missionaries was an extension of American civilization and their presence in Korea revealed, from a terracultural perspective, a clash of civilizations that broke and turned over parts of Koreans' self-understanding. Yet at the same time important remnants of the past civilization continue to add to the complexity of the new, emerging Christian landscape. For example, the simple overlay of a Christian culture and doctrines on top of a very foreign culture does not sufficiently explain the growth of Christianity. They do not account for the spontaneous reaction to Christianity where native instincts and inner cultural reflexes have combined to produce unique responses that are very difficult to manage and predict.

Mission strategies, shamanistic inclinations, and historical circumstances played important roles in shaping and structuring the development of Christian communities but they do not render the full complexity of the ideological arousal of the people. More than any other religious or social force, Korea's version of Confucianism called Neo-Confucianism contributed to creating a cultural impulse toward the stimulation of religious ideals. Centuries of exclusive Confucian training cultivated moral sensibilities that

98. Scidmore, "Korea's Religious Situation Unique," 1676.

99. Taft, "Outposts of Civilization," 547.

100. Taft, "Outposts of Civilization," 547.

increased awareness and motivation for ideological purity. Korea's Confucianism mandated an ongoing pursuit of knowledge and truth that formed
a recognizable part of the Confucian ethos.

MR. SOH SANG YUN,
*e of the Three First Christians in Korea
and the First Christian Pastor.*

Sang-yun Seo. Photo credit: Moffett Korea Collection.
Princeton Theological Seminary.

January 21, 1936. "Girls Bible Institute." Photo credit: Alice Butts Album.
Moffett Korea Collection. Princeton Theological Seminary.

2

Orthodoxy and Moral Perfection

ARCHBISHOP JEAN-BAPTISTE BUDES DE Guébriant (1860–1935) had extensive knowledge of missions in East Asia. Since joining the Paris Foreign Mission Society (PFMS) in 1883 and two years later appointed as missionary to China, de Guébriant became a renowned and influential authority of the Catholic Church's mission not only in China but also Siberia, Northeast, and East Asia.[1] In 1918, de Guébriant was one of six missionary bishops asked by the Vatican to report on the Church's situation in China and in 1921 he became the superior general of his society.[2] At the age of sixty-five, having spent most of his life leading missionary work for the Church, de Guébriant delivered a report to Pope Pius XI on May 9, 1925 that explained the origins of the Korean Catholic Church. Instead of the usual development of Christian communities through the efforts of missionaries, the Korean case, de Guébriant stated, was "an unique example of modern missionary history."[3]

Adrien Launay (1853–1927), a French Catholic historian and archivist who reported de Guébriant's presentation in *Martyrs Francais et Coreens, 1838–1846* [trans. French and Korean Martyrs], stated that the Korean

---

1. According to Don Baker, the Paris Society of Foreign Missions (Société de Missions Étrangères de Paris, or M. E. P.) was the "most important order providing priests for Korea's Catholic churches in the nineteenth century and well into the twentieth" (Baker, "Transformation of the Catholic Church," 20).

2. Wiest, "Guébriant, Jean-Baptiste Budes de," 268. De Guébriant was also appointed apostolic visitor *in missiones sinensis* in July 1919. He served as the superior general of PFMS from 1921 to 1935.

3. de Guébriant in Choi, *Roman Catholic Church in Korea*, 9.

church's uniqueness stemmed from the fact that it began independently—"without any direct evangelistic efforts."[4] Unlike "Vietnam, Japan, or China," where the Catholic Church in those countries was developed through "missionary zeal," Launay stated that the Korean church was an "accident," a "spontaneous birth" that sprouted out of the soil in a field where no fruit was expected.[5]

The appearance of a self-generated Christianity without the intervention of missionaries makes the Korean case all the more puzzling, especially in missiological studies that focuses on the ways in which people respond to missionaries, strategies, and missional movements. Christian communities are not supposed to appear by themselves without some form of external support and guidance. The independent way Koreans adopted Christianity upends our preconceived notions of how Christian communities should appear in a linear fashion: introduction of Christianity through missionaries; discipleship of converts by missionaries, teaching of church organization and leadership roles, and the building of institutions. The Korean example demonstrates that Christianity, once engaged or colliding with religious and cultural forces in the Global South, moves fluidly and at times in contradictory ways.

The work of missionaries is critical to the transmission of Christianity but it is one facet among many that engages the local culture. Unlike a newly cleared landscape that has never been used before, the Korean soil had been cultivated for centuries and the landscape has been enriched over time by the nutrients brought into the tilling process by previous generations. When seeds of Christianity were sown on Korean soil, the particular endowments in the soil fused with the seed to produce a distinctive yield.

The terracultural perspective attempts to identify the various nutrients in the soil and determine the most influential elements. By doing so, it reveals the dynamic between the seeds of Christianity and the distinctive characteristics found in the native soil. The process is hardly simple or predictable. In examining the various factors at work, we are made to

4. de Guébriant report was quoted by Adrien Launay, a historian and archivist with the Catholic Société des Missions-Etrangeres de Paris (French Society of Foreign Missions). See Launay, *Martyrs Francais et Coreens*, 9. In the 1890s, Launay published a three-volume history of the French Society of Foreign Missions that was approximately 1,800 pages (Pelley, "Colonial Benedictions," 163).

5. Launay's report is also quoted in Chung, *Syncretism*, 3–4. Don Baker, an expert on Korean Catholicism, wrote, "Because of the conditions under which Catholicism emerged in Korea, because of the hostility it endured from both the government and society at large, Korea's first Catholics did not leave us much written evidence of what precisely they believed and why they came to believe it" (Baker, "Catholic God and Confucian Morality," 101–2).

understand something of the interaction taking place beneath the surface but our understanding of missions, church growth, and discipleship leans so often on the sowers, the kind of seeds, and fertilizing strategies that we fail to recognize or activate the dormant cultural energies that may spark spiritual awakening.

The fact that planting seeds of Christianity occurs in living systems invites a host of reactions in different cultures. The receptivity of the receiving soil is determined by the amount of fertility, resistance, and resources in the land. Considering that cultures in the Global South maintain loyalty to a particular religious tradition, the introduction of foreign seeds usually triggers dynamic consequences. Nevertheless, the process of understanding the interaction enables a reassessment of the situation that factors in the receiving culture as a creative participant in the integration of Christian assumptions and ideas. By examining cultural predispositions of the receiving culture, we can explore the meaningful points of contact with Christianity that arouses a passionate response, such as the Catholic experience.

However the self-initiated way in which Koreans developed Christian communities was not only a Catholic experience, as it was repeated again and again later in Korea and the United States. More than two hundred years later, a similar phenomenon occurred when Protestant missionaries entered a country infamous for shunning foreigners, especially Westerners. Known as the "hermit kingdom," Korea maintained a strict foreign policy of isolation and Protestant missionaries were determined to bring Christianity to Korea, but much to their surprise, they discovered that Protestantism was already there. Samuel Hugh Moffett, the distinguished missionary to China and Korea and the author of the two volumes of *A History of Christianity in Asia*, wrote, "In Korea, it was the Koreans themselves, not foreign missionaries, who first brought Christianity to their own people from across its guarded borders."[6] Not only were Protestant Christians were practicing Protestantism by themselves, they were conducting evangelism on their own: distributing Christian literature and sharing the gospel to their neighbors.[7]

Horace G. Underwood arrived in 1885 as one of the first Protestant missionaries to receive permission to enter Korea but unbeknownst to him a Korean Christian heard of his arrival and tracked down his residence in Seoul. According to Underwood, Sang-yun Seo (1848–1926) one day knocked on his door. Seo "presented himself at my house, with a letter of

6. Moffett, *History of Christianity in Asia*, 2:309.

7. Seo "had come across the Yalu in 1833, but had stopped at his home on the west coast before proceeding to Seoul to distribute Christian literature" (Moffett, *Christians of Korea*, 36).

introduction from Mr. [John] Ross [of the Scottish United Presbyterian Mission stationed in Manchuria], and told me that there were a number desiring baptism in his village."[8] Seo embarked on a personal mission to entreat Underwood to follow him to Sorae, his village, right away. Samuel Hugh Moffett wrote, "Like their Roman Catholic brethren before them, Suh [or Seo] and his colleagues made their way back into and began winning their own converts before any [Protestant] missionary was able to take up permanent work in their forbidden land."[9]

Much like the Korean Catholic experience centuries earlier, Seo became a Christian in China and returning home Seo began preaching the gospel to his family and friends. In a thoroughly Confucian culture that viewed the pursuit of Confucian virtues as a private as well as a collective endeavor, the instinctive drive to uplift and edifty one another was normative in the Korean experience. He and his brother who also accepted the faith began leading others to Christianity. Soon, as the number of Christian converts increased, Seo was concerned about how to ritually incorporate these new believers since he was not a minister or priest. Underwood followed Seo to his village and discovered villagers who without formal education took the tenets of Christianity seriously enough to assume leadership in practicing them when religious authorities were not available.

On their own, Christians from Sorae traveled across villages and began sharing with their neighbors about Christianity, selling tracts and Christian literature.[10] With a cluster of villages grounded in Protestantism, Samuel Hugh Moffett wrote, "The Sorai [i.e., Sorae] congregation, unbaptized and with no clergyman, was already gathering for worship, making it the 'cradle' of Korean Protestantism."[11]

Most Korean Christians have never heard of Sang-yun Seo but his crucial role in assisting the first missionaries by teaching them Korean, translating Scripture, and traveling with them in evangelistic journeys carried significant implications for the development of Korean Christianity. As a trader who frequently traveled across Korea and abroad, Seo was familiar with Korea's routes and terrain. Seo quickly became a trusted partner in

8. Underwood, *Call of Korea*, 107–8. As a trader of ginseng and other products, Seo frequently traveled to Manchuria where he encountered Christianity by meeting John Ross and John Macintyre, both Scottish missionaries.

9. Moffett, *Christians of Korea*, 35–36.

10. "Native [Korean] Christians, most of whom had learned the truth in China, were employed to distribute and sell Christian tracts and books" (Underwood, *Call of Korea*, 136). Without ever setting foot in Korea, John Ross, while in Manchuria, completed the first Korean translation of the New Testament in 1887.

11. Moffett, "Suh Sang-Yun," 651.

ministry who personally guided Underwood to Korea's major cities, going as far as the Chinese border.[12] Later Seo assisted Underwood in developing "the first organized Korean Protestant church."[13] The renowned missionary Samuel Austin Moffett, whose legendary work in Pyeongyang is well documented, arrived in Korea in 1890 and shortly thereafter Seo took him and James S. Gale to the northern regions of Korea for three months to survey the territories for mission expansion.[14]

What is more, other appearances of self-generated Korean Christian communities have been recorded. In 1909, Mary F. Scranton, the first woman missionary in Korea, described "widower churches"—a name they gave to churches attended only by men, but not because they were welcomed.[15] Scranton wrote, "no amount of persuading on the part of the husbands and fathers was effectual in convincing the women."[16] As she investigated the situation further, she realized that no determination could be made as to how they became Christians. She wondered if someone in the village had heard of the gospel somewhere and brought it back. Perhaps a traveling pastor crossed their path. Nonetheless, these Korean Christians, according to Scranton, "organized themselves" without the aid of outside assistance and they "held their regular Sunday services and met once or twice during the week for prayer and study."[17]

Repeatedly, missionaries encountered an internal automatic response system after Koreans became Christian—the impulse to make Christianity supreme in their lives, to live out the faith into something more enriching, more satisfying, and more perfect, to tell their relatives, neighbors, and strangers of their discovery. In 1912 a woman missionary observed the phenomenon: "The Koreans are naturally very evangelistic, and as soon as they come to believe in Christ they go out at once after relatives and neighbors. They soon see that Christianity is good, and they want their friends to share with them, even though they are unable to tell intelligently about the blessings of Christianity."[18]

This chapter examines the Korean version of Neo-Confucianism as the ideological basis from which this inner sense of mission and prompting for

---

12. Some of the cities that they surveyed include Songdo, Sorae, Pyeongyang, and Euiju on the Chinese border. Underwood, *Call of Korea*, 137.

13. Moffett, "Suh Sang-Yun," 651.

14. Moffett, "Suh Sang-Yun," 651.

15. Scranton, "Widower Churches," 167.

16. Scranton, "Widower Churches," 167.

17. Scranton, "Widower Churches," 167.

18. "Our Young People (1912)," 364.

outward expression has been derived. The ease with which Korean Christians transitioned from belief to enthusiastic participation is rooted in the Confucian ethos that has been nurtured and hardwired for centuries during Joseon dynasty. The unique Korean interpretation of Neo-Confucianism viewed ideological purity in exclusivist terms with their philosophical position as the point of orthodoxy.

In Korea's Neo-Confucian orthodoxy, an enthusiastic commitment was the means to attaining the ultimate objective: moral perfection. The Confucian education and training instilled an unswerving dedication, across all social classes, of the pursuit of moral perfection, its attainment prized above all else, including monetary gain. The combination of these traits fueled a cultural ethos in which a morally aroused state was both predictable and expected. At the same time, the Confucian ethos placed a heavy burden upon the individual, at times more than what they were able to bear but practitioners of "the Way" were expected to make sacrifices to achieve the mission. In addition, the sense of the emotional and psychological toll exacted on the population expanded the people's level of tolerance for hardship.

ORTHODOXY

In the Korean mind, the distinction between orthodoxy and heterodoxy, right and wrong was very clear. In *Korea in Transition* (1909), James S. Gale observed the "appreciation of high morals . . . [and] their exalting of principles of right" among Koreans.[19] Not only are the lines clearly drawn but people were expected to enthusiastically embrace and propagate orthodoxy. Gale observed that the "coolie as well as the statesman or gifted man of letters says, '*In-eui-ye-chi-shin*.'"[20] The words imprinted on the minds of Koreans—from the lowest to the highest official—are the Five Virtues of Confucianism representing love/kindness, righteousness, ritual/rites, wisdom/knowledge, and faith.

Although Neo-Confucianism originated in Sung dynasty China with the works of Chu Hsi (1130–1200), Korean Neo-Confucian literati eventually viewed themselves as the keepers of Neo-Confucian orthodoxy or *jeong-hak* ("right learning").

Deviations of orthodox Confucian teachings, such as the Chinese and Japanese experience, "were regarded [by Koreans] as 'heretical' and,

19. Gale, *Korea in Transition*, 154.
20. Gale, *Korea in Transition*, 96.

therefore, had no solid ground on which to stand."[21] According to Isop Hong, "Everything in Korean life, including the individual's way of thinking and social behavior, had to conform to Chu Hsi philosophy; all other ideas were barred and suppressed as heresy."[22]

When the Confucian literati in China broke away from Chu Hsi's "orthodox" canon and accepted Wang Yang-ming's interpretation of Neo-Confucianism, Koreans concluded that the Chinese committed apostasy by embracing heresy. With China's intelligentsia veering off the road of orthodoxy, Koreans saw themselves as the true heirs of Confucian civilization. As unwavering adherents, Koreans came to view themselves "superior to the Chinese because they were more faithful to Neo-Confucian orthodoxy."[23] As the Joseon kingdom became "equated with civilization," the Joseon king "now represented Confucian civilization as well as the nation."[24]

As Joseon society was established on the premise that moral self-cultivation was the central preoccupation of the people, the pressure upon the Joseon kings to exhibit and exemplify sage kingship was particularly great. The king's mandate to rule rested on his ability to govern with moral excellence. The burden of perfection weighed heavily on the crown. "Not only was he expected to perfect himself; he was also burdened with effecting perfect order in his realm."[25]

As the 'father' to all the people, the Korean king's legitimacy rested on his ability to personify Confucian virtue. As the standard-bearer for the Confucian civilization, the king's moral cultivation received an inordinate amount of attention and scrutiny. Referring to the Korean king, Haboush wrote, "As the ultimate source of well-being as well as of the harmony between the moral order in the universe and the ethical and social order in the kingdom, the rectification of the imperial mind acquired a central importance."[26] As an example of a virtuous king who achieved the status

21. Chung, *Korean Neo-Confucianism*, 34.

22. Hong, "Modern Korean Thought," 320.

23. de Bary, *East Asian Civilizations*, 63.

24. Haboush, *Confucian Kingship in Korea*, 25.

25. Haboush, *Confucian Kingship in Korea*, 9.

26. Haboush, *Confucian Kingship in Korea*, 9. In her close examination of King Yŏngjo's reign, Haboush wrote that he fulfill the demand for sage kingship. "Yŏnjo's pursuit of sage kingship was predicated on his belief that the rhetoric and ideas of the sage king would render him with effective means with which to deal with the demands of his court and society. The effectiveness of his pursuit, first of all, depended on whether he could persuade his bureaucrats and subjects of the seriousness of his intent. In this respect, Yŏngjo seems to have succeeded. He pursued his ideal with single-minded commitment. His relentless construction of an image as a sage king during his fifty-two-year reign, the longest Yi reign, led to bureaucratic capitulation to his moral

as a sage-king, King Yongjo (r. 1724–1776) rejected "authoritarian and arbitrary" rule that used force to exercise his will. Instead, Yongjo sought out persuasion to win "official admiration and approval" that was achieved through his own "moral perfection."[27]

When foreign powers increased their imperialistic pressure upon Korea in the late nineteenth century, conservative leaders of the Korean government viewed the struggle against foreign imperialism as a fight between right and wrong, truth and false, and orthodoxy and heterodoxy. The rallying cry of the conservative Korean leaders was *wijeong cheoksa*, which meant "defend orthodoxy and reject heterodoxy."[28] To the conservative Korean officials, "the Confucian virtues were the exclusive hallmarks of civilization; what the West had to offer, including its commodities, were the products of barbarism."[29] When the *Shenandoah*, an American naval warship, threatened Korea by cruising into the Taedong River in 1868, Confucian scholar-officials in Pyeongyang rallied the people to uphold morality and righteousness and reject barbarian encroachment. The Confucian leaders wrote: "Lacking morals and virtue . . . these [Western] scoundrels have no idea about moral obligations. . . . How is it possible that we as righteous persons can encounter this moment and not earnestly dedicate our heart for this nation?"[30]

Staunch conservatives "were determined to uphold the Confucian orthodoxy by rejecting the West."[31] In the "Memorial of Ten Thousand Men," the "most well known of the memorials to the [Korean] throne" in the late nineteenth century, Manson Yi wrote, "Unfortunately, the heresy known as Christianity (Yesugyo), which has come from the followers of the overseas barbarians, has nothing to say about decorum or a sense of honor and is completely sweeping away the 'five human relations' (*orun*), the 'three bonds' (*samgang*), duty (*tori*), and law (*beopjik*)."[32] Furthermore, Russia, America, and Japan, according to Yi, "are all the same barbarians."[33]

---

superiority. His continued display of concern for his people seems to have earned gratitude and appreciation. His excursions into the streets in the later years of his life were greeted with spontaneous cheers, a rare phenomenon in Yi Korea" (Haboush, *Confucian Kingship in Korea*, 2).

27. Haboush, *Confucian Kingship in Korea*, 60.

28. Lew, "Historical Overview of Korean Perceptions," 115.

29. P. Lee, *Sourcebook of Korean Civilization*, 323.

30. Lew, "Enlightenment Period," 173–74.

31. P. Lee, *Sourcebook of Korean Civilization*, 290.

32. Lew, "Enlightenment Period," 178.

33. Lew, "Enlightenment Period," 179.

Hangno Yi, a senior government official, urged the king and the Korean people to "revere right learning and reject heresy" (*sung jeonghak byeok yang ijeok*).[34] Yi wrote, "The calamity caused by the Western barbarians is more serious today than any caused by floodwater or wild beasts. . . . The choice between the life of a human or that of a beast, between survival or death, is to be made in a very short time."[35] Ikhyeon Choe, a high government official who led an anti-Japanese uprising in 1906, was captured and later died of self-imposed starvation while imprisoned on the island of Tsushima. Prior to his capture, Choe in 1876 wrote to the king, "To apply the teaching of Ch'eng and Chu [two founders of Neo-Confucianism] to today's situation, peace with the bandits will without fail bring about disorder and ruination with no gain."[36]

The late nineteenth century, when Protestant missionaries arrived in Korea, shook the foundations of Korean civilization. Centuries of reinforcement in Neo-Confucian principles engendered a great sense of confidence in Korea's Confucian society. As Joseon dynasty came under imperialistic pressure, the people's absolute faith in Confucianism began to show signs of fracture. While confidence in Confucianism may have suffered, Koreans' moral sensibility of locking into an unyielding conviction of orthodox teachings and doctrines did not waver.

Protestant missionaries were amazed how Koreans, almost instantly, were able to abandon without hesitation centuries-old traditions at the moment when they concluded that the Christian teachings were the doctrinal truth. One of the major obstacles to missionary work was ancestor worship, a fundamental Confucian rite that epitomized devotion to one's parents and ancestors. Before the missionaries made an official policy regarding this issue, James S. Gale decided to ask Korean Christians how ancestor worship should be dealt with. Given how central ancestor worship was to Korean culture, Gale and other missionaries were not sure how Korean Christians would react. In a day or two, responses to Gale's request were returned and he and other missionaries were surprised at the ease with which Koreans responded to this question. Their uncompromising disposition surprised the missionaries that their responses were included in the mission report:

> Aim Soonk: I have heard the Bible and it differs altogether from the customs of the world, of which ancestral worship is the greatest. The Bible is God's Word. I intend to follow it and not sacrifice [to ancestors].

34. Lew, "Historical Overview of Korean Perceptions," 115.

35. P. Lee, *Sourcebook of Korean Civilization*, 328.

36. P. Lee, *Sourcebook of Korean Civilization*, 330.

Song Changlun: My first reason for not sacrificing is, it breaks God's commands; and my second reason is, it is foolishness.

Yang Si Yung: The New Testament teachings are an out-and-out reconstruction of our rules of action, and they prohibit offerings of any kind spread out in worship to anything, whatever it may be, and so I do not worship.

Kirun Sa Yung: I have heard God's Word, and believe it true, and I put my trust in Jesus, and hope for the guidance of the Holy Spirit. For me, of course, I must remember my parents, but offering sacrifice to them is, I know, foolishness, like offerings to idols and evil spirits, which I desire to know nothing of. What I desire to know is the Gospel of God, and how to keep His commandments and do as Jesus has done. This only do I desire to know.[37]

MORAL PERFECTION

Neo-Confucianism influenced China, Japan, and Vietnam but, in Korea, an uncompromising and all-encompassing version of Neo-Confucianism took hold during Joseon dynasty, creating Confucian sensibilities designed to arouse passionate commitment to "the Way"—a term used by Korean literati in reference to their idealistic orthodoxy. The goal was no less than moral perfection—the transition from textual knowledge to its exercise and full embodiment. Confucianism in Korea represented not only the cultural narrative within the life of the people but was also realized by that life itself, in order that its precepts may transform the soul and arouse passions with the actualization of moral perfection—a vision fervently pursued but understood to be beyond the reach and thus never fully achieved.

The encounter with Christianity and its core salvific message resonated with Koreans who perceived Christianity, with its premise of redemption and salvation, as complementary to the approach of the fundamental pursuit of moral perfection since Christian doctrines represented eternal salvation or redemption from imperfections or sins. For the Koreans who converted to Christianity, they rejected key Confucian rituals, such as ancestor reverence but their adoption of Christianity did not signal the rejection or abandonment of the Confucian worldview since their conversion emerged as the outgrowth from a Confucian landscape.

The Korean mindset during Joseon dynasty embraced a "belief in the perfectibility of man," according to Martina Deuchler, who was a leading

37. "Gensan," 162.

Pyeongyang, 1913-1920s. "Pastor Pak, of Taikee." Photo credit: Moffett Korea Collection. Princeton Theological Seminary.

"A Korean Christian Family." Photo credit: Moffett Korea Collection.
Princeton Theological Seminary.

SARIM TENACTY

As the dominant social and political force in Korea, Neo-Confucian literati turned over the landscape of the previous Goryeo dynasty and broke new ground and cultivated an energized form of Confucianism but the Confucian establishment was far from monolithic as factional disputes, regional competition, and contrasting views of Confucian propriety fragmented the homogeneity expected in a Confucian state.[52] Among the most influential agitators within the Confucian establishment were the *sarim* [trans. "forest of literati"], who not only embraced an utopian vision of Confucianism but demonstrated an unbending will to implement their reforms on Korean society.

The *sarim* were a faction within Korean Neo-Confucianism known as the "righteous oppressed," a designation that captures members' allegiance to their beliefs to the point of martyrdom. The country was already Confucianized more than any other country but the *sarim*, as ideological firebrands, insisted that Korea did not go far enough. The *sarim* criticized the established Confucian officials endlessly and they were willing to put their lives on the line for their beliefs.

Sarim's iron-will to withstand persecution and later bloody purges was instilled by their founder, Jae Gil, who, as a loyal subject of the previous Goryeo dynasty, not only refused to cooperate but also criticized the new Joseon dynasty as illegitimate, despite the fact that Confucianism formed the core of the state ideology. Even when a Joseon king called him for service to the kingdom, Gil refused and retreated to the countryside where he groomed future members of the *sarim*.

At the outset of Joseon dynasty, the *sarim* were marginalized from the political establishment but viewed the Confucian establishment as corrupt and ideologically deficient. The *sarim* mentality, according to Michael Kalton, was "a rigorous and idealistic moralism that focused on the absolute centrality of moral self-cultivation and exclusive commitment to the true Way."[53] Their single-mindedness projected a "self-conscious ambience which prevailed among the men who brought the Ch'eng-Chu school [i.e., orthodox Neo-Confucianism] to full maturity to Korea."[54]

---

52. "Still, it would be a mistake to assume that homogeneity reigned either within the Confucian community or outside it in the second half of the Chosŏn [or Joseon] dynasty. That community was marked by factional affiliation, regional distinctions, and divergent views on the propriety of hold government office" (Haboush and Deuchler, "Introduction," 3).

53. Kalton, *To Become a Sage*, 9.

54. Kalton, *To Become a Sage*, 9. Ch'eng I (1033–1107), the co-founder of the

Rejecting the lure of vestments, wealth, and status, the *sarim* waged a relentless attack on what they viewed as a compromised form of Confucianism. The impassioned breed of scholar-officials of the *sarim* "remonstrated without hesitation whenever they felt the conduct of the kings and high officials did not meet the high standards of Neo-Confucian principles."[55] Each individual from the king down to the peasant were expected by the *sarim* to an uncompromising commitment to the pursuit of the highest moral ideal, no matter the cost.

The *sarim* brought about a seemingly unstoppable movement toward their goal of moral persecution that even threats of death could not diminish. The *sarim's* constant criticism enraged the political establishment that obtained officialdom and rank through favor, family connections, political power, and lineage. The *sarim* claimed higher moral authority and they beat the drums of remonstrance without stop. They were intolerable and yet they were "unwilling to take no for an answer, continuing remonstrance on an issue for months on end and vilifying their opponents as amoral and vicious men."[56]

The relentless criticism eventually wore out the establishment's tolerance of *sarim* and began a series of backlashes on the *sarim* members but the ill-treatment only galvanized their resolve. The year 1498 was the first of *sahwa*, or the literati purges, in which *sarim* scholar-officials were tortured and executed. The following literati purges took place in 1504, 1519, 1545.[57]

The bloody persecutions did little to dampen their determination. In fact, the *sarim* persevered through all the persecutions and bloody crackdowns and by the late sixteenth century they dominated the Korean court. In fact, the purges left an indelible imprint not only on the Korean court but also on Korean society as a whole as the *sarim* interpretation of Neo-Confucianism became normative.[58] In essence, the *sarim* brand of the idealistic, yet heavily exacting, moralism gradually became the prevailing worldview in Korea. The *sarim* mentality or the uncompromising commitment to moral excellence "won general acceptance as the indisputable orthodox core of genuine Confucianism."[59]

Ch'eng-Chu school, set the precedent when he fell "victim of intense persecution and died almost a martyr" for his beliefs (de Bary, *Neo-Confucian Orthodoxy*, 14).

55. P. Lee and de Bary, *Sources of Korean Tradition,* 268.

56. Kalton, *To Become a Sage,* 11.

57. For more, see Eckert et al., *Korea Old and New,* 136.

58. "There have been many interpretations of Confucius and Confucianism but none I know of that would deny the central importance of self-cultivation and self-fulfillment in his teaching" (de Bary, *Learning for One's Self,* xi).

59. Kalton, *To Become a Sage,* 13–14. "Although the Neo-Confucian literati became

The *sarim* mentality demanded an austere personal pursuit of moral high ideals, even if it meant sacrifice—and, at times, enduring hardship and persecution for the sake of gaining the ultimate prize. Above all else, the fastidious attention to moral aims became the idealized preoccupation. Such a commitment was demanding and taxing, as it meant undergoing a continuous critical self-examination but the rigor—a mental state bent toward moral perfection—was accepted as a matter of course. The inner moral struggle shaped the character and the mental makeup, re-interpreting the notion of sacrifice as a necessary step to transformation. As a result, the relentless mental pursuit pushed towards a breaking point where it must be overcome.

When Sang-yun Seo surprised Horace G. Underwood shortly after his arrival to Korea by showing up at his house, Seo requested that Underwood come with him right away to his village in order to baptize converts. Underwood, on such a short notice, could not travel into the forbidden interior and declined the request. Seo did not give up however. Seo appeared at Underwood's house again next spring, "this time bringing the converts with him!"[60] While Underwood was pleasantly surprised at the visit, he and other missionaries were skeptical of the extent to which they understood Christianity, considering that the Christian village operated completely by lay people without the aid of missionaries or church leaders. The whole mission gathered to examine them and the three men "were found ready for baptism."[61]

The unusual nature of the visit was not lost on Underwood who asked the three Korean men if they truly understood the consequences that would befall them if they were uncovered. "We are ready," they replied, "to stand by our faith to the death."[62] At that moment, it may have been difficult for the missionaries to ascertain whether they truly meant "to the death," especially given that believers in the West do not respond to Christian doctrines in such fashion but, for Koreans, making such a profound decision took on monumental proportions that resembled the solemnity of an oath. As

---

the victims of these purges, their moralistic causes, such as the sagely rule championed by Cho Kwangjo (1482–1519), were upheld as just by later generations, and in the end their Neo-Confucian worldview prevailed among the scholar-officials of Chosŏn [or Joseon] as the Neo-Confucian orthodoxy" (P. Lee and de Bary, *Sources of Korean Tradition*, 268).

60. Moffett, *Christians of Korea*, 39.

61. Moffett, *Christians of Korea*, 39.

62. Moffett, *Christians of Korea*, 39.

Underwood proceeded with the baptismal ritual, the Methodist missionary Homer Hulbert kept watch, "guarding the door for fear of discovery."[63]

SACRIFICE

As many missionaries discovered, moral cultivation topped material wealth in terms of priority. Koreans according to Moffett "place a higher value on moral and spiritual things than upon material. The thing which appeals to the Koreans is justice, and justice has a greater appeal to them than anything of a material nature."[64] During Joseon Korea, living in relative poverty was not shameful to those who pursued the "Confucian way of life," which "incurred high costs."[65]

The missionaries noticed how Koreans distanced themselves from a life of monetary ambition and gravitated toward moral idealism. Despite the fact that the "great majority" of Korean Christians were "very poor," W. A. Noble in 1906 challenged "any people, whether white, brown, yellow, or black, to show a better record [of generosity and giving] than the Korean."[66] In 1932, Victor Peters observed among the Korean young people the disdain toward "imperialism and class privilege" while displaying a penchant for idealistic socialism. Peters wrote, "Much as they personally might wish to have money, the rich man is not their ideal. The eye of the Christian young people is caught immediately by the account in Acts of the early Jerusalem socialism."[67]

Unbeknownst to most missionaries, "extreme demands for self-sacrifice . . . made upon the individual" was a hallmark Neo-Confucian characteristic.[68] The Neo-Confucian movement produced a specialized character, "placing heavy emphasis on methods of mind-rectification, disciplining of the desires, reforming of human weaknesses."[69] Others defining characteristics of the followers of Neo-Confucianism included "moralistic religiosity," "dynamism of an intense faith," and an unwavering commitment.[70] Endur-

63 Moffett, *Christians of Korea*, 39.

64. Moffett in Huntley, *Caring, Growing, Changing,* 175.

65. Haboush, *Confucian Kingship in Korea*, 85.

66. Noble, "Korean Decadence," 176. Noble was particularly upset from reading "constantly articles written by uninformed writers who declare that Korea is a decadent nation" (Noble, "Korean Decadence," 176).

67. Peters, "Korean Young People," 93.

68. de Bary, *Neo-Confucian Orthodoxy*, 72.

69. de Bary, *Neo-Confucian Orthodoxy*, 70.

70. de Bary, *Neo-Confucian Orthodoxy*, 70.

ance and sacrifice through repression, persecution, and ostracism were common denominators "in their pursuit of the high ideal of sagehood and service to mankind."[71] Neo-Confucians, de Bary wrote, "insisted on firm assertion of the moral will, strict self-control, and the practice of an extreme self-denial which gave this early formulation of Neo-Confucian orthodoxy a stern, rigoristic quality."[72]

The sacrifice of one's material possession signaled pure motivation untainted by greed or material gain. Materialism, or at least coveting wealth, stood in opposition to Confucian morals that viewed the pursuit of wealth as impure or immoral since the person aimed for individual gain above all else instead of denying oneself in the pursuit of moral perfection. In 1893, Sang-yun Seo hosted Mackenzie, a Presbyterian missionary who recently arrived in Korea. Mackenzie heard of Seo and decided to visit him in Sorae. O. R. Avison who recorded the incident wrote that Seo "gave him the best room he had. He boarded him, taught him the [Korean] language, used to go out with him among the people and preach with him, became his helper generally." At the end of the month, Mackenzie said,

> "Mr. So [Seo], I want to pay you now for last month's work." "Well," he said, "I am not taking anything for his work; I am not working for money." "But," said Mackenzie, "I have lived in your house; you have supplied me with fuel, you have supplied me with food; you have been my language teacher; I have taken up your time and I must pay you for it; I can't have this thing go on in this way." "Well," said So [Seo], "I cannot afford to take your money." "But," said Mackenzie, "I can't have you any longer then to work for me." "Well," said Mr. So, "you pay me just what it costs for your board and I will call it square; but I can not afford to take your money for preaching. If I take your money and go out and preach they will all laugh at me; I will lose my influence and the work will stop."[73]

One of the most surprising characteristics that the missionaries encountered was the great lengths to which Korean Christians would go to follow through what becoming a 'Christian' meant to them. Without prompting, Korean Christians gave generously, at times, to the point of becoming destitute, something which the missionaries would not promote, especially considering the missionaries' deliberate display of material wealth,

71. de Bary, *Neo-Confucian Orthodoxy*, 70.

72. de Bary, *Neo-Confucian Orthodoxy*, 70.

73. *Ecumenical Missionary Conference 1900*, 2:306–7.

such as the construction of American-style houses and import of Western furniture, clothing, and foods.[74]

In traditional Korean culture, stone roof tiles were reserved for the elite and upper class while the majority of Koreans covered their houses with straw thatches. The stone tiles, which were very expensive, denoted status and wealth. When a village church in 1912, due to lack of funds, used straw thatches to cover the roof, a member of the church, "seeing that the Lord's house was faring worse than his own," went home, proceeded to manually remove the tiles from his house, and installed them on the church, while "taking the straw thatch for his own home."[75]

"Out of their extreme poverty," a missionary observed, "they are willing to give as those who are better off never think of doing."[76] With little consideration of their own welfare, they "eagerly sell their rings, hairpins, donkeys, oxen, and often mortgage their homes, in order to give to the cause of the Lord in whom they have learned to believe."[77] Others noticed how they reduce their food consumption so that they may give more for the effort. "All over Korea the people put aside handfuls of rice when preparing the daily meals, and after a measure has been thus gathered together it is sold, and the money used for the support of their pastor or their school teachers."[78]

In the early twentieth century, W. Arthur Noble, a Methodist missionary in Korea, recalled the story of a Korean who became the first convert in his village and a Christian leader to others in the village. He soon opened

74. "In another sense, missionaries strongly idealized a non-existent version of a utopian Christian America. The missionary actually living overseas remained deeply emotionally attached to the ideal of 'Christian civilization.' The culture in which the missionary had been raised could never be wholly left behind, nor did the missionary wish it to be. Indeed, according to a Luther missionary in Japan, holding on to all things 'Western' was absolutely necessary in order to be effective in the work. 'The mission home should be a Western home transplanted in the East. It may not become too much Orientalized. It should have Western furniture, pictures, musical instruments, etc., and should make its possessor feel that he is in a Western home. . . . The missionary may not be Orientalized, else he will be in danger of becoming heathenized.' For many decades, unconscious conflation of Christianity with this highly idealized and unreal home culture led to missionaries expecting converts to become 'civilized,' with American-style houses, furniture, marriage rites, hygiene, and even economic structure, and the missionaries themselves going to great lengths to hold on to the material symbols of that culture—clothing, furniture, cooking—even when ludicrous and irrational in their new setting" (Snow, *Protestant Missionaries*, 8–9).

75. "Self-Sacrifice among Koreans," 554.

76. "Our Young People (1913)," 170.

77. "Our Young People (1913)," 170.

78. "Our Young People (1913)," 170.

his house as a Christian meeting-place. Over time, more villagers converted and, to accommodate the larger number of worshippers, they decided to build a chapel. The debt from the building lingered on as the villagers exhausted their resources. One day, the leader took his ox with which he did his plowing to the marketplace, sold it, and paid off the remaining debt on the church. Noble visited the village the following spring and observed the following: "holding the handles of the plow was the old, gray-haired father of the family, and hitched in the traces, where the ox should have been, were this Korean Christian and his brother, dragging his plow through the field that year themselves."[79] The "most enthusiastic offering" was taken in 1906 at Central Presbyterian Church in Pyeongyang where people gave "deeds of lands and houses, offerings of money and rings, and promises of pay specific sums each year for a period or for life."[80]

Indeed, the ability of Korean Christians to effortlessly surpass the imaginings and expectations of missionaries was repeatedly brought home. In 1911, during an evangelistic campaign, a missionary on the field noted that the Korean Christians "were far ahead of the foreigners in zeal for the effort."[81] In an unusual twist on the mission field, Korean Christians began to create new spiritual practices and outperform the spiritual practice of missionaries. Lillias Underwood recounted how missionaries awoke "at midnight to hear Koreans singing in midnight prayer-meetings."[82] A few hours after midnight, Korean Christians gathered "at 4 a.m. morning after morning in winter."[83]

In 1912, F. H. L. Paton described the "spirit of sacrifice" among Korean Christians when he wrote:

> The further we got into the heart of Korea the more we became convinced that the people were making sacrifices for Christ that were unapproached by any other people. Thousands of men gave freely of their time and strength to act as honorary leaders of congregations, doing the full work of home missionaries, while at great toil they provided for their families and themselves. Many others rendered their already hard living still harder by giving up days of work and wages that they might go and preach.[84]

79. Noble in Jones, *Modern Missionary Challenge*, 155–56.

80. Hall, "Education in Korea," 106.

81. "Korea—The Evangelizing Zeal," 393.

82. Underwood, "Korea and the Gospel," 697.

83. Underwood, "Korea and the Gospel," 697.

84. Paton, "Picture of Korean Christianity," 615.

Without being asked to do so, Paton observed how Koreans willingly lived on "broken rice instead of whole rice" so that they could give the difference to the church.[85] When a collection was taken for a new church building in 1923, people gave generously toward the new project but a particular gift startled the Korean pastor. He "started to read it [i.e., letter of the gift] but his voice shook so he could not."[86] Instead a Sunday School teacher read the content of the letter which followed: "I am only a poor student; I have no money, but I will give my own hair that it may be sold as my gift to the church."[87]

Louisa Rothweiler who succeeded Mary F. Scranton as the principal of Ewha Academy for girls reported that a Korean woman approached her on the street and gave her "500 cash" towards the new church building. Rothweiler "was surprised at the amount she had contrived to present, knowing that the family had a hard time to obtain a livelihood, but she explained that she had first heard about the new church every time she had put the rice on to boil she had saved out a handful, until it had come to be worth this amount."[88]

It wasn't just the adults. Korean children also demonstrated the same thing. The girls at Ewha Academy heard of money being raised for a church. A missionary entered the chapel only to discover that all of the girls were sitting in their seats. On the benches were "garments of every description and hue." The missionary noted that each girls brought something. She wrote, "The benches held silk, linen and cotton garments, shoes, rings, pins, books, and countless little keepsakes dear to the owners. With little or no difficulty the articles were sold and *yen* 300 ($150) was realized."[89]

Central to the practice of Neo-Confucian principles was the denial of oneself. In Korea's Neo-Confucianism, "extreme demands for self-sacrifice," according to de Bary, was "made upon the individual."[90] All cultures praise and honor self-sacrifice as one of the highest marks of distinction. Confucianism does not have an exclusive claim to sacrifice as a virtue but Korean Confucianism mandated a response action following the acquisition of knowledge, a characteristic that distinguished itself from Chinese

---

85. Paton, "Picture of Korean Christianity," 615.

86. Conrow, "Korea Woman's Conference," 172. "The time for pledges for the new church had come. Women gave wedding rings, valued trinkets they most prized. One woman after another quietly slipped outdoors and took off the beloved part of her wedding outfit, her beautiful switch" (Conrow, "Korea Woman's Conference," 172).

87. Conrow, "Korea Woman's Conference," 172.

88. Hall, "Dedication," 185–86.

89. "Giving at Ewha Haktang," 168.

90. de Bary, *Neo-Confucian Orthodoxy*, 72.

Confucianism and other cultures. China's acceptance of Wang Yang-ming's theory of the unity of knowledge and action in Neo-Confucianism overturned Chu Hsi's insistence on the pure investigation of knowledge which became the "orthodox" position in Korea. While Wang argued that knowledge does not necessitate action, Chu reinforced the notion that knowledge demanded proper action as a response. The outpouring of extraordinary giving was an example of the reflexive reaction to gaining knowledge. The centuries of conditioning under Korean Confucianism sensitized the people of the obligation of putting knowledge into action.

CONCLUSION

In contemporary Korea, 'prayer mountains' (gido-won) have become a unique development of Protestant Christianity. Before 1945, there were only two prayer mountains which is understandable given the suppression of Christianity under Japanese colonialism. By 1982 however there were 289. While earlier 'prayer mountains' were outposts in the mountains whereby Christians could retreat to a quiet place to meditate and pray, the modern versions resemble full-scale campuses with sanctuaries, cafeterias, dormitories, classrooms, private prayer rooms, and recreational areas.

As an example of a prayer mountain, the Osanri Prayer Mountain Sanctuary, established in 1973 by the Yoido Full Gospel Church has a "main sanctuary seating ten thousand, two smaller sanctuaries seating five thousand each, three hundred private prayer grottoes, and Western-style dormitories accommodating three thousand people."[91] If transportation is a problem, Yoido provides free shuttle-bus rides "daily on an hourly basis."[92]

Visitors can stay for an hour or for months. Prayer mountains have become a sibling ministry to the church. Participants can join the early dawn prayer meetings, all-night prayer meetings, fasting sessions, worship services around the clock, and other organized events, or spend time privately on their own. Osanri is an example of a church-sponsored prayer mountain and there are others sponsored by denominations or functioning as a separate, independent prayer mountain. For many prayer mountains, a heightened sense of spiritual manifestation or healing is expected, as intense vocalized forms of supplication are expressed.[93]

91. Mullins, "Empire Strikes Back," 93.

92. Mullins, "Empire Strikes Back," 93.

93. Visitors also go to prayer mountains "for health, wealth, fertility, and success in this life." In prayer mountains affiliated with the Pentecostal tradition, charismatic gifts are cultivated. "To practice speaking in tongues, some prayer mountain centers push

The development of prayer mountains is an outgrowth of the Korean Christians' desire for greater spirituality, worship, and revelation. The intense, profound desire for God—at times revealed in loud and ecstatic ways—was a natural response for Korean Christians. The seemingly irrational lengths to which Koreans expressed their devotion were prompted by cultural conditions that demanded a passionate, emotional, and immediate response that took precedence over costs and difficulties. The unceasing drive toward moral perfection awakened their moral consciousness and aroused creative reflection to actualize their pursuit that resulted in innovative practices, such as the prayer mountains and early dawn prayers.

As discussed in this chapter, the idealistic *sarim* built an enduring and powerful ethos of pursuing their lofty ideological ideals in spite of the cost. The same stubborn resilience was exhibited by Korean Catholics and Protestants a few centuries later when they stood fast to their convictions in the face of bloody persecutions. When the Protestant and Catholic missionaries arrived in Korea, they discovered a people that, without external prompting or guidance, took charge of their religious development in a way that defied the common trajectory of religious transmission.

---

the participants in the prayer meeting to repeat 'Halleluja' seven hundred times or nine hundred times" (Y. Lee, "Analysis of Christian Prayer Mountain," 51).

1937. "Old People's Prayer Group." Photo credit: Alice Butts Album.
Moffett Korea Collection. Princeton Theological Seminary.

From left to right: Chang-nak Do (theology professor), Pyun-Hun Choi (Seoul district superintendent), Chun-do Son (first missionary sent by the Korean church to Manchuria), and Yu-soon Kim (evangelist). Choi was thrown into prison for being a Christian. During his five months of imprisonment, he converted all of his cellmates.

3

Resilience and Persecution

TODAY, ONE CANNOT TOUR any South Korean city without noticing the presence of churches. The largest church in the world is in South Korea, as well as ten of the eleven largest churches.[1] Churches in South Korea have developed in one of the world's most technologically advanced and digitally-connected countries. As a result, the fourteen Korean mega-churches with attendance of over 10,000 on Sundays provide extensive online offerings of the most advanced digital technology and many of them started global programming whereby subscribers around the world can purchase a satellite dish to view Bible studies, services, sermons, talk-shows, and children's programs around the clock.[2] Internet ministries have expanded upon streaming worship online to provide a host of services, including receiving

1. R. Kim, "Korean Missionaries," 182. "The largest Presbyterian, Methodist, and Pentecostal congregations and the second largest Baptist congregations in the world are found in Korea along with the largest theological colleges" (R. Kim, "Korean Missionaries," 182).

2. For example, the internet department of Sarang Community Church, a mega-church in Seoul with 60,000 members, has four divisions: Web planning, Web designing, broadcast production, and Web operation. Their website operates more than 200 domains with each "divided by the task and the ministry sections." The content of their website includes "sermons, broadcasts of the worship service and seminars, online quiet time, emailing service on the discipleship training, church projects, and so on. The core aspects of the Web services are internet broadcasting and Godpia.com, Sarang's portal site that provides various resources to the public and is one of most extensive Christian portal sites in Korea" (D. Lee, "Effective Internet Ministry Strategy," 133). For example, Onnuri Church, a mega-church, offers the Christian Global Network Satellite TV ministry (CGNTV).

communion, baptism, "e-prayer requests," and "e-counseling."[3] Sponsored by a large Korean church, internet ministries functions independently by providing its own multimedia content and thereby creating a unique, separate space for their online community.

Although Catholics and Protestants today number about forty percent of the South Korean population, they enjoy a level of acceptance in mainstream society not found in many Asian societies. In many countries in the Global South, Christian communities live as a minority religion often facing, at the least, suspicion or worse open hostility, persecution, and violence.

Despite the many marks of modernity that are visible on Korean churches today, both Catholicism and Protestantism first developed in an era when the decision to become a Christian came with considerable costs. Individuals considering Christianity face the very real possibility of violent repercussion especially in societies where the country's laws and customs penalize conversions. Their experience reveals the limitations of Western missiological paradigms that have difficulty relating to real-life scenarios that Christians in the Global South cannot ignore.

Based on Christendom, Western Christianity was part of the dominant state power for centuries, a reality that makes relating to marginal and oppressed Christian communities difficult. Western theologians have competed for centuries to be at the center of power and influence over their respective societies but how do you address marginalized Christian communities in the Global South that seemingly exist as outcasts of society? For them, challenging the prevailing power structure is unthinkable and their aim is to co-exist in peace with their dominant neighbors. Western theology assumed the role of the establishment while Christians in the Global South assumes a defensive posture against the establishment that often views Christians as a destabilizing and disunifying force. As the discourse on missiology turns to the Global South, perspectives that integrate the diverse ecosystems will be needed to take into account the precarious realities that accompany one's commitment to Christ.

In Korea's case, becoming a Christian was an act of defiance against Joseon dynasty (1392–1910) and later Japanese colonialism (1910–1945). They understood very clearly the implications of their decision. For the first generations of Korean Catholics and Protestants, accepting Christianity was an act of sedition, rebellion against their state, that had terrible consequences for them and their families but the costs did not deter the movement.

Their lives illuminate the seriousness with which they must negotiate the decisions before them. The terracultural model aims to understand the

---

3. D. Lee, "Effective Internet Ministry Strategy," 22.

intrinsic complexity of the interrelationship among religious, sociocultural, familial, and political obligations that actively pull at them. Intentionality with regard to decisions of ultimate significance is conditioned by time and the complexity of the moral landscape. This chapter explores how conversion and preserving faith in a society hostile to Christianity rigorously tested the country's attitudes against Christianity. In so doing, their experience provokes a critical reflection on the seriousness with which people in the Global South must confront Christianity's claims.

PERSECUTION OF CATHOLICS

During Joseon dynasty (1392–1910), Korea's royal court dispatched bi-annual diplomatic trips to China that provided opportunities for Korean diplomats, envoys, and the accompanying entourage to visit Beijing and tour the "outside world" for over a month.[4] In 1784, a "brilliant young intellectual," Seung-hun Yi (1756–1801) accompanied his father, who was the third secretary of the Korean winter solstice mission, on a diplomatic trip to Beijing.[5] While touring the city, Yi visited European Jesuit priests and learned about the Catholic faith. After a period of investigation, Yi accepted the truths of the new religion and was baptized at the age of twenty-seven by Father Louis de Grammont a French Jesuit priest in 1784.[6] Becoming the first baptized Korean in Korea, Yi was christened with the Christian name, Peter.[7]

It was unclear why Yi chose or was given the name "Peter," but his new Christian name anticipated his religious significance in Korea. In the Bible, Jesus gave Simon, one of his twelve disciples, the name *Petros* or "Peter," which means "rock" in Greek. Jesus then explained the significance of his new name as he said to Simon Peter, "You are Peter, and on this rock I will build my church (Matthew 16:18)" The young Peter Seung-hun Yi returned

4. "Although the envoys' function was diplomatic, they provided as well as pipeline for economic and culture influence, and it was the only available 'window' through which Korea came into contact with the outside. . . . The Catholic churches in Beijing, having acquired a reputation as worthy of attention, became stops on the itinerary of Korean envoys, and places where they gained knowledge of Western culture and institutions. The priests of The Society of Jesus eagerly provided the Korean envoys with requested materials, particularly translations of Western works. Approximately 167 envoys of various purposes were dispatched during the 147, up to 1783, the year Yi Seung-hun's visit to Beijing" (Choi, *Roman Catholic Church in Korea*, 19).

5. See Eckert et al., *Korea Old and New*, 170; K. Lee, *New History of Korea*, 239; Oh, "Sagehood and Metanoia," 303.

6. Choi, *Roman Catholic Church in Korea*, 25.

7. Oh, "Sagehood and Metanoia," 304; Moffett, *History of Christianity in Asia*, 2:309.

to Korea and proceeded to start—on his own—the first-known Korean church. He began to propagate the Catholic faith using the Catholic texts he smuggled into Korea that included *Tianzhu shiyi* ["The True Significance of the Lord of Heaven"], a primer of Catholic teachings and doctrines by Matteo Ricci (1552–1610), and *Qike* ["Seven Victories"], a guide to Catholic ethics by Diego de Pantoja (1571–1618).[8]

As a result of his actions, Yi was considered the founder of the Catholic Church in Korea.[9] "Within a few months," Yi and his fellow leaders in the indigenous Catholic movement "reported a thousand followers asking for baptism."[10] He baptized his friends and relatives, including Byeok Yi, his co-leader whom he named "John-Baptist"; administered sacraments; and ordained his fellow co-workers in the church as priests when Yi himself was not ordained.[11] The Korean believers proceeded to replicate Catholic rites and practices from their interpretation of Catholic doctrines.[12]

Without outside guidance or assistance, these first Korean Catholics set about creating their Christian community and applied Catholic teachings to modeling Christian discipleship. One outstanding characteristic was the egalitarian nature of the movement. The core group that sparked the Catholic movement were *yangban*—the upper, elite class. However, they began to reach across class lines, a striking feature considering Joseon's rigid social segregation that made social mobility nearly impossible. On their own, the Korean Catholic community determined that all humans, regardless what they believe, are created in the image of God. From the vernacular writings that were disseminated in the Catholic community, they believed that "human nature is in some essential sense in contact with divine nature" and "the significance of human existence is superseded only by that

8. Baker, "Catholic God and Confucian Morality," 101.

9. Jae-Keun Choi noted that while Seung-hun Yi is widely regarded as the founder of Korea's Catholic Church, Byeok Yi (1754–1786) "greatly influenced" Yi (Choi, *Roman Catholic Church in Korea,* 24).

10. Moffett, *History of Christianity in Asia,* 2:310.

11. Choi, *Roman Catholic Church in Korea,* 28.

12. Yoon explained some of the rituals of the underground Catholic community. Common practices "included saying private and public prayers, and emulating the Gospel message of a charitable life. Catholics started the day with prayers and said the Angelus in the morning, at noon, and in the evening. The rosary was also typically said before evening prayer. On Sundays and days of celebration, Catholics gathered in secret to pray. Those who could not join in the prayers said the Lord's Prayer sixty-six times, the Hail Mary ninety-nine times, or the Stations of the Cross. They often reflected on their lives as they recited the Ten Commandments. They practiced charity by looking after orphans and treating people of all classes equally, and in some cases, releasing their own slaves" (Yoon, "Martyrdom and Social Activism," 359–60).

of God."[13] One of the earliest followers was Ilgwang Hwang, a butcher, a despised class along with criminals, prostitutes, and entertainers. In addition, many *yangban* members released their slaves as part of a larger commitment to the equality of humankind.

Through their own determination, the Catholic community initiated a number of counter-cultural positions. Joseon society permitted concubines but Korean Catholics banned the practice. Catholics encouraged faithfulness and affection between husband and wife. Joseon society practiced arranged marriages but Catholics allowed their children "to choose whether or not to marry"[14]—a radical proposition considering that filial piety and the perpetuation of the family line were a few of the core tenets of Confucian culture. Abstaining from marriage was akin to abandoning one's filial duties.[15]

The unique marks of distinction formed the Korean Catholic community but questions arose regarding the particulars of doctrine and procedure, especially as the Catholic community grew from 4,000 in 1794 to 10,000 in 1800—while it was illegal and punishable offense to practice Christianity. Yi wrote a letter in 1789 to Bishop Gouvéa of Beijing that detailed the Catholic movement in Korea, described the persecution of believers, and requested guidance and assistance. The rapid indigenous growth of Catholicism in Korea "shocked the [Jesuit] missionary community [in China]."[16] They wondered, "How could the faith be spreading so rapidly in Korea without missionaries?"[17] In response, Bishop Gouvéa praised Korean Catholics for their evangelistic work in the face of persecution and recognized their baptisms as valid "lay baptisms" but also rebuked them "for the temerity in doing what they had not received authority to do."[18]

Another secret letter was sent to the Bishop a year later that asked whether or not *jesa*, a basic and fundamental Confucian ancestor rite,[19] was

13. Cho, "Human Relations," 30.

14. Yoon, "Martyrdom and Social Activism," 357–58.

15. Gari Ledyard wrote, "What is truly worth note, however, is the number and variety of cases in which women responded positively to this [lay celibate] model. . . . The society did not really have a concept of a respectable, single young women. Because of hair and dress distinctions between unmarried and married women, a single female in her late teens or early twenties would be immediately spotted; people might assume she had an incurable disease or was limited mentally and was thus unmarriageable" (Ledyard, "Kollumba Kang Wansuk," 53).

16. Moffett, *History of Christianity in Asia*, 2:310.

17. Moffett, *History of Christianity in Asia*, 2:310.

18. Grayson, *Early Buddhism and Christianity*, 74.

19. According to Donald Clark, "The 'standard' *chesa* [or *jesa* in Korean Revised Romanization] is a family ceremony that remembers one or two, or sometimes three,

something that they as Christians should be performing. In a brief response, *jesa* was deemed by the Catholic authorities as ancestor worship and therefore it was declared as idolatrous. The bishop in China forbid *jesa* among the new Korean worshippers, a decision that followed the 1742 papal ruling, *Ex quo singulari*, that "definitively" condemned ancestor worship as idolatrous superstition.[20]

Following the command, two Korean believers from the upper-class, including Paul Ji-chung Yun, refused to do *jesa* and they were thereby arrested by the royal government.[21] The refusal to perform *jesa* represented a direct challenge to the Joseon government which was founded on Neo-Confucian principles.[22] Not only did Yun refuse to perform *jesa* but he also brazenly destroyed his family's ancestral tablets—an outrageous and unthinkable act. According to Yun, "Christian truth was more absolute than Confucian morality, and the tablets were a superstition."[23] As a consequence of Yun's blatant disregard for Confucian rites and principles, King Jeongjo executed Yun and other Catholic believers in 1791. The 1791 Persecution, known as the *Shinhae* Persecution, was not the first major persecution against Catholics. The first persecution occurred in 1785, a year after Seung-hun Yi was baptized.[24]

The remaining followers petitioned the Bishop in Beijing for support and Bishop Gouvéa sent to Korea a Chinese priest, James Wen-mu Chou, in 1795 to "correct their errors and to bring them orthodox instruction in the faith."[25] Once arriving in Korea and familiarizing himself with the

---

generations of ancestors in the father's lineage. Families honor their ancestors in *chesa* ceremonies on Lunar New Year's Day and Ch'usŏk, the Harvest Festival. They also honor specific ancestors on the anniversaries of their deaths" (Clark, *Culture and Customs of Korea*, 96).

20. Oh, "Sagehood and Metanoia," 306.

21. Two cousins, Ji-chung Yun and Sang-young Kwon, were arrested, interrogated, and executed for not performing *jesa* and burning their ancestral tablets, becoming the first Christian martyrs. See Grayson, "Quarter-Millennium of Christianity in Korea," 10.

22. For an examination of a *jesa* controversy, see Baker, "Martyrdom of Paul Yun," 33–58. After his conversion, Paul Yun refused to perform *jesa* for his deceased mother and burned the ancestral tablet in 1791. His actions led to numerous anti-Christian tracts and memorials urging the ban of Christianity in Korea.

23. Moffett, *History of Christianity in Asia*, 2:311.

24. After the 1785 and 1791 persecutions, anti-Catholic persecutions continued: the Ulmyo Incident of 1795, the Sinyu Persecution of 1801, the Ulhae Persecution of 1815, the Chonghae Persecution of 1827, the Kihae Persecution of 1839, the Pyongo Persecution of 1846, the Kyungshin Persecution of 1860, and lastly Pyongin Persecution of 1866. Choi, *Roman Catholic Church in Korea*, 1.

25. Moffett, *History of Christianity in Asia*, 2:312.

coastline and caused some deaths and injuries.[39] In 1866, the American trading ship, the *General Sherman* was set on fire when it sailed inland into Pyeongyang. Two year earlier, the twelve year-old Gojong (r. 1864–1907) was enthroned in Korea and his father, the Daewongun,[40] was given regent powers for the first ten years of Gojong's kingship.

Although the Daewongun was tolerant of Catholics in the early years of his rule, he later pursued a closed-door isolationist policy as a response to the increasing pressure and threat from foreign powers to open Korean ports. When two French ships anchored off the island of Kanghwa in 1866 and easily defeated Korean defenses, ministers in the royal court advised negotiation with them. In response, the Daewongun ordered a large sign posted on one of the pillars in the royal hall that read: "The ocean barbarians have invaded. Not to fight is to advocate peace. To advocate peace is to sell out the country."[41] Other conservative ministers in the court reiterated the political slogan: "Defend Orthodoxy, Reject Heterodoxy."[42]

In the early years of Daewongun's rule, there were over 20,000 Korean Catholic followers and twelve French priests working covertly in Korea.[43] The spread of Catholicism reached every province in Korea.[44] The Daewongun was determined to "annihilate every vestige of this religion."[45] In 1866, the Daewongun unleashed a "full-scale anti-Catholic campaign" that resulted in the death of nine French priests, including Bishop Berneux, and over 8,000 Koreans—that is, "half of the membership of the church suffered martyrdom."[46] From 1785 to 1886, scholars estimated that over ten

---

39. Eckert et al., *Korea Old and New*, 194.

40. The "Daewongun [prince of the great court]" was the shortened title for Yi Ha-eung (1821–1898) who was formally known as "Heungseon Heonui Daewongun," a position granted to the father of the reigning monarch.

41. P. Lee, *Sourcebook of Korean Civilization*, 2:307. In order to galvanize public support, the Daewongun had stone markers placed across Korea with a similar message: "Western barbarians invade our land. If we do not fight, we must then appease them. To urge appeasement is to betray the nation" (Eckert et al., *Korea Old and New*, 197).

42. The slogan, *wijeong cheoksa*, is translated "Defend Orthodoxy, Reject Heterodoxy" (P. Lee, *Sourcebook of Korean Civilization*, 2:535). See Chung, "Confucian Tradition," 64.

43. Korean Catholic theology in the mid-nineteenth century had two main characteristics. First, "a pre-occupation with impending divine judgement, and secondly, a devaluation of the things of this world and an emphasis on the separate nature of the body and soul. This he says created a longing for heaven, and an emphasis on virginity" (Grayson, "Early Buddhism and Christianity," 82).

44. Moffett, *History of Christianity in Asia*, 2:315.

45. Daewongun in Moffett, *History of Christianity in Asia*, 2:316.

46. B. Kim, "Modernization and the Explosive Growth," 11.

thousand Catholics died in the century of persecutions.[47] James S. Gale, a Protestant missionary who entered Korea in 1888, met Koreans who vividly remembered the horrific execution of Catholics in 1866. Gale wrote, "[Korean] Natives still pointed out the place by the Han River where Bishop Berneux and eight priests had been beheaded."[48]

A few years after the Great Persecution of 1866–1871, the Daewongun retired from his role as Regent in favor of his son, Gojong, who assumed full kingship in 1873. Daewongun failed in his mission to eradicate Catholicism in Korea; in fact, not only did it survive the series of persecutions but Catholicism in Korea began a process of "quiet rebuilding."[49] By 1900 there were ten Korean priests; ten years later there were fifteen, and fifty-six foreign clergy."[50] At the turn of the twentieth century, members in the Catholic Church doubled that of the Protestant Church. In 1900, the Korean Catholic Church had 42,411 members; Protestant Church, 20,914.[51] In 1905, Catholicism grew to 64,000 members while Protestantism, 37,407. In 1910, the number of Catholics had grown to 73,000, a 500 percent increase over 1882.[52]

With the transition of power, Gojong ended campaigns of anti-Catholicism and signaled greater openness to Western powers and presence of foreign religions. As one of his early acts, Gojong issued an edict that prohibited the execution of Catholics "without royal consent."[53] In 1876, Korea signed with Japan the Treaty of Amity which was Korea's first modern treaty. Six years later, Korea signed a treaty with the United States in 1882.

47. "Some ten thousand Catholic Christians were martyred, including Kim Taegön [Andrew Daegeon Kim], the first Korean priest. A total of 103 Catholic martyrs were canonized by Pope Paul when he visited Seoul in 1984 to commemorate two hundred years of the Korean Catholic Church" (B. Kim, "Modernization and the Explosive Growth," 313). Also see Choi, *Roman Catholic Church in Korea*, 1, 4.

48. Gale, *Korea in Transition*, 161.

49. According to Don Baker, the persecutions left a harrowing legacy upon the Korean Catholic community as "most Catholics had become so intimidated by their century-long history of persecution that they shied away from confrontation with any political authorities, legitimate or illegitimate" (Baker, "Transformation of the Catholic Church," 17).

50. Grayson, "Quarter-Millennium of Christianity in Korea," 12.

51. Baker, "Transformation of the Catholic Church," 14.

52. "However, in 1907 the Korean Protestant community, spurred on by the Great Revival of 1907, entered into a period of rapid growth that left the Catholic community far behind, never to catch up again in absolute numbers . . . at the start of the second decade of the twentieth century the number of Protestant Christians in Korea had grown to almost twice that of Catholics" (Baker, "Transformation of the Catholic Church," 15).

53. Moffett, *History of Christianity in Asia*, 2:316.

Thereafter, Korea finalized treaty relations with seven European countries within a decade.[54]

LATE JOSEON DYNASTY

Although Gojong ceased state-sponsored persecutions, his act was not the same as legalizing Christianity. Even Gojong's signing of the US-Korea Treaty of 1882 did not change the fact that Christianity remained an outlawed religion. When Protestant missionaries entered Korea from 1884, they were fully aware of the situation. The baptism of the first Korean Protestant indicated as much. When Tohsa Noh asked Horace G. Underwood to baptize him, Underwood explained the political ramifications of the act: "You are going contrary to the law of your country. If you take this step there will be no turning back."[55] The warning did not deter Noh who became the first Korean Protestant baptized in Korea on July 11, 1886. Noh came to his decision after working for Horace Allen as his language teacher. He asked Allen for a copy of the Chinese New Testament to which Allen resisted, knowing the harm that may come from being in possession of it. Allen warned Noh, "You'll have your head cut off if they find you reading that book."[56] Noh understood the consequences but proceeded nevertheless. As one of the earliest to convert to Protestant Christianity, Baron Chiho Yun, "a nobleman by birth and a beneficiary of power and wealth under the Confucian system," became a Christian soon after his participation in the failed 1884 coup.[57] By rejecting Korea's state ideology, Yun "chose to face ridicule and even persecution."[58]

In 1894, two ordained Korean Protestant clergy "were beaten, put in the stocks and threatened with execution unless they cursed God. . . . Given one more chance to recant or be beheaded, they refused to deny Christ."[59] In 1902, George Heber Jones who was stationed in Incheon observed that "our Christians are much persecuted and molested, but they stand firm through it."[60] After discovering her son's conversion in 1906, "Mr. Pak's mother tried

---

54. After signing a treaty with the United State in 1882, Korea signed treaties with Great Britain (1883), Germany (1883), Italy (1884), France (1886), Austria-Hungary (1892), Belgium (1901), and Denmark (1902).

55. Moffett, *Christians of Korea*, 38.

56. Moffett, *Christians of Korea*, 38.

57. C. Park, *Protestantism and Politics in Korea*, 121.

58. C. Park, *Protestantism and Politics in Korea*, 121.

59. Moffett, "Place of the Native Church," 234.

60. "Mission Notes," 571.

to hang herself twice because her son had become a Christian."[61] After a man discovered that his wife had converted to Christianity, he cried out, "You want me to be cursed, do you, and all my house, down to the furthest generation?"[62] In 1906, Mrs. Samuel A. Moffet recalled a crippled "gray-haired woman of seventy" who was the "only Christian in her village, bearing witness amid the ridicule and persecution of her relatives and neighbors."[63] A widow who had given up, as a Christian, the sacrificial rites to the dead was attacked by a mob of friends and family of her deceased husband who anticipated a great feast at the widow's home at the anniversary of the husband's death.[64]

Conversion to Christianity represented not just a change in doctrine but, in most cases, a rejection of key elements of Korean culture and sacred traditions. The rejection of family rituals was particularly difficult for non-Christian family members and relatives because family rituals defined the history, culture, and genealogy of a particular family or clan. A Christian man aroused the fury of his in-laws when he rejected a superstitious practice after his wife died. As a way of honoring the dead, his wife's family placed a paper container next to her dead body to receive her departed soul. No longer practicing the superstitious beliefs, the Christian husband threw away the paper container that caused a furious reaction. The husband said, "Then they rushed on me, seized me by the hair and beat me almost to death. Every day they did this . . . thirty or forty gathered and bound me, loosened my hair, tied my hands behind my back and hung me head down behind my back and hung me head downward from the beam of the house."[65]

When a Korean man who was the head of his clan converted to Christianity, he "offered to resign his position and property to any one they should elect in his stead, but as he was the only heir and in the necessary line of ancestor worship, this was rejected."[66] As the anger brewed among clan-members, "the fury of the clan broke loose upon him. He was beaten to the ground, stamped upon and left terribly injured."[67] After he recovered from internal hemorrhages, he returned to the same village and spent three years ministering to them about Christ. Jones exclaimed, "*Eleven churches*

---

61. Sharp, "Under Persecution," 69.

62. Baird, *Daybreak in Korea,* 75–76.

63. Moffett, "Like Heaven," 69.

64. Cooper, *Evangelism in Korea*, 63.

65. "Korean's Own Story," 258.

66. "What One Christian Endured," 703.

67. "What One Christian Endured," 703.

and in 1941, over 60,000, which "represented one policeman for every four hundred Koreans."[76] Despite the deliberate attempts by the government to suppress and punish Christians, the Korean church actually grew 30 percent from 1920 to 1925 and baptized believers increased from 69,000 to 89,000.[77]

As the Japanese government strained "every nerve to make the Koreans into Japanese," they did "all in their power to throttle Christianity without openly persecuting the church or antagonizing the law that guarantees religious liberty."[78] According to a missionary, "The [Japanese] authorities do not say Koreans must not be Christians, but they indirectly do everything possible to prevent the spread of Christianity."[79] For example, laws required the church to obtain permission to operate a mission school or when hiring a pastor and a helper at a church. Without a permit, the government had cause to harass, arrest, or shut down mission schools or churches.[80]

A Korean minister was arrested for treason when he preached against the ills of smoking because "the manufacture of cigarettes is a government monopoly; to speak against their use is to injure a government institution; to injure a government institution is to work against the government; to work against the government is treason; and therefore Pastor Kil was charged with treason."[81] Under pressure from the Japanese, the missionaries "kept from responsible position in the Church" those who engaged in political activities as a way to focus on spiritual matters and to protect the Church from political repercussions.[82]

In October 1911, the colonial government "without any explanation" arrested many Koreans including over a hundred prominent Korean church leaders in the so-called the 1910 Conspiracy Case.[83] Many months after the

76. Eckert et al., *Korea Old and New*, 259.

77. Y. Lee, "Holy Spirit Movement," 59.

78. "From Korea to Chosen," 85.

79. "From Korea to Chosen," 85.

80. "From Korea to Chosen," 85. "Most of the mission schools have permits which allow them to continue as at present for ten years, but some, like Soon Chun schools, are without permits, and may be closed. . . . Hiding behind red-tape he may find many opportunities to block Christian work" ("From Korea to Chosen," 85).

81. "Korean View of Japan's Policy," 452.

82. A "memorandum" of missionaries Samuel A. Moffett, Norman C. Whittemore, O. R. Avison, George S. McCune, and C. E. Sharp to His Excellency Count Terauchi, Governor-General of Chosen, and received by Komatsu, Director of Chosen, January 8, 1912, in the Presbyterian Library, New York (Kang, "Church and State Relations," 98).

83. A missionary in the field reported: "Time after time arrests have been made, sometimes one or two and sometimes several at a time, until now there are fifty or more from our neighborhood. The parents and relatives of these men do not know why they are taken. The men themselves do not know why" (Kang, *Christ and Caesar*, 44). "All

arrests were made, the government charged the Koreans with an alleged conspiracy to assassinate the Japanese colonial governor of Korea. The arbitrary nature to which the arrests were made vacated the leadership in many mission schools. A mission school in northern Korea was forced to close after the colonial police arrested most of the teachers and kept them imprisoned for over six months.[84]

The arrest, torture, and imprisonment of mainly Korean Christians revealed the colonial government's distrust of the Christian community. A missionary who observed the conspiracy trials wrote, "If one looks at the manner in which the trials of these Korean 'conspirators' has been conducted by the Japanese officials and then at these peculiar attempts to harass Christian schools, one can not help but be persuaded that Japanese local officials in Korea are at least not any too favorable to Christian missionaries and their work."[85]

When the former Korean king, Gojong, died in 1919, a funeral in Seoul that expected mourners from all corners of the country provided an opportunity for nationalists. Working secretly underground, Korean nationalists used Gojong's funeral in 1919 as the pretext to declare throughout the country Korea's independence from Japan. Underground agents slipped through police surveillance to distribute the Korean Declaration of Independence, which was signed by thirty-three patriots, half of whom were Christians.[86] The document was distributed and read aloud in villages and cities across Korea. "The size and number of the demonstrations caught the Japanese police by complete surprise. Perhaps as many as a million people from all walks of life took part in the marches or were swept into spontaneous demonstrations that continued into the early summer of 1919."[87] A missionary who witnessed the uprising wrote, "Every element of the [Korean] population was involved in it. But when the hour of action came the people needed leaders, and in almost every place where a church was established, the Christian pastor was called upon to lead the demonstration."[88] When

---

of the accused complained of being tortured at the police station" (Kang, *Christ and Caesar*, 46).

84. "After six months they are still in prison. . . . Instead of prisoners being released, there have been more arrests and the school has been closed. Most of the arrests made in North Korea have been of Christians—leading men—those who are educated and have ability" ("Stirring Letters from Korea," 506–7).

85. "Editorial: Japanese Cloud," 859.

86. Park, *Protestantism and Politics in Korea*, 135.

87. Robinson, *Korea's Twentieth-Century Odyssey*, 48.

88. Blair, "Forward Movement in Korea," 528.

the Presbyterian General Assembly met in 1919, "most of the prominent pastors and elders were in prison."[89]

Although momentarily stunned, but the government dispatched the military to violently suppressed the movement. In the estimation of Korean historians, over 7,500 died, over 15,000 were injured, and over 45,000 were arrested.[90] A missionary who witnessed Japan's brutal retaliation saw "long lines of wounded . . . brought in [the hospital], almost daily, during March and April 1919, from the surrounding country areas where demonstrations were still going on."[91]

Embarrassed that the nation-wide demonstration was planned and organized without their detection, the colonial government increased surveillance and interrogation tactics to root-out hints of insurrection. A wide net was cast. The police freely exercised "summary powers with regard to misdemeanors, and this allowed them to adjudicate, pass sentence, and executive punishment for minor offenses."[92] It appeared every movement was held under close scrutiny. Offerings taken in the church suddenly became cause for censure or arrest after a law was passed that made public subscription of any sort illegal without a formal application and formal permission.[93] A man who bought a cow was interrogated by the Japanese police. "'Where did you get the money?' they asked. 'You must have been spying.' He was then ordered to report to the police station every single morning at nine o'clock."[94] In *The Case of Korea*, Henry Chung wrote, "An exhaustive description of Christian persecutions by the Japanese in Korea during the year, 1919, would fill a volume."[95]

It was clear who the Japanese authorities thought were behind the 1919 independence movement. The missionaries watched in horror as the police seized Christians more than any other group.[96] Among the 15,000 picked up

89. Blair, "Forward Movement in Korea," 528.

90. Robinson, *Korea's Twentieth-Century Odyssey,* 48.

91. Blair and Hunt, *Korean Pentecost,* 85

92. Eckert et al., *Korea Old and New,* 259.

93. "Offerings taken by the churches to send one or more promising students aboard for study were peremptorily forbidden, and all moneys ordered returned to the donors. In several cases where congregations had gathered money for the erection of new churches, they were forced to produce their subscription books, and every person who had subscribed was called by the police and questioned as to his reasons for making the gift" (Clark, *Korean Church and the Nevius Methods,* 165).

94. Kang, *Under the Black Umbrella,* 11.

95. Chung, *Case of Korea,* 171.

96. The March First Movement "caused the Christians to be singled out more than others" (Blair and Hunt, *Korean Pentecost,* 86). Charles Clark suggested that the Christian church became a target because it was "probably the largest closely knit social group within the nation" (Clark, *Korean Church and the Nevius Methods,* 166).

for questioning about their involvement in the protests, the police singled out 2,254 Presbyterians (14.8 percent), 518 Methodists (3.4 percent), and 54 Catholics (0.3 percent).[97] The colonial police suspected Koreans of other religions as well as they brought in 2,266 members of Cheondogyo, 220 Buddhists, and 346 self-identified Confucians.[98]

The colonial government suspected Christians the most and closely monitored the church and mission schools. A missionary observed, "For a time the police were present in every [worship] service. In many centres [sic] the Christians were forbidden to hold services."[99] If an undercover policeman heard anything in the church service that suggested or inferred anti-Japanese sentiment or yearning for Korean independence, preachers were summoned to the police station "to be interrogated in regard to certain statements they had made in their sermons."[100]

In the effort to paralyze the Christian community after the 1919 March First Movement, "practically every Christian pastor in Seoul was arrested and jailed."[101] In the aftermath of the 1919 uprising, a missionary recalled the debilitating situation in the church:

> [After the March 1919 movement], the work stopped. Everything was changed. Schools had to be closed, Bible classes could not be held, Bible institutes could not finish, trips to the country had to be cancelled, visiting in homes by missionaries was found to be inadvisable, many of our churches found their pastors, elders, helpers, and other church officers carried off to prison; missionaries lost their secretaries, language teachers, or literary assistants; every way we tried to turn, regular work seemed impossible; while, on the other hand, the Independence Movement brought upon us new and difficult problems and preoccupied our time in such a way that we have been incapable of doing the ordinary amount of work.[102]

97. Baker, "Transformation of the Catholic Church," 17.

98. Baker, "Transformation of the Catholic Church," 17.

99. Rhodes, *History of the Korea Mission*, 1:500.

100. Rhodes, *History of the Korea Mission*, 1:501.

101. Kang, "Church and State Relations," 102. "Korean Christians were active participants in this independence movement. . . . Many Christian churches became gathering places for demonstration and to hear the declaration of independence read." According to Wi Jo Kang, the "most tragic and brutal" persecution against Christian in the aftermath of the March First movement was the massacre at the village of Cheamni, near Suwon, where Japanese soldiers ordered all Christian males into the church and "fired on them with rifles and killed the survivors with swords and bayonets. Afterwards, the soldiers set fire to the church and left" (Kang, "Church and State Relations," 103).

102. "Seoul Station," 193.

With most of the church pastors and leaders in prison, "church attendance had fallen off to an alarming extent throughout the country and many
instances were reported of congregations unable to assemble."[103] When the
Methodist Koreans gathered for their Annual Conference in 1921, "only
two men [from one district] reported. . . . They received their appointments
[i.e., church assignment], and on returning to their work were arrested and
thrown into prison."[104] As the cloud of suspicion constantly hovered over
the church, non-Christians kept their distance from Christians, for fear of
interrogation and harassment by the police. Christians asked their American missionaries to stop visiting them because "it made so much trouble for
them with the police."[105]

SHRINE CONTROVERSY

After the mishandling of the 1919 independence movement, the Japanese
authorities kept a watchful eye on the Christian church. In addition to the
presence of undercover police officers in the church services, agents also
walked the halls of mission schools. Trained to detect secret codes or message in the communication, agents censored school publications and arrested any student under suspicion. A Korean high school student recalled
moving away to another village after being imprisoned and tortured, based
on suspicions of organizing a nationwide student uprising against the colonial government in 1934. After his release, he moved to a remote town but
"within a couple of days the police detective would show up to let me know
that he knew I had moved, and that he was watching me. They knew my
every movement. Every one."[106]

Louise Yim recounted in 1915 when the Japanese authorities placed
Japanese teachers at her Christian mission school to ensure the school's
adherence to the government policies, such as the singing the Japanese
national anthem every morning and bowing before the photograph of the
Japanese Emperor.[107] In his autobiography, Peter Hyun remembered the
painful day when his Christian mission school began singing the Japanese
anthem. "No! No! No!" some students shouted. The Korean headmaster
quieted the students and said, 'Unless we obey and sing the Japanese song,

---

103. Blair, "Forward Movement in Korea," 528.

104. Noble, "Christianity in Korea Today," 687.

105. Rhodes, *History of the Korea Mission*, 1:2.

106. Kang, *Under the Black Umbrella*, 48.

107. Yim, *My Forty-Year Fight*, 66.

we won't be permitted to continue our school.' All the teachers sitting on the platform broke into tears."[108]

As Japan's plan of imperialistic expansion into Asia was precipitated by the 1931 Manchurian Incident that gave Japan the cover to invade and occupy Manchuria, Japan's increased militaristic aggression signaled greater hostility toward Christians. Japan's occupation of Manchuria would later lead to the Second Sino-Japanese War (1937–1945) and World War II (1941–1945). Koreans became an integral part of the heightened wartime environment that initiated "an extraordinary effort . . . to use education to create not just loyalty to the state, but also a new sense of identity [in Koreans]."[109]

Kazushige Ugaki, the Japanese colonial governor of Korea from 1931–1936, instructed middle school principals that assembled in Seoul in 1934 to place the promotion of nationalism as the highest priority in education. Ugaki said, "It is the duty of a good subject of a nation to be loyal to the [Japanese Emperor's] Throne, to honor the national constitution, and to be steadfast in maintaining virtue, qualities which are the foundations of a good subject and form his highest duties."[110] Schools that do not highlight Japanese nationalism would be deemed, according to Ugaki, "useless" and "even dangerous" to Japan.[111] Ugaki reinforced his message by revising the Rescript on Education that intensified the assimilation of Koreans by "forcibly" inculcating the culture, values and consciousness of the Japanese empire.[112]

Christian schools were at first exempt from participating in Shinto ceremonies but, under Ugaki, the nationalistic wave enveloped them as well. In 1935, Ugaki organized a conference of Korea's educational leaders that included many missionaries. As the conference was about to begin, Ugaki said, "Before we take up the agenda we will all go by car to the new Shinto Shrine and worship."[113] "Your honor," George S. McCune, president of Union Christian College (Soongsil) interjected, "[We] must ask you to excuse us . . . it is impossible for us, as Christians, to take part in such ceremonies."[114]

108. Hyun, *Man Sei!*, 29.

109. Seth, *Education Fever*, 26.

110. Ugaki, "Speech on the Future," 91.

111. Ugaki said, "Regardless of how excellent one may be in studies and in capabilities, if lacking in these higher qualities, one is disqualified as a subject, and the school which trains such a person is not desired, since it is useless and even dangerous to the nation" (Ugaki, "Speech on the Future," 91).

112. Eckert et al., *Korea Old and New*, 315.

113. Ugaki in Moffett, *Christians of Korea*, 72.

114. Moffett, *Christians of Korea*, 72.

empire, Japan's "use [of Shinto shrines] to discipline colonial subjects was the most severe in Korea."[131]

As the colonial government mandated the Koreans' participation in Shinto ceremonies, Korean Christians faced a great moral and religious dilemma: refusal to participate only brought persecution but that meant compromising their religious convictions. Many Korean Christians and missionaries complied with the Japanese authorities who argued that the Shinto rites "were not religious but patriotic—merely 'reverence for ancestors.'"[132] However other Korean Christians, especially Presbyterians, refused to bow, an act that brought on imprisonment and torture.[133] As a result of the hard-line against Shinto worship, "some 200 churches were closed, over 2,000 Christians were imprisoned, and over fifty church workers suffered martyrdom."[134]

The Catholic church on the other hand changed their position on the issue on May 25, 1936 with the Sacred Congregation of the Propagation of the Faith that instructed Catholics in the Japanese empire. The Catholic decree declared that Shinto ceremonies were "civil affairs" that "are mere expressions of patriotic love, that is filial reverence toward the [Japanese] royal family and the benefactors of their own nation; and that, consequently, these ceremonies have only civil value and that Catholics are permitted to participate in them and behave like the rest of the citizens."[135] The decision also reversed the previous condemnation of *jesa*, the ancestor 'worship' ritual that brought on the 1791 anti-Catholic persecution.

For many Protestants, they decided to shut down their schools, rather than to worship at Shinto shrines and ceremonies. In 1936, the colonial government announced that it would not recognize the diplomas from

131. de Bary et al., *Sources of Japanese Tradition*, 2:797.

132. Clark, *Living Dangerously in Korea*, 211.

133. For detailed accounts of five Korean Christians who suffered for their refusal to bow, see Blair and Hunt, *Korean Pentecost*, 98–129. Yoonsup Kim for example was arrested eight different times. "On his release, he [Kim] continued preaching as before. He was arrested again. The torturing was more severe. This arrest-and-release policy was repeated until he had been imprisoned eight times" (Blair and Hunt, *Korean Pentecost*, 117).

134. Clark, *History of the Church in Korea*, 1. For an eyewitness account of the Japanese police's thorough involvement in the decision to declare shrine worship permissible during the 1938 General Assembly of the Korean Presbyterian Church, see Blair and Hunt, *Korean Pentecost*, 92–94.

135. Sacra Congregatio de Propaganda Fide in Kang, "Church and State Relations," 109. Don Baker surmised that the Catholic acquiescence to the Japanese demand for Catholics to participate in Shinto worship weakened the nationalistic image of the Catholic Church. See Baker, "Transformation of the Catholic Church," 17.

schools that did not participate in Shinto rituals and ceremonies. The denial of accreditation severely limited the opportunities for students since it barred "graduates from government jobs, including teaching."[136] The policy of forced assimilation also took place in the church where the Japanese authorities installed small Shinto shrines and compelled church worshippers to bow to it before the start of the church service. In addition to church services, the Japanese authorities mandated Shinto shrine bowing upon Bible study gatherings, Methodist Conference meetings, Presbyterian Presbytery and General Assembly meetings, and women's missionary society meetings. "Eventually, it came down to compulsory village, then house by house, representation and sometimes even to 'every individual' attendance at Shinto ceremonies."[137]

At the 1938 meeting of the Presbyterian General Assembly, "all four hundred delegates" were called to police stations during the Assembly. According to Samuel Hugh Moffett, "Police bluntly told them that the Assembly must pass an action approving Shrine worship. No debate and no negative votes would be permitted. When some delegates thereupon determined to absent themselves from the meeting, they were sent up under police escort. The Assembly finally approved the shrine resolution, without allowing debate or a negative vote."[138]

The vote gave further impetus for the colonial government to clamp down on Christian resistance. The failure to attend Shinto ceremonies led to the arrest and torture of Christians. Many escaped by fleeing to the mountains. Others worshipped in underground churches. Many suffered arrest and torture and, according to Moffett, "fifty paid the price of martyrdom."[139]

Eventually, the Japanese government broke all Christian resistance to the participation at Shinto ceremonies. The General Assembly of the Korean Presbyterian Church stated on November 1940: "By following the guidance of the Government and adjusting to the national policy on group organization, we will get rid of the wrong idea of depending on Europe and America and do our best to readjust and purify Japanese Christianity. . . . Like other people, the church members should attend the shrine worship."[140] The General Board of the Korean Methodist Church offered a similar statement: "It is both urgent and proper that we Christians should bring to reality the true spirit of our national polity and the underlying principle of *Naisen Ittai*

136. Clark, *Living Dangerously in Korea*, 213.

137. Blair and Hunt, *Korean Pentecost*, 90.

138. Moffett, *Christians of Korea*, 74–75.

139. Moffett, *Christians of Korea*, 75.

140. Kang, "Church and State Relations," 112.

amphibious landing in Incheon that decisively changed the course of the war, communist forces randomly killed Christians in the south.[151] The lives of Christians in northern Korea worsened after the conclusion of the Korean War (1950–1953) that divided Korea into North and South along the 38th parallel. With lines of communication cut from North Korea, one can only imagine the fate of Christians above the DMZ. According to Samuel Hugh Moffett, who was born in Pyeongyang in 1916, the North Korean communists implemented a campaign to completely exterminate Christians.[152] Moffett surmised, "Many thought that after five years of Communist persecution there would be no North Korean church left."[153]

CONCLUSION

When the Korean communists swept through Kaesong in 1950, they captured Yong-Soo Noh, a major in the Salvation Army. They beat him mercilessly and gave him one last chance: "Give up your faith in Christ," they said, "and we will set you free."[154] Major Noh stood up and, carrying a Bible in one hand and hymnbook in the other, answered, "You can shoot me, I know, but alive or dead, I am still Jesus Christ's man."[155]

The surprising self-initiated growth of Christianity in Korea was matched by the violence that followed it. Since the late eighteenth century, governments, foreign and domestic, started state-wide campaigns to suppress and eliminate Christians. All three governments—Joseon dynasty, Japanese colonial government, and North Korean—viewed Christians as a threat to the state. As a result, Christians—more than any other organization or group—became targets of intense persecution.

Similarly, in the Global South, the growth of Christianity has also meant the growth of persecution. Contemporary news reports abound with stories of Christians as objects of persecution under oppressive governments. The gap between the Global South and the West is not only the increasing gap in theological interpretations and priorities. It is more alarmingly the increasing gap in sensibility and universal concern. The church

151. Christians "were slaughtered in cold blood by the retreating communists. In hundreds of cases, as Dr Arch Campbell says, those who came out of hiding too soon to meet the conquering United Nations troops were summarily shot by the communists who had not yet completely withdrawn" (Blair and Hunt, *Korean Pentecost*, 143).

152. Moffett, *Christians of Korea*, 77.

153. Moffett, *Christians of Korea*, 77.

154. Moffett, *Christians of Korea*, 30.

155. Moffett, *Christians of Korea*, 30.

in the West has closed itself off from the harsh realities of Christians in the Global South, content with the trappings of the gilded anxieties in the First World. The West gives little consideration to the troubles in the Global South for it infuses a disquieting discord. This is so because, for one, Christians in the Global South refuses to surrender the authorship of their Christian experience to the ideal prescribed by a hostile state.

In many ways, the last one hundred years of Korea's history has left a legacy of persecution or more specifically a legacy of endurance through persecution, and an understanding of the complex nature of Christian witness and testimony. Church ministers and lay leaders were beaten, imprisoned or executed; church buildings were razed down; and Bibles and Christian books were burned. Like "noxious weeds," as King Heonjong described Christians, Korean Christians survived the worst conditions. When churches were destroyed, Christians worshipped privately in members' homes. When persecution forced Christians to flee, they fled to another province or to another country and began to spread the Christian faith to their new surroundings.

Many Korean Christians refused to yield, even though it would have eased not only their suffering but their families. To submit, however, meant, in their minds, compromising their beliefs. Starting with the Confucian *sarim* who endured series of bloody purges, the generations of forebearers laid the foundation for the reverential seriousness with which to uphold one's convictions.

"Higher Bible School Girls and Teachers." Photo credit: Alice Butts Album.
Moffett Korea Collection. Princeton Theological Seminary.

MR. APPENZELLER'S METHODIST SCHOOL AT SEOUL, KOREA.

Seoul. "[Drawing] Mr. Appenzeller's Methodist School (Pai Chai Academy)."
Photo credit: Moffett Korea Collection. Princeton Theological Seminary.

4

Education and Salvation

WHEN THE MISSIONARY VICTOR Peters wrote in 1932 of Koreans' "mania for education," he was not exaggerating.[1] Seoul had become a city of students and education was "the biggest industry that the city of Seoul has," as students outnumbered those working in factories, banks, or government offices.[2] Seoul acted as a magnet for students around the country as seven students out of ten, from Peters's estimation, were from out of town.

Among Koreans, few subjects have generated as much intense passion as education. The missionary Ethel Estey visited a Korean village in 1910 and a mob-like atmosphere erupted when she told them that she was leaving. She wrote, "I was almost forcibly held until I promised either to return soon or to send them a teacher."[3] In 1905, Korean parents demonstrated their enthusiasm for the construction of a girls' school as they "promised to support their children themselves and pay the salary of the teacher, asking the missionaries to oversee and direct the school."[4] The pioneer missionary Samuel Austin Moffett recalled the Koreans' reaction when the announcement was made that a collection would be taken to build a school: women pulled out and gave their "wedding rings, their hair, their ornaments; families have sold their rice and bought millet to eat in order to give the difference to the Lord's work."[5]

---

1. Peters, "Korean Young People," 93.
2. Peters, "Korean Young People," 93.
3. Estey, "From Northern Korea," 58.
4. Cram, "Song Do Girls' School," 26.
5. Moffett, "Native Church," 233.

The Koreans' obsession was not just about gaining education but it also reflected the Confucian veneration for learning. Annie Ellers Bunker, one of the earliest women missionaries in Korea, observed the major characteristics of Korean women: "eager to learn the new, patient in study, always willing to be taught is the Korean woman."[6] The Methodist missionary George Heber Jones described Koreans in 1896 as "scholarly people" who have "an unfeigned and voluntary admiration for learning."[7] Jones noted how this "admiration" permeated all levels of society as learning was a mark of nobility and prominence.[8] As Jones observed, education or the acquisition of education served as an important cultural marker for not only the profound respect for learning but also for socioeconomic status. Educational achievement became the most significant measurement of social respectability and symbolized power and influence of those who possess it.

Missionaries did not quite know how to make sense of the Koreans' mania for education but their zeal for education reflected the deeply rooted Confucian ethic that highly prized learning. The Koreans' obsession over education was rooted in their Confucian culture that stressed "the importance of being eager to learn or love of learning."[9] "We have seen that one of the rare claims Confucius makes for himself," according to de Bary, "is that he yields to no one in his love of learning (Analects of Confucius 5:28). To this learning of the Way he devoted himself untiringly, regardless of what other disappointments he suffered in life (8:13, 14:38, 18:7)."[10]

As discussed in chapter 2, Koreans during the Joseon period lived in an era when the Confucian culture compelled all Korean thought toward moral perfection which was achieved through rigorous self-cultivation centered on education. The Confucian sage was the paragon of human excellence. From a secular perspective, the highest accomplishment was passing the Civil Service Examination.[11] The Examination required years of painstaking analysis and meditation of the Confucian classics and passing

6. Bunker, "As I Found the Korean Women," 8.

7. Jones, "Christian Education in Korea," 559

8. Jones, "Christian Education in Korea," 559.

9. "Confucius stresses the importance of being eager to learn and distinguishes himself from other people in terms suggesting that other people are not as eager to learn as he is (Analects, 5:28). He praises highly his favorite student Yan Hui (521–481 BCE), for his eagerness to learn (Analects, 6:3; 11:7). Xunzi also sees 'love of learning' as one of the necessary qualities for becoming a gentleman (Xunxi, 2:12)" (Yao, Wisdom, 84).

10. de Bary, Trouble with Confucianism, 41.

11. In 957 AD, King Gwangjong of Goryeo dynasty was first to establish the national civil service examination (gwageo) system in Korea.

it brought glory, honor, and status—and an audience with the king for the highest achiever. The enthusiasm for education extended to all Koreans but formal education remained the exclusive space of the upper class that possessed the time to devote years to academic study and wealth to attend academies and procure private tutors.

Within this cultural context that prized education, Protestant missionaries introduced Christianity as a religion that highly esteemed sacred writing (i.e., Bible) and learning. Since Martin Luther of the sixteen century, reading the Bible had become indispensable to Protestantism. The Puritans in America in the seventeenth century not only read and memorized the Bible but they wrote "conversion narratives" to explain and convince their peers that they were part of God's elect.[12] For the Protestant missionaries of the late nineteenth century, reading and writing became an expected, normative experience for the believer. Little did they realize that education was the key for Koreans—the key that opened doors that were previous closed or inaccessible. The fact that missionaries combined the introduction of Christianity with a high-view of learning tapped into the latent educational ambitions in the Korean Confucian culture.

As Koreans discovered, one could not become a member of the church without reading and memorizing doctrines and Scripture. A Christian was expected to read, study, and apply the Bible. Reading and writing became synonymous with the Christian religion. The missionaries' most common method of evangelism was distributing religious literature. For the illiterate, the backside of the literature had the Korean alphabet printed so that Christian workers could teach them how to read the tracts. The missionaries in effect started a mass reading campaign, reviving hangul, Korea's vernacular script, in the process.

The success of missions depends on the receiving church's ability to replicate the gospel on their own terms. The process was greatly enhanced by Korea's Confucian ethos of learning and scholarship. The Protestant missions stressed characteristics that echoed in Korean culture and connecting them with Christianity inspired Confucian-based ideals. The Protestant urgency to include all corners of the Korean population to freely receive education ignited a passion for learning that was already simmering beneath the surface.

12. See Caldwell, *Puritan Conversion Narrative*.

KOREA'S CONFUCIAN CULTURE OF LEARNING

> The Master said, Be devoted to faithfulness and love learning;
> defend the good *dao* [the Way] until death. (Analects of Con-
> fucius, 8.13)

> If, you love *ren* [humanness, goodness], but you do not love
> learning, the flaw is ignorance. If you love knowledge but you
> do not love learning, the flaw is unruliness. If you love faithful-
> ness but you do not love learning, the flaw is harming others.
> If you love straightforwardness but you do not love learning,
> the flaw is offensiveness. If you love valor but you do not love
> learning, the flaw is causing chaos. If you love incorruptibility
> but you do not love learning, the flaw is recklessness. (Analects
> of Confucius, 17.8)

From the beginning, Confucius (551 BC–479 BC) promoted the full
development of human capacities through education. Over a thousand
years later, Chu Hsi (1130–1200 AD) synthesized Confucianism with
metaphysical philosophy to start Neo-Confucianism. The Neo-Confucian
tradition that became codified and institutionalized for over 600 years in
East Asia had countless Neo-Confucian scholars and teachers who supported the movement but Chu's teaching in particular was known as 'orthodox Neo-Confucianism' that became the dominant expression of Korean
Confucianism.

Like Confucius, Chu Hsi gave education "the highest priority in his
thought and scholarship."[13] The pursuit of education, however, was not the
end but rather the means to the ultimate goal: "the full, vigorous [moral]
perfection."[14] According to Chu, "The essential training should be the way
of choosing the good and cultivating the self until the whole world is transformed and brought to perfection, so that all people from the ordinary person on up can become sages."[15] The creation of a distinct Confucian culture
required the overhaul of educational system with the result that Neo-Confucianism became, according to de Bary, "the dominant force in education."
"In fact secular education," de Bary wrote, "was largely a Neo-Confucian

---

13. de Bary, "Introduction," 1.

14. Chu Hsi wrote, "But only the sage possesses the full, vigorous perfection of the
inborn nature [in its pure, original condition]; without adding the slightest bit [of further perfection] to it, all goodness is already there in its fullness" (Kalton, *To Become
a Sage*, 68).

15. Chu Hsi in de Bary, "Chu Hsi's Aim," 192–93.

society. The Confucian village schools that served as the frontlines of Confucian education "had gone out of existence" by 1910, the year Korea was colonized by Japan.[23] In the decades leading up to 1910, imperialist powers including Japan vied for influence and supremacy over the Korean court.

The traumatic series of events that crippled the Korean court also represented the geo-political shift away from China and to the West. Recognizing Korea's weak position, King Gojong opened Korea to modernization, including Western education, as a way to not only introduce Westernization into Korea but also to attract Western powers as a countermeasure against rising Japanese influence.

Introducing Western-style reforms meant abandoning centuries-old customs and practices. Gojong introduced educational reforms that reinforced the "practical application" of knowledge as opposed to metaphysical or abstract.[24] After the 1894 Gabo Reforms, an openness to globalization was introduced in government schools, as the learning of foreign languages from primary and middle schools to normal schools was initiated. In 1895, Gojong issued the *Decree of Nation Building Through Education* in which he stated:

> When one looks at the state of affairs in the world, one finds that in all those nations that maintain their independence through wealth and power and thus have gained ascendancy, the citizens are enlightened in their knowledge. Enlightened knowledge is attained through excellence of education, and so education truly is of fundamental importance in preserving our nation.[25]

The king's attempt to introduce Western education in Korea was underway but the influence of government schools remained largely confined to the capital and the children of the upper class. Efforts by the royal government to disseminate Western education to a wide audience remained largely unfulfilled. About this time, American Protestant missionaries began entering Korea with the promise of starting Western-style schools at little or no cost.

---

23. Paik, *Protestant Missions in Korea*, 392.

24. Kang, *Land of Scholars*, 481. King Gojong's three main principles of education were moral education, cultivation of the body, and cultivation of knowledge.

25. King Gojong in K. Lee, *New History of Korea*, 331.

LITERACY AND EDUCATION IN AMERICAN PROTESTANT MISSIONS

In 1901, Cameron Johnson, an American Southern Presbyterian missionary stationed in Japan, visited mission stations throughout Korea and gained greater insight into Korea's culture of learning. Johnson attended a worship service during which the Korean minister announced the scriptural passage from which he would be preaching. Johnson observed that "instantly every Bible was opened and the text found and marked."[26]

In 1902, the renowned missionary statesman Robert E. Speer met a twenty-four-year old blind Christian who never received formal education. Although the Korean young man was blind since the age of three, he managed to memorize portions of the Bible by listening to people reading scripture. The young man said, "I think of the gospel all the time. In my little room at the gate others read them to me."[27] Speer wondered how a blind young man knew the Bible so well without any learning apparatus so he quizzed him with random questions:

> "Do you know what is the fifteenth chapter of Luke?"
> "O, yes," he replied; "the parables of the lost sheep, the lost coin, and the prodigal son."
> "And do you know in which chapter in Matthew is the story of the feeding of the five thousands?"
> "Yes; in the fourteenth," was his instant reply.[28]

The fact that missionaries in Korea introduced the Bible as sacred text resonated powerfully with the Confucian mindset that esteemed canonical texts above all other litearture. When missionaries began preaching about the authority of the Scriptures, the Koreans were already culturally conditioned to, first, revere sacred writings and, secondly, put into practice the knowledge taken from the words the sacred text. The Confucian culture of learning reinforced the necessity of applying what was learned. The concept of knowing something just for the sake of knowing was foreign in the Korean version of Neo-Confucianism. Koreans gave little room for misgivings about the sacred text. If one was convinced of its truth, they were conditioned to pursue it seriously and to dedicate their lives chasing after it.

The Methodist missionary George Heber Jones in 1902 recounted the experience of Korean Christians going over the parable of the unforgiving servant (Matthew 18:23–35). In Jesus's parable, a man refused to forgive

26. Johnson, "When I Went to Church in Korea," 200.

27. Speer, "An," 116–17.

28. Speer, "An," 116–17.

a small debt from his servant even though he was forgiven an enormous debt by his lord. After hearing the parable, a Korean man, almost like an automated response, "immediately made a literal and personal application to himself."[29] The man proceeded to call "to his home all who were in his debt, and when they had assembled he read them the story and told them the application he had made of it. He freely released them from their obligations to him, and bringing out the papers he held against them burned them before their wondering eyes."[30] The man underwent radical change after gaining knowledge of biblical truth; the response was immediate and without reservation.

In 1910, the missionary J. Wilbur Chapman was probably exaggerating when he wrote, "Every missionary in Korea unquestioningly believes the Bible to be the Word of God. He accepts it as such and faithfully preaches its truths to the people, and they are accepting salvation in Christ in a marvelous way."[31] Nevertheless, Chapman's observation reflects the theological tenor of the missionaries in Korea. Walter Erdman, a missionary in Korea, reinforces Chapman's view when he wrote, "The Korean Church has from the first been a scriptural church founded on a belief in the absolute authority of the scriptures."[32]

Arthur Judson Brown, who traveled to the Far East as the secretary of the Foreign Mission Board of the Northern Presbyterian Church, observed in 1919 that the orthodox line was "sharply drawn" by their missionaries. Brown wrote, "The area of duty in both doctrine and practice is strictly defined [by the missionaries], and every professing Christian who does not keep within it is counted a heretic."[33] Furthermore, Brown described the uncompromising orthodox outlook of the missionaries:

> The typical missionary of the first quarter century after the opening of the country was a man of the Puritan type. He kept the Sabbath as our New England forefathers did a century ago. He looked upon dancing, smoking, and card-playing as sins in which no true follower of Christ should indulge. In theology and biblical criticism he was strongly conservative, and he held

29. Jones, "Korean Class Leader," 128–29.

30. Jones continued, "Modern exegesis would say that the humble Korean class leader had not mad the proper application of the teaching of Christ in the parable. This may be true. But who shall say that Christ did not visit that Korean hamlet the day young Chong burned up his neighbor's notes and look with joy on a man seeking to follow him" (Jones, "Korean Class Leader," 128–29).

31. "Man and the Call," 259.

32. Erdman, "Bible Classes and Bible Institutes," 365.

33. Brown, *Mastery of the Far East*, 541.

as a vital truth the premillennarian view of the second coming of Christ. The higher criticism and liberal theology were
deemed dangerous heresies. In most of the evangelical churches
of America and Great Britain, conservatives and liberals have
learned to live and work together in peace; but in Korea the few
men who hold 'the modern view' have a rough road to travel,
particularly in the Presbyterian group of missions. The Koreans
converts naturally reproduced the prevailing type.[34]

On the mission field, Protestant missionaries took for granted that
literacy was essential to Christian formation. Reading the Bible has long
been crucial to understanding the historical relationship of literacy with
Protestantism. Since Martin Luther's *sola scriptura* (Latin: "by scripture
alone") during the Protestant Reformation, reading the Bible and religious
literature became so common that it was accepted as a natural part of the
Protestant experience. Protestant missionaries have long recognized literacy
as an integral component to mission work and a major force behind evangelistic efforts. The central role of Christian literature, especially the Bible, for
the dissemination of Christianity, preparation of church membership and
leadership, and practicing the faith demonstrates the way literacy served as
a precursory measure for Christian formation in the church's culture.

The Methodist missionary Henry G. Appenzeller procured a Western-
style printing press in Korea in 1888. Appenzeller requested Franklin Ohlinger, a fellow Methodist missionary, to go to Japan to purchase one and
to start operating it in the basement of Pai Chai Academy, the school Appenzeller had started. "Mr. Ohlinger visited Japan, made the necessary pur-
chases, and was at work before the Korean Government had time to make
the usual objection that the importation 'of such machines was prohibited
by the treaty.'"[35]

Understanding Protestantism's historical and established relationship
with literacy can offer explanatory models that echo the Confucian reverence for sacred texts. The ways in which missionaries stressed the memorization of Scripture and internalizing its message showed striking parallels in
their relation to Confucian culture. In 1902, George Heber Jones observed
the reverence Koreans had for books and learning. Jones wrote, "Books, being scarce, are prized highly, and when a book like the Bible falls into the
hands of one who really undertakes to study it, the result is most beneficial
to the man."[36] Anna Pierson in 1911 described the ease with which Koreans

34. Brown, *Mastery of the Far East*, 540.
35. "Korea," 3:512.
36. Jones, "Korean Class Leader," 128.

took to the reading of the Bible with seriousness and solemnity when she wrote: "The secret of the strength of the Korean Church lies in the fact that the Bible is their *daily food*. The Christians read it day and night and are among the greatest Bible lovers in the world."[37] In 1911, Samuel A. Moffett described the seriousness and veneration with which Koreans received the Bible. Moffett wrote:

> First of all—it is a Bible loving and a Bible studying church, receiving the Scriptures as the Word of God and resting in simple faith upon His promise of salvation from sin through His Son Jesus Christ. I do not hesitate to state my conviction that what has been the chief factor in the transformation of the spiritual life of the Koreans and what has placed the Korean Church in its proper place in evangelization has been the great system of Bible Training Classes. The Bible is of course the greatest factor in evangelization in all countries, but it has certainly occupied a rather unique position in the work in Korea, and the Korean Church derives its power, its spirituality, its great faith in prayer, and its liberality from the fact that the whole church has been as it were saturated with a knowledge of the Word of God. These Bible study and training classes constitute the most important factor in educating, training, and developing the whole church, all its membership, young and old, literate and illiterate, is given systematic education and training."[38]

In *The Bible and Missions* (1920), Helen Barrett Montgomery surveyed the influence of the Bible in Korea. Montgomery wrote that Korean Christians were "pre-eminently Bible Christians."[39] In 1908, a journalist from the United States observed the Korean church and wrote, "In devotion to the Bible the Korean Christians put the Churches at home to blush."[40] In *Korea for Christ* (1910), George Davis wrote, "The Korean Christian is a man of one Book, and that Book the Bible."[41] Another missionary in 1914 described how Korean Christians unreservedly accepted the Bible as the "truth." He wrote,

> The missionary body of Korea has as a whole been characterized by an unreserved acceptance of the Bible as the truth of God, believing the poetical parts are divinely inspired songs;

37. Pierson, "Korea—Land of Opportunity," 270.
38. Moffett, "Native Church," 228–29.
39. Montgomery, *Bible and Missions*, 121.
40. Ellis, "Korea," 98.
41. Davis, *Korea for Christ*, 51.

the historical parts are accurate accounts of what happened to
actual persons, not relegating Adam to the myths and Abraham
to the shades, nor putting Job and Jonah in a class with Jack and
Jill. . . . In spite of the strong tide of destructive criticism there
has been little wavering in the teaching of the Word in Korea.
The Korea missions consider that the Bible is to be accepted as
a whole, and is not like a moth-eaten bolt of cloth, from which
may be cut, according to human will and judgment, here and
there, a usable remnant.[42]

Essential to the Protestant missionaries' plan for missional success was
to teach the lower classes to read. In the effort to make Christianity available
to the widest audience, commoners and lower classes who were for the most
part illiterate were the largely untapped mission group. Missionaries quickly
discovered that it was much easier than it appeared.

Despite the fact that the lower classes had been illiterate for centuries,
the Confucian culture instilled a widespread desire for learning. The impact
of the turnaround in literacy played a key role in accelerating the teaching
of Christianity. In 1911, Anna W. Pierson, a Presbyterian missionary in Korea, claimed that the literacy movement had made reading in Korea "almost
universal."[43] Pierson continued, "Even those who have had no education
and have passed middle age, when they become Christians, can learn to
read their Bibles in a few weeks."[44]

The impetus to propagate Christianity throughout Korea created a
grassroots literacy movement that inspired a cultural revival of hangul, Korea's native vernacular script. Wm. Theodore de Bary called hangul "one of
the most ingenious writing systems ever devised."[45] The invention of hangul,
the only script in world history "of which the inventor and the date of promulgation are recorded and known,"[46] was commissioned by King Sejong (r.
1418–1450) and distributed with explanation of its usage to the public in
1446. King Sejong called for creation of hangul to combat illiteracy among
the people and to raise their level of education but it had fallen into disuse

42. Toms in T. Lee, "Beleaguered Success," 333.

43. Pierson, "Korea—Land of Opportunity," 271.

44. Pierson, "Korea—Land of Opportunity," 271.

45. According to Wm. Theodore de Bary, the development of *hangul* was "one of
the most ingenious writing systems ever devised. . . . In its rational structure, economy
of means, and functional efficiency, this alphabet of the native language demonstrated,
independently of Chinese learning, how the Neo-Confucian philosophy of principle
lent itself to new forms of secular learning—as testified to in the explanatory note accompanying its promulgation" (de Bary, *East Asian Civilizations*, 61).

46. Pae, "Korean Writing System," 338.

among the Confucian literati who favored hanmun (Sino-Korean script), the lingua franca of the East Asian scholarship and the symbol of classical Confucian learning.

William E. Griffis, a founding member of the American Academy of Arts and Letters and the American Historical Association, observed that Korean classical learning culture resembles "mediaeval Europe. It is extra-vernacular. It is in Latin—the Latin of the Eastern Asia—the classic tongue of the oldest of living empires."[47] Like Latin, hanmun was often connected with classical learning reserved for academic inquiry and formal learning.

Missionaries realized early on that hangul which was based on the phonetic science of encoding the place, manner, and voicing of every consonant best served their goals of literacy and wide readership.[48] John Ross a Scottish missionary stationed in Mukden, China helped usher the revival of hangul by producing a Korean hangul primer, then translations of the Gospels of Luke and John, eventually in 1882 the whole New Testament printed in hangul. Missionaries in Korea adopted hangul and it became, according to Homer Hulbert, a Congregationalist who served with the Methodist Episcopal Mission, the "sole means of written expression" among the missionaries and their converts.[49] Missionaries initiated a literacy campaign that succeeded in mobilizing and sustaining a very large-scale campaign that spurred the people's ability to read and memorize the Bible, read and sing hymns, and distribute Christian literature as a tool for evangelism.

As missionaries structured the path for converts to become members of a church, one could not become one unless he or she could read. Prior to becoming a full member of a church, a Korean was first a probationer for six months or longer to determine if he or she demonstrated the proper qualities. In preparation for membership, a probationer attended catechumen

47. Referring to the place of classical Chinese in Korean history, William E. Griffis wrote, "[Korean] culture resembles that in mediaeval Europe. It is extra-vernacular. It is in Latin—the Latin of the Eastern Asia—the classic tongue of the oldest of living empires. This literary instrument of the learned is not the speech of the modern Chinamen, but the condensed, vivid, artificial diction of the books, which the Chinese cannot and never did speak, and which to be fully understood must be read by the eye of the mind" (Griffis, Corea, 339).

48. "Each Hangul letter makes a sound, representing transparent letter-sound correspondences. Each Korean consonant has a name and represents one sound, but each vowel has the same name as the sound it represents. The names of Korean basic consonants consists of the syllables in a CV (consonant + vowel) VC (vowel + consonant) or CVC (consonant + vowel + consonant) form. In general, each consonant starts with its own sound and ends with the sound value of the letter made at the syllable-final position" (Cho, "Early Literacy Policy," 201). For a detailed examination of hangul, see Kim-Renaud, Korean Alphabet.

49. Hulbert, History of Korea, ED 39.

class where one had to read and repeat the Lord's Prayer, the Apostles' Creed, and the Ten Commandments. The failure to read, memorize, and recite key biblical passages and fundamental theological principles usually meant disqualification but exceptions were later made for those fifty years old and older. They were excused from the reading portion but they were not exempt from memorizing and reciting passages.

When the probationers approached the end of their term and approached full membership, missionaries rigorously interviewed and examined the probationers for membership. In 1911, William Ellis, a journalist from the United States, was surprised at the 'severe' requirements as he wrote,

> And such examinations! I sat through one for several hours, having questions and answers interpreted, until the atmosphere became too thick for me, and the company too numerous—for there were more living organisms present than showed on the Church rolls. Into the little room, perhaps six or ten feet, there were crowded (seated on the floor of course), the missionary, four elders, the candidate, the journalist—and the others, unseen, but not unfelt. I have sat in many session meetings, but never have I seen such close, searching and difficult questioning of the candidates. At first, it seemed to me entirely too severe, and I remonstrated with the missionary; but he knew better than I, for they are determined to have a pure Church in Korea. If what I personally observed is typical, as I have reason to believe it is, then the Church in Korea has the narrowest door of all the Churches in the world.[50]

The Presbyterian missionary Daniel L. Gifford compared the interviews for church membership as being comparable in rigor with the examination of candidates for ordination in the United States.[51] If they successfully passed the examination, they were baptized and became members of a church. Following church membership, the women took Home Study Courses that required Bible-reading on a continuous basis. "The women missionaries prepared and printed books of questions on various books of the Bible, taking them chapter by chapter and making the questions answerable only from the Word itself, since the women had no other book save

50. Ellis, "Korea," 97–98.

51. "The sessional examinations for admission to the church—I can speak with certainty for Seoul—are made very thorough, something between the similar examination of candidates in the home-land and the ordeal through which the young minister passes when examined by his presbytery for the licensure to preach" (Gifford, *Every-Day Life in Korea*, 142).

the Bible. These questions were studied at home and the answers prepared awaiting the coming of the missionary on her fall and spring trips visiting the churches."[52] In addition to Bible classes, the missionaries also offered "courses in reading, writing, simple Arithmetic, Geography, Hygiene, Physiology, Church History, and mission to a limited extent."[53]

In many cases, missionaries confessed that they were overwhelmed by the tremendous response of Koreans to the religious and educational opportunities given to them. When 250 Korean women attended a Bible training seminar in 1906, they could not all squeeze into a church for a Sunday preaching service. For those who could not get inside, they sat "on straw mats outside, rain or shine."[54] To their amazement, missionaries witnessed Korean women sitting outside in the cold, determined to hear the religious message. A missionary wrote, "We have as cold weather here as in Chicago, and many of them are thinly clad."[55]

52. Cooper, *Evangelism in Korea*, 69.

53. Cooper, *Evangelism in Korea*, 70.

54. "Editorial Notes (1906)," 30.

55. "Editorial Notes (1906)," 30.

"Korean Graduates [of Seminary]." Photo credit: Moffett Korea Collection.
Princeton Theological Seminary.

CHRISTIAN TRACTS

The missionaries' dependence upon literature underscores the depth of their identification of literacy with of the power of the written word. Their effective usage of Christian tracts, leaflets, and literature inspired mass readership and circulation. In many instances, Koreans became Christians by simply reading Christian literature. In 1901, a Korean learned that his village leader became a Christian. Curious, he borrowed a Christian book to learn about this new religion. He said, "I took it home and studied it, and became amazed at the pure truth and simple teachings."[56]

Chang Sik Kim, the first Korean Protestant to be ordained, recalled how reading religious literature played a critical role in his conversion.[57] The pioneer missionary Franklin Ohlinger gave Kim the Gospel of Matthew, turned to the fifth chapter, and challenged him to "study it from there on."[58] Ohlinger effectively used religious literature to further stimulate Kim's interest in Christianity. When Kim became more interested as a result of reading the Gospel of Matthew, Ohlinger gave him the next piece of literature, "The Bible Catechism." After many conversations about Christianity, Ohlinger then began to teach Kim Christian theology and doctrine by using Christian texts. Trained as a child in the Confucian academy that instilled a solemn disposition toward learning and a rigorous memorization of the classics, Kim plunged deeply into Christian literature, consuming it without restraint. Kim said, "I studied till I could almost repeat from memory the whole of the four Gospels."[59]

In Salmone Paik's case, her unusual conversion story involved a mystical experience in which Jesus appeared to her in a dream and instructed her to read a passage of the Bible. When the mysterious figure first appeared, she did not know who it was since, as Paik explained, "there were no Christians in our village and I had never heard the name of Jesus."[60] The person said, "I am Jesus, follow me." Bewildered, Paik asked 'who are you' and Jesus

56. Noble, "Early Life and Conversion," 209.

57. Kim, "Korea's First Ordained Protestant Minister," 99. "It was under the appointment of Bishop Mallelieu, August 1892, that Dr. Hall began his work. Seven years later [i.e., 1899] I was ordained a minister [in the Methodist church]. . . . In 1901 I was appointed evangelist of the West Pyeng Yang district living at Chinnampo. In 1904 I was appointed District Superintendent of the Yeng Byen District and held that position for six years and then was appointed evangelist at Suwon of the Kyengki Provence, where I remained till last Annual Conference when I was transferred to Haiju" (Kim, "Korea's First Ordained Protestant Minister," 100).

58. Kim, "Korea's First Ordained Protestant Minister," 99.

59. Kim, "Korea's First Ordained Protestant Minister," 99.

60. Smith, "Story of Paik Salome's Conversion," 38.

responded, "I am the Son of God."[61] In the dream, Jesus showed her a book. Opening the book, Jesus "placed his finger by a certain line [of the book] and pointed as he read saying, 'Ask, and it shall be given you; seek, and ye shall find; knock and it shall be opened unto you' (Matthew 7:7)."[62]

As missionaries made inroads into the lower classes, illiteracy was a major hindrance to the development of Christian formation. As a precursor to the study of Christian doctrines and literatures, missionaries conducted classes to teach people how to read. In 1910, the Methodist missionary Mary Hillman described a women's Bible class in Yeju where many were "unable to read." Hillman wrote, "We introduced the study of the Korean alphabet as a regular period, those who could already read spending the time in writing."[63] It is not surprising that Koreans of this era closely associated the Christian religion with literacy.

As they traveled extensively across Korea, the Korean Bible Women served on the frontlines of evangelism and the delivering of rudimentary education. They "visited from house to house, and told the gospel story, and sold Gospels, and likewise distributed tracts."[64] Understanding that many of the women they encounter may not read, the tracts were made so that a gospel message or the Lord's prayer was printed on one side and the Korean alphabet on the other.[65] If they met someone who did not know how to read, they would use the tract to instruct them of the Korean alphabet.

The Bible Women made numerous contributions as their work intersected evangelism, literacy campaign, and women's movement. The Bible Women understood that teaching literacy to women was looked with disdain in some circles and they carefully distributed their tracts to ensure that they did not incur suspicion or hostility. The women who received the tracts hid them "away in their sewing baskets" and "secretly studied them."[66] As a result, the Christian work of educating women took on a subversive note. Despite acquiring the ability to read as adults, they persisted by learning "to read by writing the characters on the ground with little wooden twigs while feeding the fire for boiling the rice and heating the floors."[67]

From the beginning of Protestant missions in Korea, missionaries used the written word as the fundamental instrument of evangelism. When

61. Smith, "Story of Paik Salome's Conversion," 38.

62. Smith, "Story of Paik Salome's Conversion," 39.

63. Hillman, "In Journeyings Oft," 41.

64. Wasson, *Church Growth in Korea*, 25.

65. Cooper, *Evangelism in Korea*, 66.

66. Cooper, *Evangelism in Korea*, 66.

67. Cooper, *Evangelism in Korea*, 66.

the pioneering missionaries, the Methodist Henry G. Appenzeller and the Presbyterian Horace G. Underwood first explored the Korean interior in 1887, they carried along with them a supply of "medicines, books, and tracts," which "were sold on the way."[68] As W. J. Hall and George H. Jones prepared to embark a seven-hundred-mile trip into the Korean interior in 1892, their ponies "were loaded with books, medicines, and a small quantity of provisions."[69] In a women's hospital, "278 copies of Gospels and other books" were sold and 130 books were given away in one year.[70]

The Korean Religious Tract Society reported in 1885 for its first annual report that over 890,000 pages of tracts and leaflets had been published.[71] In an issue of *The Korean Repository* in 1896, the Korean Religious Tract Society, which was overseen by C. C. Vinton, W. M. Baird, W. B. McGill, and S. A. Moffett, included their list of tracts for sale including: including "*Calendar for 1896*," "*Plan of Salvation*," "*Pilgrim's Progress*," and "*True Saviour* [sic]."[72] Horace Underwood translated and wrote a number of tracts, such as "*The Saving Faith Catechism*," "*Leading the Family in the Way*," and "*Salient Principles of Christianity*."[73] In the same 1896 issue of the *The Korean Repository*, the Methodist Tract Society sold the following tracts: "*The Methodist Catechism*," "*Articles of Religion*," "*General Rules and Ritual of the Methodist Church*," "*Nast's Larger Catechism*," "*Bible Picture Book, Old Testament Studies*," "*Korean Primer*," "*Tract on Faith*," "*Entering Door of the True Doctrine*," "*Baptismal Catechism*," and "*New Testament Catechism*."[74] In 1888, Underwood wrote to John Ross, the Scottish missionary in Mukden, Manchuria, requesting an additional 1,000 copies of the *Corean Catechism* that Ross wrote in the Korean hangul script.[75]

68. "Korea," 3:511.

69. Hall, "Journey in Korea," 538. Provisions "were put into boxes about the size of a small trunk, and one box fastened on each side of the pony, which left a place in the center for our blankets, upon which we rode when tired of walking. As our ponies could not travel faster than walk we were able to go on foot most of the journey."

70. "Korea," 83–84.

71. *Korean Repository* 2, 75.

72. *Korean Repository* 3, 345.

73. Paik, *Protestant Missions in Korea*, 246.

74. *Korean Repository* 3, 344.

75. Paik, *Protestant Missions in Korea*, 246. Although John Ross (1842–1915) was stationed in Mukden, China [or in the Manchurian region of northeast China], he greatly influenced the development of Christianity in Korea. Before American Protestant missionaries began mission work in Korea, John Ross helped convert Korean travelers in Manchuria. Working Korean converts in Manchuria, Ross translated the first Korean New Testament of the Bible. His translation of the Bible as well as the *Corean Catechism* were secretly taken to Korea by Koreans and disseminated. Ross evidently

Little did Henry G. Appenzeller realize at the time of his purchase of a printing press in 1888 that it would make a dramatic impact not only on Christian literature but also on the broader Korean society. In the basement of Pai Chai Academy, Appenzeller started the Tri-lingual Press and later the Korea Methodist Publishing House. In 1894, Appenzeller's Press reported printing nearly two million pages.[76] As one of Appenzeller's major projects, he along with William Scranton and Horace G. Underwood undertook the work of translating the Bible into Korean from earlier versions.[77]

In addition to the volumes of tracts, catechisms, hymnals, Bibles, books, Sunday School lessons, textbooks, and leaflets, the Tri-lingual Press published regularly missionary magazines and academic journals such as *The Korean Repository, Korea Methodist, The Christian News, Methodist Christian Advocate, The Korea Review,* and *The Korea Mission Field.*[78] In particular, the Northern Methodist Book Store in Seoul reported selling 3,024 volumes from May 1899 to April 1900, earning $498.07 dollars.[79]

The success of the printing industry was so great that a missionary declared in 1902 that "Christian influence controls the literature of Korea."[80] The missionaries took advantage of the Koreans' attraction to literature and opened book rooms across Korea whereby Koreans can browse books and

---

had a gift for languages. He had knowledge of eleven languages including Mandarin, classical Chinese, Manchu, and Korean.

76. Paik, *Protestant Missions in Korea,* 249.

77. "Mr. Appenzeller and Dr. Scranton were now engaged, as members of a Committee of Translation, to render the Scriptures into Korean, it having been found that previous translations made by Rev. John Ross, in Mouken, were imperfect and ill adapted to the needs of the great work of the evangelization of Korea" ("Korea," 3:521). The National Bible Society of Scotland published John Ross's Korean translation of the Gospels of Mark and Luke in 1884. Rijutei published a Sino-Korean and *hangul* translation of the New Testament by 1885. W. D. Reynolds explained the reasons for revising Ross and Rijutei's versions. "The Ross and Rijutei versions were of necessity almost wholly the work of Korean scholars translating from Chinese and Japanese Scriptures, without adequate revision by a foreigner, versed in both the original and Korean. However grateful we must always feel for these pioneer translations, the stilted style, abounding in Chinese derivations and provincial expressions, with frequent errors, obscure renderings, queer spellings and archaic type, caused the early missionaries to resolve to make a new translation rather than waste time patching up the old" (Reynolds, "Contribution of the Bible Societies," 127).

78. For a brief explanation of the development of these publications, see Paik, *Protestant Missions in Korea,* 340–44; "Korea," 3:519–20.

79. Paik, *Protestant Missions in Korea,* 342.

80. Paik, *Protestant Missions in Korea,* 342.

investigate the claims of Christianity. In 1898, the Northern Presbyterian Mission alone operated twenty book rooms.[81]

The Tri-lingual Press, which was the only mission press in Korea, also had the monopoly of the printing business in the capital.[82] Among the publications for the general public, the Korean newspaper, *The Independent* (Dongnip Sinmun) had an enormous impact through its advocacy of nationalism, independence, and self-determination. Homer Hulbert, who took over the Tri-lingual Press in 1893 after Franklin Ohlinger returned to the United States, helped Jae-pil Seo and Chiho Yun to edit and publish *The Independent*, Korea's first vernacular newspaper. Although the newspaper was published for only three years, from 1896 to 1899, *The Independent*, which "combined its zealous calls for reform with a pro-Christian message," helped prepare many future leaders of Korea's independence movement.[83] Appenzeller's encouragement and support of *The Independent* indicated his political commitment toward Korean independence (a topic that will be discussed in chapter 6).

BIBLE TRAINING CLASSES

As more Korean Christians began to take leadership over the church and its affairs, they shaped the educational system after its own cultural character. The Korean example in which Korean Christians applied their local knowledge to the developing formation of new Christian structures demonstrates how local perspectives not only informs and guides the organization but also bridges the traditional/new dichotomy.

As part of the larger effort by Korean Christians to develop Christian discipleship, Bible training classes were introduced across the country with basic training starting at local settings. Interestingly, the levels of the Bible training class paralleled the divisions of educational hierarchy during the Joseon period when the village Confucian academies, known as *seodang*, flourished across the country.

At the village *seodang*, children became acquainted with elementary Confucianism. Even before they read the original work of Confucius and Mencius in hanmun, children learned and mastered the 'One Thousand Hanmun Characters,' a primer to teach children the most common hanmun characters. When the child has outgrown the instruction of the village teacher, he moved to *seowon*, the county Confucian academy where

---

81. *Korean Repository* 5, 416.

82. Paik, *Protestant Missions in Korea*, 342–43.

83. Schmid, *Korea Between Empires*, 47.

the student received advanced Confucian learning.[84] Many *seowons* were founded by Korean Confucian luminaries that served as important learning centers for particular branch or faction within Korean Neo-Confucianism.[85] Most students would finish their formal training at the *seowon* but a few select entered *Sungkyunkwan* in Seoul, the foremost Confucian institution of national higher learning in Korea.

When Korean Christians created Bible training classes, they showed structural similarities with the Joseon educational system. The Bible training classes were organized first in local churches across Korea. By 1910, local classes in the villages numbered "no less than a thousand."[86] If they successfully completed the courses at the local village level, they moved on to district Bible classes that usually lasted for a week. After district classes, participants attended a large gathering usually in a large city, such as Seoul or Pyeongyang. Then "more than a score" of general classes that drew people from all districts were organized, "where sometimes 1,000 or 1,200 Christians gather from long distances to listen to God's Word expounded by the missionaries and leading Korean teachers."[87] Exceptional students could receive training by gaining admission to a Christian college or seminary.

In 1911, Samuel A. Moffett noted that the general classes began with a group of seven people but had grown to "500 in Seoul, 800 in Taiku, 1,000 each in Chai Ryung and Pyeng Yang, and to even 1,300 in Syen Chun, while for women, [general] classes in Songdo, Fusan, Taiku, Kongju, Pyeng Yang and Syen Chun have numbered from 150 to 700, some of the women walking even 200 miles in order to attend them."[88] The wide network of Bible training classes that connected small villages to higher levels of Christian learning made George Davis declare that the system of Bible training classes was the "cornerstone" of the Korean church.[89]

84. K. Lee, *New History of Korea*, 180.

85. For example, the Sosu Seowon located in Sunheung was built to commemorate Hyang An, who first introduced Neo-Confucianism to Korea. The Okcheon Seowon in Suncheon was built to memorialize Kim Geongpil, a sarim scholar who was exiled for his convictions.

86. Davis, *Korea for Christ*, 39.

87. Davis, *Korea for Christ*, 39.

88. Moffett, "Native Church," 229.

89. Davis, *Korea for Christ*, 39. According to Walter Erdman, there were major flaws to the Bible Class system. Erdman wrote, "We speak of our Bible Class system and the name implies a greater degree of systematization than really exists, for one is surprised to find on consultation with workers from different parts of the country that there is an utter lack of uniformity of method, and usually complete absence of any other than an accidental relation between the various kinds of classes and between the classes and the Bible Institutes. Divergence of method and difference in degree of development of

According to Samuel A. Moffett, the Bible training classes, as a sys-tem, originated "with the Koreans themselves."[90] The classes began in 'two county classes' and thereafter they "spread all through the country until tens of thousands of days of preaching were subscribed."[91] The Bible training classes, Moffett stated, constituted "the most unique and important factor in the development of the Korean Church."[92] From the classes that attracted a large pool of Christians across Korea, Moffett and other missionaries re-cruited "evangelists, helpers, and Bible women."[93] In special cases, Korean pastors, teachers, and evangelists were "exclusively invited" and "the class becomes an informal theological seminary."[94]

According to a report from the Union Methodist Bible Class for wom-en in the autumn of 1914, the ten-day class enrolled 225 women who were assigned to their respective grade which depended upon their successful completion of the previous grade.[95] Each of the six grades followed a similar schedule: evangelistic services in the first hour; two hours of Bible study; singing and 'physical culture' at noon; practice of evangelism in the field; and medical lectures 'by native physicians from Severance Hospital.'[96]

At one general class, "over 5,000 Gospels" were purchased by 500–700 Korean men with the purpose of going back to their village and distribut-ing them "to unbelievers as a means of leading them into the light."[97] The distribution of religious literature by local Koreans became an effective tool in the work of spreading Christianity.

The self-initiative demonstrated by Korean Christians extended to included children's ministries. J. Fairman Preston reported in 1919 that his church in Suncheon hosted over 500 children in ten Sunday School programs that were "run entirely by the native Christians."[98] The emphasis on literacy in the Sunday Schools was evident from their religious curriculum

---

Church life are so marked in the different sections of the country that a very long dis-cussion would be required to cover the whole situation, and it is hoped merely that this paper may start us to thinking along lines that will lead to a greater systematization and correlation of our classes and schools" (Erdman, "Bible Classes and Bible Institutes," 365).

90. Davis, *Korea for Christ*, 40.

91. Davis, *Korea for Christ*, 40.

92. Davis, *Korea for Christ*, 40.

93. Davis, *Korea for Christ*, 40.

94. Dennis, *Christian Missions and Social Progress*, 137.

95. "Union Bible Class Work," 26.

96. "Union Bible Class Work," 26.

97. Davis, "Great Movement in Korea," 824.

98. Preston, "Extension Sunday School," 112.

that depended upon the reading of Scripture, reciting catechism, and repeating Scripture memory verses. In all of these cases, the teaching of hangul, or Korea's native script, became a fundamental tool in their religious work.[99]

CONCLUSION

For the Protestant missionaries in Korea in the late nineteenth century, literature was indispensable for evangelism and Christian formation. As a result, a great deal of effort went into creating a new religious identity that had literacy and literature as the standard of the Christian experience. The missionaries' desire to create a literate landscape struck a responsive chord in a population steeped in reverential awe with Confucian writings.

Korea's Confucian culture of learning which has been a neglected area of study in Korean Christianity was of particular importance in connecting with the cultural sensibilities of the Korean people. One could not be a Christian without reading and writing and, combined with the missionaries' reverence for the Bible as sacred literature, Christianity's vibe with Confucianism was unmistakable as it energized their Confucian imagination. Missionaries encountered a people with an instinctive love of learning that strongly complemented Christianity's tradition of learning and scholarship.

As the Joseon dynasty collapsed, Confucianism's preeminent place in Korean society also ended but Koreans still retained their reverence for learning and scholarship as witnessed by observers and missionaries in their travels. In the transition, Koreans appetite for learning shifted to Western education and knowledge as missionary accounts provided dramatic reports of the magnetic allure of education, and to the extraordinary lengths to which they would go to acquire it.

And let us not overlook the power of the missionaries' assumption that everyone deserves to read and learn. The missionaries made it very clear that they wanted to reach and educate the lowest classes that had been woefully neglected by Korea's establishment in spite of the fact that the Confucian mandate for the higher classes was to educate those below them. Throughout the centuries during Joseon dynasty, the upper class successfully maintained their status and privilege by blocking pathways to social mobility, most notably education. Ironically, the foreign missionaries outdid the Confucian establishment in making education available to the masses.

For the Koreans excluded from formal education, becoming a Christian represented a sense of liberation that went beyond spiritual considerations. In addition to finding redemption in Jesus Christ, the chance to

99. Preston, "Extension Sunday School," 112.

attain education helped fulfil a key cultural benchmark. Christianity made the unreachable, available and the disenfranchised, welcomed. Christianity stood for a spiritual as well as cultural wholeness that satisfied cultural yearnings that had long been denied. The assimilation of educational priorities into Korean Christianity was remedial and therapeutic.

Pyeongyang, 1913-1920. "A Straw Horse—They Hope the Small Pox Spirit Will Ride Away on (put on the door during the illness)." Photo credit: Moffett Korea Collection. Princeton Theological Seminary.

Seoul, 1890s. "Mulberry Palace—Inside West Gate, Seoul." Note the totem pole on the right. Photo credit: Moffett Korea Collection. Princeton Theological Seminary.

5

Shamans, Gods, and Demons

PAUL G. HIEBERT (1932–2007), who was one of the world's leading missiological anthropologists, argued that the Western world has a "blind spot" that prevents Western missionaries from understanding "let alone answer, problems related to spirits, ancestors, and astrology."[1] Born in India to missionary parents and himself a missionary to India, Hiebert understood first-hand the limitations of the Western mind when confronted with cultures that operate in a cosmology filled with spirit beings.

"As a Westerner," Hiebert wrote, "I was used to presenting Christ on the basis of rational arguments, not by evidences of his power in the lives of people who were sick, possessed and destitute."[2] Since the Enlightenment, the Western mind, grounded upon scientific empiricism that reinforces materialistic naturalism, interprets the world through a mechanistic prism that denies the existence of spiritual beings or forces that interact with human beings for good or ill.

In 1909, the Presbyterian missionary James S. Gale noted the disbelief prevalent among missionaries, at least initially, of the unmistakable active presence of idol worship in Korea. Gale wrote, "America has heard idols, has seen them in museums, has looked on them through the pages of Scripture, but to see an idol actually in command of his own and at work would be thought almost an impossibility."[3] Gale wrote of the incredulity felt by missionaries who discovered a world of idol worship that they imagined

1. Hiebert, "Flaw of the Excluded Middle," 35.
2. Hiebert, "Flaw of the Excluded Middle," 35.
3. Gale, *Korea in Transition*, 152.

having existed in ancient Israel of the Bible coming to life. "What grinning teeth and glaring eyes meet you on the highways and byways of Korea that you unconsciously associate with Dagon, Moloch, Chemosh, and Baal, and other gods and idols to whom Israel bowed down."[4]

When natives turned to missionaries about how to deal with plagues, curses, witchcraft, black magic, or spirit possessions, the missionaries failed to show the interconnections between Christianity and the spirit world. In the face of the supernatural forces afflicting the people, the missionaries' response "often denied the existence of these spirits rather than claim the power of Christ over them."[5] However to people for whom a spirit-filled reality dominates their consciousness, "there had to be an answer."[6] To deny their existence did little to change the minds of people who experienced their influence and power.

Given that the Western world no longer affirms or validates the existence of spirits interacting in our empirical world, "it is not surprising," Hiebert wrote, "that many Western missionaries have no answers within their Christian world view."[7] As an example, Hiebert asks, "What is a Christian theology of ancestors, of animals and plants, of local spirits and spirit possession, and of 'principalities, powers and rulers of the darkness of this world' (Eph 6:12)?"[8] Obviously the Western missionary has no answer for these types of questions. Having learned that Christianity does not relate to their real-world conditions, the native returns "to the diviner who gave them definite answers, for these are the problems that loom large in their everyday life."[9]

When Protestant missionaries entered Korea from the late nineteenth century, they encountered a world filled with fetishes hanging on houses, ancestor shrines from the local to the national level, folk tales of ghosts and apparitions, pairs of grim-looking totem poles planted to ward off evil spirits, and sorcerers and diviners on the streets offering their services or

---

4. Gale, *Korea in Transition*, 152.

5. Hiebert et al., *Understanding Folk Religion*, 90.

6. Hiebert, "Flaw of the Excluded Middle," 39.

7. Hiebert, "Flaw of the Excluded Middle," 45.

8. Hiebert, "Flaw of the Excluded Middle," 45.

9. Paul Hiebert, "Flaw of the Excluded Middle," 45. Hiebert urges the development of "holistic" theologies that take into account the spiritual realm. "First, it points out the need for missionaries to develop holistic theologies that deal with all areas of life, that avoids the Platonic dualism of the West, and takes seriously body and soul. On the highest level this includes a theology of God in cosmic history: in the creation, redemption, purpose and destiny of all things" (Hiebert, "Flaw of the Excluded Middle," 45–46).

ever-ready to make house-calls. Missionaries attacked the native practices as pagan, heathen, demonic, and/or superstitious, something to be cleansed and eliminated. However, as Hiebert pointed out, missionaries did not develop a theological framework from a Christian world view that addressed critical questions of the spirit realm that Koreans perceived to be very real and influential.

As an example, how would Western missionaries respond when Korean converts in 1906 reported that they are being "tortured" by the devil because "they gave up his service."[10] Confronted with phenomena that defied rational categories, the cases of the paranormal were simply unexplainable. The Presbyterian missionary Annie Baird in 1913 witnessed a Korean woman in fits that neighbors claimed was demon possession. Baird wrote, "Fine drawn psychological explanations as to what her complaint may have been were of little concern to her or myself."[11] Baird continued, "All we really knew or cared much about was that, whereas she had been oppressed and she was now free and well, and we are united in giving the glory to God."[12]

The objective of missionaries was a spiritual one in nature but they were untrained for the task of dealing with a hostile spiritual universe and with people suffering within. Despite their unpreparedness, the missionaries in Korea had to quickly adapt to the supernatural context. When confronted with a situation in which Koreans asked her to deal with a demon possessed person, Annie Baird admitted, "I had never expected to play the role of exorcist of evil spirits, but my mind was made up in an instant that if I had any power, be it no more than mere animal magnetism, this poor creature should get the benefit of it."[13]

Missionaries entered a world where the people are deeply entrenched in a spirit-filled world that governed the people's welfare. All around them, missionaries viewed how Koreans paid their respects and offerings to the spirits. From a terracultural perspective, Koreans, already well introduced to the activities of the spirit realm, interpreted the Christian God in contrast with the pantheon of gods that existed among them. Which god was stronger? Was the Christian God any different from any of the countless gods that they pay obeisance to? Why should they consider the Christian God when they already had a system of engaging and appeasing the spirits?

Missionaries that were affiliated to "all the historical churches" espoused the missionary doctrine *tabula rasa* that viewed non-Christian

---

10. Lewis, "Holocaust of Fetishes," 134–35.

11. Baird, *Inside Views of Mission Life*, 131.

12. Baird, *Inside Views of Mission Life*, 131.

13. Baird, *Inside Views of Mission Life*, 130.

cultures as having little redeemable traits and thereby traditional customs and practices had to be eliminated or cleared out before the seeds of Christianity could be sown.[14] Missionaries in Korea were no exception. They condemned native customs as superstitious and demonic and imprinted an American version of Christianity.

By roundly criticizing native beliefs, the missionaries created the expectation of Christianity's dominance over the spirit world in the minds of ordinary Koreans but they did not establish procedures or practices that dealt with the occult and demonic possessions. Filling the gap, Korean Christian workers, especially Bible Women, confronted the spirit realm. Native workers understood all too well the spiritual battles Koreans faced with spirit forces.

The missionaries boldly proclaimed the salvific work of Jesus Christ but, as members from a civilization that no longer believed in an active spirit-filled cosmology, they refrained from demonstrating the power that the scriptures mentioned. However, Koreans took the claims of the Bible seriously and expected spiritual power to be exercised, such as having authority over unclean spirits and casting them out. Furthermore, a terra-cultural transition was taking place. By converting to Christianity, Koreans were shifting their cosmological allegiance. No longer were they paying obeisance to demonic spirits. They now believed in a more powerful God.

In doing so, Koreans were eyewitnesses to the manifestation of power overcoming demonic possessions and spiritual strongholds. Koreans saw first-hand the superiority of the Christian God over the spirit world. The evidence of power of the Christian God over the spirits gave significant credence to the claims of missionaries. Within the missionary community, the engagement of the spirit realm produced an internal debate regarding the validity of such approaches but to the Korean Christian workers who were on the frontlines of the spiritual battle there was no doubt what Christianity stood for: the power to overcome spiritual bondage to which they were felt powerless against in the past.

---

14. John Pobee noted, "all the historical churches by and large implemented the doctrine of *tabula rasa*, i.e., the missionary doctrine that there is nothing in the non-Christian culture on which the Christian missionary can build and, therefore, every aspect of the traditional non-Christian culture had to be destroyed before Christianity could be built up" (Pobee, "Political Theology," 168).

SPIRITUAL REALM IN MISSIOLOGY

Hwa Yung, who retired as the Methodist bishop of Malaysia in 2012, affirms Hiebert's assessment of Western theology's rejection of a spirit cosmology but considers the "blind spot" to be far more pervasive than many would like to acknowledge. Yung writes that "Asian theology (or, for that matter, African or Latin American theology) hardly, if ever, touches on this realm of reality."[15] Yung asks whether Asian theology which reflects the discursive form of Western theology is capable to grappling with the everyday issues of its communities. Most of the Asian theological writings have "so neglected" the supernatural realm that, Yung writes, "it gives rise to the question whether they adequately understand, let alone address, Asian realities."[16]

The fallout from this neglect will further widen the gap between academic theology and the every-day experiences of people. It will render Christianity impotent to not only thoughtfully reflect on the nature of supernatural activity but also offer real compelling remedy to the realities. In addition to the epistemological problem, Simon Chan calls for a genuine reflection on 'Asian' theology. Chan writes, "This highly selective understanding of what constitutes Asian theology must be challenged, not only for its uncritical assimilation of Enlightenment epistemology and the resultant lack of theological discernment, but also for the way it totally ignores vast swaths of Christian movements in Asia: the evangelical and Pentecostal movements in much of Asia and, more specifically, the indigenous Christian movements in India, Japan and China."[17] Unless a shift in theological formulation takes place, Christianity, Yung writes, "will be perceived as evangelistically powerless and pastorally irrelevant, in dealing with many of the questions posed by Asian worldviews."[18]

However, the ability to construct a theology that incorporates a supernatural perspective is obstructed by the fact that Western theology rests upon a rationalistic philosophical theology within the limits of reason alone. As a result, supernatural explanations are dismissed or pushed "to the periphery of Christian thought" that render the Christian message incapacitated to effectively evaluate and address them.[19] Charles Taber writes,

---

15. Yung, *Mangoes or Bananas?*, 73–74.

16. Yung, *Mangoes or Bananas?*, 73–74.

17. Chan, *Grassroots Asian Theology*, 24.

18. Yung, *Mangoes or Bananas?*, 73–74.

19. "Western Christianity has, by and large, pushed miraculous healing and spiritual explanations for everyday events to the periphery of Christian thought, preferring scientific theorising and other secular values and beliefs" (Johnson, "Korean Christianity," 75).

"The superiority of Western civilization as the culmination of human development, the attribution of that superiority to the prolonged dominance of Christianity, the duty of Christians to share civilization and the gospel with the 'benighted heathen'—these were the chief intellectual currency of their lives."[20] As long as the prevailing form of Christianity remains Western in praxis and theological framework, the particularities of the non-Western context will not receive the kind of attention that scrutinizes their compatible and reconcilable characteristics with Christianity.

The dominant way of knowing in the West has deemed a supernatural cosmology, along with the larger network of non-material qualities such as consciousness, meaning, value, emotions, self, and spirit, as, at best, unknowable or, at worse, illusion and irrational. The historian Douglas Sloan wrote that "a purely quantitative, mechanistic, and instrumental way of knowing, by definition, cannot deal with the qualities of experience."[21] The conception of knowable reality has been, according to Sloan, "extremely narrow" and as a result a cosmology of the spirit realm is beyond the ken of rational and empirical understanding.[22]

Fused with positivism, modernism and the notion of superior civilization, Christianity in the West assumed a crucial link with culture. "In the Western world there was no doubt," wrote the outstanding missiologist David Bosch, "about which religion stood at the pinnacle. In almost every respect every other religion—even if it might be termed *praeparatio evangelica*—was deficient when compared with Christianity."[23]

Western Christianity survived the Enlightenment but was overthrown from the pedestal by the ascendance of scientific rationality and empirical scrutiny. Protestant missionaries retained the belief in the supernatural but it was greatly reduced by the claims of reason and science that in many ways undermined any attempt to bridge the two worlds.[24] Supernatural realities such as witchcraft, magic, spirit possessions, and occult became naïve traits of a bygone era that no longer exist. As an example of the shift in cultural

---

20. Taber, *World is Too Much*, 71.

21. Sloan, *Faith and Knowledge*, viii.

22. "The dominant conception of knowing that has shaped modern consciousness and culture, while quite powerful, has been extremely narrow. In the prevailing modern view of how and what we can know, the qualitative, the mechanical, and the instrumental are accorded full standing" (Sloan, *Faith and Knowledge*, viii).

23. Bosch, *Transforming Mission*, 479.

24. Protestant missionaries "retained their faith in God and the domain of the supernatural, but they also placed great value on science and reason. They built churches to focus on religious matters, and schools and hospitals in which they explained nature and disease in naturalistic terms" (Hiebert et al., *Understanding Folk Religion*, 90).

perspectives, later generations would conclude that the residents of Salem that conducted the witch trials in the seventeenth century were swept away in a mood of paranoia stemming from backward traditions.

When Protestant missionaries started arriving in Korea from the late nineteenth century, they must have felt as if they stepped back in time. Imps, goblins, bogeys, trolls, ghosts, and phantoms were only imaginary figments of the Western mind, often relegated to the pages of folk stories and fairy tales but missionaries entered a world where they discovered those beings not only interacted with individuals but also menaced and terrorized people to no end. In 1909, the pioneer missionary James S. Gale illustrated the sentiment of many in the missionary community when he noted, "We have come to realize that there are demons indeed in this world, and that Jesus can cast them out; to learn once more that the Bible is true, and that God is back of it; to know that his purpose is to save Asia."[25]

SPIRITUAL REALITY IN KOREA

Koreans lived in a world that took the phenomenology of the spirit world seriously as part of the natural order. Koreans assumed that the spirit realm controlled or influenced people's lived experience but Korea was not alone. Outside of North America and Europe, the unquestioned belief in a spirit cosmology was common throughout the world. In 1887, J. P. Jones, a missionary in India, asked "Is there such a thing as being possessed of a devil? They who say 'No' are very few in India."[26] Jones explained, "The bulk of the people here strongly believe it because they think they almost *daily* see instances of it."[27] In the West Central African Mission of the American Board, a woman missionary in 1887 told Chitwi that it was "nonsense" to believe that demon possession was the cause of infertility in a woman. Chitwi "repeated my remark to the other young men, and they laughed long and loud at my ignorance."[28] The missionary's mind however changed after she witnessed startling manifestations. She wrote, "If I had never before believed in a personal devil I should no longer doubt his existence, for if that woman was not an incantation of the evil one himself, then I am mistaken."[29] In

25. Gale, *Korea in Transition*, 89.

26. Jones, "Devil Possession in India," 395.

27. Jones, "Devil Possession in India," 395 (emphasis mine).

28. "African Superstition," 115–16.

29. She described the scene: "Her eyes nearly came out of her head, her tongue protruded, and while six women tried to hold her to secure her garment about her, she, in spite of their efforts, would leap into the air with superhuman strength. When

Mexico a missionary wrote in 1912 that "the devil is also a very real being to them."[30] In 1887, a missionary in China explained the elaborate and structured organization of spirit beings: "The Taoists teach that the spirit-world is just like the Chinese Empire in its government. . . . Each of the 1,600 cities of China has its city god, also each of the 100,000 great market towns; and not a few of the million villages have their village gods."[31]

The missionary E. M. Cable described how a Korean man, named Kim, became a Christian through a vivid dream in which "a man dressed in long black garments and wearing short hair approach him and hand him a book."[32] Kim who had never heard of Christianity or met a missionary was in Incheon on business and stayed at an inn where a Bible colporteur presented him with a Bible. During their conversation, Kim explained his puzzling dream and the Bible colporteur, who realized the physical description of the man in the dream matched him, replied, "O, that is easy to interpret. I am the man that you saw in your dream last night, and I have been sent by the Holy Spirit to speak to you and sell you this book."[33] The colporteur explained the gospel of Jesus Christ and Kim "at once decided to become a Christian." To follow up on Kim, Cable traveled northwest to Kim's village. Cable was amazed to discover that "all the families of this village" were Christians except one but Kim informed Cable that "it would not be long before this one would decide for Christ."[34] Cable noted that his visit was "the first time a missionary had ever visited Mr. Kim's village." All on his own, Kim helped to convert his entire village, using his conversion story and the New Testament that he bought from the colporteur.

Dreams carried important messages from the spirit realm. Visions brought specific instructions and apparitions were not fiction but interaction from another dimension of reality. The medical missionary Dr. W. G. McGill recounted a testimony of a Korean boy who became a Christian in

---

released she threw herself on Mrs. Kapey, leaping, screaming, waving her hands, and going through all sorts of gymnastics. Then running to the bushes she tore two of the fowls from their fastenings, threw them in Mrs. Kapey's face, struck her on the head, back, and limbs, then leaping in the air ran off to the woods and back again, going through the same performance till, exhausted, she fell on her face in the dust. Meantime the ochimbanda woman on the mat by the side of Mrs. Kapey had uttered a loud scream, rolled in the dirt, threw herself on Mrs. Kapey, seized the third fowl by the head, eat Mrs. Kapey with it, swung it in the air, etc., till its head was wrung off. She too fell exhausted" ("African Superstition," 115–16).

30. Wallace, "Personal Work in Mexico City," 19.

31. Baldwin, "Taoism," 171.

32. Cable, "Bible in Korea," 105.

33. Cable, "Bible in Korea," 105.

34. Cable, "Bible in Korea," 105.

1902. The boy described his radical decision to cut off his hair as a sign of his commitment to Christianity. The boy said, "When I said that I would cut off my hair, the devil said, in the person of a man that works with me, 'That is good: you can see it and buy a hat [as a way to tempt the boy to profit from the act].' I said, 'I will not sell it, for I am cutting it off to show that I am a Christian.'"[35]

In 1912, Florence Starr visited Korea and took note in her tour that "along the way we find shrines for the devil spirits."[36] She observed, "Beside the shrines are piles of stones thrown there by passers-by, to attract attention of the evil spirits away from them. A little tree or branch has tied to it many rags, indicating prayers made to the spirit."[37] From all quarters of the country missionaries received reports of the prevalence of spirit worship in Korean culture. When Horace G. Underwood visited a seaport in 1886 and made his way toward the city, Koreans stopped him and "by gestures earnestly requested not to proceed."[38] Underwood realized that they stopped him for his sake. Pointing to the totem poles, Koreans told Underwood that the poles were "guardians of the road who would take his life if he attempted to pass, as they were there especially to keep out foreigners."[39]

The totem poles acted as guardians of the village and kept away evil spirits. The Koreans demonstrated the seriousness with which they believed the powers of the totem poles by their reaction to Underwood's insistence that he will go into the city. Underwood wrote, "They stood back aghast, evidently really believing that he would be stricken dead, if he attempted to pass. To their astonishment the passage was made without mishap."[40]

William Griffis in *Corea: The Hermit Kingdom*, noted that "the air is far from being empty" as it is "thickly inhabited with spirits and invisible creatures."[41] James S. Gale found pairs of totem poles usually facing each other nearly everywhere he went in Korea. He wrote, "Here, there, and everywhere in Korea are posts seen by the wayside, cut roughly with grinning teeth, horrible face, and most ferocious eyes and ears. They are placed there to keep devils from passing."[42] Gale surmised that they "were the strong

35. "Experience of a Korean Christian Boy," 129.

36. Starr, "Korea Through a Visitor's Eye," 269.

37. Starr, "Korea Through a Visitor's Eye," 269.

38. Underwood, *Call of Korea*, 88.

39. Underwood, *Call of Korea*, 88.

40. Underwood, *Call of Korea*, 88.

41. Griffis, *Corea*, 327.

42. Gale, *Korea in Transition*, 86.

defense of Korea's poor people through the generations gone by against the countless forces of the unseen world."[43]

When cholera broke out in 1895, Gale noted how Koreans introduced intangible ways to block the spread of the disease, including digging ditches "across the roadway to make sure that no spirit should pass."[44] Believing that diseases were caused by evil spirits and demons, Koreans gave diseases the honorific titles *mama* (your majesty) or *sonnim* (guest).[45] When Gale encountered a group of very sick people, he asked the grandmother to explain what happened to them. She replied, "His Excellency the spirit of smallpox is with us."[46] Her comments were a reminder of the rites and she "hastened to make her evening sacrifice of rice cake" for the smallpox spirit. A spirit specifically attached to a particular illness—or even geographic locations— was a common belief throughout Asia. In 1887, a missionary in China wrote that the Chinese have "sixty-three gods of diseases" as well as having "gods of fire, pestilence, medicine, cities, roads; of day and night; gods of small-pox, liver complaint, colic, and measles."[47]

Koreans believed that totem poles had supernatural power and they also received the honorific title 'General.'[48] With the outbreak of cholera in 1895, inscriptions were written in front of the totem poles: "This is the general who is after the cholera devils."[49] The action to scare away demonic spir-

43. Gale, *Korea in Transition*, 87.

44. Gale, *Korean Sketches*, 243–44. "Another mark of heathenism is the idea that the exposure of decapitated bodies will serve as a preventative of evil doing. One day when riding past the execution ground beyond the East Gate, I saw a number of human heads on the roadway, trampled by the horses, the grass about bespattered with blood, and a little further on were the bodies with the ravens feeding on them" (Gale, *Korean Sketches*, 67).

45. "Koreans attributed every ill by which they are afflicted to demonical influence" (Bishop, *Korea and Her Neighbors*, 405). Horace Allen, a physician, qualifies Bishop's claim when he wrote, "Koreans believe that some diseases, such as smallpox, are caused by evil spirits" (Allen, *Things Korean*, 204). "Both smallpox *kwishin* and measles *kwishin* were raised to the status of gods and worshipped in shamanic rites. A principle income source for *mudang* was the *mama-baesong-kut* (a ceremony for sending off the smallpox spirit)" (Oak, "Healing and Exorcism," 102).

46. Gale, *Korean Sketches*, 135.

47. "There are sixty-three gods of diseases; twenty-five gods of the body, such as god of the tongue, nose, ear, back, feet, etc. Only think of having to worship all these gods! and their images are ugly enough to frighten any child" (Baldwin, "Taoism," 171).

48. "Usually they are called by the name of General, General this, and General that. Frequently they stand in pairs, side by side, or facing each other, one the General and the other the General's wife. Down his front runs the inscription, 'The General of Heaven,' while down the front of his wife it says, 'Mrs. General of Hell'" (Gale, *Korea in Transition*, 86–87).

49. Gale, *Korean Sketches*, 243–44.

its of disease was also observed by Horace N. Allen who wrote that Koreans smeared substance "over the front door and the walls of the house where it could be seen and thus alarm the evil spirit so he would be afraid to enter."[50]

Most often associated with the mediation between the spirit and human worlds, shamanism is often described as Korea's indigenous religion but shamanism is a part of the larger constellation of religious understanding that encompassed Korean folk religion. As missionaries observed totem poles, shrines to devil spirits, customs to ward off evil spirits, rice offerings to the gods, and prayers to the spirits, they expressed aspects of Korean folk religion that did not require the participation of a shaman. However, shamans (*mudang*), sorcerers, and geomatists were part of the unofficial low-born class of religious practitioners that Koreans turned to for divination, fortune, and medical and mental concerns.

Korea's folk religion, despite the lack of institutionalization, organization, or doctrinal coherence, flourished among the people that paralleled the Hellenistic culture of the New Testament. While in Athens, Paul was "greatly distressed to see that the city was full of idols. (Acts 17:16)" While Paul spoke at Areopagus in Athens, he came across the inscription 'to an unknown god' (Acts 17:23) written on an altar that indicated the countless number of deities the Greeks acknowledged. In a similar way, Koreans viewed the effort to secure and retain the good will of innumerable spirits as fundamental to their existence, lest they should bring misfortune onto themselves.

Lillias H. Underwood, wife of Horace G. Underwood, observed that Koreans "worship and fear an infinite number of all sorts of evil deities— gods or demons, who infest the earth, air and sea, gods of various diseases, and all trades."[51] George Heber Jones stated simply: "There are more gods than people in Korea."[52] As the Greeks worshipped and honored their gods in diverse ways, such as festivals, games, and sacrifices, the Korean gods, in a similar fashion, "must be propitiated with prayers and sacrifices, beating of drums, ringing of bells and other ceremonials too numerous to mention."[53]

In *Daybreak in Korea,* Annie Baird recorded a conversation between an old Korean woman and a missionary who asked her, "You all know about God, of course?" Offended by the question, the old woman retorted, "Do you take us for animals?" The missionary responded, "You all know him but do you worship him?" She replied, "Why should we? He's too far away. The

50. Allen, *Things Korean*, 207.

51. Underwood, *Fifteen Years Among the Top-Knots*, 9.

52. Jones, *Korea*, 51.

53. Jones, *Korea*, 51.

demons are nearer."[54] The 'God' the old woman referred to was 'hananim' ('heavenly lord or ruler') who was recognized in Korean folk religion as the supreme god but was perceived to be impersonal and distant.[55]

The British explorer, writer, and naturalist Isabella Bird Bishop (1831–1904), who traveled to Korea, China, Japan, Vietnam, Singapore, and Malaysia, observed the common belief in demonology in the East:

> Underlying all the faiths of the East there is a faith, an active belief, perhaps stronger than the whole of them, and that is the belief in demons. It underlies every creed, it is the belief in the women's houses. The women are the great agents for keeping up demon-worship, by bringing up their children to offer offerings daily to the fetishes of the demons in the women's houses. One knows that all sickness is regarded as the work of demons, as a demoniacal possession, and is treated as such, and the priest and the sorcerer are sent for when sickness enters a house, and by cruel measures and incantations the spirit is supposed to be driven out of the sick person.[56]

George Heber Jones presented a compelling portrait of the spirit sensibilities of Koreans.

> In Korean belief, earth, air, and sea are peopled by demons. They haunt every umbrageous tree, shady ravine, crystal spring, and mountain crest. On green hill-slopes, in peaceful agricultural valley, in grassy dells, on wooded uplands, by lake and stream, by road and river, in north, south, east, and west, they abound, making malignant sport out of human destinies. They are on the roof, ceiling, fireplace, kang, and (84) beam. They fill the chimney, the shed, the living-room, the kitchen, they are on every shelf and jar. In thousands they waylay the traveler as he leaves home, beside him, behind him, dancing in front of him, whirring over his head, crying out upon him from earth and air and water. They are numbered by thousands of billions, and it has been well said that their ubiquity is an unholy travesty of the Divine omnipresence. This belief keeps the Korean in a perpetual

---

54. Baird, *Daybreak in Korea*, 62.

55. The Protestant missionaries in Korea coopted the Korean word *hananim* and used it for the Christian God. "The name *Hannonim* is so distinguished and so universally used, that there will be no fear, in future translations and preaching, of the unseemly squabbles which occurred long ago among Chinese missionaries on this subject" (Ross, *History of Corea*, 355). For an analysis of the word *hananim*, see Oak, *Making of Korean Christianity*, 33–84.

56. Bishop, "Missionary Spirit and Life," 369.

state of nervous apprehension, it surrounds him with indefinite terrors, and it may truly be said of him that he passes the time of his sojourning here in fear. Every Korean home is subject to demons, here, there, and everywhere. They touch the Korean at every point in his life, making his well-being depend on a series of acts of propitiation, and they avenge every omission with merciless severity, keeping him under the yoke of bondage from birth to death.[57]

As Jones and other missionaries have noted, every place or corner in the house could conceivably be occupied by spirits.[58] Calamity could befall on individuals and families at any moment. "Not a day goes by," Gale added, "but the spirit of some animal must be propitiated."[59] Gale continued, "They throw rice into the well to quite the dragon, and offer sacrifices to *Ma-ma*, the god of smallpox and to other unclean spirits."[60] Gale's personal assistant woke him up one night, "saying that he could not sleep, because devils were throwing sand against the window, and that they were coming out of an old tree behind the house."[61] Gale noted how Koreans believe that a tree is "the abiding place of various kinds of evil spirits. Inside of the bark and roots, everywhere in fact, legions of these are secreted."[62]

The fluidity of Korea's folk religion illustrates the limitations of a discursive focus but the existence of a spirit cosmology that varied in types and formations was never doubted. In addition, the content, intensity, and expression of religiosity were conditioned by regionalism as particular characteristics of the local community contributed to the formation of individualized experiences. The Korean life was guided by chance or a stroke of good fortune. To increase the odds, Koreans relied on 'luck.' Homer Hulbert wrote, "Lucky days, lucky hours, and lucky moments; lucky quarters, lucky combinations, lucky omens; luck or ill-luck in everything."[63]

57. Jones in Gale, *Korea in Transition*, 83–84.

58. Horace G. Underwood wrote, "Every hill, every path, every mountain, every stream, every house site, house, kitchen, and almost every room has its deity or demon; and surrounding by this host of enemies, it is to be wondered at that the Korean has as good as time as he has" (Underwood, *Call of Korea*, 85).

59. Gale, *Korean Sketches*, 243.

60. Gale, *Korean Sketches*, 243.

61. Gale, *Korean Sketches*, 77.

62. Gale, *Korean Sketches*, 77. Horace G. Underwood wrote, "Spirit or demon trees are found everywhere, and in a marked way is the Ginko or Maidenhair fern tree an object of worship among the Koreans" (Underwood, *Call of Korea*, 87).

63. Hulbert, "Korean Almanac," 67–73. William Elliot Griffis wrote, "The unlucky days are three in each month, the figure of ill-omen being five. They are the fifth, fifteenth, and twenty-fifth. On all extraordinary occasions there are sacrifices,

Koreans operated on the unquestioned belief that spirits, in varying roles and purposes, constantly interacted at the human level. To the Koreans, Gale stated in 1896, "these demons are as real as the earth beneath their feet and I am thankful that we have a Gospel that can take away their fears."[64] Not only are they perceived as real, Horace G. Underwood noted that "the belief in demonical possession is common" among Koreans.[65]

Koreans walked a conceptual tightrope in relation to the spirits. Getting overly close or familiar with any spirit brought disaster, even with those that bring fortune. They "should never be made a companion of or spoken to in a loose or frivolous way."[66] Particular protocol regulated how Koreans interacted with spirits. Gale wrote, "Never propitiate it in advance, but only on the appointed day, and then strictly in accordance with form."[67]

Koreans demonstrated little love or affection toward the spirits but they respected and honored them to avoid giving any offence to them. Koreans remained careful to make appropriate offering or worship, lest they feared incurring their wrath that manifested itself in a plurality of ways that could bring misfortune, sickness, or disease. In 1901, a young Korean, named Tyeng Skil, described his family's religious practices prior to his conversion. In the main room of his house was "a small slip of paper pasted to a cross beam."[68] Beside the slip of paper was "a small basket filled with clothing of bright colors" that represented the dwelling of many spirits.

The offering was designed to satisfy or pacify spirits intent on doing harm. "My mother," Skil noted, "tried to impress upon me that the hospitality in providing the basket and paper had often been the means of appeasing the evil spirits of disease, and they should, accordingly, be always regarded gratefully and reverently."

While his mother viewed the appeasement of these spirits as a way to ward off sickness and disease, his father worshipped the same spirits to protect him from his travels as a peddler. Skil wrote that his father would take the basket and place it "in the middle of the floor, stand in front of it, place the palms of his hands together, raise them high above his head, and make a low salaam, bringing him to his knees and his head to the floor. The action was accompanied with the words, 'Ah, bright spirits, let not they wrath beset

---

ceremonies, and prayers, accompanied with tumultuous celebration by the populace. The chief sacrifices are to heaven, earth, and to the King or Emperor of Heaven (Shang Ti of the Chinese)" (Griffis, *Corea*, 327).

64. "Gensan," 161.

65. Underwood, *Call of Korea*, 89.

66. Gale, *Korean Sketches*, 156.

67. Gale, *Korean Sketches*, 156.

68. Noble, "Early Life and Conversion," 208.

me on the journey. Withhold they hand of misfortune and disease till my return.'"[69]

The whimsical nature of spirit activity that randomly afflict people made Koreans ever watchful of causing offense to the spirits. Violations against the spirits could result in minor mischievous pranks to destruction. Koreans told James Gale that "devils set fire to the house by throwing a ball of living flame against the thatch. This ball the *tokgabi* have brought all the way from Pluto's furnace. Dishes go clash, bang, in the kitchen without visible cause, while water is heard being dashed against the wall."[70]

There were benevolent and kind spirits that were guards, healers, and helpers but more often than not they were fickle spirits with the intention to bring about mischief, vengeance, harm, or destruction. Gale encountered coolies who feared no man but they had one weakness. Gale wrote, "His enemies are *tokgabi* and *kwisin*, which might be translated 'little devils.'"[71]

Goblins, imps, and leprechauns offer the nearest Western equivalent to *tokgabi*. The traveler and journalist William Eliot Griffis wrote in *Korean Fairy Tales* (1911) that "Tokgabi is the most mischievous sprite in all Korean fairy-land. He does not like the sunshine, or outdoors, and no one ever saw him on the streets."[72]

The constant possibility of an assault—intentional or random—weighed on the minds of Koreans and ritualistic appeasement was practiced extensively in dealing with the spirit realm. For example, repeated disasters may indicate the discontent of spirits and, as a way of placating them, a family may "exhume their ancestor's bones and bury them elsewhere, thinking thus to conciliate the spirits."[73] To defend themselves against attacking spirits, Koreans enrolled the assistance of 'guardianships.' Guardian spirits of various forms are enticed by food, prayer, and characters pasted on walls. Many animals and mythical figures are associated with the role of guardian

---

69. Noble, "Early Life and Conversion," 208.

70. Gale, *Korean Sketches*, 67.

71. Gale, *Korean Sketches*, 66. For more information on the subject, see Gale, *Korean Folk Stories*. The volume has 53 folk stories.

72. Tokgabi "lives in the sooty flues that run under the floors along the whole length of the house, from the kitchen at one end of it to the chimney hole in the ground at the other end. He de-lights in the smoke and smut, and does not mind fire or flame, for he likes to be where it is warm. He has no lungs, and his skin and eyes are both fire-proof. He is as black as night and loves nothing that has white in it. He is always afraid of a bit of silver, even if it be only a hairpin" (Griffis, *Korean Fairy Tales*, 6).

73. Gale, *Korean Sketches*, 216.

including dragons, venomous snakes, weasels, swine, "and unclean animals of every kind."[74]

Given the circumstances, shamans, sorcerers, or geomantists were frequently the recourse of Koreans to repel or exorcise spirits that caused possession, illness, or disease or procured, simply, for fortune-telling. In 1905, the Methodist missionary Henry G. Appenzeller noted "blind men, sorceres, feeling their way along the street, with a long staff to the house of some high official, to cast out, by means of wand and divining tortoise box, some foul spirit that brought misfortune or serious illness to the family; or perchance he may be on a more congenial mission of selecting a lucky day for the nuptials of two high contracting parties."[75]

Even though missionaries dismissed the spirit realm of Korean folk religion, Koreans nevertheless turned to missionaries for their authority in the matter. A 1896 report stated that "men have come to Mr. [James] Gale complaining that the quiet of their households was disturbed by nocturnal visitations of spirits."[76] The report continued, "Various persons have become, as they supposed, possessed by demons. Exorcists in all such cases ply their trade. Houses are set on fire, water is dashed about, iron kettles are pushed one within another."[77]

ELIMINATION OF FETISHES

As an important step of joining a Protestant church was the elimination of fetishes that were kept by Koreans as a charm, guardian, or object of worship of spirits. The concept of 'fetish' encompasses all of the household gods and spirits. Henry G. Appenzeller noted "the small stake in the yard around which straw is wrapped, and capped with a discarded sandal, and a small piece of white paper with a sentiment on it to act as a charm." Appenzeller explained, "This stake represents a form of fetichism and is placed there to

74. "Also from the years of sacrifice in the home, comes the idea of a guardian spirit, which is worshiped by food, prayer, and characters posted on the walls. A species of venomous snake so commonly makes its home under the tiles, and is seen winding in and about the roofs of Korean huts, that they have associated with him this guardianship, and one of the commonest kinds of worship is prayer and offering to the serpent. To this has been added a host of other spirits, such as the guardian dragon, which they worship by dropping food into the well, his supposed retreat. In this guardianship they include weasels, swine, and unclean animals of every kind, giving to each so many days in the year, thus making a constant round of religious ceremony" (Gale, *Korean Sketches*, 216–17).

75. Appenzeller, *Korea Mission*, 14.

76. "Gensan," 161.

77. "Gensan," 161.

the honor of the god of site, whose good will is assumed by proper obeisance and sacrifices."[78]

George Heber Jones explained the ritual:

> When a Korean erects a house, he must first recognize the pro-prietorship of a spirit which he believes to occupy the land upon which he builds, so with great ceremony and sacrifice he installs in his house, as the representative of this spirit, a sheet of paper or a piece of cloth, attached to the main beam that supports the roof. After being installed by these rites, this piece of paper or roll of cloth becomes sacred, and the Korean lives in constant fear of it. In eating his meal in the room where it is enshrined, he is careful not to turn his back upon it. When sickness overtakes him or any member of his family, his first thought is that it is due to the anger of this spirit, and before medicine is taken or a physician is consulted, sacrifice is offered to the spirit to propiti-ate its anger.[79]

Koreans believed the accumulation of fetishes increased their fortune and protection. When an old Korean woman converted to Christianity, she collected a pile of fetishes including "old wornout straw shoes, pieces of rag rotten with filth, scraps of paper written over with prayers and incantations, human bones, images made of straw, pieces of gourds and broken dishes, and spirit-garments of silk and gauze."[80] They were all collected and "stuck away in dark corners [of the house] in the hope that the spirits would find them and be pleased."[81]

The Methodist missionary Charles Morris observed that "a Christian burned up all the paraphernalia of his devil worship, and instead of what we destroyed we pasted on the walls of his home the Lord's Prayer, Apostles' Creed, and Ten Commandments in the Korean language. Since then regular Sabbath and midweek services have been held in that house."[82]

---

78. Appenzeller, *Korea Mission*, 13.

79. "There are several other spirits connected with the household life of the Kore-ans, such as the earth-lord, the god of luck, the god of life, the kitchen god. These are represented by a booth of straw, a black earthen crock, a small bag of rice, a fish head, or various articles of clothing. As these several gods are enshrined in every house, they outnumber the inhabitants" (Jones, *Korea*, 50–51).

80. Baird, *Daybreak in Korea*, 100.

81. Baird, *Daybreak in Korea*, 100.

82. Board of Foreign Mission, *Annual Report*, 363.

SPIRITUAL AUTHORITY OVER SPIRITS

Koreans attached great significance to the power of anyone who could drive out demons since demonic affliction was considerable. The oppressive preoccupation with demonology was, according to George Heber Jones, "our chief problem in the country."[83] Jones continued, "The fear of the demons rests like a cloud over their entire life." In a context where Koreans viewed problems fundamentally of spirit origins, Koreans turned to shamans who were the professionals in engaging the spirit realm. Shamans would perform rituals and ceremonies called *kut* in attempt to expel demons but they were successful, according to Underwood, in "very few" cases.[84] The shaman was an intermediary between the material and spiritual worlds and sought good fortune for their patrons. The position of the shaman interestingly was for the most part filled by women (Korean: *mudang*) instead of men (Korean: *baksu*)[85] which stood in contrast in the wider shamanistic world (including Mongolia, Japan, Siberia, indigenous Canadians, and Native Americans) where men for the most part functioned as shamans.[86]

Not only was the *kut* tailored for the particular issue but it was also unique to the specific patron. The shaman did not cast out demonic spirits in the biblical sense but rather, through a series of *kut* she engages and cooperates with the spirit realm by making offerings, paying homage, entertaining, worshipping, dancing, or praying in order to bring about a desired outcome.[87]

83. Jones, "People on the Chelmulpo Circuit," 283.

84. Underwood, *Call of Korea,* 89. Many missionaries noted how Korean families go broke paying shamans to heal loved ones with diseases. "To instance but one item, most sicknesses are supposed to be demons or the afflictions visited by demons. Under this delusion the country people spend more money in propitiatory sacrifices to exorcise the afflicting demon than in medicine to cure the disease. Many a family has wrecked an entire fortune on the altars of this brutish superstition in the vain attempt to save some loved one's life" (Jones, "People on the Chelmulpo Circuit," 283).

85. *Mudang* (female shamans) outnumbered *baksu* (male shamans) at an approximate ratio of seven to three. Choi, *Understanding of Korean Shamanism*, 222–26.

86. W. H. Weinland, a Moravian missionary working with the Yuutes in Alaska, wrote, "Of medicines they possess none, their only source of relief in case of sickness being the 'shaman' or medicine-man, who generally informs them that there are under the influence of some other 'shaman,' but cure the disease itself he cannot" ("Country and People of Alaska," 488).

87. "The shaman directly communicates with spirits. The Shaman is the priest who can sense the spiritual world and exercise spiritual power, and accordingly, remove calamities and call in blessings. These interactions with the spirit world take several forms from individual counseling sessions at the Shaman's shrine (usually his or her home) to elaborate rituals called Kut. Different Kut serve different purposes, such as trying to conceive a son, ending a drought, paying homage to ancestors, blessing a new

Some *mudang* specialized in dealing specific situations or illnesses. However, when Christianity appeared on the scene, one can imagine the experience of those who witnessed a spiritual power stronger than demons and evil spirits. It was a phenomenon that Koreans have never seen before. In the missionary literature, witnessing the power of the Christian God was enough for many Koreans to convert. The Methodist missionary Jane Barlow stationed in Haeju reported in 1926 how "two girls were delivered from demon possession," and as a result their families "now regularly attend the services and study classes."[88] Barlow mentioned that the mother-in-law from the same house, "being so impressed with the power of God manifested in her family that she cannot rest until others suffering in the same way have had the opportunity to be delivered too."[89] In other words, the manifestation of God's power made her an evangelist as she became an enthusiastic witness to the gospel. "As a result of [mother-in-law's actions], new believers have been added to the church."[90]

The pioneer medical missionary Rosetta Sherwood Hall chronicled a young woman who became insane. Her family brought in a *mudang*, who for 20 days danced and attempted to drive out the spirits "but to no avail." The family "also burned her in various places 6 nights in succession so deeply that the ulcers made were not yet healed."[91] Desperate and having exhausted all options, the family appealed to Hall, "promising to carry out [her] directions faithfully, which they did."[92] Under Hall's care "she began at once to improve" and as a result her family and three of their neighbors began to attend church.[93] Already, "five members from these have been baptized."

Rumors started circulating concerning the ability of missionaries and Christians to cast out demons from people. Horace G. Underwood wrote, "The news has gone widely abroad that the Jesus of the Christians drives

business, or healing the sick. Shaman are invited by both the patron and the spirits for the interaction. A Kut may last for several hours or more than a day and involve as many as eleven acts called kori with different costumes, offerings, songs, feats of balance, and spirit interaction in each. While its purpose may be serious, a Kut is meant to be both entertaining and engaging for both the patron and the spirits In order to be effective the Shaman must know the patron's family ancestry. With very little formal institutionalization of Shamanism, each Shaman's Kut is unique and each is tailored to the specific situation and patron" (Choi, *Shamanism*, 43–75).

88. Barlow, "Evangelistic Report of Haiju District," 29–30.
89. Barlow, "Evangelistic Report of Haiju District," 29–30.
90. Barlow, "Evangelistic Report of Haiju District," 29–30.
91. Hall, "Report IX," 21–22.
92. Hall, "Report IX," 21–22.
93. Hall, "Report IX," 21–22.

out demons."[94] Underwood's observation is noteworthy for several reasons. Few missionaries could have imagined that the ability to drive out demons would become one of the important ways Koreans believed in Christianity. In 1895, James S. Gale also recognized demonic activity to be of utmost importance in Korean culture when he noted that "the idea of possession and demon influence has a great place here in life."[95] A year earlier, Gale witnessed the Donghak Uprising, a massive peasant rebellion that threatened to topple the government. The Uprising channeled the people's discontent but it also gain popularity as a religious movement with extraordinary abilities. "One cause of their popularity," Gale observed, was that they "professed to have power to cast out devils."[96]

The news of fearless Korean Bible Women driving out demons became legendary. So much so that when cases of illness or demon possession broke out, Koreans turned to Bible Women instead of *mudang*.[97] The Methodist missionary Ella Lewis noted how Sarah, a Korean Bible woman, visited three people who were said to be demon possessed. Their families promised Sarah that they would become Christians if she and her companions drove them out. Sarah proceeded to drive them out and "the next Sabbath these families were well represented at the services."[98]

Annie Baird reported a Korean woman tormented by "demoniacal characters." "All day and much of the night she sat with head bowed and eyes closed, unable to resist the terrible fascination which they exercised over her."[99] She and her family resorted to shamans but "all the arts of the heathen exorcists had been tried without avail."[100] Finally, after they exhausted all conventional options, "some one suggested that she be taken down to the Christian village at the foot of the mountain."[101] The Korean "church sisters" prayed over the woman and they succeeded in expelling demons but not completely, so they sent the woman to Annie Baird, the missionary. Baird admitted she "never expected" to be an exorcist of evil spirits but nevertheless she treated the woman with prayers and compassion

94. Underwood, *Call of Korea*, 89.

95. Gale, "Korea," 230.

96. Gale, "Korea," 230.

97. Bible Committee of Korea, *Annual Report*, 27.

98. Lewis, "Holocaust of Fetishes," 134–35.

99. Baird, *Inside Views of Mission Life*, 130. Baird described how the woman was distressed by demons familiar in Korean folklore. "Ever since the birth of her child she had been tormented by two devils, one a woman, and one a big boy, both well-known demoniacal characters to all Koreans" (Baird, *Inside Views of Mission Life*, 130).

100. Baird, *Inside Views of Mission Life*, 130.

101. Baird, *Inside Views of Mission Life*, 130.

until she was delivered.[102] In 1898, James S. Gale reported that many "beset by evil influences, come in great terror and ask some way of deliverance." "Our remedy," Gale wrote, "is to read from the New Testament, translating the English into Korean as we proceed. They listen with eagerness, and I have seen those who were in bondage transformed entirely while dwelling on these stories from the Gospel."[103]

Horace G. Underwood recounted an incidence in the "extreme north" of Korea where a newly married young girl was said to be demon possessed. Shaman exorcists were brought in but to avail. Finally, one of the neighbors said, "The Jesus they worship over the hills drives out devils."[104] The mother "eagerly seizes the opportunity" and brings her daughter to the Christians. The Korean Christians prayed two or three times a day with no results. The neighbors made fun of the Christians, "Your Jesus God can't do what you claim."[105] The Christians redoubled their efforts "having decided that they will, without ceasing, continue until their end is attained."[106] Then, "it is a little before the midnight following," Underwood recalled, "when the possessed girl quickly arises and passes out of the chapel door. She proceeds to the shrine, where the village devils are worshipped, and seating herself, addresses the Christians sneeringly with the words, 'You dare not enter and pray for me here.' They at once get down on their knees to renew their prayers, and shortly she falls prostrate in their midst, to rise healed."[107] Underwood concluded, "This Shamanism is the most obstinate enemy that the missionaries have to meet in Korea."[108]

In 1896, two distressed Korean women came looking for Harriet Gale, wife of James S. Gale. The women claimed that their homes were "full of evil spirits" that terrorized them. "They could not sleep for the strange sights and sounds. Sometimes it would seem as if sand were being dashed against their windows, water seemed to be poured out on their roofs, dishes and

---

102. Baird, *Inside Views of Mission Life*, 130. Baird wrote, "I drew her close my side, stroked her shoulders and arms and held her hands in a close clasp. She looked up at me dully, without the least change of countenance. The next Sunday the little scene was enacted as before, but on the third Sunday when I put my arm around her, her face relaxed into a smile. On the fourth Sunday she failed to appear, and when I asked after her I was told that she had gone home cured" (Baird, *Inside Views of Mission Life*, 130–31).

103. Gale, *Korean Sketches*, 247.

104. Underwood, *Call of Korea*, 90.

105. Underwood, *Call of Korea*, 90.

106. Underwood, *Call of Korea*, 90.

107. Underwood, *Call of Korea*, 90.

108. Underwood, *Call of Korea*, 90.

other utensils were thrown about the house."[109] The women rushed to find her because they heard from James Gale's preaching that Jesus had cast out devils and they wished to be set free. Harriet Gale "taught them for some hours, reading passages in the New Testament which referred to demon possessions, and told them that the spirt of God was able to remove all their fears."[110]

The missionaries' capability to cast out demons made a strong impression upon Koreans that, in turn, generated greater interest and respect for Christianity. Interestingly, the unquestioned belief in demon possession brought Koreans, according to James S. Gale, "closely into touch with Christian thought."[111] The connections Koreans made with the biblical accounts of demon possession are not surprising. The New Testament is replete with references to people afflicted with demon possession and to demons as causes of illnesses and diseases.[112] In Mark 5:1–5, Jesus was confronted by a demon-possessed man who dwelled among the tombs. The man broke through "shackles and chains" and constantly, "he was screaming among the tombs." In *Inside Views of Mission Life* (1913), Annie Baird described an incident in which "a young fellow in the neighborhood, becoming possessed of an evil spirit, had roamed naked about the hills, tearing up the earth from his father's grave."[113]

In the four Gospels of the New Testament, the cultural awareness of demonic activity was so strong that fits of irrational rage, volatile and violent outbursts, unusual or strange sightings, and extreme erratic behavior were attributed to demon possession. Jesus himself was not above being accused of being demon possessed. An agitated crowd shouted, "He [Jesus] has a

109. "Gensan," 163.

110. "Gensan," 163.

111. Gale, *Korea in Transition*, 152. Not only the cultures of biblical times (both Old and New) but ancient civilizations across the world believed a cosmology filled gods, spirits, and demons. For example, in the Song of Moses (Deut 32:17), it says, "They sacrificed to demons where were not God, To gods whom they have not known, New *gods* who came lately, Whom your fathers did not dread." In the Hellenistic era of the New Testament, the Greeks divided the world of the gods and spirts into three divisions: 1. Theos were heavenly beings with god like powers, such as Zeus and the Olympians; 2. Daimon were earthly level powers, such as Heracles and Achilles, that carried out earthly functionaries; and 3. Daimonions were the lowest level. Cited over 60 times, 'Daimonions' is the most common Greek word used by New Testament writers to describe demons.

112. Not all illnesses are attributed to demon possession, but there are cases in the Bible where demon possession was the root of a particular illness or condition. As an example: "Then a demon-possessed man who was blind and mute was brought to Jesus, and He healed him, so that the mute man spoke and saw" (Matt 12:22).

113. Baird, *Inside Views of Mission Life*, 116.

SHAMANS, GODS, AND DEMONS 155

demon and is insane. Why do you listen to Him?" (John 10:20). His cousin, John the Baptist, was likewise similarly accused. Jesus said, "For John the Baptist has come eating no bread and drinking no wine, and you say, 'He has a demon!'" (Luke 7:33). As Jesus made enemies with the Pharisees, the religious leaders, they accused Jesus of having demonic power when they said, "This man casts out demons only by Beelzubul the ruler of the demons" (Matt 12:24).

The Bible verse that would have shocked and amazed Koreans was the superiority of Jesus over demons. Many verses illustrate how demons were subject to Jesus's authority. A demon possessed man suddenly burst out in a loud voice to Jesus, "Let us alone! What business do we have with each other, Jesus of Nazareth? Have You come to destroy us? I know who You are—the Holy One of God!" (Luke 4:34). In another passage, the crowds "were amazed" and said, "Nothing like this has ever been seen in Israel" (Matt 9:33). Furthermore, Jesus gave authority to his followers to cast out demons in his name (Mark 3:15; 9:38; Luke 9:1; 10:17).

The revelation that the Christian God is superior to demons marked the decisive turning point for many Koreans. Having lived under demonic activity that rendered them powerless against them, Koreans discovered a pathway apart from demonic oppression.

In addition, the Protestant missionaries encouraged converts to become active participants in ministry including deliverance. Commoners with little or no education now took part in asserting authority over demons. Annie Baird described how Korean church leaders offered prayers "without ceasing" for ten days for a demon possessed young man. "On the tenth day, after a mighty struggle, the devils left him and he was restored to his right mind."[114] In another village, Baird noted how Korean Christians "united" in prayer "for persons afflicted with demons."[115] Baird wrote, "Many of them were healed in answer to prayer exactly as they were in Jesus's time."[116]

---

114. Baird, *Inside Views of Mission Life*, 116.
115. Baird, *Inside Views of Mission Life*, 319.
116. Baird, *Inside Views of Mission Life*, 319.

Andong, 1957-1958. "Girls Choir." Photo credit: Moffett Korea Collection. Princeton Theological Seminary.

1931. "Outdoor Sing—Bible Class for Country Women." Photo credit: Alice Butts Album. Moffett Korea Collection. Princeton Theological Seminary.

BIBLE WOMEN

Unique to the history of Korean Christianity was the Christian work of former *mudang*. Many Bible Women were former *mudang* or shamanists who were well-acquainted with the shamanistic arts. Shamans also known as witch doctors or medicine men in other cultures were traditional healers who used witchcraft or mediated with spirits for various human conditions. As purveyors of the demonic realm, these former *mudang* "knew well what it meant to wrestle against principalities and powers."[117] Many of these Bible Women gained renown for their spiritual authority and power over demonic spirits. The deployment of former *mudang* represented quite a reversal for these women who previously served the interests of demonic spirits and communicated with them. As Bible Women, they now harnessed the power of God and exercised authority over them. Switching sides, they became powerful instruments of spiritual deliverance.

The 1907 Report of the British and Foreign Bible Society noted that "whenever there were demon-possessed people, they pleaded to Bible Women for help."[118] In 1914, the missionary Hanna Scharpff noted how Sin Tu, a Bible woman, "has a special power in exorcising evil spirits."[119] Dealing with demonic powers, according to Mary F. Scranton, became a specialty of Korean Bible Women. Scranton wrote, "When anyone gets tired of trying to propitiate the evil spirit, it is the Bible woman who must come and take down the fetishes and burn them. They are called upon to cast out devils, as well as to offer the fervent effectual prayer for the healing of the sick."[120] In her 1899 Report, Louisa Rothweiler wrote, "A man and wife were pointed out to me who had been possessed by evil spirits; but after the Bible woman had prayed with them, the evil [sic] spirit departed, and they, as well as their families, rejoice in a Savior who has power to cast out devils and to fill the heart with his own presence."[121] "A thing which the people dared not do themselves," Scranton wrote in 1907 that Bible Women were called to their homes to collect and burn the fetishes."[122] The Methodist missionary E. Irene Haynes in 1929 reported, "this spring the people in two of the homes asked the pastor and Bible woman to come out and burn all their fetishes"[123]

---

117. Hall, "Report IX," 21–22.

118. Scranton, "Korea," 394.

119. Scharpff in Strawn, *Korean Bible Women's Success*, 127.

120. Scranton, "Mead Memorial Church," 26–27.

121. Rothweiler, "Korea," 36–37.

122. Scranton, "Sang Dong," 10–11.

123. Haynes, "Evangelistic Work," 35.

As examined further in the next chapter, Korean Bible Women exercised authority over evil spirits and demonstrated not only to women but to Koreans all across the country that there was a stronger power. Annie Baird described one such convert who took the scriptural passages of casting out demons as "the word of God."[124] Although none of the missionaries would vouch for the existence of spirit world that Koreans inhabited, the missionaries' insistence of taking the Bible as the word of God lent unswerving credence to the biblical message of deliverance. The former *mudang*, now Christian, "read in the Gospels that Christ cast out demons and bestowed like power upon his disciples, she accepted the commission and exercised it with unquestioning faith."[125] She traveled across Korea with the reputation of casting out demons and "now her fame spread as a fearless follower of the Lord Jesus Christ.[126]

In 1922, the Methodist missionary Hanna Scharpff recounted the story about the "The Conqueror" for the *Woman's Missionary Friend*. A young Korean woman who had recently become a Christian had a son who became very ill. As common for this period, the family called for a shaman (*mudang*) that missionaries called sorceress. To cure the boy, the *mudang* performed the *kut*, the rite performed with dances, loud prayers, and songs. When the *kut* did not cure the boy, the *mudang* "pleaded with the evil spirits who were supposed to have caused the sickness, trying to chase them away."[127] When the *mudang* finished, without success, the Christian mother stepped forward and said, "Now let me try" and prayed earnestly. "Very soon all the boy's pain disappeared. Like a conquerer she turned to the beaten sorceress and asked, 'Tell me now who is better and more efficient, you and all your evil spirits or God in heaven?'"[128]

The *mudang*, presuming the Christian woman to be another but different form of shaman intermediary, asked "what her charms were" to which the woman replied, "The God of the Christians."[129] The Christian woman's father-in-law, who witnessed the entire event, said, "Yes, that is right. I believe it, too, for here we have the proof." Despite the evidence, the father-in-law's ingrained belief in ancestor worship prevented him from becoming a

---

124. Baird, *Daybreak in Korea*, 102.
125. Baird, *Daybreak in Korea*, 102.
126. Baird, *Daybreak in Korea*, 101.
127. Scharpff, "Conqueror," 401.
128. Scharpff, "Conqueror," 401.
129. Scharpff, "Conqueror," 401.

Christian. He said, "I do not want to die like a dog, who does not receive any worship when he lies under the ground."[130]

Annie Baird recalled the ministry of Sim Ssi, an old Korean woman who converted late in her life. Sim fearlessly tackled demon possession. She confronted a woman with demon possession. She and two helpers "knelt, face downward to the floor, and the two others followed her in long and earnest prayers. Every time they mentioned the name of Christ, the woman hissed and spat, and struck at them with hands and feet."[131] After the prayers, Sim Ssi began singing hymns that had "peculiar expulsive power with regard to demons."[132] The prayers and singing turned into hours and it was approaching midnight.

> The poor demoniac was placed in the midst of them, and under Sim Ssi's leadership, the attention of all was concentrated upon her and their prayers went up in her behalf. During the early hours of the evening she was perfectly quiet beyond an occasional snarl or whimper, but as midnight approached she grew very restless, turning constantly from side to side in a way that suggested the motions of a wild animal in a cage. When midnight came old Sim Ssi rose and made a gesture of command. The praying ceased and dead silence reigned. Then Sim Ssi called out in a loud voice: "Thou foul spirit, I adjure thee in the name of Jesus of Nazareth, come out of her!"
>
> At the words the woman was thrown backwards on the floor, where she lay screaming and writhing for a moment, and then all sound and motion ceased. She was like one dead, and the rest of the company were frightened, but Sim Ssi, always self-possessed and dauntless, called for water and sprinkled her face and chest. Presently life came back to her, and she sat up, very weak, but quiet and sane. The demon had taken his departure, never to return, for from that hour Toulchai Umuni and all her family joined themselves to the little company of believers, and walked thereafter among the redeemed.[133]

130. Scharpff, "Conqueror," 401.

131. Baird, *Daybreak in Korea*, 104. Sim Ssi "approached a Korean woman and asked her, 'Are you possessed of a demon?' The question was repeated several times, each time in a louder tone, before the woman seemed to hear. Then she answered: 'Yes, I am. Oh, have mercy on me! Don't kill me!' 'I'm not going to hurt you,' said Sim Ssi; 'I'm going to help you get rid of this demon.' 'Oh, let me be, let me be!' came from the woman's lips. 'I want to stay. I will stay. Let me alone!' 'I'll give you so long and no longer,' replied Sim Ssi, with perfect assurance. 'When I say the word you will have to get out.'"

132. The hymns are "I am so glad that our Father in heaven" and "Tells of his love in the book he has given" (Baird, *Daybreak in Korea*, 104).

133. Baird, *Daybreak in Korea*, 105–6.

Mary F. Scranton wrote that the faith of Korean Bible Women was "often greater than that of their teachers."[134] The spiritual power demonstrated by Korean Bible Women was "highly respected" and they "are believed to have the ability to offer up prevailing prayer."[135] Scranton wrote that the Korean Bible Women were called upon "to cast out devils, as well as to offer the fervent effectual prayer for the healing of the sick."[136]

As Bible Women made the burning of fetishes a part of their ministry, it became a unique ceremony that combined Christianity with pressing native concerns. At the supernatural level, it marked the individual's shift in allegiance to another power—a spiritual turn that Koreans did not take lightly. Ella Lewis and her Bible woman "moved on to another, where we had been asked to perform the same ceremony."[137] At one location, the woman of the house "went out to a corner of the yard and pulled down a little straw roof which covered a crock half filled with barley chaff. This she emptied in the fire place and proceeded to take down a stick, half covered with a dirty fringe, which was put with the chaff and the whole burned. . . . Then we sang 'I need thee every hour' and 'My soul be on thy guard.' These hymns are thought by the native Christians and Bible-women to have great power over evil spirits."

CONCLUSION

Today, the Sung Rak Baptist Church in Seoul, with a membership of about 170,000, is considered as one of the "fastest growing" megachurches.[138] Ki-dong Kim, the founder of Sung Rak, is renowned for his ministry of spiritual deliverance. He has been known to lead nine hundred exorcism meetings since 1961. At Sung Rak, "all-night prayer meetings, revival meetings, exorcisms, healing, and speaking in tongues are the regular fare at this Baptist Church."[139]

Elements of supernatural deliverance continue today but modern South Korea, as one of the most digitally and technologically connected countries in the world, bears little resemblance to Korean society of the early twentieth century when an active demon-filled cosmology filled and terrified Korean minds. Demons are "everywhere," wrote James Gale.

134. Scranton, "Day Schools and Bible," 53.
135. Scranton, "Day Schools and Bible," 53.
136. Scranton, "Day Schools and Bible," 53.
137. Lewis, "Holocaust of Fetishes," 134–35.
138. Mullins, "Empire Strikes Back," 91.
139. Mullins, "Empire Strikes Back," 91.

Koreans "accept it as a something not to be questioned any more than their own existence."[140]

In the West, the Enlightenment ushered in the "disenchantment of the world"—to use Max Weber's phrase. The stripping of the world of its magical and animistic beliefs from the natural world was, to a great extent, fait accompli. Although the missionaries believed in God's supernatural abilities, they for the most part subscribed to rationalistic religion that relied upon empiricism and scientific approaches.

The West's rejection of a supernatural cosmology also raises question about contemporary relations between the West and the Global South where many countries still recognize supernatural forces at work. The West's reliance upon empirical evidence is decidedly at odds with the Global South's comfort with supernatural explanations. Skepticism of the supernatural gives an impression of triviality to the weighty issues and concerns that many in the Global South invest with more credence.

From a terracultural perspective, the Koreans' unquestioned belief in the oppressive presence of demonic spirits was a reality that could not be ignored when preaching about the authority of the Christian God. While the reality of demonic activity terrorized Koreans, it was also the key to their conversion as James S. Gale wrote, "Another fact that brings the people closely into touch with Christian thought is their understanding of demon possession."[141] The system of spiritual oppression motivated Koreans to experiencing God.

The missionaries were cognizant of the disparity between what they and Koreans thought about demons and gods, yet, despite the missionaries' absence of a theological framework on the matter, Koreans deduced the superiority of the Christian God over theirs simply by exercising their conviction from reading passages in the Bible that related to demon possession. From the perspective of Koreans, the Christian God overpowered and defeated the gods and demons that have been oppressing and terrorizing them for centuries.

140. Gale, *Korea in Transition*, 152.
141. Gale, *Korea in Transition*, 152.

From Sarah E. Gearhart

THREE GENERATIONS OF KOREAN CHRISTIANS

"Three Generations of Korean Christians." The grandmother is holding a New Testament. Photo credit: Alice Butts Album. Moffett Korea Collection. Princeton Theological Seminary.

"Christian Women." Photo credit: Moffett Korea Collection.
Princeton Theological Seminary.

6

Missional Outliers

Korean Bible Women

You are making a great mistake.[1]

—An Anonymous Korean to a missionary in the *Story of the Woman's Foreign Missionary Society of Methodist Episcopal Church*, 1898

When American missionaries entered Korea in the late nineteenth century, many Koreans disapproved but this quote by a Korean was hardly typical. This is not the voice of an angry Korean Buddhist, Confucian, or shamanist who was reacting against the disruption caused by the introduction of Christianity, a foreign religion, upon Korean families and traditions. Anonymous was not an anti-Christian at all but, rather, a supporter of mission work who simply recognized a major flaw with how they approached missions.

Suggesting an alternative to what the missionaries have been doing, the anonymous Korean asked the missionaries, "Why don't you work the other way?" In other words, instead of focusing on men, why not women? In proposing a new model of doing missions, the suggestion compelled missionaries to come to terms with their own biases. Anonymous' comments were less a critique of missionaries than a question of strategy. Viewing

1. Baker, *Woman's Foreign Missionary Society*, 342.

women as having superior cultural sensibilities that aided the transmission of Christianity, anonymous concluded: "If you want to win Korea, win the women. Win the mothers, and all Korea will be Christian."[2]

Anonymous' confidence challenges the status quo that assumed a natural division between men and women that extended into the mission field. As the Korean Bible Women revealed, they are not only well suited to missional work but also proved indispensable in the early decades of Protestantism's entry into Korea.

Korean Bible Women were outliers on the mission field: many of them were widows from the lower classes, uneducated and impoverished. Their lives lie outside the mainstream and their marginality all too consistently imposes a position of lesser status and authority. Despite the little recognition in the academic literature, Korean Bible Women represented a vital force that propelled Christianity's expansion in Korea.

Korean Bible Women overturned conventional ideas about the primacy of missionaries in the development of Christian communities and, in turn, created space for marginalized women to construct new identities based on the egalitarian principles of Christianity and on the correlative notion that it is important to society that all people are redeemed and transformed by God regardless of one's estate.

This chapter turns to the crucial role of Korean Bible Women in shaping the critical first decades of Protestantism's growth. The Korean Bible Women were often leading the charge into the untouched regions of the country. As such, they were the ones who entered the wilderness and broke the landscape, enabling those who followed to till the land. Korean Bible Women possessed none of the markers of authority on the mission field: they were laity, not ordained; received very little formal education; and rose from the ranks of lower class. Nonetheless, few could have anticipated the extraordinary success achieved by Bible Women.

The Korean Bible woman, coming from poor, uneducated, and widowed backgrounds, re-defined their marginality as assets. The same characteristics that defined their outlier status now opened doors to wider missional horizons. Missionaries chose them for the task because of their availability but little did they know that they were extremely well-suited to bring Christianity to a country which was made up of mostly commoner and lower classes. As missionaries surprisingly discovered, the army of Korean Bible Women marched on the frontlines of Christian expansion, leading a populist movement while enduring hostility and persecution.

2. Baker, *Woman's Foreign Missionary Society*, 342.

BIBLE WOMEN'S MINISTRY

"What would we ever do without our Bible women!" exclaimed Marguerite G. English, the Methodist missionary stationed in the Pyeongyang East District.[3] "They are doing a magnificent work for the bringing in of Christ's kingdom," English added. English's enthusiastic endorsement came after she reported that three whole families in one place decided to believe "and there are forty-five other new believers in that place" as a result of the work of Bible Women.[4] Missionaries in Korea observed the self-initiative of Korean women. Mary F. Scranton, who is credited with starting the Bible woman system in Korea in 1888,[5] wrote, "Past experience teaches us that when the Korean woman once gets 'fairly started' in the good way she zealously labors to induce her friends and neighbors to become 'partakers of like precious faith.'"[6] Although Korean Bible Women held no official position in the church leadership, they nevertheless were viewed with having spiritual authority and power by the people. Abigail, a Korean Bible woman, noted how she was in constant demand. "Some new believer will ask her [Abigail] to go and 'cleanse her house from evil spirits,' or some one will come from a sick house and ask her to go and pray, or sit up with a child or whoever is sick."[7] Mary F. Scranton wrote that Sarah, a Korean Bible woman, "is in great demand for the visitation of the sick."[8] Sarah "goes about the work firmly believing that the 'prayer of faith will save the sick' and cast out the devils."[9]

The term 'Bible Women' referred to lay women who were trained to assist in the work of evangelism but in reality they filled in to do anything that was needed. In many cases, they acted as missionaries as they traveled to far and remote places in Korea to preach the gospel. The Methodist missionary Lulu Miller reported in 1926 that a Bible woman "conducted all of the [church] services" on an island called Acham off of Incheon since no one qualified was available.[10] On a Sunday morning, someone from the island

3. "Pyeng Yang East District," 41.

4. "Pyeng Yang East District," 41.

5. Yun, *Hanguk Gamnikyo*, 104. Also cited in Strawn, "Korean Bible Women's Success," 118. The Bible woman system was started by Mary F. Scranton but the first Bible woman's training school was started by Louisa C. Rothweiler in 1902. See Chaffin, "Union," 17. In 1905, the school was officially called Seoul Methodist Women's School (Seoul Gamnigyo Yeohakdang). See Yang, "Chogi Chundo," 102.

6. Scranton, "Widower Churches," 167.

7. Foote, "Biblewomen," 339.

8. Scranton, "Missionary Work among Women," 316.

9. Scranton, "Missionary Work among Women," 316.

10. Miller, "Chelmulpo District," 9–10.

"would not allow her to lead the service because she was a woman."[11] The Bible woman consulted the Methodist District Superintendent of Incheon, Chan-heung Kim, who "told her to lead all of the meetings even though this man might cause her trouble."[12]

The roles of Bible Women were many but evangelism and teaching, especially to other women, was understood to be their central emphasis. However, their flexible approach allowed them to work in the most diverse contexts: Bible Women led singing classes and prayer meetings, taught Korean language lessons in classrooms, preached sermons on Sundays, did visitations and called on the sick, worked as a house matron for girls at a school's dormintory, led Bible studies and Sunday school classes, and assisted with orphanages. They were ready and willing to do everything, even menial tasks. They filled the gaps on the mission field more than any other person in the church and mission organization. It was not unusual for Bible Women to teach classes in the mornings and then travel to the countryside on evangelism trips in the afternoon.

The Presbyterian by-laws of 1896 defined the Korean Bible woman as a "Christian woman employed in the distribution of Christian literature, and in biblical instruction."[13] Missionary literature distinguishes Bible Women who were employed by missionaries and churches, those who received traveling stipend only, and volunteer Bible Women. Among those in employment, missionary sources note that they may "live on their small and inadequate salary."[14] Volunteer Bible Women may assist with local church ministries or partner with other Bible Women for special mission projects.

---

11. Miller, "Chelmulpo District," 9–10.

12. Miller, "Chelmulpo District," 9–10. Korean leaders were integrated early into Methodist missions, as demonstrated by the incorporation of Koreans as district superintendents—key leadership positions, a level below of bishops in the ecclesiastical structure. A district superintendent was in charge of a district or a geographic region. In 1915, of six district superintendents in Korea, three were Koreans: Pyeng-hyen Choe (Chemulpo District), Chang-sik Kim (Yeng Byen District), and Pak-won Paik (Wonju and Kangnung Districts) ("Reports," 31–55). By 1926, Korea missions expanded to thirteen districts that included northern Korea and Manchuria. Of the thirteen, nine districts were led by missionaries and four were by Korean District Superintendents: Chan-heung Kim (Chelmulpo or Incheon District), Pyung-chai Kim (Chunan District), Yu-soon Kim (Haiju District), and Hyung-sik Pai (Manchuria District, office in Harbin) (*Minutes* [1926], 205–8). In 1927, of the thirteen Methodist districts, six districts were led by Koreans: Chan-heung Kim (Chemulpo District), Pyung-chai Kim (Chunan District), Yu-soon Kim (Haiju District), Hyung-sik Pai (Manchuria District), Chong-Oo Kim (Seoul District), and Hong-sik Cynn (Wonju District) (*Minutes* [1927], 309–313).

13. Huntley, *Caring, Growing, Changing,* 126.

14. "Objects of Intercession," 209.

In 1909, a missionary in Pyeongyang described how the mission school has grown remarkably, "chiefly through the efforts of an unsalaried woman" who devotedly gathered the children every morning.[15]

The versatility of Bible Women was illustrated when the pioneer woman missionary Mary F. Scranton dispatched Korean Bible Women to a "widower church," named for the fact that no women attended the church. The women of the village would not join the church, despite repeated pleas from the men.[16] In many cases, the Bible Women were the only church leaders remote villages encountered. In 1910, Abigail, a Bible woman, was going from "house to house" when she discovered "a home in deep trouble": the eldest son of a family, aged twenty-two, became "insane."[17] His parents were desperate. Abigail made "made arrangements that the son should go with her some distance to the home of one of our colporteurs. There he was prayed for, taught to read, and kindly treated until his reason returned. God blessed this ministry of love to the good of the afflicted home, so that the father is now a faithful Christian and others in the village are professing believers."[18]

In her 1926 Report of the mission work in the Wonju and Kangnung Districts, the Methodist missionary Louise O. Morris wrote of how the Bible Women have been working independently "with practically no help from the missionary."[19] On their own, Bible Women were "teaching, travelling, keeping the home study course going, leading the Missionary Societies, holding night schools, and doing personal work."[20] Morris added, "They have taught in the District Institutes and held the local classes."

15. "Korean Mosaics," 311.

16. Scranton, "Widower Churches," 167.

17. Foote, "Village Prayer-Meeting," 355.

18. Foote, "Village Prayer-Meeting," 355.

19. Morris, "Report of Wonju and Kungnung," 76.

20. Morris, "Report of Wonju and Kungnung," 76.

Pyeongyang. "Morning Bible Class." Photo credit: Moffett Korea Collection.
Princeton Theological Seminary.

BIBLE WOMEN'S BACKGROUND

Korean Bible Women were a highly motivated group from a variety of socioeconomic backgrounds. In the beginning, however, the ranks of Bible Women were filled mostly by women from the lower classes that had little or no education. As it turned out, being born in the lower classes was an advantage to church work and evangelism since the mobility of women from higher classes was severely restricted while none of the laws of seclusion applied to the lower classes. Kate Cooper, a woman missionary stationed in Korea in the early twentieth century, wrote that the "first Bible women were women of no education, with no equipment save that they knew they had been saved from sin through the name of Jesus, and that they wanted others to receive a like salvation"[21] Cooper's description of first Bible Women offers clues to the humble origins of a powerful Christian movement started from the lower classes of society.

Without educational qualifications and the ability to receive a formal education, Bible Women's operated outside the leadership structures of mission organizations and local churches, yet with their simple task of traveling, preaching, and teaching they represented an army of evangelists that went to areas and locations neglected by others. Later, women missionaries established courses and schools for Bible Women but in the early stages they were trained informally in the homes of women missionaries. They were expected to memorize the Lord's Prayer, Apostle's Creed, and the Ten Commandments, as well as narrating their conversion experience. As formal education became the norm, attending Bible Academy or Bible Institute required money which many women from the lower classes did not possess. Louis Hayes in 1935 noted that most Bible Women were trained in Mission Bible Institutes but "not all of our most faithful and successful workers are receiving a diverse and quality education."[22]

The first Bible school for women, started by Mary F. Scranton, was later expanded to become the Seoul Methodist Women's School in 1905.[23] The need for greater training for Bible Women was apparent and various mission boards began to develop institutes and schools across Korea. The Women's Bible Institute in Pyeongyang, started by the Presbyterian missions, had two departments: regular and preparatory in 1910.[24] Women who did not graduate from elementary school received rudimentary biblical

21. Cooper, "Bible Woman," 6.

22. Hayes, "Korean Bible Woman," 151.

23. S. Lee, *Methodist and Sinhak Dahaksa*, 136–38.

24. Best, "Course of Study," 152.

training in the preparatory department. The regular department offered advanced courses in church history, ethics, music, gymnastics, and home education.[25]

The fact that institutes and schools offered advanced courses indicated that women from various socioeconomic backgrounds became Bible Women. When Edith Blair opened registration for the Ten Days of Bible Study in Pyeongyang in 1918, she observed that there were "old women and young, middle aged women and girls, women in silk and women in coarse cotton, women with bundles on their heads and babies on their backs, women foot sore from many weary miles of rough roads, alone and in groups of two, four or half a dozen, all pouring into the Bible Institute on the opening day."[26] The wearing of silk signaled wealth and upper class while course cotton indicated working class background.

As the expectation of literacy increased, Bible Women began their education with Bible classes and progressed to Bible institutes and then to Bible Women training schools, which eventually developed into seminaries. The Presbyterian missionary Margaret Best, in describing the courses at the Pyeongyang Presbyterian Women's Bible Institute, noted in 1910 how their education extended well-beyond biblical and religious courses as the curriculum incorporated mathematics, writing, hygiene, physiology, and cooking.[27] The Methodist Woman's Bible School in Seoul also taught what they termed "liberal arts" courses such as psychology, sociology, music, geography, and physiology.[28]

Nellie Pierce, a missionary in charge of a Bible School for women in Pyeongyang, noted in her report after opening her school she began the study of the Book of Acts. Pierce wrote, "My plan is to take up the life of Paul chronologically. In this way we have studied First and Second Thessalonians, First and Second Corinthians."[29] She noted that all classes were held in the morning since the afternoons were reserved for the women to visit the members of the church, "teaching the catechisms and telling to all with whom they come in contact the story of the cross."[30] The system, developed by the Woman's Foreign Missionary Society, enabled these graduates to find work. Pierce wrote that Lulu Frey, a Methodist missionary in Seoul, "has charge of five of these women. Of the others some are at work in Mead

25. Best, "Course of Study," 152.
26. Blair, "Care of Babies and Children," 79.
27. Butts, "Report of Workers' Class," 11; Best, "Courses of Study," 152–54.
28. Chaffin, "Macedonian Cry," 9–11.
29. Pierce, "Report IV," 10–11.
30. Pierce, "Report IV," 10–11.

Memorial church, the rest itinerating on the Southern District. Part of the time, three only have been able to go into the country."[31]

BIBLE WOMEN'S UNIQUE ADVANTAGE

The role that Bible Women had in promoting Christianity to women is tied closely to the access they had to domestic interiors and their ability to experience them as spaces of religious engagement and interaction, something rarely extended to their male counterparts. As A. G. Welborn, a woman missionary, observed, even looking at a woman in the public was a grave offense. In 1915, Welbon noticed that a Korean man was about cross paths with a woman on the road and he "quickly turns his back and holds up his fan so that he may not be guilty of the discourtesy of gazing at a woman. He may even turn down a side street until you [i.e., a woman] have passed."[32]

For the first twenty-five years of resident Protestant missionaries in Korea, they lived in Joseon dynasty when the country was ruled by a king and strict gendered spaces separated men and women, even in their homes. The men's quarters was the *sarangchae*, literally meaning "the outer room," and the women's space *anbang*, meaning "inner room." It became quickly obvious to foreigners that male and female interaction was forbidden. A male missionary making a pastoral visit to a Korean home asked if he could also greet the lady of the house and he was politely told that social decorum prohibited such interactions. Not surprisingly, male missionaries promptly "appealed to the Mission Board [in the US] for single women to be sent out since men were not allowed by custom to speak to women."[33]

Homer Hulbert observed the strict separation of the sexes in the early twentieth century:

> After a young bride arrives at the home of her husband, she will have free access to the private rooms of her new father and mother, even as their own daughters do, but neither her father nor any other man except her husband will ever step inside her private rooms, except under stress of sickness or other imperative cause. If any of her male relatives are to see her, it must be in the rooms of her father and mother. This does not apply to the young brothers of her husband, who may come into her room

---

31. Pierce, "Report IV," 10–11.
32. Welbon, "Yang Ban Lady," 6.
33. Cooper, *Evangelism in Korea*, 61.

upon invitation up to the age of thirteen, after which they too are excluded.[34]

When Protestant missionaries started entering Korea from 1885, street evangelism was forbidden. The best option to reach women was their home but only women were permitted to enter women's space. Korean culture also placed respect and admiration for elders, thus making widows more effective in interacting with other women. In 1895, Margaret Bengel Jones wrote, "There seems by one way in which to reach the women of Korea and that is to visit them in their homes."[35]

In her early years of ministry for women, Mary F. Scranton, before she was able to acquire a female helper, used a male assistant. She overcame the Korean custom by adopting a "new plan." Scranton wrote, "So now I shut him up in a room by himself until they are seated and ready to listen. Then I arrange a screen between them and the place where he is to sit, and in this way the women's ideas of seclusion are held sacred, and the speaker's voice can be heard as distinctly as though he were visible."[36]

In the rigid gender separation that governed Korean society, Korean Bible Women deftly navigated through forbidden cultural spaces. "Standing outside of the paper-covered door of the inner room [i.e., women's private room or *anbang*], she [a Bible woman] coughed in Korean style to attract attention and opened the door with the request for permission to enter. Having gained entrance and a seat on the floor, the approach to the telling of the 'Good News' is never a long postponed or a difficult one."[37]

Women's exclusive inner room served many purposes, including as a private meeting place for conversations between women. Female visitors

---

34. Hulbert, *Passing of Korea*, 351. "Before marriage, [Korean] girls were not only instructed in Confucian ideology, but also experienced its practical consequences. After the age of seven, girls could no longer associate with boys or men. They were more and more confined to the inner quarters of the house where they received instruction in domestic duties from their mothers and grandmothers" (Deuchler, *Confucian Transformation of Korea*, 258). Korean girls "kept to the women's quarters, and out of doors rode in closed palanquins or kept their faces covered (in later days with the famous green coat worn over the head" (Pratt and Rutt, *Korea*, 508). "Korean women are as much secluded as any women of the East . . . and the sexes of a family are separated after the age of eight or ten years" (Carpenter, "Koreans at Home," 439).

35. Jones, "Korean Bride," 55.

36. Scranton, "Korea," 47. The strict separation would eventually loosen but in 1888 Methodist missionaries decided to form a church for women in respect to local customs. Scranton: "On account of the rigid seclusion of a large part of the women of this land, it has seemed necessary to organize our little band [Methodist term for a group of believers] into a separate church" (Scranton, "Korea," 47).

37. Cooper, *Evangelism in Korea*, 65.

were taken into the inner room as a practice of hospitality where hosts were expected to deference to the concerns of visitors. The inner room therefore became an effective conduit for woman-to-woman evangelism. Later, women missionaries would use this cultural women's network to invite Korean women to their Western-styled homes to introduce and preach the gospel.[38] In 1905, a missionary described an instance when a Bible Woman visited a particular house to speak about the gospel. A *mudang*, or a female shaman, was already in the inner room. The Bible Woman shared the Good News and as a result the *mudang* believed and converted.[39]

The British and Foreign Bible Society Annual Report for 1913 stated: "every door is open to [the Bible Women], even if the only place where they can meet the women is in the kitchen."[40] George Heber Jones recalled the conversion story of a Korean woman who overheard as a girl the gospel preached by a Bible woman. Jones wrote, "From the kitchen the girl had heard the Bible woman tell the older folks the story of Christ and His suffering for us and it sank deep in her young heart."[41]

Despite their lack of training and education, Korean Bible Women moved their audiences with their impassioned narrative of their conversion experience. Many accounts describe Bible Women's previous experience in abusive marriages and troubled past before encountering Christ. Before becoming a Bible woman, Gikyu Sim's conversion offended her parents-in-law so much that one occasion they beat her so severely that she "spent more than three months in the hospital."[42] Lulu Chu, a Bible Woman, previously considered "becoming a shaman as a way to escape her abusive married life, even though shamans were in the lowest of social classes."[43] After her conversion, Chu learned to how to read and became a language instructor at the Haeju School for Girls.

Chu even began to train other Bible Women. Understanding that Bible Women lacked formal education, their strength was not theological conversations but rather their personal narrative and impassioned belief in the power of the gospel. Lulu Chu advised women to speak of their personal experience: "For those in persecution, exhort them with the stories of your

---

38. The curiosity of a Western house drove many Korean women to visit a woman missionary's home. "When Rosetta Sherwood Hall first arrived in [Pyeongyang] in 1894, at least fifteen hundred women and children came to [her home to] see her and her baby" (Ahn, *Awakening the Hermit Kingdom*, 192).

39. J. R. Moose detailed this event in Moose, "Mrs. Kim and Mrs. Change," 88–89.

40. British and Foreign Bible Society, *Reports of the Korea Agency*, 20.

41. Jones, "Report VII," 19.

42. S. Kim, "Study of Bible Women's Impact," 15–16.

43. D. Lee, *Stories of Early Christian Women*, 80.

own persecution. For those in suffering, encourage them with the stories of your own suffering, and for those in mental illness, comfort them with the fact that you used to suffer mental illness. For anyone in trials, tell them that by faith Jesus Christ was saved from all the trials of the world."[44]

BIBLE WOMEN AS MISSIONARIES

With numerous Bible Women dispatched in circuits all over the country, they served on the frontlines of Christianity's expansion across Korea. A woman missionary in 1916 requested prayers for the army of Bible Women assigned to various corners of the country in which "many of whom [are] at lonely posts and in the midst of great difficulties."[45] She acknowledged the danger involved with their work that went "beyond the conventional boundaries of a woman's life and bearing responsibilities that are new to the women of the Orient."[46] Margaret Best recorded in 1913 that 93 women studied at the Bible Institute and most of them volunteered to travel to the country to teach Bible classes.[47] The evangelistic spirit of Korean Bible Women to willingly sacrifice time and effort for the gospel had a profound effect upon the how Koreans were introduced to Christianity.

The Bible Women represented a new model of emissaries in the Korean Christian landscape. The image of Bible Women boldly traveling to foreign and risky places—at times alone—paralleled with the experience of women missionaries of the Woman's Foreign Missionary Society (hereafter WFMS) who were often their mentors and supervisors. Called "the greatest Woman's Missionary Society in the country,"[48] the WFMS, during its seventy years (1869–1939), sent out 1,559 single woman missionaries around the world. The WFMS only recruited single women so that they will devote exclusively to "women's work for woman" on the mission field without home responsibilities.[49]

44. L. Kim, "Bible Woman," 51.

45. "Objects of Intercession," 209.

46. "Objects of Intercession," 209.

47. Best, "Country Bible Classes For Women," 103.

48. Quote by Helen Barrett Montgomery, the pioneer Christian social activist who became the first woman president of the Northern Baptist Convention in 1921 (Hartley, *Evangelicals at a Crossroads*, 93).

49. Dana Robert, a leading historian of missions, wrote of the independence with which women organized a world-wide network of women-led mission work. "By 1870, a system of branch organizations was worked out whereby Methodist women across the country could run their own regional operations and pay for their own mission projects and personnel, coordination of the enterprise being left to an Executive Committee.

Mary F. Scranton was a widow who arrived in Korea in 1885 at the age of fifty-two. Her age did not stop her from taking an evangelistic trip for thirty-two days, a feat that actually impressed the villagers that she encountered. Scranton "visited a village where the people were much moved that a woman of such an age should undertake such a work for their sake. In the two days spent there, twelve men, with their households, the most influential in the village, decided to become Christians."[50]

Like Scranton, the women missionaries of the WFMS modeled the trailblazing ethic that Bible Women would emulate on the mission field. In her autobiography, Louisa Yim recalls in the early twentieth century when a single woman missionary surprised everyone by coming to her village to preach the gospel. Yim quotes her father:

> There is a strange lady . . . from far, faraway Yang Kook [America]. . . . She is a large lady. Her face is covered with chalklike powder. Her nose is large and of different shape than ours and her eyes are blue and her hair golden. She is going to tell us about her God and all of us shall go down and listen to her.[51]

Although the primary aim of WFMS missionaries was to reach women, Yim's experience highlights the common practice of WFMS missionaries traveling and preaching wherever they went. The woman missionary stayed at Yim's village for only a day but it resulted in her father's conversion to Christianity. Furthermore, the experience of a traveling single woman preacher made an indelible impression upon Louisa Yim. She wrote, "I stood close by as they loaded her things on an oxcart and cried as she disappeared down the road. I wanted more than anything else in the world then to be just like her, to go from place to place telling the wonderful stories that made people happy."[52]

Two WFMS missionaries, Paine and Snavely, traveled more than 1,700 miles, mostly by boat off the shores of Incheon to many untouched islands along Korea's west coast in 1908.[53] D. A. Bunker, a male missionary in Ko-

---

The branch system provided for a de-centralized organization with a high degree of local autonomy and grassroots participation in the local churches. Each branch had its own corresponding secretary who communicated with the missionaries appointed by that particular branch. In effect, major decisions were made by the consensus of volunteers at the home base rather than by denominational officials." (Robert, *American Women in Mission*, 139).

50. "Korea," 185.

51. Yim, *My Forty-Year Fight*, 24.

52. Yim, *My Forty-Year Fight*, 27.

53. "This district [islands and Haeju province, headquartered in Incheon] has one hundred and thirty-six churches, and although Miss Paine and Miss Snavely last year

rea in the early twentieth century, learned a startling fact when he visited what he thought were remote islands on the western coast untouched by the Christian message. Traveling to an island, he discovered Christians were already residing there. When he asked them if he was the first foreigner on the island, they replied, "There has been a woman preacher here by the name of Hess," evidently, a woman missionary from the Woman's Foreign Missionary Society.[54] Bunker remarked, "Whatever direction I went, my way had been pioneered by someone under the Woman's Foreign Missionary Society."[55]

WIDOWHOOD AND BIBLE WOMEN

When the Methodist Bible school graduated four women in 1912, they were aged 40, 50, 51, and 52.[56] Even though Protestant missionaries have carried on with mission work in Korea for more than twenty-five years, it is not surprising that the graduates in 1912 were older. In the early years of Protestant missions, women missionaries found it nearly impossible to recruit young women since they married in their early teens. A missionary wrote, "It is difficult to secure competent young women who truly desire to remain in single blessedness for the long term of six years. Young widows prove the more satisfactory pupils."[57] WFMS missionaries, who employed Bible Women more than any other missionary organization, "preferred" widows since they would be "without home responsibilities" and can devote full-time to the mission work.[58] Furthermore, Korean custom stigmatized the re-marrying of widows, thus making them more available for the kind of ministry that missionaries envisioned. Even today, illiterate widows would not be considered ideal candidates for ministry but the Woman's Foreign Missionary Society, more than any other mission organization, developed a keen terracultural sense of thinking outside the range of normal missional paradigm and, in the process, raised up the most effective evangelistic force in early Korean church history.

Being free of familial duties and obligations, widows gave more time to ministry and shouldered more responsibilities. Lulu Frey, in praising the

---

traveled more than 1,700 miles, mostly by boat, they were unable to visit them twice" ("Words of Remembrance," 12).

54. "'WFMS' in the Lead," 287.

55. "'WFMS' in the Lead," 287.

56. Huntley, *Caring, Growing, Changing*, 126.

57. Edmunds, "Training Native Nurses," 154.

58. Cooper, "Bible Woman," 8.

work of her Bible Women, wrote that they are "all women unencumbered by household duties giving their whole time to their work."[59] In 1909, a woman missionary remarked surprisingly at the results when she challenged a group of devoted Christian women if they would freely give a "tenth of their time in preparing for and holding classes throughout the country."[60] It was a "great success," the missionary wrote. "Glowing reports have reached me from the villages they visited."[61]

Among her notable group, she mentioned an exceptional woman who exceeded "far more than" she asked. The woman "plans to be at home one month out of three, and all the rest is her freewill offering to" travel and preach. "During the last three months she has taught in four classes, visited between two and three hundred homes, brought over a hundred to believe and personally invited several hundred more."[62] Kate Cooper, a woman missionary in Korea, described the ideal Bible woman: "She must be able to give her whole time and service to the Lord's work; she must be a woman whose life has proven her to be a doer of the word and a follower of the Master, not for any earthly gain but because of her love for the salvation of souls. She must be a graduate of a Bible institute able to teach."[63]

Examining their number in a fifty-year span, from 1895 to 1945, there were 1,215 Korean Bible Women, of whom 717 were affiliated with the Methodist Church, 209 with Presbyterian Church, 138 with Holiness Church, and 151 with other churches.[64] It is not surprising that the Methodist Church had the most number of Bible Women. The Woman's Foreign Missionary Society, a woman's mission society within the Methodist Church, made reaching women their exclusive focus and agenda. In the year 1927 alone, the Methodist Korea Mission reported 121 Bible Women.[65]

Older, wiser, and exceptionally knowledgeable about navigating through Korean culture, Bible Women proved to be indispensable assistants to women missionaries. For example, gaining fluency in the Korean language was a challenge for many missionaries and Bible Women accompanied them on evangelistic trips and served as guides, protectors, and translators. In her

59. Lulu Frey, "Report II," 4.

60. "Tenth Classes," 318–19.

61. "Tenth Classes," 318–19.

62. "Tenth Classes," 318–19.

63. Cooper, "Bible Woman," 8.

64. Strawn, "Korean Bible Women's Success," 118.

65. In 1927, the Methodist Korea Mission reported a total of 1,326 preachers: 84 Korean pastors, 37 local Korean preachers, 18 other ordained pastors, 365 local preachers, 608 exhorters, 121 Bible women, 19 male missionaries, and 49 female missionaries ("Statistical Summary," 351).

1902 report, Alice Hammond, a woman missionary, admitted that "I have felt my hands somewhat tied because of my inability to speak the language [when visiting the homes of church members]."[66]

Despite the fact that Bible Women operated as laywomen, their tireless effort to expand the footprint of Christianity at a critical time in Korean church history cannot be overstated. Serving as the women missionaries' "right-hand woman," the Bible Women provided invaluable work such as creating an audience for the missionaries. In this cross-cultural encounter, Bible Women used their cultural knowledge to not only ease any suspicions but also generate interest in the gospel message. A missionary wrote, "I have received many Korean guests through or with her."[67]

Margaret B. Jones, wife of the pioneer missionary, George Heber Jones, wrote in 1894 that she "made in all about four hundred visits [to Korean homes] since last Annual Meeting" with "Helen, our Bible woman."[68] Kate Cooper, a woman missionary with the WFMS, wrote in 1917 that Bible Women were "invaluable" assistants to a woman missionary. After the missionary traveled to a village, gathered a crowd, and finished preaching, the Bible woman "would preach to crowd after crowd the whole long day."[69]

The Bible Women provided critical local knowledge that enabled women missionaries to navigate cultural boundaries with sensitivity and awareness. When Susan Ross wanted to visit Korean homes, her Bible woman persuaded her against it because the Korean women "would be so embarrassed by coming upon them in the dishabille [state of being partially or very casually dressed] to which they let themselves down in August heat that I could do them no good."[70] Ross later commented that as the winter cold forced women into their homes "it was not so easy to approach perfect strangers as it had been when we would find the women in their yards or sitting in their open doorways."[71]

Mary F. Scranton said, "I have been greatly assisted by my Bible women."[72] Lulu Frey, the woman missionary who developed Ewha Academy into Ewha College, wrote, "Most of the work has been done by our five Bible-women whom I might call the five fingers of my right hand, so useful

---

66. Hammond, "Report V," 14.

67. Avison, "Bible Woman's Work," 212.

68. Jones, "Mission Work on the Chemulpo Circuit," 414.

69. Cooper, "Bible Woman," 8.

70. Ross in Clark, "Mothers, Daughters, Biblewomen, and Sisters," 170.

71. Clark, "Mothers, Daughters, Biblewomen, and Sisters," 170.

72. Scranton, "Missionary Work among Women," 316.

have they all been to me."[73] Their usefulness and effectiveness derived partly from the fact that their outlier status as lower or lowest social class enabled them to travel freely across the country, as opposed to women of nobility or higher class whose mobility was severely restricted. Their marginality enabled these Bible Women to have access to a wider audience as they traversed the country on foot.

The women missionaries' dependence upon Korean Bible Women underscores the crucial role Bible Women played in the expansion of Christianity. Nellie Pierce, who led the Bible Woman's Training School, reported in 1902 that the work of traveling evangelism fell to the Bible Women. Pierce wrote, "More and more, until we are reinforced by workers from home, we relegate much of this part of our work to our Bible women."[74] The invaluable contribution of Korean Bible Women enabled women missionaries to focus their energies on other aspects of mission work. Pierce added, "Were it not for these [Bible] women who go in our stead into these far distant places, I feel the work could not be touched. They go to places we cannot go and at times, we cannot go."[75]

Through the evangelistic campaigns undertaken by Bible Women, many remote Korean villages became Christian but there were not enough Korean clergy or pastors, especially in far-off places. In these cases, the Bible Women were willing to travel to small churches in isolated locations and serve as the church pastor. They preached on Sundays, conducted visitations, and offered pastoral care.

As a whole, Christianity in Korea grew faster than anyone expected. The speed with which Christian communities in Korea expanded demanded enlarging the roles of Bible Women. Lulu Frey noted that women probationers, a step before full inclusion in a local church, were examined for membership by the women missionaries but first the probationers were "taught by Bible women."[76]

The unique versatility of Bible Women allowed them to work in any capacity. Considering the multitude of roles on the Korean mission field, the Bible Women were the "go-to person" who had the ability to perform whatever task was before them. The Bible Women worked alongside medical missionaries and nurses in clinics, assisting the staff in any way with the patients.

---

73. Frey, "Report II," 4.

74. Pierce, "Report IV," 10.

75. Pierce, "Report IV," 13.

76. Frey, "Opportunities in Korea," 286.

Her [Bible Woman] work consisted in first attending morning worship at the hospital and then teaching in-patients at any and all times convenient to the patient, according as she was well enough to listen and understand; then in meeting all the women who came to the clinic every day, teaching them and finding out where they live, accepting invitations to visit them at their homes. She visited patients who had gone out from the hospital, even in villages many miles from here, where sometimes she had to remain over night and come back next day, always inviting all she met to come to our Sunday morning services or any of our church services where most convenient."[77]

Dr. Rosetta Sherwood Hall, a medical missionary with the WFMS, wrote that Susan No, her Bible woman "is my right-hand helper in all the work; she conducts a service with the patients in the waiting room before dispensing, sells the books, and dressing surgical cases, and accompanies me when needed in my out-calls."[78] In addition to Susan No, Hall reported that another Bible woman visited 107 homes as follow up to the "medical work in the homes of our patients."[79]

SELF-INITIATIVE OF BIBLE WOMEN

An aspect of the work of Bible Women that is little known is that, despite their marginal status, exercised autonomy and authority on the field. The independent way Bible Women at times demonstrated leadership at the local levels reveals complexity in how Bible Women influenced the development of Christian communities. On her own, a Bible woman in 1902 accompanied her husband who traveled long distance as a colporteur. During the two-month trip, she taught women along the way and "doing her best to fill the lack of a foreign woman's teaching."[80]

Stories of Bible Women creating their own pathway abound, and whole programs were developed under their leadership, underscoring the notion that Bible Women not only working independently of missionaries but also shaping the Christian landscape, such as training other women to complement her work. In 1909, Mary Nora, a woman missionary, described how Sarah, her Bible woman, regularly visits twelves villages and teaches an average of forty women in each. In the villages, Sarah "began a little school

77. Avison, "Bible Woman's Work," 212.
78. Hall, "Kwang Hya Nyo Won," 15.
79. Hall, "Kwang Hya Nyo Won," 15.
80. Rhodes, *History of the Korea Mission*, 1:334.

for girls, and this is now merged into a larger one where one of Sarah's pupils does her much credit as a pupil teacher. Sarah has not only taught her women, but inspired and helped some of them to teach others also, so that her work is carried on in the villages she can only visit once or twice a month."[81]

In 1910, a newly formed country church near Pyeongyang, with fewer than forty members, was too small to financially support a Bible woman. Chan-Il Oh, a Bible woman willing to visit the church on a part-time basis, attended "the church one week each month to cultivate relationships with the women of the area."[82] Through her efforts, membership grew to more than one hundred, enabling the church to hire both a full-time pastor and a Bible woman.

Over time, the competence demonstrated by Bible Women facilitated the passing of many of the work done by missionaries to Bible Women. For example, the Presbyterian Church recorded that in the year 1912 "Korean Women leaders alone taught five thousand seven hundred women in one hundred sixty-six country classes."[83] M. Switzer reported in 1919 that most of the Bible classes for women in the Daegu District of the Methodist Church were taught by Bible Women.[84] Just as she was personally mentored by Mattie Wilcox Noble, a women missionary of forty-five years in Korea, Sadie Kim took up the task of mentoring other Korean Bible Women, including Tabetha Kim, Isabelle Lee, Circus Kim, and Dorcas Kang.[85]

The amazing growth of converts and churches led by Korean Bible Women was fueled in part by the stellar reputation that preceded them. The Bible Women's passionate preaching and willingness to sacrifice themselves for the gospel generated respect and admiration among Koreans which in turn produced goodwill and greater openness to the Christian message. For example, when a village heard that a Bible woman was coming, "the news generally resulted in nearly all the village people gathering."[86] Kyung-chik Han, founder of Young Nak Presbyterian Church and one of the most respected pastors in Korea, recalled as a boy the excitement of hearing that a Bible woman was coming to preach. He remembered, "Her preaching was engraved deep in my heart, even though I was young."[87]

81. Nora, "Bible Women," 360.

82. Swallen, "Native Bible Women," 119.

83. Rhodes, *History of the Korea Mission*, 1:159.

84. Switzer, "Bible Classes for Women," 150–52.

85. Kim, "Story of My Life," 102–4.

86. Chu, *Presbyterian Women in Korea*, 92–93.

87. Chu, *Presbyterian Women in Korea*, 92–93.

TRAVELERS FOR THE GOSPEL

Considering that 70 percent of Korea is mountainous terrain, Korean Bible Women exhibited an Olympian ability to travel, mostly on foot, long difficult journeys. In 1914, a woman missionary wrote, "The [Korean] Bible women have waded waist-deep through streams; they have walked over mountain passes knee-deep in snow; they have walked until their feet were so badly swollen that it was impossible to go farther; they have been lost in the mountains all night; but all are rejoicing in the privilege of service."[88]

In 1909, Mary F. Scranton sent two Korean Bible Women to "far-off villages" more than one hundred and sixty miles from Seoul. In order to reach these remote villages, there were "mountains for them to climb, streams to be forded, over some of which they must be carried on men's backs."[89] According to Scranton, the women did not fear the arduous journey that meant potentially encountering robbers that preyed upon travelers passing through the mountains. They safely returned to Seoul after visiting the villages and reported to Scranton: "We prayed a great deal, and God has helped us and brought us home in safety and with happy hearts over the work we have done in his name."[90] As a result of their extensive trip across six towns, fifty-two women were converted and pledged to attend church.[91]

The Bible Women who made these trips expended a great deal of energy in reaching fellow women. The missionary community was startled at the willingness of mostly older women to toss out caution and boldly go where few have gone before. A woman missionary stated in 1912 that a Bible woman in three months "visited 669 homes and taught 1,355 women." In addition, "she also holds a weekly prayer meeting in four different places."[92] In describing her two Bible Women, Josepha and Madeline, Nellie Pierce reported that Josepha traveled "over seven hundred and twenty five *li* [approximately 225 miles] and taught aside from the women of the church about five hundred ninety women" in a trip of six weeks.[93]

Leaving the comforts of home, Bible Women survived grim, makeshift living conditions and shortages of decent food and clothing. A woman missionary noted, "Oft times they live alone in a tiny little room, subject to the opposition, malice and suspicion of those who do not understand. Here

88. "Bits from Korea Reports," 54.

89. Scranton, "Widower Churches," 167.

90. Scranton, "Widower Churches," 167.

91. Scranton, "Widower Churches," 167.

92. "Our Young People (1912)," 364–65.

93. Pierce, "Report IV," 10–11.

they cook their own food, wash their own clothing, do their own sewing when the long day of ministry is over."[94]

Mamie D. Myers, a WFMS missionary of the Methodist Episcopal Church, South, stationed in Pyeongyang, reported that nine Bible Women under her supervision visited, from October 1912 to August 1913, 4,772 non-Christian homes, 3,878 Christian homes, and 339 new believers' homes. In all, they visited forty-two villages, preached to 3,070 people, taught 616 Sunday school classes, led 69 to study church courses in the country, and organized twenty-four services.[95]

Undeterred, Bible Women accepted their harsh reality and explored the outer limits of Korea. Another woman missionary in 1909 wrote that four Bible Women under her supervision "have visited and taught in more than six thousand homes" during the year.[96] Dorcas Kim Kang became a Methodist Bible woman in 1900 at the age of fifty-two. She was first assigned a circuit (or a geographical route in which an individual was responsible) of seventeen churches that stretched 195 miles but that was not enough. In the following year, the entire Hwanghae province "was added to her circuit, and she had to walk 1,450 miles to reach all the places under her care."[97]

The Methodist approach to missionary expansion was establishing "circuits" or geographic pathways that connected towns and villages. For the Methodist Episcopal Church, South, two main churches in Seoul served as the central point of their circuits in the early twentieth century.[98] Using these main churches as the launching point, circuits expanded that later developed into districts. Forty-two districts were created in and around these two main churches. According to Mrs. J. P. Campbell in 1917, nine Bible Women worked with women missionaries of the Methodist Episcopal Church, South. In eleven months, Campbell reported that these Bible Women visited the homes of 5,884 church members and 2,497 nonbelievers. They visited 673 villages and preached the gospel message to more than 11,253 people.[99] Campbell reported that five of the nine women graduated from the Bible school.

94. "Objects of Intercession," 209.

95. Myers, *Woman's Missionary Council*, 259.

96. Maskell, "Work in Korea," 323.

97. Huntley, *Caring, Growing, Changing*, 126.

98. The two churches are Water Gate and Water Mark Churches. Woman's Missionary Council, *Fourth Annual Report*, 258.

99. Woman's Missionary Council, *Fourth Annual Report*, 258.

CONCLUSION

The Korean Mission Field was a monthly periodical that served the missionary community by regularly providing updates of missionaries and their families, news about Korean society, culture, and politics, and reports on the Korean mission field. In the 1935 issue, Louis B. Hayes chides his fellow missionaries in regard to their perception and treatment of Korean Bible Women:

> Whether the Korean Bible Woman is the highly trained, efficient, versatile church worker, or the humble, tireless country evangelists, the spirit is the same and God uses both types equally well. We as missionaries owe them our greatest respect and affection, and recognition of the wonderful work they are doing. We like to tell how marvelously the church is growing in Korea, how many hundreds of new believers are admitted each year, how many new churches established; but do we give full credit to the nameless, tireless, faithful Korean evangelist, man or woman? And are we doing all we can to make the Church realize the value of these trained workers, and that the worker is worthy of his hire?[100]

Despite Hayes's urging, Korean Bible Women's contributions continue to receive little recognition. During their years of pioneering ministry, they not only reached gender-specific spaces but they crossed many cultural and geographic boundaries that enabled many Koreans to learn about Christianity for the first time. They were outliers who harvested on the margins of the mission field. In the beginning, missionaries turned by necessity to older, widowed women of lower classes but their decision to empower and mobilize Bible Women became a game-changer on the mission field. Bible Women were leading the vanguard in the great spiritual battle that broke and turned over the native landscape.

The Korean Bible Women were innovators who established new patterns of initiative and activity. They challenged prevailing models of gender roles and drew from the melding of a variety of cultural and Christian influences to create new paradigms. They provide narratives from the receiving church that are often dismissed by scholars but they serve as an important reminder of how marginal figures of society can profoundly alter the religious landscape.

Unfortunately, the title and role of 'Bible Women' have diminished in Korean churches today in favor of professionally trained staff. Yet students

---

100. Hayes, "Korean Bible Woman and Her Work," 153.

of missions would do well to remember the Bible Women who plowed the field ahead for others who would eventually replace them. The Bible Women may be now a chapter in Korean church history but they represented an important episode from the past when women emerged from humble backgrounds to become a powerful Christianizing force.

December 26, 1929, Pyeongyang. "Christmas at a Country Church." Photo credit:
Alice Butts Album. Moffett Korea Collection. Princeton Theological Seminary.

7

Political Mobilization and Nationalistic Christians

A RANDOM SURVEY TAKEN in 1997 revealed surprising results. A poll asked the students at Korea University in Seoul whom would they choose if they could clone anyone in world history. Among countless options, the answers could have been a sundry of possibilities but the results were clear by a large margin. Students overwhelmingly voted for Kim Gu (1876–1949), the renowned Korean nationalist and independence fighter with 113 votes, followed by Mother Teresa with seven votes.[1]

The admiration from the student poll for Kim Gu, a heroic militant crusader for Korean independence from Japanese colonialism, was not an aberration. For South Korea's young people, Kim remains "the most respected figure in the history of Korea."[2] Few however know that he was a Christian. Kim converted to Christianity as an adult but that did not deter his use of violence as a means to achieve his nationalist goals: Kim killed a Japanese army lieutenant in 1896; orchestrated two bombing in 1932 that killed a number of Japanese high officials; and even attempted to take the life of the Japanese Emperor.

Kim Gu embodies a seemingly contradiction between his hawkish militarism and Christian faith. The contradiction is magnified by the fact that the historiographical narrative of Korean Christians reinforces a widely-held perception of pacifism. The complicated relationship between militant Korean nationalists and their Christian faith was one of the reasons

---

1. Lee, *Developmental Dictatorship*, 313.
2. Lee, *Unfinished War*, 14.

for their absence in the scholarly literature. The historian Chung-shin Park, in *Protestantism and Politics in Korea*, reiterated this point when he wrote, "For some reason the Christian background of these individuals is not mentioned at all, or only tangentially, in the literature."[3]

The Christians' reputation for non-violent activism was solidified during the March First Movement of 1919, a nation-wide protest that the Japanese colonial government brutally suppressed. Although many Koreans called for an armed insurrection against the Japanese on March 1, Korean Christian leaders convinced fellow Koreans to stand down and, instead, stage a peaceful demonstration.[4]

The perception of Korean Christians as pacifists overshadows the nationalist legacy of not only Kim Gu but many others. Little known are Korean pastors and evangelists, such as Donghui Yi and Eunhyeong Yeo, who "played the leading role in organizing" the Koryo Communist Party and the Korean Communist Party.[5] In 1922, Gyusik Kim and Eunhyeong Yeo attended, as representatives of the League of Korean Christians, the First Congress of the Toilers of the Far East in Moscow.[6] Another puzzling figure is the founder of North Korea, Kim Il Sung, who came from a Christian background: his father married the daughter of a "prominent" local Presbyterian family; both parents were Christians; and both parents participated in "Christian-led nationalist groups" that engaged in anti-Japanese activities.[7]

The missionaries in Korea, caught in the crossfire between the Japanese colonial government that viewed their presence as threat to their colonial rule and the Korean people that looked up to them for guidance and leadership, remained neutral in political affairs and disavowed any interest in political engagement. The Japanese colonial government had reasons to be suspicious of Korean Christians and by extension foreign missionaries. Despite the fact that Korean Christians were a small percentage of the Korean population, many of the leaders of the Korean independence movement were surprisingly Christians.

Time and again, the Japanese police interrogated missionaries to determine any political interference but Korean Christian nationalists,

3. C. Park, *Protestantism and Politics in Korea*, 160.

4. The non-militant approach to the March First Movement left many Koreans, including Christians, disillusioned with the church. The failure of the church's approach to independence "revealed the church's naivete, fragility, and limited capacities in the real world" (C. Park, *Protestantism and Politics in Korea*, 150).

5. C. Park, *Protestantism and Politics in Korea*, 143.

6. C. Park, *Protestantism and Politics in Korea*, 143.

7. Buzo, *Guerilla Dynasty*, 2. For an analysis of Kim's "strong tie with Christianity" as a youth, see Choe, "Christian Background," 1082–91.

recognizing the situation, organized their efforts without involving missionaries. The development of Korean Christian nationalists, seemingly without collaboration from missionaries, complicates our understanding of the transmission of Christianity. The missionaries repeatedly restated that their work was not political but spiritual.[8] Nevertheless, the Korean Christian community inspired some of the most outstanding Korean nationalists in modern history.

Studies in church planting often presume a predictable trajectory of outcomes. Terraculturalism challenges the linear understanding of missional development as the Korean example illustrates the ways Christianity in the local context may develop in unintentional ways. The effect of sowing of Christianity in foreign soils reverberates in ways that are difficult to control or predict. Crystallized in-between the pages of the Bible are combustible themes, such as deliverance, liberation, and redemption that may trigger responses in ways that are not foreseeable. The Protestant missionaries entered Korea during the most tumultuous period of Joseon dynasty. A failed coup d'état, the assassination of the Queen by a foreigner, and one of the largest peasant uprising in Korean history were a few of the debilitating events that perilously crippled the country. At a moment of national crisis, Korean Christians were inflamed with radicalism and revolutionary fervor and gravitated toward nationalistic ideals.

MISSIONARIES AND KOREAN POLITICS

Robert Maclay arrived in Seoul on June 24, 1883 as the first Protestant missionary to enter Korea after the signing of the US-Korea Treaty of 1882, the first Korean treaty with a Western nation. Maclay, a pioneer missionary with the distinction of having been the superintendent of Methodist missions in China, Japan, and Korea, first entered Korea while Christianity was still illegal. Many in Seoul still remembered the executions of Catholics only a little more than a decade earlier.

Given Korea's recent suppression of Catholics, the US-Korea Treaty of 1882 predictably had no "toleration of religion" clause. In other words, the previous edicts issued by the royal government were still binding: Christianity was an illegal and outlawed religion. However circumstances changed dramatically since the last persecution as Korea was increasingly threatened by foreign imperialist powers, encroaching upon Korea's sovereignty.

---

8. During the Japanese colonial period, "the main current in the [Korean] Protestant church community was opposed to political involvement" (C. Park, *Protestantism and Politics in Korea*, 147).

Robert Maclay entered Korea with no assurances but he understood that Gojong was more open to mission work as part of a larger acceptance toward Westernization.[9]

With the assistance of Ok-gyun Kim, a pro-West reformer who pressed upon the King to modernize the country, Maclay gained an audience with King Gojong who granted him approval of educational and medical work. A year later, Ok-gyun Kim orchestrated the ill-fated 1884 Gapsin Coup that rankled the highest levels of the Korean government. A series of debilitating events followed, including a major domestic uprising and an international war on Korean soil, that further crippled the country, leading eventually to the Japanese colonization of Korea in 1910.

After Maclay gained royal approval for Protestant missions, missionaries slowly but steadily began taking root in various locations throughout the country. However, the missionaries could not avoid the increasing political upheaval that engulfed Korea. As early as 1897, John Sills, the US Ambassador to Korea, warned missionaries in Korea to restrict themselves "to their legitimate avocations."[10] In other words, stick to spiritual matters and do not interfere in political matters. In a letter sent to every US citizen in Korea and published in *The Independent* on May 15, 1897, Sill advised missionaries "to strictly refrain from any expression of opinion or from giving advice concerning the internal management of the country, or from intermeddling in its political questions. If they do so, it is at their own risk and peril."[11]

The message sent by the US Foreign Mission Boards, the governing church body that sent and supervised the missionaries, was also unequivocal: abstain from political matters. The work of missionaries was strictly and clearly limited to spiritual questions and the Board was wary of missionaries and lay Christians stepping outside of their boundaries. Arthur Judson Brown, who served as Administrative Secretary and later as General Secretary of the Presbyterian Board of Foreign Missions (1895–1929), learned from European governments that "persistently and notoriously sought to

9. King Gojong would grant Maclay permission to start educational and medical mission work in Korea but the issue remained contentious depending upon the political influence in the court. When Yuan Shih Kai exerted influence over the Korean government, the president of the Korean Foreign Office sent a memo to the American Minister, dated April 24, 188, which stated in part: "Teaching religion and opening schools of any kind are not authorized by the [US-Korea] treaty, therefore we forbid severely any school whatever except it be authorized by our Government, and we will not allow religion taught to our people" (Pollard, "American Relations with Korea," 455–56).

10. Dennett, *Americans in Eastern Asia*, 572.

11. Dennett, *Americans in Eastern Asia*, 572.

advance their national interest through their missionaries."[12] Brown was especially critical of the effect of political participation on the local people. The result of politically-active missionaries, according to Brown who was speaking from the Chinese experience, was that the "average Chinese official regards all missionaries as political agents [of foreign governments] who are to be watched and feared."[13]

In the Korean context, any hint of pro-Korean nationalistic sentiment from the missionary community was an anti-Japanese one and it would have incurred the aversion of the new colonial rulers. By abstaining from political involvement, the missionaries lent the perception that they were of little political threat to the government under which they legally operated. Brown further extended and reinforced the non-political position to the lay Christians. In Korea, where the people experienced political turmoil, Brown advised lay Christians to eschew conflict and accept their new Japanese government. Brown in 1902 wrote, "The missionaries strongly believe, with the Boards at home, that . . . it is better for disciples of Christ to patiently endure some injustice than to carry Christianity in antagonism to the government under which they labor."[14]

Reinforcing the consensus of opinion in the missionary community, a missionary in Korea wrote, "It is one of the cardinal principles of Protestant missionary societies that their missionaries must not engage in political disputes or take sides in national controversies in the lands where they labor. Almost without exception the foreign missionaries adhere to this principle, even at the risk of being greatly misunderstood by their native friends and converts."[15] Lillias Underwood, wife of the pioneer missionary Horace G. Underwood, wrote in *Fifteen Years Among the Topknots* (1904) that "the missionaries, one and all, whether from a wish to uphold Japanese rule, or a desire to save useless bloodshed, are unanimous in using all their influence to quiet the [Korean] Christians and to induce them to prevent uprisings and revolts."[16]

In the aftermath of the Japan-Korea Treaty of 1910 that concluded the Japanese annexation of Korea, the missionaries helped cool the public's anger by urging a peaceful transition through "law-abiding [acceptance] and without reproach than for evil-doing."[17] A missionary wrote, "It is one of the

---

12. Brown, *New Forces in Old China*, 236.

13. Brown, *New Forces in Old China*, 236.

14. Brown, *Report of a Visitation*, 6.

15. "Missionaries and Politics in Korea," 220.

16. Underwood, *Fifteen Years Among the Topknots*, 297.

17. "Missionaries and Politics in Korea," 220.

cardinal principles of Protestant missionary societies that their missionaries must not engage in political disputes or take sides in national controversies in the lands where they labor. Almost without exception the foreign missionaries adhere to this principle, even at the risk of being greatly misunderstood by their native friends and converts."[18]

The missionaries carefully avoided any hint of inciting political uprising while at the same time encouraging their flock to accept the new political reality. The church historian, L. George Paik noted the missionaries' efforts to steer clear of political controversy, such as Wade Koons who assured Koreans "that their duty was to obey the Japanese and to do so with a 'sweet mind' and not to work for independence, and we have in no way tried to discredit or hamper them in their reforms."[19] Koons continued, "I have spent hours explaining to the church officers and teaching men advantages of Japanese rule, and I cannot think of one who has been kept from it."[20]

As one of the few associations permitted to operate in Korea after the Japanese colonization, the church attracted the attention of insurrectionists who wished to find cover within the church walls. To shield the church from the unwanted political involvement, church leaders determined that those focused on political and social issues as "unfit for the church."[21] Arthur Judson Brown surveyed the situation and concluded that the missionaries "used their great influence to induce the Koreans to acquiesce in Japanese rule."[22]

According to San Kim, a Korean Christian in the early twentieth century, the message was clear: the church was not "a place to discuss issues of society, labor, peace, or international affairs."[23] With encouragement from the missionaries, Korean pastors delivered a pacifist message to their parishioners. As an example, Rev. Chongmin Chae, a leading pastor in the northwestern region, emphasized the division between spiritual and secular pursuits, reinforced with biblical language. In 1936, Chae wrote,

> My Lord and Savior, Jesus, did not make His church as institution for production. . . . He did not order His church to create a secular movement. Then, why do church ministers today try to make stones into bread? Do today's churches desire to be

18. "Missionaries and Politics in Korea," 220.

19. Rev. Wade Koons wrote a letter under date of February 4, 1908 (Paik, *Protestant Missions in Korea*, 415).

20. Paik, *Protestant Missions in Korea*, 415.

21. C. Park, *Protestantism and Politics in Korea*, 147.

22. Brown, *Mastery of the Far East*, 574.

23. C. Park, *Protestantism and Politics in Korea*, 147.

institutions for production? The day when the church becomes
an institution for production, it will be a den of robbers.[24]

When the ranks of Korean insurrectionist forces, known as the 'Righteous Army,' swelled in the aftermath of Japanese colonization, the Presbyterian missionary Charles Allen Clark condemned militant action and prevented his church members from joining the movement. In 1908, Clark wrote, "Our position has been that the church is a spiritual organization and as such is not concerned with politics either for or against the present or any other government. . . . We set ourselves rigidly against it [i.e., joining the Righteous Army] and we have held our church and almost to a man our members rigidly from going into it."[25]

The missionaries were well aware of their influence over their followers: they could fan nationalistic and militant flames or douse them. Their influence alarmed the Japanese who were cognizant of the fact that the masses were ready to strike on their command. Despite the missionaries' commitment to refrain from "any public utterance on the Japanese occupation of Korea," the missionaries remained under constant suspicion as the Japanese viewed them as outside of their authority and control. For example, when a Korean assassinated Ito Hirobumi in 1909, Japanese newspapers blamed Horace G. Underwood for inciting anti-Japanese sentiment.[26]

According to a missionary in 1910, Japan would have had a "tenfold more difficult task in Korea" if missionaries had encouraged armed retaliation against the Japanese.[27] Brown wrote, "Indeed it has often been said that if it had not been for the missionaries, a revolution would have broken out when Korea was annexed to Japan."[28] Missionaries convinced the renowned Korean church leader, Seon-ju Kil, to pacify the battle-ready Koreans in the north who were ready to stage a bloody attack upon the Japanese after Gojong's abdication in 1907. According to a missionary, Kil "pressed home

24. Chae in C. Park, *Protestantism and Politics in Korea*, 147.

25. Clark in Paik, *Protestant Missions in Korea,* 415–16.

26. Horace G. Underwood "has only recently returned to Seoul, and the story is therefore wholly without foundation, as printed in Japanese papers, that he has had anything to do with stirring up anti-Japanese sentiment or is in the most remote way responsible for the assassination of Marquis Ito. Dr. Underwood is a Christian statesman; and, with the other missionaries, is busied with the spiritual regeneration of the Koreans, and does not interfere in the political affairs" (Paik, *Protestant Missions in Korea,* 415–16).

27. Paik, *Protestant Missions in Korea,* 415–16.

28. Brown, *Mastery of the Far East,* 574. "The Japanese fully appreciate this; but they are restive under a situation in which foreigners apparently have power to make or unmake a revolution among their own subjects" (Brown, *Mastery of the Far East,* 574).

on the [Korean] people that 'the powers that be are ordained of God,' and with the assistance of the Christian church he turned the fury of the whole north, and delivered Korea from tremendous bloodshed."[29] Some Korean Christians began to distance themselves from missionaries and Christianity as they detected an unwillingness to assist Koreans in the cause for independence. A missionary reported that his "inability to give definite help has often interpreted itself to the Korean mind as lack of interest in them, or feebleness of love, causing many to split off, at time, and seek other affiliations."[30]

MISSIONARIES AND NATIONALISM

Although the non-violent perspective of Korean Christianity, reinforced by missionaries and Korean church leaders, dominates the narrative, less well known are the indirect ways missionaries informed (and thereby disseminate) notions of nationalism, democracy, and self-determination. The Presbyterian missionary James S. Gale, in critiquing the weaknesses of the Korean mind, bemoaned in 1902 that "neither does the independence of the West appeal to the Korean"—a fact that revealed Gale's engagement with Koreans on the topic of independence.[31] Gale surmised that Koreans needed to be awakened to the belief in independence since Koreans were culturally conditioned to view 'independence' with only negative presuppositions, such as "suspicion, mistrust of each other, lawlessness, etc."[32] As a result, the Korean, instead of relishing independence, "conceives of life as a condition of subjection only."[33]

The Koreans' interactions with foreign missionaries were not limited only to religious topics. Missionary accounts detail a cross-cultural exchange in which wide-ranging topics were covered, including the diverging governmental systems between the West and Korea. Deliberately or unwittingly, Koreans received a political education from the missionaries. When engaging Koreans on the topic of politics, Gale did not resist speaking about the superiority of the American government. Gale boasted, "The glory of the American eagle, with his *E pluribus unum*, he thinks to be sheer madness."[34]

29. Northern Presbyterian Report for 1908 in Paik, *Protestant Missions in Korea*, 416.

30. Paik, *Protestant Missions in Korea*, 351.

31. Gale, "Korean Mind," 110.

32. Gale, "Korean Mind," 110.

33. Gale, "Korean Mind," 110.

34. Gale, "Korean Mind," 110.

Gale's presumption of the superiority of American civilization was directly linked to Christianity as the basis for the greatness. The Protestant missionaries circulated globally on the crest of this confluence of Christianity, culture, and civilization that were inextricably intertwined. Eugenia McInturff, a missionary in Japan, demonstrated the confidence of the West in a conversation with a native in 1888. McInturff said, "The best you have in Japan are Christian men, and the greatest nations in the world are Christian nations; and Japan is much greater now than ever before, because Christianity is making her home here."[35]

In the Korean context where Japan was taking imperialistic steps toward the Korean peninsula, most missionaries abided by the mandate to refrain from political activity by their government and mission boards but there were those who openly challenged Japanese rule over Korea and actively supported Korean independence. In 1897, the editors of *The Japan Times* criticized a "certain class" of missionaries who openly advocated Korean independence.[36] Henry G. Appenzeller and George H. Jones, both of the Methodist mission, and Homer B. Hulbert, a Congregationalist who was affiliated with the Methodist mission, wrote in *The Korean Repository*, "We are evidently spotted; our names are in the black-book, guilty of very grave offences."[37]

The editors of *The Japan Times* accused the missionaries of crossing the line—engaging in political affairs when they should abstain. According to the Japanese editorial, "Heedless of the repeated admonitions of their government at home, and in lamentable disregard of the duty they owe to a higher authority, they have debased themselves by meddling in the political intrigues of the peninsular kingdom."[38] With their inexcusable involvement in Korean politics, the editors of *The Japan Times* criticized the missionaries for "mingling with the servants of the Devil."[39]

Appenzeller, Jones, and Hulbert at first welcomed Japanese influence in Korea. They were initially encouraged by the modernizing changes Japan introduced to Korea; they "always believed in the reforms inaugurated by Japan."[40] However the Japanese assassination of Korea's Queen Min in 1895 and the "duplicity of her minister" in the aftermath raised serious questions

35. McInturff, "Something About Japanese Idolatry," 93–94.

36. Quoted in "Unnecessary Anxiety," 274–75.

37. "Unnecessary Anxiety," 275. Appenzeller and Jones were the co-editors of *The Korean Repository*. Hulbert was the manager of *The Korean Repository*.

38. "Unnecessary Anxiety," 275.

39. "Unnecessary Anxiety," 275.

40. "Editorial (1897)," 277.

about their intentions.[41] Hulbert in particular viewed the introduction of Japanese civilization as "retrograde," a "degrading" moral experience that equated modern civilization with "a finer method of getting what one wants without paying for it."[42]

In response to the accusation that they were colluding with "the servants of the Devil," Hulbert, Appenzeller, and Jones said, "The murder of a queen, in her own private apartments, in the grey of the morning, we readily grant would be likely to place any one in an 'exceptional position,' and if any missionary, and especially an American, was guilty of 'mingling with the servants of the Devil' on that morning let us have his name, so that we may help to drive him from the country."[43] Marking their allegiance, Hulbert, Appenzeller, and Jones, in the same editorial, addressed the Koreans: "We are with you."[44]

Perhaps the most impassioned demonstration for Korean independence by a missionary occurred when Hulbert advocated freedom for Korea through his trips abroad as an emissary for the kingdom. In 1905, Gojong sent Hulbert to Washington DC as his emissary in a futile attempt to dissuade President Theodore Roosevelt, American law-makers and media of supporting the Japanese takeover of Korea.[45] However, with President Theodore Roosevelt's firm and vocal support of Japan, Hulbert found no politicians in the Capitol willing to stand up against the president and he also discovered that media outlets refused to publish his pro-Korean articles "unless previously approved by Washington."[46]

After Japan became Korea's Protectorate in 1905 without Gojong's consent and took over Korea's foreign affairs, Hulbert urged Gojong to bring Korea's case before the international tribunal at the 1907 Second Peace Conference in Hague. After "selling all his possessions" to raise funds for the trip, Hulbert secretly led a Korean delegation to Hague by rendezvousing with the Korean members in Valdivostok and crossing Russia into Europe.[47] Although they reached Hague in time, they were refused entry into the Conference since Korea was now a protectorate and no longer a

41. "Editorial (1897)," 277.

42. Hulbert continued, "What with her morphia, her swarming prostitutes, her lawless traders, her partial officials and her utter contempt of the better side of the Korean, Japan has been degrading Korea rather than lifting her up" (Hulbert, "Japanese and Missionaries in Korea," 208).

43. "Unnecessary Anxiety," 275.

44. "Unnecessary Anxiety," 275.

45. Hulbert, *History of Korea*, ED 45–48.

46. Hulbert, *History of Korea*, ED 47.

47. Duus, *Abacus and the Sword*, 208.

sovereign nation. However, they managed to circulate "to all of the delegates [at the Conference] except Japan a summary of Korea's case . . . which was largely a restatement of the Emperor's original note."[48] In addition, Gojong's document was also "published in full" in the *Courrier de la Conference*, "a daily journal published in The Hague and devoted entirely to Conference affairs."[49] The Hague Incident, as it was later called, brought world-wide embarrassment to Japan and, as a consequence, Gojong was forced to abdicate in favor of his imbecile son in 1907. For his treasonous actions, Japan expelled Hulbert from Korea in 1907. In the United States, Hulbert continued his campaign for Korean independence and was finally able to return in 1949 to Korea where he died and was buried.[50]

APPENZELLER AND KOREAN NATIONALISM

A close associate of Hulbert's was Henry G. Appenzeller, a missionary who worked together with Hulbert on many projects.[51] On November 21, 1896, Appenzeller participated in the cornerstone dedication ceremony for the Independence Arch, a memorial gate in Seoul that was designed by Seo Jae Pil (Philip Jaisohn) to symbolize Korea's desire for independence. The ceremony started with a song entitled 'Korea' by the Pai Chai Glee Club. "Next, Henry Appenzeller prayed in Korean for 'Divine blessing upon Korea' and asked protection for Korea's independence."[52]

Before his untimely death in 1902, Appenzeller cultivated at Pai Chai Academy, a high school that he founded, an ethos of militaristic preparation, political activism, and intellectual engagement.[53] In a stark contrast to Korea's traditional schools that reinforced the recitation and memorization of classics, Appenzeller introduced formal military training and exercise among his Korean students. Appenzeller enlisted the assistance of a sergeant

---

48. Hulbert, *History of Korea*, 53.

49. Hulbert, *History of Korea*, 52.

50. Homer B. Hulbert (1863–1949) is buried at the Seoul Foreign Cemetery with the inscription on his tombstone: "I would rather be buried in Korea than in Westminster Abbey" (Millett, *War for Korea*, x).

51. For example, Hulbert and Appenzeller worked together to develop the Trilingual Press, a Western-style printing press that became the primary source for many journals, magazines, books, and newspapers.

52. Liem, *First Korean American*, 173–74.

53. "Pai Chai" is not romanized in the Revised Romanization of Korean because the original Pai Chai schools in Korea continue to use to spell their schools as "Pai Chai." If rendered in the Revised Romanization of Korean, it would be spelled *Baejae*.

from the US Marines who came "over every afternoon" to Pai Chai to train them.[54]

The Pai Chai students displayed their militaristic prowess when they performed "an exhibition drill" during the 1897 Commencement Exercises.[55] The instruction in military drills greatly inspired the Koreans and, as a result, many mission schools, for boys and girls, adopted military drills as a part of their academic training. For example, during the 1906 "Field Day" at Pyeongyang where lower school boys demonstrated their various skills, the boys performed military drills. A missionary who witnessed the drills noted that the boys were "trained by Koreans entirely."[56] The military drill exercises were not an ancillary program; they were, according to E. M. Cable, a fixture in the school curriculum in 1906. Cable observed that the non-Christian Korean parents became so enthusiastic over the military drill exercises that they purchased "all the necessary equipments for military drill."[57]

Another characteristic of Pai Chai Academy was the combative and engaging tone that fostered political and social activism. Under the tutelage of Seo Jae Pil, a Christian and a leading Korean nationalist who served as a faculty member at Pai Chai, students started *Hyeop Seonghoe* (or Mutual Friendship Society) in 1896, a student's version of the Independence Club.[58] The student society "which had only 13 members in 1896, grew to some 200 members within a year."[59] During the 1897 Commencement exercises at Pai Chai, members of the *Hyeop Seonghoe* debated whether the "Orient [should] accept, in the main, the civilization of the Occident."[60] The people attending the commencement observed that "logic, wit, sarcasm and appeal were used with the skill of clever debaters and the large audience frequently interrupted the speakers with vigorous applause as they made their various points."[61] After two members of each side finished presenting their arguments, "a popular vote was then taken [from the audience] and the question

54. The Korean students at Pai Chai "are drilled by the Sergeant of the U.S. Marines who comes over every afternoon and trains them. Long live Pai Chai" ("Notes and Comments," 260).

55. "Closing Exercises of Pai Chai," 274.

56. Best, "Year at Pyeng Yang," 250.

57. Cable, "Longing for Education," 144.

58. Seo Jae Pil (Philip Jaisohn) founded the newspaper, *The Independent*, as well as the Independence Club, an open public forum designed to engage the public and stimulate debate on a number of social, political, and religious issues.

59. C. Park, *Protestantism and Politics in Korea*, 123.

60. "Closing Exercises of Pai Chai," 273. The closing exercises at Pai Chai went very long, from 3pm to 8pm.

61. "Closing Exercises of Pai Chai," 273.

[whether or not Korea should accept Western civilization] carried overwhelmingly in the affirmative."[62]

During the school year, the *Hyeop Seonghoe* met every Saturday to discuss and debate important topics of their day, including "Korean writing in mixed script, educating wives, sisters, and daughters, freeing slaves, making roadside speeches to the public, and refraining from getting married until the age of twenty."[63] In contrast to the Confucian preoccupation with rote learning of the minutiae of an ancient language, young students at Pai Chai learned to formulate, articulate, and debate their ideas before audiences. In addition to Pai Chai Academy, the art of public speaking and debating, according to Chung-shin Park, "were practiced in all churches and mission schools at that time."[64] In other words, students in mission schools—both young men and women—engaged in the debate of the civic issues of their day, developed a keen sense of political affairs, and learned to be confident leaders of their peers.

CHRISTIANITY AND NATIONALISM

The full spectrum of Korean Christian leadership would be seen later during the preparation, organization, and execution of the March First Independence Movement in 1919. The signing of the Korean Declaration of Independence that sparked that Movement triggered a three-month, nation-wide peaceful protest against Japanese colonial rule. Thirty-three signers placed their names on the Declaration that would seal their fate. Of the thirty-three, sixteen were Christians; fifteen followers of Cheondogyo (the Way of Heaven); and two Buddhists.

The unusually high number of Christians who signed the Declaration did not go by unnoticed by the Japanese who discovered, upon investigation of the Movement that Christians played a major role, leading to the "high proportion of Christians among those arrested in the 1st March Movement."[65] Immediately nearly every Christian pastor in Seoul was arrested and jailed. Samuel Hugh Moffett wrote of the aftermath: "Soldiers [of the Japanese colonial government] stopped passers-by and asked, 'Are you Christian?' If they answered 'Yes,' they were beaten. If they answered 'No,' they were released. In rural areas, the brutality was unspeakable."[66]

62. "Closing Exercises of Pai Chai," 273.

63. C. Park, *Protestantism and Politics in Korea*, 123.

64. C. Park, *Protestantism and Politics in Korea*, 123.

65. Matsuo, "Japanese Protestants in Korea," 587.

66. Moffett, *Christians of Korea*, 70.

While the Japanese authorities identified Christians as leaders of the Movement, they mistakenly presumed the missionaries, "especially the Americans," to be the mastermind behind the insurrection. Even in July, after four months of protests, the Japanese authorities stated: "There is no doubt that the riot this time was supported and led by missionaries residing in Korea."[67]

To the Japanese authorities, the idea that Korean Christians themselves planned and orchestrated a covert nation-wide protest, without detection by the police, seemed implausible. However, a thorough, internal investigation absolved the missionaries. "Only ten out of about four hundred missionaries were suspected of having been involved." [68] The conclusion of the investigation allayed fears of missionaries behind the Movement but the Japanese authorities remained convinced that the missionaries at the same time did not endorse or support Japanese efforts.

Like an uncontrollable wildfire, peaceful demonstrations of the March First Movement spread spontaneously across the country. Lulu Frey, the principal of Ewha Academy, "bolted" the main gates of the school in order to prevent the girls from joining the protest in the streets and getting arrested by the Japanese police. However, the Korean girls "en masse, ordered it to be opened, [and] the gateman opened it."[69] Frey ran to the gate and "stood there with arms outstretched and announced, 'Well, girls, you will go over my dead body.'" Although some girls returned to their rooms, many stormed the streets where they were later arrested and detained.

As Korea witnessed the biggest upheaval since Japan assumed control over Korea, Frey dismissed school after a few days after March 1st but that did not quell the nationalistic fervor as the girls returned home to share the news of what was happening in Seoul and "many [girls] became leaders in their own communities." Frey's instincts proved correct as severe punishment awaited those who participated. Frey wrote, "Induk Pak and Julia Syn, two of our teachers, were in prison for long terms. Months afterward, Yu Kwansoon, a little 16-year-old girl, died in prison."[70]

The action at Ewha was an example of the greater nationalistic participation of Korean girls across the country. As Japan slowly clamped down on the population, the Japanese government listed 471 Korean girls and women as having participated in the 1919 movement.[71] The high number

67. Matsuo, "Japanese Protestants in Korea," 587–88.

68. Matsuo, "Japanese Protestants in Korea," 586.

69. Clark, "Mothers, Daughters, Biblewomen, and Sisters," 179.

70. Clark, "Mothers, Daughters, Biblewomen, and Sisters," 179.

71. Robinson, *Korea's Twentieth-Century Odyssey*, 48.

gave, according to the historian Michael Robinson, "strong evidence of the increased participation in nationalist activities of a new generation of women who attended or had graduated from the new schools for women that mushroomed in the 1910s."[72]

CHRISTIAN NATIONALISM

Despite the effort of many missionaries in Korea to stifle nationalistic impulses among their flock, Korean Christians demonstrated unusual patterns of nationalism that were significantly more intense than others in the population. In 1909, the missionary Lulu Miller recounted the testimony of a Korean who, as an expression of his pride as a Christian, "put up the Christian flagstaff in front of [his] house."[73] While touring Korea in 1897 as a representative of the Board of Foreign Missions, Robert E. Speer remarked that Korean patriotism was "one of the most interesting and striking features of the Korean Church."[74] Patriotism was proudly displayed on bamboo poles where small Korean flags flew to mark "the residences of Christians or were flying over churches."[75] The appearance of Korean Christian nationalism surprised Speer who noted that it developed "without missionary pressure."[76]

The amazement expressed by Speer and other missionaries who witnessed the nationalistic outburst indicate the diverse and unexpected ways Korean Christians relate faith to nationalistic concerns. Even with missionaries' efforts to suppress nationalistic impulses, Korean Christians were often on the frontlines of nationalistic activity. So much so that Koreans associated nationalism with Christians. The close relationship of Christianity with Korean nationalism prompted some Koreans to convert to Christianity. A Korean Christian activist wrote, "We accepted Christianity for we hoped independence lay in the church. It is only through Christ's intervention that an opportunity at hand is before us. This is an order, rarely given, which no one under the sun can afford to disobey."[77]

Despite missionaries' attempts to blunt the emergence of nationalism among believers, their attitudes nevertheless evoked nationalistic passions. For example, "Christian civilization" was an important expression that

72. Robinson, *Korea's Twentieth-Century Odyssey*, 48.

73. Miller, "Over Charcoal Fire." 173.

74. Speer, *Missionary Principles and Practices*, 253.

75. Speer, *Missionary Principles and Practices*, 253.

76. Speer, *Missionary Principles and Practices*, 253.

77. C. Park, *Protestantism and Politics in Korea*, 133.

encapsulated the spirit of the missionary movement of late nineteenth and early twentieth centuries.[78] The missionaries' understanding of Christianity was never far from Christianity as a socio-political culture. It was taken for granted that missionaries operated on the presumption that God acted upon the world stage and invigorated nations that honored God.

The missionaries derived a part of their inspiration from disseminating the virtues of American civilization. In 1899, L. H. Stewart, a missionary, illustrated America's divine purpose: "We believe that God has given us this continent, upon which he has planted a pure, spreading Christian civilization, that the life blood of our holy religion may circulate through all nations."[79] The outcome of individual salvation was of course the baseline for the mission work but Protestant missionaries understood a larger cultural, societal, and political purpose in which the 'Christian civilization' meant reforming nations according to Christian ideals. A missionary working with Muslims in Tunisia wrote in 1912, "Civilization and education are two strong stakes which, early attached to the plant, will do much toward training it upward with a strong, straight stem."[80]

At stake was nothing less than the destiny of civilizations in which missionaries viewed America as a major if not the leading stakeholder in leading the battle.[81] "The greatest event of the twentieth century now before us is," wrote John Henry Barrows in 1899, "between Christian civilization, as represented by pure homes, biblical ideals, popular enlightenment, and popular freedom, on the one hand, and the barbarism or semicivilization of Asia, on the other, where human rights are denied, opportunities restricted, womanhood degraded, where superstition, deceit, idolatry, and impurity

---

78. A missionary in China wrote in 1911, "There is no question but what if the heathen nations are to be redeemed, if pagan civilization is to be transformed and replaced by a civilization Christian in principle and in practice, we must reach and influence and hold the children" ("New China's Plea for Education," 135). "The advance of Christian civilization is coincident with the spread of the knowledge of Christian truth, and Christian missions have produced a body of sincere disciples of Christ who are to be the salt of the new China that is just at hand" (Longden, "Developments," 437).

79. Stewart, "Our Home Missions," 134.

80. Hammon, "Crooked Trees," 308.

81. "They need thorough reconstruction, and any attempt to build up a real Christian civilization in Cuba must begin with fundamental principles on all lines" (Ninde and Leonard, "Report on Cuba," 175). "These downtrodden people shall one day rejoice in a civilization which is truly Christian, and which shall lift them up out of material, political, social, and spiritual degradation" (Robinson, "Some Experiences of a Missionary," 273). Writing about the Holy Lands in contention between the Turks and the West, S. Ralph Harlow asked in 1922, "How is it that Christian civilization can stand by while hundreds of thousands of our fellow Christians are done to death with every cruelty that the minds of fiendish men can invent" (Harlow, "Holy Places," 865).

are almost universal."[82] H. G. Jackson in 1899 spoke of the Christian civilization as a precursor to eternal destination when he wrote, "They must have
the Gospel and a Christianity civilization to save them from the miseries of
their present conditions. . . . The Gospel has to do with man in *this* life, and
the mission of the Church is to redeem *this* world and bring it to Christ,
and thus will lost Eden be restored, and man be fitted for the life to come."[83]

"There can be no doubt," according to James Mudge, "that missions are
the very greatest power at work in the world to-day for the uplifting of the
nations that were in heathen darkness into the noonday light of Christian
civilization." Mudge continued, "And the true progress of mankind is un-
questionably bound up in the bundle with the spread of vital Christianity."[84]
In 1898, Henry Loomis, a missionary in Japan, wrote, "There is also, no
doubt, a growing conviction that Christianity is the basis of the highest type
of civilization."[85] At the same time, missionaries understood the difference
between Westernization as the adoption of Western technology and institutions and Christian civilization. The missionary George Miner wrote in
1899, "To give the Chinese 'Western civilization' without Christianity would
be like putting a two-edged sword into the hands of children."[86]

As Korea teetered on the brink of collapse at the turn of the twentieth century, a growing consensus emerged in Korean society that viewed
the adoption of Western learning, technology, and methods was essential
to save the nation. Many Koreans "believed that the *only* way to recover
independence was to modernize and enlighten Koreans, and many organizations were established for this purpose."[87]

In this regard, Korean Christians received the most exposure to Westernization through their experience with missionaries and mission schools.
A missionary in Korea in 1912 expressed this sentiment when he wrote,
"There is no evidence that they [Japanese authorities] have desired to per-
secute the Christians as such, but are naturally suspicious of the more intel-
ligent, independent classes of which these Christians are composed. They
also look with critical eyes on the schools and churches under missionary
control, and, without cause, consider them hot-beds of treason."[88]

82. "Outlook in Asia," 234.

83. Jackson, "Methods of Arousing Missionary Interest," 309.

84. Mudge, "Debt of Progress to Christianity," 341.

85. Loomis, "Bible and Christianity in Japan," 465.

86. Miner, "Reforms and Christian Education," 496.

87. "The organizations that formed during this period were established to build
more schools and train female leaders" (Yoon, *Korean Christian Women's Movement*,
21 [emphasis mine]).

88. "Stirring Letters from Korea," 505–6.

Considering how missionaries' self-understanding seamlessly inter-twined Christianity and civilization, it is no surprise that Korean Christians saw no contradiction between having a fervent faith in God and express-ing nationalistic sentiments. Before the Japanese colonization of Korea in 1910, J. O. Paine who was one of the missionaries in charge at Ewha Girls' Academy noticed that the girls—without her knowledge—were praying on their own. After a few days, Paine asked the girls what they were fervently praying about each day and they replied, "We are praying for our country."[89] At a heightened moment in Korean history when the people sensed the real possibility of their country's collapse, turning to God urgently was not only common but also a rallying call to bring fellow Koreans together in prayer and unity. An Ewha student told Paine that she had stayed at a non-believer's home over the winter break. Eventually, she won them over as they "allowed her to have prayer each day." Furthermore, "at noon they had gathered together while she prayed for the country.[90]

Korean Christian women responded to their country's plight by start-ing a national debt redemption movement. Their aim: to raise money to free the country from foreign debt. "They collected their jewelry, rice, and cash and formed organizations such as Kam Sun Hoi and Tal Hwan Hoi."[91] Their concerns did not stop with economic concerns. They aimed to advance gen-der equality and education by building more schools.

In 1910 when Japan colonized Korea, less than two percent of the Ko-rean population was Christian. There were an estimated 200,000 Christians out of thirteen million Koreans.[92] Although Korean Christians were a tiny minority in Korea, their political leadership was significant in at least three ways: first, because of their unique experience in forming and mobilizing organizations; and second, because of the prominence of Christian leaders at a national level; and third, because the church became the de facto center for assembly and dissemination.

Korean church leaders through their country-wide network of churches, schools, and associations found themselves well placed to make important contributions to advance the cause of Korean independence. The Korean church was one of few organizations where a large assembly of hun-dreds of Koreans could gather. Chung-shin Park wrote, "Because there were virtually no civic organizations for reform endeavors and also because many reform activists were members of the religious community, enlightenment

---

89. Paine, "Ewha Haktang-Seoul," 5.

90. Paine, "Ewha Haktang-Seoul," 4–5.

91. Chu, *Presbyterian Women in Korea*, 76–77.

92. Paik, *Protestant Missions in Korea*, 423.

ideas spread naturally throughout churches, church-operated schools, and other institutions affiliated with the church."[93]

In many ways, the Korean church leaders were a major force behind the independence movement as they formed a web of operatives that connected pockets of resistance groups in Korea. Most Koreans had very little experience in leadership of organizations but Korean church leaders had years of experience leading classes, organizing assemblies, and preaching before an audience. Evangelism was one of the hallmark characteristics of the Korean church and church leaders were unafraid of speaking boldly in public with inspiring messages. As a result, evangelizing or speaking on behalf of the nation for the cause of independence came easily. All of these traits learned as they became Christians became invaluable skills in advancing the cause of independence.

As the single-largest organization in Korea, the Korean church built an extensive network that proved conducive to transmitting covert messages. For example, Rev. Soon Hyun's position, as the Superintendent of all Methodist Sunday Schools throughout Korea, enabled him to "travel unnoticed" across the Korean provinces.[94]

Working undercover as an agent of the independence movement, Hyun was "chosen to cross the country from church to church organizing and alerting the people to the planned uprising [i.e., March First Movement]."[95] The missionaries were well-aware of the Koreans' aspirations for independence and the tensions sometimes caused missionaries to stamp out overt nationalistic activity. For example, the Epworth League, an interchurch youth organization in the Methodist church, was later disbanded by the missionaries after the Epworth League evolved into an independent and powerful organization with political agendas.[96]

In her autobiography, Louise Yim, as a high school student, first learned about Korea's independence movement from Pastor Kim who secretly informed Yim about the guerilla forces in the mountains, the preparation and plans to wage war against Japan, and the work of the provisional Korean government in Shanghai. The knowledge of independence stoked the flames of patriotism among the girls at Yim's mission school. After learning about the bravery of Korean patriots, Yim said, "I suddenly felt that my dreams

---

93. C. Park, *Protestantism and Politics in Korea*, 122.

94. Hyun, *Man Sei!*, 5, 66.

95. Hyun, *Man Sei!*, xi.

96. Methodist Episcopal Church North Report (1906) in Paik, *Protestant Missions in Korea*, 352.

were not just those of a child and I knew that I had a place in the scheme of [Korean] liberation."[97]

As was common among mission schools, organizing school plays and dramatic productions was part of the school curriculum. Yim's school decided to pursue the biblical account of Queen Esther as a Christmas play. The teachers selected Yim to play Esther. In the biblical story, Esther pleaded desperately to save the Jews from extermination. When Yim acted as Queen Esther, she embodied the movement of her people who desired freedom from Japanese colonization.

Even though it was only a school play, Esther's words "took on new meaning" and conveyed hope to a downtrodden people.[98] The re-telling of the biblical story evoked a political consciousness that was subversive and empowering at the same time. As she played Esther, Yim said, "When I pleaded with King Ahasuerus to save the Hebrews, the words became a plea for Korea. And the meaning of my lines, though I did not mention Korea, was clearly understood by the audience. Quite often they interrupted by speeches with applause and when I came off the stage at the end some of my classmates came over to embrace me and one said, 'With such words we can free Korea!'"[99]

The mission school was more than a place of learning. It also served as an incubator for the transmission of knowledge, providing a crucial space for not only for students but also for teachers, pastors, and parents. The Japanese authorities banned the study of Korean history during the colonial period but, privately, knowledge of Korea's past was learned in secret. There was no doubt that learning Korea's history was a subversive act that would surely lead to arrest. Yim remembered the exciting and fearful moments when Pastor In Chun Kim would take a few of the girls aside to a secret location to teach them about Korean history.[100]

Korean Christians became skillful in encoding Christian language with double meaning and that under religious lyrics rested a deeper political meaning. Although public discussion of independence was prohibited, 1,000 to 2,000 Koreans gathered in Seoul as an act of defiance and recited together the Lord's Prayer in unison.[101] Korean ministers used the pulpit as a weapon against tyranny by evoking biblical narratives to illustrate the fight against the tyrannical forces of evil. When Rev. Soon Hyun preached a

---

97. Yim, *My Forty-Year Fight*, 58.

98. Yim, *My Forty-Year Fight*, 55.

99. Yim, *My Forty-Year Fight*, 55–56.

100. Yim, *My Forty-Year Fight*, 58.

101. I. Kim, *Christian Church of Korea*, 156.

salvific message, calling upon the people to 'Follow Jesus, for He shall make you free,' the Korean audience understood the double meaning of freedom that underscored the sense of loss that all Koreans experienced.[102]

Listening to a powerful sermon by a Korean preacher in 1907, W. L. Swallen, a missionary in Korea, observed how the preacher used the biblical allusion of Egypt and the slavery of Israel as an unmistakable voice for Korean freedom. Swallen wrote, "Egypt is the shadow of the power of sin just as Japan represented a symbol of evil in their situation. Just as the people of Israel got acquainted with the power of evil and sin, the Korean people are learning about the nature of evil."[103]

Rich with references of war, God-inspired victories, overcoming adversity, colonization by foreigners, and successful uprisings against foreign rule, the Bible gave ample ammunition to Korean ministers to empower Koreans and to preach a message of national salvation without overtly saying it. The empowering Christian teachings also provided a buffer against the deprecating information delivered by their colonial rulers who depicted Koreans as "an inferior race" that needed the "guidance of a superior race to bring about 'civilization and enlightenment.'"[104]

A Korean who as a youth attended Sungin Commercial High School in Pyeongyang, which was founded by the Protestant nationalist Mansik Cho, described how his Christian school raised the students' "awareness of and pride in being Korean and fostered a sense of active resistance against the Japanese."[105] During his weekly speeches to the students, Cho "could not come out and say that the Japanese were our unwelcome masters and we should resist, but in the form of a sermon from the Bible, he said those things. . . . We did not mistake his message."[106] As a result of their nationalist activism, the Japanese authorities gradually closed down many of the Christian schools, calling them "strongholds of actual or potential anti-Japanese sentiment."[107] L. George Paik, who lived through the colonial period, described how Korean preachers used biblical language to disguise their nationalistic rhetoric:

102. Soon Hyun's "most compelling call was, quoting Jesus, 'Follow me and I shall make you free.' Koreans everywhere ached for their freedom. Even more than the attraction of education in the American missionary schools, it was this yearning for freedom that moved the people to flock to Christian churches"
(Hyun, *Man Sei!*, 4–5).

103. Swallen, *Sunday School Lessons*, 4.

104. Shin, *Ethnic Nationalism in Korea*, 42.

105. Kang, *Under the Black Umbrella*, 46.

106. Kang, *Under the Black Umbrella*, 46.

107. Myers and Pettie, *Japanese Colonial Empire*, 296.

> When one looks at the language and deeds of Christians, they profess that the people of Israel under the oppression of Egypt succeeded in their exodus for national independence and liberation under God's help and under the leadership of Moses. They teach the biblical story that during the war with another nation the people of Israel were vindicated by David, the Apostle of Justice who destroyed the giant Goliath. And whenever they congregate together, they sing hymns, 'Believers are like soldiers of the Army!' and 'The Army of the Cross.' This language was easily construed to be rebellion oriented, as Christian leaders now saw.[108]

CONCLUSION

In 1905, a former student of Henry G. Appenzeller wrote (in English): "As far as spiritual salvation is concerned, Christianity is the only foundation upon which the future prosperity of our country can be based."[109] In response, Appenzeller wrote, "He is simply stating a historical truth."[110] The identification of Christianity with the strength of a country represented the mindset of many Koreans who looked to Christianity for national deliverance. As Appenzeller's response indicated, the conjoining of Christianity with American civilization reflected the assumptions of American missionaries.

When Protestant missionaries arrived in Korea from the late nineteenth century, they walked into a middle of a political maelstrom generated by domestic and foreign problems. The political crisis that unfolded had serious consequences for Korea's sovereignty. As Koreans considered their situation, many turned to modernity or Westernization as the answer and, for those who viewed America positively, their openness to Christianity increased. For American missionaries in Korea, the superiority of the American civilization was taken as a certainty. As Korea became weaker and crept closer to being colonized, Koreans' confidence in traditional institutions also collapsed. In its wake, many Koreans turned to Christianity for personal and national salvation.

The association of the superiority of American civilization with Christianity as its cornerstone was not surprising to Koreans. After all, Koreans presumed the superiority of Korean civilization with Neo-Confucianism as the foundation before it crumbled at the turn of the twentieth century.

108. Paik in Suh, *Korean Minjung in Christ*, 34.
109. Appenzeller, *Korea Mission*, 34–35.
110. Appenzeller, *Korea Mission*, 35.

Koreans witnessed the decline of Joseon dynasty while encroaching imperial powers vied for control. The political situation produced a crisis of national proportions involving nothing less than the existence of the Korean state and identity. The impending collapse of nationhood engrafted an urgent nationalistic concern to Koreans' Christian formation.

In the face of national tragedy, missionaries, especially those who proactively promoted the American civilization, played a significant role in clarifying Western political ideals. Having had Joseon dynasty with Neo-Confucianism as the sole philosophical framework for over 500 years, Koreans were unaccustomed to competing ideologies. At such a time, Christianity as a civilization, institution, and nation-wide organization represented a political lifeline and offered the chance to partake in the outcome of the nation.

On June 3, 1973, Billy Graham closed his five-day crusade to a crowd estimated to exceed 1.1 million—the largest in Billy Graham's ministry.

Yoido Full Gospel Church in Seoul. The world's largest congregation.

8

Contemporary Korea

Kyung-chik Han, an outstanding Korean church leader, was born in 1902 in a farming village northeast of Pyeongyang. Died in 2000, Han's life spanned nearly the entirety of the twentieth century. Han experienced the chaotic series of events that profoundly shaped how Koreans understood and practiced Christianity. And, in a way, his life journey mirrors the experience of Korean Christianity in the twentieth century.

Han was born while Korea was still ruled by a monarch of the Joseon dynasty. As a boy, he witnessed the collapse of his country that became part of the Japanese empire. With the help of a missionary, Han went to the United States to attend College of Emporia and Princeton Theological Seminary. Upon returning to Korea, he discovered that the Japanese colonial government remained suspicious of him and blocked him from positions of leadership.[1] The euphoria brought on by Korean independence in 1945 as a result of the Japanese defeat in World War II dissipated as the communists in northern Korea rose to power in the wake of the political vacuum.

Han assisted his mentor Man-sik Cho to start the Christian Social Democratic Party (later re-named Social Democratic Party) in northern Korea. The political participation of Christians was met quickly with resistance and violence from the communists. In one instance, communists fired

---

1. As a student of the renowned nationalist, Man-sik Cho, Han was marked by the Japanese police. According to Samuel Hugh Moffett, the Japanese police blocked Han's appointment to teach at Union Christian College. "So Han went instead to the far north, to a pastorate on the Yalu River. But again the Japanese interfered. Police ousted him from his pulpit, and he retired to the country, farming with his own hands the land of a combined old folks home and orphanage, of which he became the director" (Moffett, *Christians of Korea*, 22).

upon thousands of demonstrators, many of them Christians. Fortunate to evade the bloody suppression, Han escaped to Seoul in October, 1945 where he started the Young Nak Presbyterian Church that quickly grew in attendance. Only three weeks after the dedication service of Young Nak's new church building,[2] the communists crossed the border, ushering three years of the Korean War (1950–1953) that left the country divided, decimated, and impoverished.

While the end of the Korean War brought peace, Koreans struggled to come to terms with the devastation of a war that ripped the country apart. Like Han, Koreans from the north fled as refugees to the south only to discover later the permanent division of Korea into North and South. From the ashes of war, Han's Young Nak Church grew and it became in the 1950s the largest church in Korea with over 6,000 in Sunday attendance.[3] The 1960s saw unprecedented economic development and prosperity as well as growth of churches, as freedom of religious practice was finally achieved in post-War South Korea. In 1992, when Han received the Templeton Prize for Progress in Religion Award, Young Nak was the largest Presbyterian congregation in the world with a membership of over 60,000.

Korean Christians since the 1940s have experienced a period of intense social and political conflict that subjected them to a wide range of circumstances that helped define the framework from which to understand their theological location. The shifting political fault lines invariably shaped the contours of socio-political consciousness that nurtured theological formation and outlook.

Decades of oppressive Japanese colonial rule took a heavy toll on Christians. The nightmarish experience of Christians under colonial rule ended when Japan was defeated during World War II but their relief was short-lived as communists quickly mounted a formidable political machine in northern Korea. Shortly after the end of World War II, Korean Christians faced the dystopian turn as Korean communists indiscriminately targeted Christians for execution. The ravages of war created widespread destruction, tore countless families apart, and left more than 2.7 million civilian deaths.

2. Moffett, *Christians of Korea*, 24.

3. The Young Nak Church, "where six thousand people flock to hear him [Han] preach every Sunday, making his congregation the largest in Korea" (Moffett, *Christians of Korea*, 21).

END OF JAPANESE COLONIAL CONTROL

The years leading up to World War II (1941–1945) were marked by unprecedented crackdown on Christians by the Japanese colonial government.[4] The worst persecution of Christians occurred during Japan's imperialist expansion into China and Manchuria. Already engaged in the Second Sino-Japanese War (1937–1945), Japan "embarked on a breathtaking program to mobilize Koreans of all walks of life."[5] The colonial policy during the third period included the forced assimilation of Koreans "into the organic structure of the [Japanese] Empire."[6]

Previously, Christian schools were able to preserve some autonomy but not during an era of heightened nationalistic consciousness. The Japanese government had no tolerance for dissension and, in an effort to galvanize all under Japan's imperial religion, attendance in Shinto ceremonies became compulsory. Students also recited the Pledge of Imperial Subjects that declared, "We are the subjects of the great empire of Japan. We shall serve the Emperor with united hearts. We shall endure hardships and train ourselves to become good and strong subjects of the Emperor."[7]

When students started classes in the morning, they lined up in the school-yard facing the principal who was standing on an elevated platform. Upon the principal's signal, the children sang the Japanese national anthem. The principal then delivered and led the students in a series of slogans that were loudly chanted: "Obey and sacrifice for the Emperor!" "We are a great Japanese people!" "Defeat America and England!" or "Japanese Victory!" A student recounted that "every single day the principal gave a homily and we

---

4. Japan's colonial rule of Korea (1910–1945) is divided into three periods: 1910–1919, *Budan Seiji* (Military of Dictatorial Colonial Government); 1919–1930, *Bunka Seiji* (Cultural Rule); and 1931–1945, *Naisen Ittai* (War-time Mobilization and Assimilation). See Eckert et al., *Korea Old and New*, 254–320; Brudnoy, "Japan's Experiment in Korea," 165–88; Page, *Colonialism*, 320.

5. "The mobilization [of Koreans] was designed to insure total obedience and enthusiastic participation" (Eckert et. al, *Korea Old and New*, 316).

6. Brudnoy, "Japan's Experiment in Korea," 185. As the first "modern" Asian country, Japan justified imperialism by arguing that they were in the best position to help "civilize" other Asian countries. "By suggesting that the Japanese were better able to introduce the Koreans to 'civilization' than the Westerners, the Japanese privileged their own earlier 'backwardness.' As the first Asian people to break free of the thrall of Western imperialism, the Japanese had a kind of 'yellow man's burden' to help their fellow Asians acquire the new knowledge and technology that would make them strong" (Duus, *Abacus and the Sword*, 432).

7. Kang, *Under the Black Umbrella*, 115.

all bowed east toward Tokyo and the Emperor and shouted 'Tenno Heika Ban Zai'—'Long Live the Emperor.'"[8]

Christians and churches were brought under close surveillance through an elaborate and expanded police force that exercised broad authority to arrest people even for minor offenses. The last years of Japanese colonialism witnessed increasing stranglehold on the Korean churches. As an example, a large number of church leaders were scheduled to be executed on August 18, 1945 but Japan's surrender on August 15 led to their release.[9]

About a month before Japan surrendered, Japan attempted to deal a "final blow" to Christians when it consolidated all Korean churches and denominations into "one tightly controlled organization, the united 'Korean Christian Church of Japanese Christianity'" that subjected all Korean Christian churches under Japanese church authority.[10]

COMMUNIST SUPPRESSION OF CHRISTIANITY

Japan's surrender brought the US and the former-Soviet Union to Korea. Japan ordered a complete withdrawal of its troops on August 10, 1945.[11] At a meeting of the State-War-Navy Coordinating Committee on the evening of August 10–11 in Washington DC, a decision was made to divide the Korea peninsula at the thirty-eighth parallel into American and Soviet occupation zones. President Harry S. Truman approved the plan on August 13; Premier Joseph Stalin on August 14.[12]

The arbitrary division of Korea at the thirty-eighth parallel signaled the formation of two distinct spheres of influence. The communist ideology which had been suppressed under the Japanese was now freely disseminated across northern Korea. As early as 1926, Yu-soon Kim the Methodist District Superintendent of the Haeju District (the Hwanghae Namdo Province in North Korea which is adjacent to the South Korean border) reported that

8. Kang, Under the Black Umbrella, 115.

9. Moffett, Christians of Korea, 75–76.

10. Moffett, Christians of Korea, 75.

11. "On August 11, the Soviet forces attempted to land at Chongjin, a port city in northern Korea near the East Korea Bay in the Sea of Japan. The Seventeenth Area Army decided to withdraw and halt the Soviets at Wonsan, more than 200 miles south of Chongjin" (Koshiro, Imperial Eclipse, 249–50).

12. When Soviet and American personnel arrived in Korea, they discovered the government of the Korean People's Republic (KPR) already in place as well as a wide-array of political organizations.

"younger members" of the church "have been led away by Communistic thought, which has come from neighboring countries."[13]

In 1930, Hyung-sik Pai, the Methodist District Superintendent of Manchuria, reported that the "communists in Manchuria became active and in December the Chinese police were forbidding meetings of every kind even of those including church services."[14] In particular, Koreans in Manchuria were becoming communists and the Chinese police cast a wide net over Koreans, sweeping up Christians along the way. Pai wrote, "Because of the presence of Communists among the Koreans in many places the Chinese are driving out the Koreans."[15] As the communists engaged in "ruthlessness in destruction of life and property," innocent Koreans were arrested and killed. Pai noted, "Sixteen were killed recently after their arrest."[16]

By the end of World War II, the communist network expanded widely in the north and it was not long before they suppressed the efforts of Christians to engage in political activities. In 1946, they prevented Christians from organizing politically. Kyung-chik Han's Social Democratic party was crushed and disbanded. In Pyeongyang, Hwa-sik Kim's Christian Liberal party was prevented from mobilizing and later he and forty of his colleagues "died in prison or disappeared."[17]

Like the Japanese colonial government's plan to control and manage churches, the communists created the Christian League, an organization that consolidated all Christian churches together under communist supervision. The Christian League assumed obeisance to the communist party but when Christians boycotted the League the communists enforced a mandatory membership for all church leaders. The Christians in the north resisted all efforts to be incorporated into the communist political machine and after exhausting all attempts to control the Church the communists proceeded to exterminate Christians, "the third and final stage of their religious policy."[18] The indiscriminate killing of Christians became reality for Christians not only in the north but also in the south when the communists during the Korean War temporarily occupied most of the Korean peninsula. Samuel

13. "Reports of the District Superintendents," 318.

14. "Manchuria District (1930)," 245.

15. "The Chinese police are not to be trusted and they will not protect the Koreans though paid for it" ("Manchuria District [1930]," 245).

16. "Ten more have been arrested in the neighborhood of Yungotap and will probably be killed. When pursued by the authorities the [communist] leaders all flee and the farmers who stay behind are the ones who stand the brunt of the suffering" ("Manchuria District [1930]," 245).

17. Moffett, Christians of Korea, 77.

18. Moffett, Christians of Korea, 77.

Hugh Moffett estimates that over four hundred Protestant ministers alone were killed during this period.[19]

When the Korean People's Army (KPA) crossed the DMZ on June 25, 1950, it was not the first armed clash between the two sides. And in some cases, South Korean forces had initiated skirmishes with communists along the border and "fighting had been fierce along the Thirty-eighth parallel for more than a year, including particularly pitched battles in the area of the Ongjin Peninsula in the summer of 1949."[20] The Korean War ended in 1953 but in its wake 66 percent of Seoul was destroyed. The streets of Seoul were littered "Russian tanks, American tanks, mortars, [and] the remnants of artillery."[21] Roads were "gutted out with shell holes, dust a mile high, and most of all, people."[22]

For many Korean church leaders, the evil of communism left an indelible imprint on their consciousness. Communists targeted Christians more than any other civilian group. For example, Bishop Yoon-soon Kim of the Korean Methodist Church was captured and killed by the communists in 1950.[23] South Korea lived under the threat of communism and many turned to Christianity for spiritual comfort and deliverance. In March 1950, Protestant churches under the sponsorship of the Korean National Council of Churches (KNCC) joined together for the "Save the Nation Evangelical Crusade" crusade. In three months, from April to June 1950, all the major cities in South Korea were visited. In all, more than 25,000 made public confessions as "the average number of converts gained in each meeting [of the crusade] was higher than the crusades led by Billy Graham in Los Angeles (1949) or any other Youth for Christ rallies in the United States during the same period of time."[24]

On June 25, 1950, an estimated 75,000 soldiers from the communist north invaded the south that started the Korean War and, facing little resistance, they nearly conquered all of the country. General Douglas McArthur's surprise amphibious landing in Incheon flanked the communists' position in 1950 and drove them back as far as the Yalu River that bordered China which had their own communist revolution a year earlier in 1949.

19. Moffett, *Christians of Korea*, 77.

20. Armstrong, *Tyranny of the Weak*, 10.

21. "Within two years after their inauguration (August 15, 1948), President Syngman Rhee and his cabinet had to evacuate Seoul in June, 1950, because of the Communist invasion. When they returned in October, the city was in ruins, 66 per cent destroyed" (Rhodes, *History of the Korea Mission,* 2:62).

22. Rhodes, *History of the Korea Mission,* 2:38.

23. Moffett, *Christians of Korea*, 114.

24. Haga, "Rising to the Occasion," 96.

Just when it seemed that McArthur would take all of Korea, Chinese troops poured across the Yalu and pushed the UN forces back to the 38th parallel, a boundary that still remains in place today. Korean Christians in the north, desperate to escape the impending communist slaughter of Christians, made their way to the south. Samuel Hugh Moffett estimated that "four and a half million refugees fled into South Korea in those few months."[25]

Included in the massive exodus of humanity was the "greatest rescue by a single ship in the annals of the sea," according to the US Maritime Administration when Captain Leonard LaRue evacuated over 14,000 refugees from the North Korean port of Hungnam in a freighter ship designed to carry only 60 passengers in December 1950.[26] LaRue viewed the horde of humanity crowding at the port in fear of the incoming communists and turned his ship, *SS Meredith Victory*, a freighter ship transporting supplies, to pick up the refugees.

The sea was littered with mines but the sailed south with no mine detectors, no doctor (five babies were born during the voyage), no interpreter, no lighting in the holds, no heat, and no sanitation facilities. However, not a single passenger was lost. Among those onboard were the parents and the older sister of the current president of South Korea, Moon Jae-in. LaRue, who after the Korean War became a Benedictine monk in 1954 and spent the rest of his life at St. Paul's Abbey in Newton, New Jersey, thought a lot about the ship at sea and said, "I think often of that voyage. I think of how such a small vessel was able to hold so many persons and surmount endless perils without harm to a soul. The clear, unmistakable message comes to me that on that Christmastide, in the bleak and bitter waters off the shores of Korea, God's own hand was at the helm of my ship."[27]

DIVIDED KOREA, DIVIDED CHURCH

Korea's liberation from colonial rule delivered the first taste of freedom in thirty-five years but the controversial issues of legitimacy and collaboration hung over the church in the years following the end of World War II. Take for example, the complicated legacy of Helen Hwal-lan Kim (1899–1970)— the first Korean woman to receive a PhD in 1931, the founder of the Korean daily *The Korean Times*, and the first Korean president of Ewha University, the largest women's university in the world. As part of the 100th anniversary of Kim's birth, Ewha officials planned in 1998 to annually bestow the

25. Muller, *Wearing the Cross in Korea*, 79.

26. Blume, *Historical Dictionary*, 324.

27. LaRue in Gilbert, *Ship of Miracles*, 129.

'Kim Hwallan Award' (with a USD $50,000 cash prize) to a woman or a woman's organization that advanced the causes of women around the world. The announcement provoked a series of protests against Kim including the burning of her effigy at the front gate of Ewha University.[28] All of the negative press succeeded in postponing the award and in a few years the University officials decided to drop the award. Several years later on March 25, 2005, protests against Kim flared up again when Ewha students gathered around Kim's statue on campus to denounce her pro-Japanese activities and demanded that the University replace her with another alumnus who had a spotless record during the colonial period.[29] The historian Theodore Jun Yoo asked, "How could such a luminary figure, respected for her pioneering efforts in advancing women's rights and access to education, be equally infamous for her collaboration with the colonial government?"[30]

Japan's surrender in 1945 uncorked euphoric expressions of unimaginable joy and, yet, at the same time exposed raw emotions fueled by the suffering endured during the colonial period. As the Korean liberation offered Christians the first opportunity in a long time to lead their churches without interference, stories of the faithful who, without compromise, endured enormous suffering at the hands of the Japanese were now coming forth and provoked consternation within the Korean Church that now was forced to reckon with the past.

A similar dilemma played out in the larger Korean society where accusations of collaboration tainted those who cooperated with the Japanese. In the aftermath of Korean liberation, remnants of Japanese colonialism were promptly destroyed. Korean dismantled and chopped down Shinto shrines. Crowds "tore down the wooden shrines, hacked them to pieces, and right there on the wide courtyards, they burned them to the ground."[31] Children who had never spoken Korean were learning it for the first time. A woman who was fourteen-years old at Korean liberation said, "I was young, and I had never spoken in my entire life. Since I didn't know a single word of Korean, I repeated the sixth grade just to learn my own native language."[32]

Korean Christians also began the efforts to reclaiming what had been lost or forgotten. Many of the top denominational leaders had been imprisoned or killed but those who could remember the past institutions

---

28. Kwon, "Feminists," 43.

29. Students demanded a statue of Gwan-seon Yu to replace Kim's. See Yoo, *Politics of Gender*, 202.

30. Yoo, *Politics of Gender*, 202–3.

31. Kang, *Under the Black Umbrella*, 147.

32. Kang, *Under the Black Umbrella*, 145.

resurrected old denominational structures and organizations but not without significant conflict. The decades-long systematic oppression against Christians left many in the church bitter, divided, and, in many ways, broken. The Korean Church which had withstood tremendous persecution in the past found itself unable to move on from the past. The in-fighting within the Church spiraled downward into cycles of dissent and fragmentation.

Samuel Hugh Moffett remembered the mood in the church in the years following post-liberation. Moffett wrote, "Years of struggle against outside enemies had so drained the people emotionally and physically that they no longer had the strength and the love to forgive and forget after a family quarrel. What would have been minor irritations in normal times now were magnified into major issues, and quarrels led straight to divorce."[33]

The Methodists managed to gradually heal the wounds but not without a painful process. In February 1946, a group of Methodist leaders who resisted Shinto worship condemned those who participated in the "Japanized" united church. Their efforts to reconstitute the Korean Methodist Church "fell apart" as the majority in the Methodist Church chose "to forgive and elect to office some who had been guilty of wartime collaboration."[34] A minority in the Korean Methodist Church broke away to form the Constitutional Methodist Church in 1950 when dispute over the election of bishop to succeed Yoon-soon Kim created disagreement. However, the schism ended in 1959.

"Far more serious, and immeasurably more damaging to Protestant prestige and evangelistic effectiveness and even perhaps to the faith of some believers," according to Samuel Hugh Moffett, "were the schisms that tore the Presbyterian Church in Korea into four jagged pieces, not to mention some smaller fragments."[35] In 1951 the Koryo Presbyterian Church separated from the Presbyterian Church in Korea on the grounds that the parent church was "too liberal, too ecumenical, and too tainted with Shinto collaborationism."[36]

The ultra-conservative factions within the Presbyterian Church drew a hardline along theological and political lines.[37] The parent Presbyterian

33. Moffett, *Christians of Korea*, 113.

34. Moffett, *Christians of Korea*, 113. "The minority group withdrew to form the Rehabilitated Methodist Church—a schism that was bridged three years later" (Moffett, *Christians of Korea*, 113).

35. Moffett, *Christians of Korea*, 114.

36. Moffett, *Christians of Korea*, 114

37. Moffett laments that the ultra-conservative faction was encouraged by Orthodox Presbyterian missionaries who themselves broke away from the parent Presbyterian church in America on similar grounds of liberal theology. Moffett wrote, "The

Church censured the ministers guilty of collaboration and removed them from their pulpits "for months of penance and repentance," but it was not enough to unite the brokenness as the purists claimed that collaborators were permanently tainted, regardless of how much they repent.[38]

In the following years, the parent Presbyterian body witnessed more defections. The creation of the Presbyterian Church in the Republic of Korea in 1954 occurred with the excommunication of the administrators and faculty of Hankuk Seminary when they refused the mandate of the General Assembly to disband and merge with a conservative seminary. Instead, members of Hankuk Seminary organized and started a separate Presbyterian denomination.

Another debilitating effect of the numerous divisions was the eroding of authority and discipline within the church. The option to start a new denomination enabled Korean Christians to bypass mechanisms of accountability within ecclesiastical standards. Without an overarching system of governance, individuals felt unfettered to pursue their own interests, a scenario which did not exist in the early twentieth century when missionaries exercised strict discipline among the ranks. For example, the Presbyterian missionary H. G. C. Hallock in 1902 noted how a Korean church leader "who was taking care of this whole district, fell into the sin of disobedience and deceit."[39] As a result, he "was suspended, and later excommunicated."[40]

The "most virulent schism of all" took place in 1959 when a minority group within the parent Presbyterian group, spurred on by Carl McIntyre, a "the *uber*-fundamentalist" renowned for creating schism, created a rival assembly and decided to split the church than to face charges of ethical misconduct.[41] Moffett wrote, "Fighting and shouting, the dissidents withdrew to form the Anti-Ecumenical Assembly that accused missionaries and Korean Christian leaders alike of heresy, pro-communism, and ecclesiastical vaticanism."[42] Unfortunately, the Protestant Church never overcame the

---

dissidents were supported by fundamentalists mission bodies related to the Orthodox and Bible Presbyterian schisms in America, which were all too eager to accuse other Presbyterians of liberalism" (Moffett, *Christians of Korea,* 114).

38. Moffett, *Christians of Korea,* 114.

39. Hallock, "Country Church in Korea," 119.

40. Hallock, "Country Church in Korea," 119.

41. Mcintyre "was the *uber*-fundamentalist, largely incapable of agreeing even with other fundamentalists." He and J. Gresham Machen separated from the Presbyterian Church for liberalism in the late 1920s and early 1930s but he felt Machen compromised and, when Machen died in 1937, he started his own church, the Bible Presbyterian Synod. In 1955, he "was ejected from this church because of his dictatorial leadership style" (Hendershot, "God's Angriest Man," 375).

42. Moffett, *Christians in Korea,* 115.

legacy of intra-church disputes and denominational splintering as outbreaks continue to occur since then.[43]

The complex legacy of discord and strife within the Church left many to wonder if the trauma of the Korean War, funding from abroad, or Western ecumenical rivalries were a factor. Others point to Western missions' "narrow oneness in their theological emphases," "doctrinaire creedalism that exalts orthodoxy at the expense of ethics," or Korea's regionalism and history of factionalism.[44] Whichever the motive, the pattern of discord has become a diasporic phenomenon as Korean immigrant churches in the United States experience similar creation of seceding congregations produced by internal conflicts and competition. On the other hand, Don Baker attributed Protestantism's "extraordinary surge" in Korea to the denominational schisms and break-ups since they created more opportunities for pastors, building of more churches, and, invariably, increase of church members. The creation of a new subdenomination, according to Baker, "built new churches and trained its own group of ministers to staff them." As a result, "over half of all halls of worship and 45 percent of all clergy in Korea were Protestant" by 1960.[45]

Despite the history of fragmentation that would seem to suggest a debilitating effect on Korean Christianity, the Korean Church maintained an evangelistic outward-looking approach that shaped the overall mission. In the aftermath of the widespread destruction caused during the Korean War, all Christian denominations embarked on a save-the-nation campaign, refugee relief activities, reunification efforts, and new efforts of revival and evangelism.[46] Kyung-chik Han, for example, formed the Christian National Salvation Assembly "to promote and coordinate patriotic relief activities among Christians."[47]

The Korean example remained one of the most successful mission fields in the modern period and in the post-War era Korean churches became a regional Protestant "superpower," especially in relation to mission

43. At the end of the twentieth century, there are "nearly one hundred different Protestant denominations and subdenominations" (Baker, "Sibling Rivalry," 283).

44. Moffett, *Christians in Korea,* 117–18.

45. "The 5,011 Protestant churches and 10,964 Protestant clergy that year [1960] gave the Protestant community a significant advantage over the Catholic Church, which had only 1,858 churches and 1,394 priests and there could not reach as many potential converts" (Baker, "Sibling Rivalry," 297).

46. For an examination of the Church's efforts in the unification movement, see Yi, "Korean Protestants and the Reunification Movement," 238–57; Min, "Division and Reunification," 258–79; Cho, "Christian Mission Toward Reunification," 376.

47. Haga, "Rising to the Occasion," 97.

work.[48] As an early sign of the increased prestige as a missionary-sending church, American Presbyterian missionaries in Ghana asked Samuel Hugh Moffett in 1960 for "lesson materials and textbooks available from the Korean experience in the [mission] field" and a Korean pastor or church leader to assist in the missionary activities.[49]

A 2006 article in *Christianity Today* stated that "South Korea sends more missionaries than any country but the US and it won't be long before it's number one."[50] According to the Korea World Missions Association, 26,677 Protestant missionaries from South Korea are working in 170 countries as of December 2014.[51] In comparison, only 93 missionaries were sent by Korean churches in 1979. Interestingly, the United States has become the mission field destination for many South Korean missionaries.[52] Although the number of missionaries sent by the Korean Catholic Church remains much smaller than the Protestants, it is increasing "about 10 percent annually."[53]

The academic literature on Korean Christianity tends to focus on the early decades of growth at the turn of the twentieth century and rightfully so considering that period as the origins of Protestantism but the Korean Protestant Church during the mid-1960s through the 1970s experienced the greatest growth. At the start of the Korean War in 1950, Protestant membership was 500,198.[54] Ten years later, the Protestant Church grew 24.6 percent to 623,072 in 1960. The 1960s represented the unprecedented expansion as the Protestant Church multiplied four-fold to 412.4 percent in 1970 with membership of 3,192,621.[55] Membership more than doubled fifteen years later with 6,489,242 in 1985.[56] In the other words, the Protestant population

48. Freston, *Evangelicals and Politics*, 61.

49. Yoo, *American Missionaries, Korean Protestants*, 213.

50. Moll, "Missions Incredible," 28–34.

51. Park, "Missionary Movement," 24.

52. In 2014, the University Bible Fellowship (UBF) sent the largest number of missionaries (1,740 missionaries in 93 countries) among all South Korean mission organizations (Park, "Missionary Movement," 25). The United States has become a critical destination for UBF missionaries. For an insightful study of the work of UBF on American college campuses, see Kim, *Spirit Moves West*.

53. "According to the 2012 Bishops' Conference, 183 Korean priests were engaged in mission to foreign nations and 400 more were serving the Korean diaspora. The number of Koreans serving overseas with missionary congregations—both founded in Korea and elsewhere—was around 700; the vast majority of them were religious sister" (K. Kim, "Significance of Korean World Mission," 48).

54. B. Kim, "Modernization and the Explosive Growth," 310–11.

55. B. Kim, "Modernization and the Explosive Growth," 310–11.

56. B. Kim, "Modernization and the Explosive Growth," 310–11.

during the Cold War and years of authoritarian rule in South Korea "doubled every decade."[57] However, in contemporary South Korea, the numbers have leveled off and signs of recession are appearing. According to the Korean National Statistical Office, in 2005, there were 8,616,438 Protestants or 18.3 percent of the population and 5,146,147 Catholics or 10.9 percent.[58]

SOCIAL JUSTICE AND MINJUNG THEOLOGY

On March 15, 1960, Syngman Rhee was elected president of South Korea for his fourth term but his presidency quickly unraveled in little more than a month after the elections when the brutal death of a seventeen-year old student demonstrator sparked a regional protest that spread nation-wide. The last straw was the government's shooting of unarmed student demonstrators that killed about 130 and wounding another 1,000 in Seoul alone.[59] Less than two months after the election, Rhee resigned on April 26, 1960. Myon Chang was elected Prime Minister of the Second Republic of South Korea on July 29 as the country adopted a parliamentary system of government as a way to curb abuses of presidential power as exhibited under Rhee's rule.

Less than a year later, Major General Park Chung-hee successfully led a military coup on May 16, 1961 that ended the Second Republic and proceeded to win elections as president. When Park was elected for the second time in 1967, he promised to abide by the 1963 Constitution that limited the presidency to two consecutive terms and step down in 1971. Park's party, the Democratic Republicans, however, successfully amended the Constitution to allow for three consecutive terms. In 1971, Park won the election for his third term but in December 1971 Park took steps to broaden his political power.[60] Having dissolved the legislature a month earlier, Park in November

57. Haga, "Rising to the Occasion," 104.

58. "According to a government report, there were 22,072 Buddhist temples, 60,785 Protestant churches, 2,386 Catholic cathedrals, 730 Confucian shrines, and 548 Won Buddhist temples. Alternatively, there were 41,362 Buddhist priests, 124,310 Protestant ministers, 13,704 Catholic priests, and 11,190 Won Buddhist priests in 2005" ("Today's Religious Situation in Korea," 674).

59. The seventeen-year-old "had apparently been struck and killed by a tear gas canister in March during one of the demonstrations against the elections, and his body had been dumped into the bay by the police to protect themselves from charges of brutality. This ghastly discovery, which immediately brought the citizens of Masan into the streets and into confrontation with the police, provided the spark that ignited the rest of the country" (Eckert et al., *Korea Old and New*, 354–55).

60. "The mounting criticisms and dissent against cold war orthodoxy did not change Park. To prevent South Korea from becoming 'another South Vietnam,' which had aligned with the United States only to be abandoned by it in the midst of military

1972 established the *Yushin* Constitution that expanded his authoritarian rule while eliminating limits on re-election. Park also enacted the Special Law for National Security, a law that gave a wide range of dictatorial powers. "With this special law, South Korea no longer had even a semblance of democracy."[61] Park's assassination in 1979 led to a series of political maneuvers by the military elite to fill the vacuum but in the end Major General Chun Doo-hwan outwrestled his rivals for power and usurped the office of president in a coup. Chun proceeded to dissolve Park's *Yushin* period by promulgating a new constitution in 1981.

It was during the era of *Yushin* Constitution, characterized as a dictatorial regime, that minjung ["people's"] theology was developed. Like liberation theology that originated from Latin America in reaction to the brutal authoritarian rule of military dictators and juntas, minjung theology addressed the social injustices of the common people during the *Yushin* period. The term "minjung" was used to identify with the disenfranchised masses.[62] Minjung was first used during the Joseon dynasty, according to Tong H. Moon, a minjung theologian, to describe everyone excluded from the oppressive and exclusive rule of the yangban or upper-class which was more than 90 percent of the population.[63] During the Japanese colonial pe-

conflict, Park called for 'recharging the security state.' Describing South Korea as in a state of war because the armistice of 1953 had not been replaced by a peace treaty among the warring parties of the Korean War, Park established new reserve forces 2.5-million-men strong to defend the rear area. The president also set up the Student Corps for National Defense with the goal of operating military training programs on campuses, and the defense industries were promoted as never before. Then, in December 1971, Park declared a state of emergency and enacted the Special Law for National Security" (Im, "Origins of the *Yushin* Regime," 253).

61. Im, "Origins of the *Yushin* Regime," 247. The special law gave Park "the power to declare a national emergency, to order economic emergency measures by presidential decree, to prohibit outdoor demonstrations, to restrict the freedoms of speech and the press, and to limit the collective action of workers" (Im, "Origins of the *Yushin* Regime," 247).

62. Inferences to liberation theology and Marxist thought in minjung theology are not a coincidence. "Furthermore, unlike their first-generation predecessors, many second-generation *minjung* theologians openly and programmatically borrow from Marxist theories as they construct their version of Minjung Theology" (W. Kim, "Minjung Theology's Biblical Hermeneutics," 227).

63. Moon in A. Park, "Minjung Theology," 2. While parallels with the Latin American experience exists, A. Sung Park sees more similarities with the American Black experience. Park writes, "The main of their [Latin American] oppression, however, comes from the economic dimension. The problems of the Korean Minjung, somewhat similar to those of the Black in the United States, cannot be solved by the elimination of poverty. Their problems are multi-dimensional. The Minjung are made up of political outcasts, laborers, women, the poor, the illiterate, the illegitimate, etc. The concept of 'Minjung' is broader than that of the Latin American poor" (A. Park, "Minjung

riod, every Korean was minjung except for those who profited from the system by colluding with the colonial government. The minjung of the *Yushin* period are the exploited, oppressed, impoverished, and dehumanized by the industrial and political elite that enrich themselves on the backs of the commoners.

During the Korean War, Korea was one of the poorest countries in the world as its GDP per capita in 1950 was about $60, a figure that was lower than Somalia or Ethiopia. From 1945 to the late 1960s, South Korea received in foreign aid a total of $13 billion as its main source of income but with rapid industrialization it became an aid donor, providing $696 million in 2007 and $803 million in 2008. In the process, South Korea became "the only nation that has converted itself from an international aid recipient to an aid donor."[64] By 1990, South Korea became the thirteenth largest economy in the world, joining the ranks of the G20—the meeting of the top twenty wealthiest countries in the world.[65] In 2010, South Korea became the first non-G8 member to host a G20 Summit.

Yet, the "Miracle on the Han River" presents a glossy front as the unprecedented economic growth mask the exploitation of laborers that enabled the miracle to take place. With low wages and long hours of work, as much as seventy hours a week, the laborers remained a marginalized, impoverished part of the population, without the skills and education needed to climb out of their condition while at the same time disadvantaged from acquiring those skills. Subjected to an unconstrained job competition that lacks security and protections, the laborers found themselves with minimal protection from the state. At the same time, attempts to fight against exploitation were met with punishment, including imprisonment.

The emotional connection with suffering, that Koreans term "han," lies at the heart of minjung theology. "Han" according to a renowned minjung poet Chi-Ha Kim "is Minjung's anger and sad sentiment turned inward, hardened and stuck to their hearts. Han is caused as one's outgoingness is blocked and pressed for an extended period of time by external oppression and exploitation."[66] Locating han as the source of theological inspiration,

---

Theology," 8).

64. Heo and Roehrig, *South Korea's Rise*, 26.

65. Heo and Roehrig, *South Korea's Rise*, 34.

66. Kim in A. Park, "*Minjung* Theology," 3. "While there is no English equivalent, han is often translated as sadness, sorrow, resentment, bitterness, grief, or regret. The term expresses both personal sorrow, such as hunger, poverty, discrimination, or serious illness, and "shared suffering" felt collectively as Koreans throughout history, for example from continual foreign invasions and occupations, including the exceptionally atrocious Japanese occupation (1910–1945)" (A. Kim, "*Minjung* Theology.")

minjung theologians explore the contextual tensions within Korea's cultural and historical complexity to bring about transformation in constructing God's kingdom.

When Chun became president, he continued the authoritarian practices of his predecessor, most notably his crackdown of demonstrators in the city of Gwangju where in 1980 over 2,000 people were killed. The structures of oppressive political power became the focus of minjung activists as they locked arms with the democratic movement against authoritarian regimes. Criticizing the government over autocratic policies and abuses in human rights became precarious and "most [minjung theologians] were forced out of their positions in universities, Christian seminaries, and social movement organizations."[67]

As the socio-political reality in South Korea has changed over time, minjung theology "has turned its attention to more contemporary issues, such as socioeconomic polarization and the human rights of foreign migrant workers and marriage migrants."[68] In the 1990s and 2000s, the political outlook brightened as South Korea became more democratic and, as a result, interest in minjung theology has waned but minjung theology has gained credence in the theological literature, especially in relation to liberation theology.[69] Many theological scholars have cited minjung theology as an Asian example of contextual local theologies developed in the Global South, such as dalit theology.[70] Others view minjung theology as an example

67. Chang, "Carrying the Torch," 204.

68. A. Kim, "*Minjung* Theology."

69. Simon Chan noted the limitations of contextual theology. "Many Asian theologies appear to be caught in a time warp because of the way they define the theological task. If the theologian's task is essentially a reflection on context—whether social, political or economic—such an approach can ostensibly produce interesting theologies if one believes that the various contexts are where God is at work. For instance, M. M. Thomas's reflection on the Asian Revolution in the 1960s and '70s was predicated on the belief that the Asian Revolution was where God was working to prepare Asians for the gospel. Asian theologies of liberation are similarly predicated. But time and again these theologians have been proven wrong—sometimes terribly wrong (as we have seen in Song and Ting)" (Chan, *Grassroots Asian Theology*, 25). Chan also critiqued minjung theology for its elitist outlook. Minjung theology "promotes the views of the intelligentsia and largely ignores the views of the ordinary people themselves, especially the ordinary members of the church. It's the elite theologians who define the problem of the Minjung and decide what they really need: their problem is that they are victims of an oppressive social system, and what they need is a certain kind of political liberation. . . . But if the Minjung should desire a more spiritual kind of liberation, or if Asian women should desire to pursue the ideal of motherhood and family, they are accused of having 'false consciousness' and therefore all the more in need of liberation" (Chan, *Grassroots Asian Theology*, 27).

70. Minjung theology is frequently included in the discussion of global contextual

of the theological struggle for liberation along the lines of black theology or feminist/womanist theology.[71]

CONTEMPORARY KOREA

Recent surveys and studies on religion in Korea depict a gloomy picture of the state of Protestantism. A Gallup Korea poll in 2015 found that 69 percent of Koreans in their twenties expressed no religious belief which 14-percentage-point higher ten years earlier in 2005 when 45 percent professed belief.[72] The survey reflects in part the recognition in the Protestant community that the Protestantism may have reached a plateau despite ongoing evangelistic efforts. Young-hoon Lee, the successor to David Yonggi Cho at Yoido Full Gospel Church admitted that "right now [in 2017], we have a little slowdown and stagnation period," in reference to Christianity in contemporary Korea.[73]

The news that Protestant membership decreased by 140,000 from 1995 to 2005 sent shockwaves in the community that had long been accustomed to evangelism and growth. "The current crisis of Korean Christianity" is the sentiment share by many in the Protestant community and it acknowledges the sense of urgency and immediacy necessary to accomplish the church's mission.[74] The phrase "a deep recession and slowdown" was used to describe the current dilemma in the Protestant Church by a scholar who concluded that the "church crisis of decline is entrenched by the immaturity of psychological and spiritual development among Church leaders and laity."[75] An-

---

theologies. "Soon, 'contextual' theologies, advocating social equality and economic justice, emerged across the continents, wherever Christian people began to read the Bible through liberation lenses: Anti-apartheid theology in South Africa and Namibia, *Minjung* theology in Korea, *Dalit* theology in India, and Palestinian liberation theology" (Nessan, *Vitality of Liberation Theology*, xiv–xv. "Minjung theology is one of the most provocative and challenging theologies to emerge in recent years" (Paul, *Ubuntu God*, 101). "The dynamic definition of *Minjung* can include Deaf people as subject to hearing people and so we, like *Minjung* theologians, can look for *Minjung* in the Bible as a people with whom we can identify and whose stories can engage with ours" (Lewis, *Deaf Liberation Theology*, 130).

71. "Both black theology and *minjung* theology emerged in periods of protest. . . . *Minjung* and black theology, Roberts asserts, focus on the experience of suffering and connected with suffering is the theme of theodicy" (Smith, "Minjung," 207–8).

72. Cho, "More South Koreans."

73. Bell, "Biggest Megachurch on Earth."

74. Choi, "Christian Worldview," 188.

75. Son, "Crisis of Church Decline," 575. Not only is Korean Christianity experiencing a slowdown, but also Koreans are beginning to view Christianity as an "unreliable

other argued that "Korean Protestant churches need to stop producing more seminary students than needed and must carefully plan church planting."[76] A sociologist of religion argued that "the crisis of Korean [Protestant] churches is in the loss of spirituality, morality, and communalism."[77] The missiologist Joon-sik Park states that Protestantism's response so far "have been reactive and shallow; the churches have not yet engaged in the critical theological self-reflection necessary for the renewal of the church at a more fundamental level."[78]

The situation has prompted soul-searching and introspection, provoking conversations and challenging perspectives on the state of the church. The situation is regarded for the most part as self-inflicted and self-perpetuated. The top-five responses to a Gallup Korea survey about the state of the Korean Protestant church revealed insightful findings: 91.9 percent said too many pseudo-religious churches exist; 87.9 percent pointed to church splits; 84.7 percent cited fighting over church finances; 79.6 percent cited the low quality of pastors; and 79.6 percent mentioned that church expansion, including buildings, is prioritized above the search for truth.[79]

The recent scandals involving some of the megachurches, including Yoido Full Gospel Church, have tarnished the prestige and trustworthiness of Protestant Christianity.[80] In 2017, a Korean feature movie titled "Romans 8:37" depicted a large fictional church in which two powerful pastors fought for control over the church's vast wealth and political influence. As the tug-of-war compelled church members to pick a side, the church divided into two camps and each side waged a vicious battle that included tactics such as allegations of embezzlement, bribery, sexual abuse, and even heresy. The movie, while fictional, sheds light on many of the structural problems that are contributing to internal stress and social marginalization. For one, the lack of accountability and oversight has created little fiefdoms whereby local autonomous jurisdictions operate independently, immune or oblivious to how harmful public perception may damage the overall effectiveness of the church. Keun-Won Park critiqued the easy adoption of intra-church competition within the Protestant community. Park wrote, "The preoccupation with numbers of converts and church buildings has brought us

religion."

76. Chung, "Reflection on the Growth and Decline," 332.

77. Lee, *Crisis and Hope of Korean Churches*, 7.

78. Park, "Korean Protestant Christianity," 59.

79. Gallup Korea in Kim, "Modernization and the Explosive Growth," 327.

80. In a highly publicized case, David Yonggi Cho of the Yoido Full Gospel Church was convicted in 2014 of embezzling $12 million from the church. His sentence was suspended but his son was sent to jail.

to a point where churches often attempt to lure members away from other congregations. On account of these practices, the Christian church today is again experiencing a loss of credibility, particular among non-Christians, who are highly critical of the 'salesmanlike' methods adopted in soliciting converts."[81]

A senior pastor of a small church in Seoul stated, "The general public in Korean society, they do not trust Christians anymore."[82] While the statement may sound extreme, there is evidence to suggest that Protestantism is suffering from the worst public perception in its history. A 2017 survey released by the Korean National Association of Christian Pastors revealed the approval rating for Protestantism was 9.5 percent; for Buddhism, 40.6 percent; and Catholicism, 37.6 percent.[83] When asked what they perceived to be the biggest challenges for churches, 24 percent cited "self-interested pastors" and 16 percent mentioned "self-centeredness" and "focusing far too much on expanding in size."[84] The survey asked non-Protestants how they viewed the Protestant church and the words "selfish," "materialistic," and "authoritarian" were commonly expressed.[85]

These characteristics stand in sharp contrast to more than half-century ago when Korean Christians were known for their selflessness, commitment to the highest ideals,[86] perseverance through suffering, heroism, and defiance against the Japanese empire. For example, under the dark cloud of

81. "Non-Christians perceive Christians as fighting a battle between evangelism and mission. As it is often expressed humor, much to our embarrassment: 'Jesus is fighting with Christ.' This is due in part, of course, to the fact that the major Presbyterian denomination has divided in the Jesus and Christ denominations. We hear of denominations accusing others of heresy and most unfortunately there is little cooperation in mission among churches, even among churches belonging to the same denomination" (Park, "Evangelism and Mission in Korea," 102).

82. Bell, "Biggest Megachurch on Earth."

83. Yim, "Sadly, Churches in South Korea."

84. Yim, "Sadly, Churches in South Korea."

85. Yim, "Sadly, Churches in South Korea."

86. "The Korean Protestant church has had a long tradition of human liberation, dating from the early years of its mission. Therefore, those who long for basic human rights and individual freedom tend to look to the Korean church tradition for human liberation. This tradition of human rights activities has continued in various Protestant organizations such as the National Council of Churches (NCC), Urban Industrial Mission, Korean Christian Student Federation (KCSF), and YMCA, and more. Such human rights activities initiated by the church organizations have increased the institutional credibility and public support among a wide range of people—intellectuals, university students, and common people, especially factory workers, laborers, and women, who had been oppressed under the patriarchic system" (B. Kim, "Modernization and the Explosive Growth," 324–25).

the *Yushin* Constitution, pastors and church leaders created the 1973 Theological Declaration of Korean Christians that challenged Park's authoritarian government and specifically the National Security Law that curbed democratic procedures and human rights. Knowing full well the possible outcome of challenging their authoritarian government, the Declaration directly confronted Park's *Yushin* system as it stated: "The present dictatorship in Korea is destroying rule by Law and persuasion. . . . Our present position is that no one is above the law except God. . . . If anyone poses himself above the law and betrays the divine mandate for justice, he is in rebellion against God. The present regime is destroying freedom of religion."[87]

While the Protestant Church faces a formidable challenge in the foreseeable future, the Catholic Church on the other hand has fared better. As Protestantism's luster is fading, Catholicism is characterized as progressive, anti-regime, above corruption, and more democratic.[88] Although Korean Catholics during the Japanese colonial period remained "passive" and accepted Shrine ceremonies as patriotic rituals, the authoritarian regime during the *Yushin* Constitution awoke Korean Catholics' consciousness.[89] In the 1970s, Bishop Haksun Chi suffered arrests and beatings for his opposition to the *Yushin* system but he remained steadfast in resistance, a posture that inspired fellow Catholics including the future president Kim Dae-jung who was kidnapped while in Japan and nearly executed if not for the international pressure upon the Park administration to relent.

As an example, Chun Doo-hwan, who succeeded Park, "waged a large-scale war against Catholics" after Catholics priests offered refuge to those responsible for the 1982 Busan United States Information Service (USIS) Arson Incident. Kim Dae-jung wrote, "At first, the Catholic Priests

87. Chang, "Carrying the Torch," 214.

88. The poor reputation of Korean Protestantism "has reached the all-time low of its century-long presence. Indeed, a survey regarding perceptions of Korea's Protestant churches found that both Protestant church-goers and the rest of the Korean population agree in perceiving a preoccupation with: quantitative growth; too many denominations and a lack of co-operation amongst churches; church individualism; and the churches' inability to provide their members with practical support and guidance for everyday life. Protestant church-goers further expressed the view that clergy are greedy and self-centered" (Han et al., "Serving Two Masters," 334).

89. Don Baker notes the peculiar reversal in reputation. During the Japanese colonial period, "Catholic missionaries, for their part, appeared to prefer to keep their flock isolated from the temptations of the secular world and there did not have as many followers with modern ideas such as nationalism. . . . Over the course of the thirty-five years Japan ruled Korea, there were several incidents in which Catholics sat on the sidelines while Protestants stepped into the front ranks of the forces fighting against Japanese attempts to force Koreans to act the way Japanese wanted them to act" (Baker, "Sibling Rivalry," 294).

Association did not get involved. But, as the fact that the police brutality tortured the arrested and distorted facts about the incident became known, religious leaders confronted the regime head-on."[90]

The Korean Catholic Church reached a milestone in 1974 when it reached a million members. In a little more than ten years, Catholic membership increased to nearly two million in 1985. From 1985 to 1995, the number of Catholics grew more than 50 percent (1,865,397 in 1985 to 2,951,000 in 1995).[91] In the ten-year period from 1995 to 2005, the number of Protestants declined 1.6 percent to 8,616,000. In contrast, Korean Catholics in the same period increased by 74.4 percent, from 2,951,000 to 5,146,000.[92]

Recent statistics however have documented a decline which has caught the attention of the Catholic leadership. On April 13, 2018, the Catholic Bishops' Conference of Korea (CBCK) release figures that represent "the slowest rate of growth in the last decade, leaving church authorities concerned about a continued wind-down."[93] *The Union of Catholic Asian News* reported that "the number of [Catholic] baptisms has steadily declined since 2008 [except 2014]."[94] In addition, the information indicates that more Korean Catholics are elderly as 18.4 percent are aged 65 or older while two years earlier 12.6 percent were 65 and older. In 2017, 19.4 percent fewer people attended mass compared to the previous year.[95]

CONCLUSION

Young-hoon Lee who succeeded David Yonggi Cho in 2008 as the senior pastor of Yoido Full Gospel Church, the world's largest congregation, delivered a sermon in 2017 in which he stated that he regularly prays for North Korea and how its survival depends upon people there believing in Christ. Then he mentioned South Korea's prosperity, referring to the rising income levels, and pointing out that South Korea's prosperity was the outcome of Christians in the South praying and exercising their faith.[96]

90. Kim, *Conscience in Action*, 276.
91. Park, "Korean Protestant Christianity," 59.
92. Park, "Korean Protestant Christianity," 59.
93. "South Korean Church Frets."
94. "South Korean Church Frets."
95. "South Korean Church Frets."
96. Bell, "Biggest Megachurch on Earth."

Lee's anti-North Korea and pro-capitalism message is not surprising when considering that South Korea's Protestant establishment since the Korean War remained staunch anti-communist and, in response to communist ideology, embraced capitalism in part to demonstrate the impotency of communism. The decision for church leaders, at least in the beginning, was an ideological one to counterbalance what they viewed was an evil system in power.

Many Protestant church leaders, such as Kyung-chik Han, witnessed first-hand communists' reign of terror in the north before they fled to the south as refugees. In the decades that followed, they waged a single-minded campaign against communism, especially those in South Korea that harbored sympathy toward communist North Korea or antagonism toward US military presence in South Korea. However, this ideological posture has its costs.

On June 13, 2002, an anti-American backlash was unleashed after a US Army armored vehicle struck and killed two Korean fourteen-year old schoolgirls. A US court martial acquitted the American soldiers involved of negligent homicide and public anger against the American military boiled over into rallies, vigils, and boycotts. Demonstrators hurled firebombs into a US military base and the protest received widespread domestic and international coverage. "Priests, monks and entertainers" participated in the growing protests.[97] "The leader of the South Korean Catholic Priests' Association for Justice (CPAJ), Reverend Kyu-hyun Mun, told a rally that the road accident had led many to question the very presence of US forces."[98]

On the other hand, the Protestant Koreans conducted a counter-demonstration against the protestors. The General Association of Christian Organizations, a Christian umbrella group, organized a rally attended by 30,000 mostly Protestant Christians in front of Seoul City Hall to condemn the anti-American demonstration and to oppose the withdrawal of US troops from Korea. The counter-demonstration, led by a clear anti-North Korea, pro-America position, held up posters that read: "We oppose the anti-American movement" and "Lord, give North Korea real political change."[99]

For many Koreans in South Korea, the Protestant Christians' actions seemed reactionary and out-of-touch but the position taken by church leaders remained unchanged since the Korean War. As a result, Korean Protestants became intensely anti-North Korea and viewed the US as an

97. "Anti-US Protests Grow in Seoul."
98. "Anti-US Protests Grow in Seoul."
99. Lee, "Tens of Thousands."

indispensable ally that fought for South Korea's freedom from what would have been a certain conquest of Korea by North Korean communists. "Following the Korean War, South Koreans came to view the Americans as saviors, and the Americans' religion, Christianity, as a source of strength and wealth."[100]

The unwavering belief in economic prosperity and anti-communism served as crucial counter-weights against a threatening neighbor. When the Korean War concluded in 1953, North Korea's economy for the first two-decades after the War actually thrived and gave North Korea "an impressive rate of economic growth far beyond that of the South," a fact that may surprise people, especially considering North Korea's GDP per capita is $2,000 today, one of the lowest in the world.[101] Comparatively, South Korea's GDP per capita broke through the $2,000 barrier only in 1983, but then it increased on a torrent pace. It broke $10,000 in 1994 and $20,000 in 2006. South Korea's GDP per capita is on the cusp of exceeding $30,000 as South Korea concluded 2017 with $29,742.

In other words, North Korea's economy was superior to South Korea in the years following the Korean War. The fact that the Korean War ended with an armistice (and not a peace treaty) exacerbated the sense of inferiority as the countries remained technically still at war. Rising to the occasion, the Protestant Christians claimed the mantle of promoting national security and prosperity by preaching economic growth to the aspiring middle-class, endorsing measures to improve heavy industries, and pushing governmental policies that kept a hardline against North Korea. The Protestants viewed the authoritarian regimes of the 1960s and 1970s with alarm but—at least, in the minds of many Protestants—the South Korean military leaders stood solidly alongside the US with an anti-communist and pro-industrialization platform.

However, the political reality has shifted considerably in South Korea in the decades after the Korean War. The Cold War has ended. The

100. Hazzan, "Christianity and Korea."

101. "Two years after liberation, North Korea embarked on an ambitious project of planned economic growth, concentrating on construction, steel, chemicals, mining, and other heavy industries. The regime remained committed to the Stalinist path of production thereafter. For more than twenty years, a program of heavy industry, limited consumer goods, withdrawal from the capitalist world-economy, and planned production seemed to work well, giving North Korea an impressive rate of economic growth far beyond that of the South. By the 1970s, however, such a development path was showing limited returns, and by the 1990s the North Korean economy was in a seemingly intractable state of crisis. The very success of the planned economy in its early years contributed to the difficulty of economic reform in the DPRK in the decades to come" (Armstrong, *North Korean Revolution*, 137).

former-Soviet Union has collapsed. Communist China has abandoned Maoist economic policies for capitalism. North Korea is not the grave threat that it once was and the prospect of a war on the peninsula appears less likely than in the past. A major reason for the lessening of the North Korean threat has been South Korea's economic and democratic transformation that has placed an embarrassing contrast on North Korea's poverty and abuses.

In many ways, the Protestant Christians' prayers have been answered but their uncontested acceptance of economic prosperity has been questioned. What is the church's mission after a strong middle-class has been achieved? What is Protestant Christianity's response to its perception "as a religion of individual success and national prosperity"?[102] "The core of the teaching in the Protestant church," one Korean church scholar wrote, "was recognized as enjoying material blessings and prosperity by accepting Christ as Lord."[103]

The nation-wide destruction of the Korean War often served as the basis for the pursuit of economic prosperity but what do you do when the country manufactures luxury cars, builds one of the most sophisticated cell phones, and leads the world in many sectors of technology? The uncritical promotion of wealth has led to a host of unintended and unforeseen consequences on the overall health of churches and Christians. The problematic dynamics of growth-minded expansionism that elevates quantity over quality necessitate a reassessment of the notions that have been carrying on uncritically since the mid-twentieth century.

The excesses brought on by materialism and greed has been the target of criticism by Protestant scholars and church leaders.[104] The decline in Korean Protestantism is attributed to "the 'impossible' task of serving two masters—God and money."[105] The Korean Protestant church, according to Byong-suh Kim, "is now too big and too rich." Kim explained, "It became overly materialistic, oriented to the accumulation of wealth and expansion of church properties. Nonbelievers no longer look up to the church as the institution they can resort to for solutions to their problems. They consider big organizations to be self-serving, guilty of collective selfishness."[106] Young-gi Hong referred to the adoption of church growth strategy and theology in Korean Protestantism as "McDonalization" in which the

---

102. J. Kim, "Christianity and Korean Culture," 134.

103. J. Kim, "Christianity and Korean Culture," 134.

104. Park criticizes the "predominately commercial and materialistic thinking within the Korean church" (Park, "Evangelism and Mission in Korea," 103).

105. Han et al., "Serving Two Masters," 334.

106. B. Kim, "Modernization and the Explosive Growth," 326.

"preference for what is big" prevails.[107] Under such free-market-like conditions, churches are compelled to "compete against one another to achieve a
larger slice of the religious market share in an uncertain society."[108]

As the mega-churches compete to enlarge their fold and to build a
larger facility with the latest technological advances, the situation exacer-
bates the inequality among churches as the gap between the 'haves-and-
have-nots' widen. Church leaders are driven to increase their flock as the
church size implicitly communicates success. In a Darwinistic turn, the
culture breeds a 'survival-of-the-fittest' mentality in which neighboring
churches are viewed as rivals and competitors instead of as a collective missional undertaking.

The churches in South Korea face numerous challenges but it is easy
for forget that Korean churches in the last years under Japanese colonialism
lost their autonomy when they were assimilated and merged into the "Korean Christian Church of Japanese Christianity." As a result, the Japanese
government controlled and regulated all Korean churches. Furthermore,
the dominance of Japanese Shinto over the Korean Christian church was
illustrated by an incident that Samuel Hugh Moffett recounted as "a bizarre
and frightening spectacle." A Shinto priest "led a procession of Christian
pastors to the Han River for the opening ceremony of purification."[109]

After Korean liberation, the multiplication of denominations caused
by conflict and disagreements may partly reflect the fierce resistance to
oversight fostered during the Japanese colonial period. The propensity of
Korean churches to divide is just one of numerous characteristics of Korean
Christianity in the twentieth century. Despite the many problems, Korean
churches have accomplished something rare: an Asian country as one of
the top missionary-sending countries in the world. Korean Christianity has
become a crucial factor in world missions. For example, China is projected
to be the world's largest Christian country by 2050 and Korean missionaries
made their mark by training and strengthening Chinese Christians.

As Philip Jenkins noted in *The Next Christendom*, the global landscape
of Christianity has been transformed by profound regional shifts which is
not to say that Christianity in North America and Europe will disappear but
the most vigorous growth is occurring in the Global South. As the Korean
experience indicates, the growth of Christianity in the Global South is not
without controversy. However, the future of World Christianity appears
more unpredictable than ever. The diverse cultural landscape of churches

107. Hong, "Encounter with Modernity," 243.

108. Hong, "Encounter with Modernity," 243.

109. Moffett, *Christians of Korea*, 75.

around the world presents a multi-directional trajectory that will be difficult to coalesce but, as long as churches remain faithful to the core message, the diverse expressions of faith will continue to manifest itself most visibly from areas of the world where it has been most intensely engaged.

May 5-7, 1939, Kauai. Christian Young People's Council.

Founded in 1921, the Korean Methodist Church and Institute in New York City is one of the oldest Korean churches in the United States. The South Korean government recognized the church as an overseas historic site for its political role in Korean history. In the first decades of the church, political activism was central to the church's identity as some of the most important overseas political figures, such as the future president Syngman Rhee, attended the church.

Conclusion

IN THE INAUGURAL 1917 issue of *The Korea Magazine*, the founding editors, S. A. Beck (Methodist), James S. Gale (Presbyterian), W. G. Cram (Methodist), and W. A. Noble (Methodist), recounted an important visit from the Board of Foreign Missions, an organization that sets the broad agenda, holds missionaries accountable, and oversees the work of missionaries around the world. During their visit to Korea, a question was asked to the Board, "What do you regard as the greatest lack on the part of the missionary?" "Quick and incisive" was the answer: "A knowledge of the people among whom he lives."[1]

The Board member's response indicates the deficiency of local knowledge of the people to whom missionaries seek to serve. For one, the inadequacy exposes the limited awareness in understanding or responding to contingencies in the native church. In addition, the inattention to local knowledge shifts the attention away to missional strategies and personnel, resulting in the over-reliance of external forces as the primary missional actor without taking into account the cardinal role played by the conditions experienced by those on the receiving end. Certainly strategies and approaches are important to missional work but from what ideological position was it formed? Who is speaking, from what part of the world, and with what presumptions about the respective native culture?

---

1. "The Magazine makes no pretension to possessing any superior knowledge, but it is sincerely interested in the East, and has an earnest desire to aid in its interpretation. We, Occidentals, must remember that the Far East represents the oldest civilization in the world, a civilization that has come down by a continuous line, not through centuries only, but through long millenniums, and surely nothing could be more interesting or profitable to those who desire to deal with the mind and spirit of a race, than to read into their souls and to see what their ideals are, what their hopes, their fears, their longings. This is the wish of the MAGAZINE, to interpret sympathetically the great world in which we live, and of (3) which we really know so little. It is not too much to say that while we modestly think we have something to teach Asia, we must also admit that Asia has much to teach us" (*Korea Magazine*, 2).

Terraculturalism transcends the limitations of missional methodologies by taking seriously ethnographic distinctions and the artifacts of local cultures. Terraculturalism assumes the premise that a religious vacuum does not exist anywhere. Centuries of cultural development, building layers upon layers of complex traditions inform the religious landscape.

Terraculturalism makes visible the process taking place in the native soil from the environment's perspective. It reveals the challenges of cross-cultural engagement as it attempts to examine underlying social pressures and cultural expectations. The incorporation of cultural footings into missional interpretations allows for thematic resonances that produce creative expressions of the gospel in local contexts. Recognizing the cultural pillars that form their self-understanding, the work of examining points of contact could be identified, discerned, and explored for application.

Terraculturalism analyzes how deep attachments to particular ideals create responses to the different aspects of the Christian message. In this book, for example, the devotion to sacred writings and nationalistic concerns was examined as important points of contact between missionaries and Koreans. The missionaries on the whole dismissed demonology and spirit cosmology as superstition but the visible manifestation of the superiority of the Christian God over demons was the tipping point for many Koreans to believe in Christianity. Even though missionaries did not present the gospel as the liberator to demonic oppression, Koreans nevertheless found the claims of Christianity more truthful and convincing after the Christian God demonstrated authority over their demons and gods. Not enough recognition is given to native church workers, especially Bible Women, who, having keen awareness of the power of Korean folk religions, fought a spiritual battle on the frontlines.

Once known as the "hermit kingdom" for its isolationism, Korea from the late nineteenth century faced overwhelming pressures from global powers. The start of international trade and transnational networks also opened the opportunity for Koreans to migrate to Hawaii as laborers on the sugar plantations. From 1903 to 1905, thousands of Koreans established residency in Hawaii, marking the start of Korean American history.[2] As Korean Americans migrated to the West Coast and to other urban areas, churches became the center of the burgeoning communities, especially after the 1965 Immigration Act that opened an unprecedented number of Korean immigrants to the United States.

---

2. Scholars separate three distinct periods in Korean American history. While scholars vary on the start of the second period, they unanimously agree that the year 1903 marked the beginning of Korean American history. See Yoo and Chung, *Religion and Spirituality*, 2; Choy, *Koreans in America*; Kim, *Korean Diaspora*.

Throughout Korean American history, the Protestant church became a powerful symbol of community, uniting Korean immigrants in their efforts to aid Korean independence to supporting immigrants in adjusting to life in America. In the decades following 1903, the church became the primary institution in the fight against Japanese colonialism. Korean preachers stirred nationalistic passions and raised considerable funds for Korean independence. From the 1970s, when Koreans by the tens of thousands entered the United States each year, the church evolved into an important ethnic institution within a racialized American society. While the Korean church preserved ethnic identity, the church also played an important role in assisting immigrants in assimilating to American culture.

The Korean American experience illustrates how Christianity became the majority religion of immigrants. The collective consciousness, centered on the family, was noticed by the Methodist missionary Minerva Guthapfel in 1906 who found it "strange and an inspiring sight to see Koreans coming into the church by families."[3] The missionaries in Korea noticed a similar pattern: Koreans viewed conversion to Christianity as more than an individual act; conversion and church participation involved the whole family. Guthapfel wrote, "Missionaries in Korea see this so frequently that it ceases to be strange and becomes the end toward which faith and effort are put forth."[4]

The collective familial consciousness so evident among Christians in Korea was now expanded into an ethnic consciousness among Korean immigrants who lived in a diverse American society. The missionary Lulu Miller in 1909 recounted the story of a Korean Christian who suffered persecution from his family three years ago as a result of his conversion. "But now," he proudly declared, "my whole family believes in Jesus Christ and six families in the neighborhood have also become Christians. . . . The Wednesday night and Sunday services are held in one of the rooms of our home."[5]

Korea's Confucian culture reinforced through its rituals and principles a strong social fabric that tied one's affection and obligation to their family. From the Korean Catholics in the late eighteenth century to recent Korean immigrants in the United States, converts immediately turned to their families to bring Christianity to their attention. While all societies recognize the importance of families, Korean Confucianism generated a commitment to one's family that, at times, exceeded one's own personal concerns.

---

3. Guthapfel, "How They Come," 82.

4. Guthapfel, "How They Come," 82.

5. Miller, "Over Charcoal Fire." 173.

In Korean culture, folk stories abound with tales of sons and daughters who with ardent filial affection sacrificed their own welfare for the betterment of one's parents and siblings. In the twentieth century, as Koreans immigrate to the United States, familial collectivism continues to be integral to a widely shared cultural understanding. In the 1970s, for example, the percentage of Korean immigrant families with children was higher than "any other Asian group."[6] As Koreans had done earlier, Korean immigrants joined churches in America which in many ways became an enlargement of the familial ideal.

1903–1905 HAWAIIAN PLANTATIONS

In 1903, the *SS Gaelic* was the first ship that transported Koreans to Hawaii but that voyage almost never happened due to the lack of interest among Koreans despite promotions by the American recruiter that advertised Hawaii's lush tropical climate and the opportunity to earn wages while working on the sugar plantations. No one signed up. Koreans remained "suspicious and 'believed only a fraction' of what they heard."[7] Who knew if they were telling the truth? What would really happen on that strange, exotic land? No Korean had ever migrated so far from home. They would be leaving their families behind. Who would do the ancestral rites?

The "unknowns" were too much and the migration might not have ever happened if not for the intervention of George Heber Jones, a Methodist missionary who played a crucial role in Korean American history. Jones was coincidentally stationed in Incheon, the port-city where he became well-known and established a church. The sociologist In-Jin Yoon wrote, "The intervention of the Reverend George H. Jones of the Methodist Episcopal Church of Incheon was crucial in overcoming the initial resistance."[8] Not only did Jones allay fears of the migration and encourage his church members to go but Jones, who was "very fluent" in Korean, began to promote it to the people of Incheon.[9] "Of all American missionaries," wrote

6. Ryu, "Koreans in America," 216.

7. Patterson, *Korean Frontier in America*, 48. According to Patterson, "For some, fear of the unknown was an inhibiting factor, most having never been far from home. Others hesitated because they thought ill of leaving their relatives and deserting the graves of their ancestors. Still others feared the distances involved; it was one thing to emigrate north to the Vladivostok area but quite another to cross several thousand miles of the Pacific Ocean, perhaps never to return" (Patterson, *Korean Frontier in America*, 48–49).

8. Yoon, *On My Own*, 51–52.

9. Soon Hyun, who attended Jones's church, recalled that Jones "could speak the

the sociologist Hyung-chan Kim, "Reverend George Heber Jones of the Methodist missions was the most influential with Korean emigrants."[10]

In the end, more than fifty members of his church and twenty workers from the Incheon port-city decided to be the first group to travel overseas.[11] On a Monday in December 1902, when Koreans gathered at the Incheon seaport to await the arrival of their ship, Jones set up "tents" to give them training and orientation of life overseas as well as giving the departing group prayers and words of encouragement as they were about to embark on a historical journey. Jones wanted "to inspire them with laudable ambitions and prepare them for the strange experiences so soon to overtake them."[12] Before Jones gave "them in parting his heartfelt blessing," he gave the leaders of the group "letters of introduction to the Superintendent of Methodist Missions in Hawaii."[13] Jones had already alerted the Methodist missions in Hawaii of their impending arrival but the letters provided additional means of support and extended the transnational Methodist connection.

Onboard the SS Gaelic were 102 Korean passengers, 51 of whom were from Jones's Nairi Methodist Church in Incheon. During the ten-day voyage across the Pacific Ocean, the Korean Christians held Christian services in the ship's steerage where people were "herded together in the three-tiered bunks, sweating, vomiting, and eliminating."[14] Despite being cramped into the "dark steerage hold of a ship," they evangelized fellow Koreans as they "carried on Christian work among their fellow emigrants."[15] As a result of their influence, eight Koreans converted during the trip. With eight persons added to their fold, a total of fifty-eight out of the 102 were Christians.[16] The Korean Christians abroad the SS Gaelic set a precedent as Christians traveling to Hawaii on successive trip across the Pacific shared their testimony. There was "at least one Christian minister," according to Korean witnesses, "who gave inspiration and hope to the despairing immigrants . . . on every immigrant ship that carried Koreans to Hawaii."[17]

Korean language very fluently" (Soon Hyun in Patterson, *Korean Frontier in America*, 49).

   10. Kim, "History and Role of the Church," 49.

   11. Patterson, *Korean Frontier in America*, 49.

   12. Wadman, "Educational Work among Koreans," 146.

   13. Wadman, "Educational Work among Koreans," 146.

   14. Pai, *Dreams of Two Yi Min*, 34.

   15. Patterson, *Korean Frontier in America*, 50.

   16. Jones, *Korea*, 108.

   17. Choy, *Koreans in America*, 97.

After the *SS Gaelic*, recruiting became easier. With a group already in Hawaii and proof of satisfactory conditions, as evidenced by pictures of satisfied Koreans taken in Hawaii, nearly a dozen recruiting offices were opened "throughout Korea by 1905."[18] However, the geo-political situation made Korean emigration to Hawaii short-lived, as the transportation of Koreans to Hawaii ended in 1905 when Korea forfeited authority over its foreign affairs when Japan became Korea's protectorate.[19]

Japan's decision to stop the Korean migration to Hawaii was motivated in large part to assist the large Japanese population already in working on the Hawaiian plantations. By 1894 the Japanese became three-fifths of the total labor force on the Hawaiian plantations.[20] In 1902, of the 42,242 sugar cane workers, Japanese laborers numbered 31,029, or 73.5 percent of the total sugarcane plantation population.[21] Making up nearly three-quarters of the total labor population, Japanese laborers began to strike for better wages and conditions. Instead of negotiating with the Japanese, the plantation association recruited Koreans to diversify and divide the labor population. By 1905, Koreans represented one of the smallest ethnic groups in Hawaii's labor pool but they made up eleven percent of the total plantation workforce.[22]

Although the migration of Korean laborers to Hawaii ceased in 1905, Japan permitted Korean women or "picture brides" to Hawaii afterwards. In all, an estimated 1,100 "picture brides" emigrated to Hawaii and mainland US.[23] Among the "picture brides," a significant number were Christians. In Louise Yim's autobiography, she recounted Pastor Kim hosting a Korean matchmaker from Hawaii at his home. Yim and her classmates, who attended a Christian mission school for girls in the Korean town of Jeonju, received the offer of marriage from the matchmaker who showed pictures of the bachelors and described life on the Hawaiian plantations.[24] Although Yim declined the offer that she described as "tempting," especially given the opportunity to escape life under Japanese colonialism, two of Yim's

---

18. Choy, *Koreans in America*, 92.

19. The Protectorate Treaty "was imposed on the Korean government virtually at gunpoint, thereby raising questions about its legality. It placed the external affairs of Korea under Japanese direction and management" (Ch'oe et al., *Sources of Korean Tradition*, 2:289).

20. See Conroy, *Japanese Expansion into Hawaii*, 145–46.

21. Yun, "Early History of Korean Immigration," 39.

22. Yoo, "Nurturing Religious Nationalism," 107.

23. Hurh and Kim, *Korean Immigrants*, 40. For further reading on Korean American picture brides, see Chai, "Picture Bride from Korea," 37–42.

24. Yim, *My Forty-Year Fight*, 79–80.

classmates from the mission school consented and they left for Hawaii.[25] With the addition of women and children, it is estimated that the Korean population in Hawaii surpassed 7,000 by 1910.[26]

"STARTING CHURCHES EVERWHERE"

When the *SS Gaelic* arrived in Honolulu, Rev. George Pearson, the Methodist superintendent of the Hawaii mission, was already there at the port to welcome them ashore.[27] Pearson assisted the Koreans to settle into the plantations but, as seen from previous examples of self-initiative in Korean history, the first group of Koreans took steps to care for the next ship that carried Koreans. The next ship arrived in March 1903 and the Korean Christians were ready for them: they "started 'informal' worship services together with the Korean immigrants from the second boat not long after they settled in the Kahuku-Waialua area."[28]

Koreans were assigned to various plantations across the islands and, "without any external prompting," Koreans started churches in nearly every plantation where Koreans resided.[29] In the summer of 1903, "about fifty" Koreans organized a church on the Kahuku plantation that met every Sunday morning with Chi-pong Yun as their preacher.[30] Just like the Catholics of the eighteenth century and Protestants in the nineteenth century who mobilized Christian communities without the aid of clergy or outside instruction, Korean Christians who labored on the sugar plantations rose to the challenge and, like Yun, began to preach and teach to their flock. In 1905, the Methodist missionary society reported that among the six or seven thousand Koreans scattered over the islands, "sixteen hundred to two thousand" were enrolled "as members and probationers."[31]

The growth of Christianity on the Hawaiian islands took place without church buildings. Koreans gathered at what was termed "kitchen churches"

---

25. Yim, *My Forty-Year Fight,* 80.

26. 6,048 men, 637 women, and 541 children (Hurh and Kim, *Korean Immigrants,* 39).

27. By an arrangement made between the Protestant denominations in Hawaii, the Congregational and Anglican Churches were assigned the Chinese population while the Methodists were given the Japanese and Koreans. See Murabayashi, *Korean Ministerial Appointments,* 7.

28. Murabayashi, *Korean Ministerial Appointments,* 8.

29. Patterson, *Ilse,* 56.

30. Patterson, *Korean Frontier in America,* 49.

31. "Hawaii," 385.

for meeting quietly in the camp kitchens on Sunday mornings. "Boarding-house kitchens" became a popular space for worship on Sundays.[32] When the number of worshippers outgrew boardinghouse kitchens, they began to seek the formal organization as churches. On November 3, 1903, Koreans in Honolulu petitioned George Pearson, the superintendent of the Methodist mission in Hawaii, for a place to worship.[33] As a result of their inquiry, Pearson helped start a week later the "Korean Evangelical Society in Honolulu."[34] In April 1905, the Society received the full status as a church.

A 1905 Methodist missionary report noted a remarkable development on the Hawaiian plantations. The chapels in Oahu "have all been built and dedicated free of debt and without any charge to the Missionary Society."[35] It is not unusual for churches in the United States to receive funding to build local churches but for Koreans working on the plantations as laborers to collect the necessary money to build chapels was an achievement. The report added that two church edifices on the island of Kauai "have been erected without any expense to the Missionary Society, and two more are under way."[36]

The remarkable growth may give the perception that Koreans are in-clined toward Christianity but that was hardly the case as Korean Christians met at times stiff resistance. Instances of harassment and violence against Christians were reported at various locations. In Kohala, Christian workers in 1905 "suffered much through fierce persecution."[37] One was "beaten with stripes, and the other brutally kicked, and both left for dead."[38] The preach-ing of the gospel meant confronting the vices among the Koreans. The 1905 missionary report cited that "gambling and drinking are common practices" and how "immoral influences prevail among" Koreans. "The camps are in-fested with ringleaders in all bad things, so that as laborers they have lost

---

32. Patterson, *Ilse*, 56.

33. Kim, "Church in the Korean American Community," 51. "Efforts to establish a congregation began on November 3, 1903, when a group of Koreans in Honolulu chose An Ch'ung-su and Yu Pyong-gil to negotiate with a superintendent of the Methodist mission for a place of worship" (Kim, "Church in the Korean American Community," 51).

34. Murabayashi, *Korean Ministerial Appointments*, 9.

35. "Hawaii," 385.

36. "Hawaii," 386.

37. "Hawaii," 386.

38. "Hawaii," 386.

caste among the managers, and their reputation is very bad."[39] The report concluded that the church "lived through it all and grown rapidly."[40]

The wide-spread presence of Korean churches across the islands demonstrated the extent of the reach of Christianity. The missionary George Heber Jones went to Hawaii in 1906 to follow up on the Korean community and a reunion between he and former members of his Incheon church took place. As he became acquainted with the situation, he realized they surpassed his expectations. Jones wrote, "One third of all the Koreans in Hawaii are professing Christians."[41] Not only was the Korean Christians creating a vibrant community but they were also positively impacting the larger island culture. Korean Christians, Jones wrote, "dominate the life in the camps on the Islands of Oahu, Kauai and Maui where they are stamping out gambling and intoxication."[42]

In 1906, the Korean Christians started publishing a monthly newsletter that was "distributed among thirty-six Korean churches" on the islands.[43] Between 1903 to 1918, "approximately 2,800 Koreans were converted to Christianity and thirty-nine churches were established in the Hawaiian Islands alone."[44] "This numerical growth," according to the sociologist Hyung-chan Kim, "is a remarkable achievement in view of the fact that the total number of persons of Korean ancestry in the Islands during this period was less than 8,000."[45] By 1945, the Koreans in Hawaii were "overwhelmingly Christian."[46] A long-time resident of Hawaii, Tai-youn Kim said, "There was always a Christian church" where Koreans lived and the Korean church became the "center of the Korean community."[47]

As way of comparison with other ethnic groups in Hawaii, the 1905 church document from the Methodist Episcopal Church reported one Anglo congregation with one hundred people as full members on the Hawaiian islands.[48] Among the Japanese, there were six congregations with 119 full members.[49] Among the Koreans, there were twelve congregations with

39. "Hawaii," 386.

40. "Hawaii," 386.

41. Jones, "Koreans in Hawaii," 405.

42. Jones, "Koreans in Hawaii," 405.

43. Kim and Patterson, *Koreans in America,* 10.

44. Kim, "Church in the Korean American Community," 50.

45. Kim, "Church in the Korean American Community," 50.

46. Yoo, "Nurturing Religious Nationalism," 107.

47. Choy, *Koreans in America,* 97.

48. "Hawaii," 383.

49. "Hawaii," 387.

201 full members.[50] Counting the Sunday School for children and adults, probationers, inquirers, and baptisms, John Wadman, the superintendent of Hawaii who succeeded Pearson at the end of 1904, wrote, "We have enrolled from sixteen hundred to two thousand as members and probationers."[51] Wadman continued, "In all we have established over thirty Mission stations [among the Koreans], and have now in our regular employ ten evangelists and four teachers."[52] A milestone was reached in 1931 when Dora Moon and Chung-Song Lee Ahn became the first Korean women local pastors in Hawaii. Recognized and licensed by the Methodist Church, they were appointed to congregations where they were authorized to administer the sacraments, officiate funerals, and other church duties.[53] A year later, Dora Moon helped start the Korean Missionary Society that raised funds for the purpose of assisting churches and families in Korea.[54]

Before they arrived in Hawaii, Koreans came from villages where most of their families lived for centuries. Yet, when they entered Hawaii, they created new communities. Unbound by traditional roles and expectations, Koreans, especially women, became instrumental in developing community organizations aimed at assisting and improving the welfare of their community, such as the Korean Women's Association and Women's Missionary Association.[55] Margaret K. Pai remembered her mother's leadership in the Methodist Ladies Aid Society that had extensive coverage throughout the islands. The Society aimed to provide a network of services to reach "every Korean family in the community."[56] Pai wrote,

> Although the immigrants were all poor, so dedicated were the Society members that no family went without food or a roof over their heads (immigrant men often lost their jobs); a mother who became ill could depend on other mothers to help her; and a mother with a newborn baby did not have to rise from her bed until she was strong. All these services were rendered despite the fact that every woman was burdened with heavy responsibilities of her own.[57]

50. "Hawaii," 387

51. "Hawaii," 385.

52. "Hawaii," 385.

53. Choe, "History of the Korean Church," 48.

54. Choe, "History of the Korean Church," 48.

55. Kim, "Korean Independence Movement," 67.

56. Pai, *Dreams of Two Yi-Min*, 7.

57. Pai, *Dreams of Two Yi-Min*, 7.

Helen Chung, a member of the Korean Christian Church and the Korean Women's Relief Society, remembered the "spirit of giving" among the women. She said, "My mom and the others worked hard all day and then came to the church at night to make kimchee and other food to sell so that they could raise funds for the church and for Korea. People would come by the church all the time, not just on Sundays, and whenever you needed to find someone, you usually could find them there."[58] The attachment to Korea, their homeland, continued decades after their arrival. For example, the Women's Relief Society sent "over 700 tons of goods to Korea" in 1946.[59] The Korean Women's Relief Society began in 1919 when forty-one representatives of "various Korean women's societies throughout the islands met in Honolulu to merge their efforts."[60] According to the historian David Yoo, "the primary aim of the [Korean Women's] Relief Society was to provide support for women and children in Korea and for the provisional government in Shanghai."[61]

In 1907, the first women's organization was formed and it evolved into the Korean Women's Educational Association in 1909. Duk Hee Lee Murabayashi, the vice-chairwomen of the 2003 Centennial Committee of Korean Immigration to the United States, recalled the primary purpose of the Korean Women's Educational Association: "education, education, education."[62] Murabayashi noted the nationalism of the women as an important factor in the promotion of education. She said, "They had lost their country and they saw education as the only means they had to regain their country's sovereignty."[63]

EDUCATIONAL AND NATIONALIST CHURCH

The limited opportunities on the plantations for Korean children to receive a formal education compelled Korean communities across the islands to raise funds for their children's schooling despite their meager wages. The close-knit Korean community produced a collectivist ethos that facilitated the growth of schools. The Korean community in each respective camp formed a strong bond, as Bernice Kim, a community leader, noted in 1934

58. Yoo, "Nurturing Religious Nationalism," 113.
59. Yoo, "Nurturing Religious Nationalism," 113.
60. Yoo, "Nurturing Religious Nationalism," 113.
61. Yoo, "Nurturing Religious Nationalism," 113.
62. Adamski, "Better Life."
63. Adamski, "Better Life."

when she said that "each camp was like a small unit of the old Hermit Kingdom transplanted to another land."[64]

When the Koreans sought the establishment of a formal school for the children, Korean Christians petitioned John Wadman, the Methodist superintendent, in 1905 for the start of an elementary school in Honolulu where many Koreans migrated after fulfilling their contract obligations. With Wadman's approval and support, the Korean Compound opened on Punchbowl Street in 1906.

The Korean Compound which offered instruction through eighth grade also taught Korean language and Bible study classes in the afternoon.[65] Although the Koreans received only 75 cents a day as wages on the plantations, "many laborers contributed money for scholarships, 25 cents here, $1 there."[66] As the Korean Compound also housed the pastor of the Korean Methodist Church and the office of the Methodist superintendent in Hawaii, the school became the main Korean school in Hawaii.

To advance the education of their children and to help them avoid a life on the plantations, the passing of cultural knowledge became a central concern. "Usually taught by the Methodist pastor," Korean language classes became a staple on every island.[67] The Korean-language schools "were held in the late afternoon or evening, where students were taught not only language, but also Korean history, customs, and ethics."[68] A woman born in 1907 recalled her days in the Korean school: "We all were taught to speak and write Korean, our native language, and in order to acquire perfection father sent us to the village language school. . . . That faithful old Confucius scholar eagerly bent to penetrate our stubborn minds to the wonders of the ancient classics."[69]

From the perspective of religious participation Koreans had the highest average number of Sunday School attendance among all Methodist Episcopal Churches in Hawaii with 605 in 1905.[70] In comparison, Japanese had 276 and whites 64. In fact, the Methodist church in Hawaii had more Koreans than any other group as Koreans "constituted 64 percent of the total Methodist congregation in Hawaii."[71]

64. B. Kim, "Koreans in Hawaii," 409–413.

65. B. Kim, "Koreans in Hawaii," 409–413.

66. B. Kim, "Koreans in Hawaii," 409–413.

67. Patterson, Ilse, 117.

68. Patterson, Ilse, 118.

69. Patterson, Ilse, 118.

70. Ch'oe, "History of the Korean Church," 42.

71. Ch'oe, "History of the Korean Church," 42.

Working ten hours a day, six days a week with a half an hour for lunch, a Korean adult received sixteen to eighteen dollars a month.[72] A Korean laborer on the plantation wrote, "We worked in the hot sun for ten hours a day, and the pay was fifty-nine cents a day. . . . When we got back to the camp [after quitting work at 4:30pm], we ate, washed, and then went directly to bed."[73] Due to the difficult conditions on the plantations, approximately a quarter of the Korean plantation population left each year. The Korean plantation workers dropped to 3,615 at the end of 1906; 2,638 or 6 percent of the plantation labor in 1907; 2,638 or 4.5 percent of the plantation labor in 1908; 2,125 or 4.5 percent of the plantation labor in 1908; and only 1,700 remaining in 1909.[74]

Hyung-soon Kim, a worker on the plantation recalled that Korean laborers were "treated no better than cows or horses. . . . Every worker was called by number, never by name. During working hours, nobody was allowed to talk, smoke, or even stretch his back. A foreman kept his eyes on his workers at all times. When he found anyone violating working regulations, he whipped the violator without mercy."[75] A Korean woman recalled, "I'll never forget the foreman. . . . He said we worked like 'lazy.' He wanted us to work faster. . . . He would gallop around on horseback and crack and snap his whip."[76] Hong-gi Lee recalled, "I lived in the camp: it was just like the army barracks; wooden floors and we slept on wooden beds or just on the floor, with one blanket over the body. Usually four single men lived in one room."[77]

The workers in the fields were closely monitored by foremen or camp police who galloped around armed with a snake whip. The whip symbolized his authority to punish those who refuse to comply with demands of the plantation. According to the *Hawaii Herald*, "Some of them bear marks which they say were made with a whip."[78] Hong-ki Lee "who had come to

---

72. Choy, *Koreans in America*, 94; Patterson, *Korean Frontier in America*, 17. As a note of comparison, Ko Shigeta, a Japanese laborer who entered Hawaii in 1903 at the age of seventeen, received fourteen dollars a month as he worked on Oahu's Aiea plantation. Ko said, "Fifty of us, both bachelors and married couples, lived together in a humble shed—a long ten-foot-wide hallway made of wattle and lined along the sides with a slightly raised floor covered with a grass rug, and two *tatami* mats to be shared among us" (Okihiro, *Cane Fires*, 28).

73. Pang, "Korean Immigrant," 19–24.

74. Patterson, *Korean Frontier in America*, 56.

75. Takaki, *Pau Hana*, 74.

76. Takaki, *Pau Hana*, 74.

77. Choy, *Koreans in America*, 96.

78. Takaki, *Pau Hana*, 74–75.

Hawaii in 1903, described his German luna [Hawaiian for foreman] as very strict. 'If anyone violated his orders," Lee said, "he was punished, usually with a slap on his face." Other Korean laborers reported harsh methods to make them work as they felt they had been "too roughly treated."[79]

Hawaii was nearly four thousand miles from Korea but Koreans in Hawaii remained intensely drawn to the political drama that unfolded in their homeland. Having emigrated to Hawaii while Korea still retained its sovereignty, Koreans in Hawaii grieved when Japan colonized Korea; they gladly bore the burden of obligation to assist the exiled Korean independence movement. With their country in peril, they became hyper-aware of not only the political conditions in Korea but also of their own political standing.

Koreans left their country with Korean passports but, Korea now being part of Japan, they were no longer valid. The Japanese embassy offered Koreans in Hawaii representation from the Japanese consulate. Rejecting their offer, Koreans requested from their king representation from their homeland as early as 1905. In a letter dated May 1, 1905, the Korean community in Hawaii requested the Korean royal government to send a consul to Hawaii and added that the Korean community in Hawaii would "provide all funds for establishing and operating a consulate."[80] However, Japan's control of Korea's foreign affairs after the Protectorate Treaty prevented King Gojong from dispatching a Korean diplomat. Instead, the Japanese authorities appointed the "Japanese consul in Honolulu as honorary Korean consul."[81] The Korean community dismissed the appointment and continued to petition the Korean government for a Korean consul. Not only was the Korean government hamstrung by Japanese political pressure and prevented from appointing a Korean consul but the Japanese authorities ended all emigration to Hawaii in June 1905.[82]

The news of Japanese colonization of Korea in 1910 left the Korean community in Hawaii devastated but at the same time the hope of Korean independence united and galvanized the community. As the largest concentration of Korean expatriates outside of Asia, Hawaii became a hotbed of political activism and training grounds for Korean nationalist leaders as

---

79. Takaki, *Pau Hana*, 75.

80. *Hwangsong Minbo* in Son Young Ho, "Search for Ethnic Identity," 4. Yun, "Early History of Korean Immigration," 37.

81. Yun, "Early History of Korean Immigration," 37.

82. "In fact, it [Japan] attached great importance to the Korean government's decree banning immigration to Hawaii because this greatly reduced the competitors to the Japanese [on the Hawaiian plantations]" (Yun, "Early History of Korean Immigration," 39).

they "threw themselves into the nationalist movement with a fervor unmatched by any other overseas nationalist movement."[83]

The establishment of Korean communities built on Protestant Christianity became fused with fervent nationalism—a phenomenon that transformed the character of the community as well as its members. Take, for example, Soon Hyun, a member of George Heber Jones's Incheon church and a passenger on the *SS Gaelic*, who became a traveling preacher and an important member of the transnational Korean independence movement. At first, Soon Hyun, was recognized for his outstanding work when he was employed as an interpreter by the plantation.[84] The work as an interpreter afforded him the opportunity to visit many plantations. Networking with Koreans in other plantations, Hyun organized "Self-Rule Associations" on the islands and conducted English classes in the evenings for the community.[85] The superintendent of the Methodist Mission in Hawaii recognized Hyun's leadership and recruited him to work for the church as a pastor. Accepting his invitation, Hyun was appointed by the Methodist Church to the island of Kauai where he traveled like a Methodist circuit-rider on horseback, covering "the island from one end to the other, taking care of the sick, arranging schooling for the children, and conducting religious services."[86]

Hyun's multiple roles that he practiced as a pastor to the Korean community was not uncommon. The Korean pastor performed religious duties, taught English classes, functioned as a community activist, and organized political activities. The Korean pastor acted as a "medium" between Koreans and the plantation manager.[87] Individuals and families "constantly" turned to the pastor "for advice and aid."

Leading the political mobilization were Korean pastors and church leaders. Soon Hyun preached the gospel "with his ringing voice and fearless sermons" and his "most compelling call" to the audience, according to his son, was "Follow me and I shall make you free"—a quote from Jesus that unmistakably implied nationalist aspirations.[88] Using religious language to express a political message, Hyun's call to freedom addressed the spiritual

83. Patterson, *Ilse*, 100.

84. Patterson, *Korean Frontier in America*, 49.

85. According to his son, Soon Hyun "organized a 'Self-Rule Association' to help preserve their cultural identity as Koreans. In the evening, after work, he conducted classes in English for the workers" (Hyun, *Man Sei!*, 27).

86. Hyun, *Man Sei!*, 27.

87. "Certain individuals and families constantly go to him for advice and aid. He is the medium through which these individuals keep in touch with the plantation manager" (Patterson, *Ilse*, 67).

88. Hyun, *Man Sei!*, 4.

woes as well as reinforcing the political yearnings of a people. In Hawaii, Korean Christian pastors, like Soon Hyun, were often the leaders of political activism for Korea's independence, preaching Christ and country. Soon Hyun, who traveled to Korea, Manchuria, and Shanghai on behalf of the independence movement, "never failed to take up a special collection and send the money each month to Kim Koo in Shanghai [where the Korean Provisional Government resided]."[89] The fusion of Christ with ethnic nationalism is not surprising, given that Christian ministry is conducted within a cultural outlook at a particular time to put the gospel message contextually closer to the people for whom it is addressing.

Tensions brewed between the Japanese and Korean communities in Hawaii but their common Christian expression in the Methodist denomination helped eased tensions. Every year, the Methodists in Hawaii gathered together for the Annual Conference that included delegates from all churches, including Korean and Japanese. In addition, Hawaii's district superintendent hosted events and activities for all churches in the district. The fact that the Methodist Church brought together Koreans and Japanese alike under one faith helped break down walls of suspicion. Many Korean and Japanese who became church ministers in Hawaii knew each other while going through the licensing process in the church as they took the same classes for the course of study. In the 1913 Methodist church records, candidates on their first year of the course of study included three Japanese and four Koreans: Iwataro Arauchi, Y. C. Cha, C. S. Kim, K. M. Lee, S. W. Park, Kaminosuke Tanaka, and N. Yamada.[90] In the second year of the course of study listed four Koreans and two Japanese: K. Anzai, H. S. Cho, Y. T. Cho, C. H. Lim, S. Toda, and S. I. Lee.[91]

Living in Hawaii allowed for increased familiarity with Japanese neighbors but the topic of Korean independence from Japanese colonialism dominated the discourse and mood in the Korean community. Soon Hyun's sermons, according to his son, "never failed to combine Christian faith with Korean aspirations for national freedom."[92] Margaret Pai remembered her father and other Korean men gathering in large numbers and talking "endlessly about independence and the latest news" and the "freedom movement."[93] When Louise Yim visited Hawaii, she preached at the Korean Christian Church where she described the conditions in colonial Korea and

89. Hyun, *Man Sei!*, 165.

90. "Hawaii Mission," 153; "Hawaii," 386.

91. "Hawaii," 386.

92. Hyun, *Man Sei!*, 27.

93. Pai, *Dreams of Two Yi-Min*, 43.

expressed her plans to build a women's college in Seoul. After her message, an old man sacrificed his burial money in order to donate to the cause of women's education in Korea. The old man said, "I have carried it with me for years lest I should die suddenly. Take it for your school."[94] Yim described the enormous generosity of Koreans in Hawaii: "Almost all the Koreans in Hawaii wanted a share in the building of the school."[95]

To mobilize the nationalistic efforts of Koreans on the islands, the first political organization was started on August 7, 1903 with the founding of *Shinmin Hoi*, or new people's society. The *Shinmin Hoi* was started by Soon Hyun and Hong Sung Ha who both later became local preachers in Hawaii's Korean churches.[96] Koreans' entry into political activities was beset with problems from the beginning. The development of one political organization spawned a growing body of political societies. The societies were "fragmented politically because of the continuing factionalism in the Korean community."[97] By 1907, twenty-four Korean organizations were formed with agendas of political activism and mutual benefit. The twenty-four organizations came together in 1907 to adopt a resolution calling for greater unity.[98] Two years later in 1909, the Korean organizations merged together to create the Korean National Association (KNA). The KNA "was the first united organization in the United States proper to coordinate various efforts of Koreans in their struggle for national independence."[99]

IMMIGRANT CHURCHES IN THE POST-1965 ERA

To illustrate the prominent role of churches, a Korean in Hawaii said it seemed as if "every Korean wanted to live near the church, and almost every Korean went to church on Sundays to meet each other and to help those in trouble."[100] Certainly Koreans went to church for religious reasons but the Korean church was more as it encompassed a wide array of cultural and social services that enhanced the quality of life.

As the first generation fulfilled their labor contracts, fewer Koreans thereafter wanted to remain on the plantations. Their children found other

94. Yim, *My Forty-Year Fight*, 196.

95. Yim, *My Forty-Year Fight*, 196.

96. Hong Sung Ha, the leader of Shin Min Hoe, "was appointed as a local preacher" at the Korean Methodist Church in 1903. See Patterson, *Ilse*, 57.

97. Patterson, *Ilse*, 57.

98. Kim and Patterson, *Koreans in America*, 94.

99. Kim and Patterson, *Koreans in America*, 95.

100. Choy, *Koreans in America*, 97.

work on the islands. Families would seek their fortunes by moving to the West Coast on the mainland. The Korean American population remained small and was concentrated for the most part in Hawaii and the West Coast until the passage of the 1965 Immigration Act that greatly increased the influx of Korean immigrants to the United States.

To illustrate the impact of Korean immigration after 1965, the Korean Methodist Church (later re-named Christ United Methodist Church), the biggest Korean church on the islands, experienced a period of unprecedented growth after 1965. Christ UMC expanded its sanctuary size to 500 in 1979.[101] When church attendance continued to increase in the 1980s with adult attendance over 600, Christ UMC approved an ambitious project to construct a new building and sanctuary "at total cost of $5.7 million."[102]

Prior to 1965, the order of countries that sent the most number of immigrants to the United States was the United Kingdom, Germany, and Italy. Ten years after 1965, the order became the Philippines, South Korea, and China.[103] In the year 1973, the percentage of Asian immigrants equaled for the "first time" the percentage of European immigrants.[104] In 1970, the Korean American population rose above ten thousand for the first time in United States history.[105] In the year 1974 alone, the total number of Korean immigrants surpassed the combined number prior to 1965.[106] In 1985, the number of Korean immigrants comprised 6.2 percent of the total US immigration.[107] In the 1990 census, there were 787,849 Korean Americans.[108]

Like the experience of Korean churches in Hawaii, the immigrant churches also became the "center of the Korean community."[109] As the Korean population swelled, mostly in urban and adjacent areas, a striking

---

101. Choe, "History of the Korean Church," 61.

102. Choe, "History of the Korean Church," 61.

103. Hurh and Kim, *Korean Immigrants in America*, 53.

104. "The Asian share of total immigration to the United States increased from 7.6 percent (1961–1965) to 27.4 percent (1969–1973), equaling the European share (27.3 percent in 1969–1973) for the first time in the American history of immigration" (Hurh and Kim, *Korean Immigrants in America*, 53).

105. I. Kim, *New Urban Immigrants*, 26.

106. Hurh and Kim, *Korean Immigrants in America*, 210.

107. Kitano and Daniels, *Asian Americans*, 111.

108. Jo, *Korean Immigrants*, xi.

109. Kim, "Miju Haningyohoiwa Haninsahoi." Scholars of Korean American Studies conclude that the Korean church is the center of the community. Bong Youn Choy also wrote that Korean Churches are the "centers of the Korean community" (Choy, *Koreans in America,* 257). For more information on the significance of the church on the Korean immigrant community, see Min, "Introduction," 1–14; Hurh and Kim, *Korean Immigrants in America*; Kim and Patterson, *Koreans in America.*

parallel development took place in the increase of ethnic churches in Korean communities across America. In one year, from 1976 to 1977, Korean churches in the United States grew from 264 to over 400.[110] The number of Korean churches in Southern California, the region with the highest Korean population, "increased 20 times" from "11 churches in 1965 to 215 in 1979."[111]

In a 1978 study of the Korean immigrant community in the Chicago metro area, the religious participation of Korean immigrants exceeded all Asian groups, except Filipinos. For example, 71 percent of the Korean population, compared with 28 percent of the Japanese and 32 percent of the Chinese, were affiliated with a Korean ethnic church.[112] In the early 1980s, studies of the Los Angeles and Chicago communities revealed that 70 percent of Koreans in Los Angeles and 78 percent in Chicago were affiliated with Korean churches.[113] Of those who attended church, 84 percent in Los Angeles and 78 percent in Chicago went to church at least once a week.[114] In 1990s, studies showed 75 percent of Koreans continued to participate in ethnic churches, a "remarkable" statistic in American religious life.[115]

Recognizing both the unique uprooted circumstance and the importance of nurturing their immigrant existence, the Korean church evolved to take on a vision that encapsulated pertinent social and emotional concerns. In *Being Buddhist in a Christian World*, Sharon Suh described how Korean Buddhist temples paled in comparison to Korean Protestant churches. Mrs. Jin, a fifty-year old devout Korean American Buddhist, said, "At church, they do a lot of things to help immigrants. But Buddhism [is not like that]. When I first came to the US and went to Sa Chal, we didn't know where anything was! Even though we went to the temple, the monks didn't ask us when we came to America, where we lived, what we did and what we needed etc." Such interaction would have been unwarranted in Korea but in America, where immigrants are rendered invisible, a simple greeting or acknowledgement brings solace to those coping with life on the margins. Mrs. Jin continued, "I heard that at the church, when the minister sees people

110. Hurh and Kim, *Korean Immigrants in America*, 129.

111. Hurh and Kim, *Korean Immigrants in America*, 129.

112. Hurh, *Korean Americans,* 107. Hurh based the statistics on B. Kim, *Asian Americans.*

113. Hurh, *Korean Americans,* 107.

114. Hurh, *Korean Americans,* 107.

115. C. Kim, *Bitter Fruit,* 166.

coming and going, he will greet them and tell them to have a good week. At the temple here, it is just about giving money and leaving!"[116]

According to a research of the Korean immigrant community in Queens in 1997 and 1998, 79 percent reported that their religious background was Christian with 62 percent claiming Protestantism and 17 percent Catholicism.[117] Among Korean Christians, a remarkable 98 percent was affiliated with a particular ethnic church. Furthermore 83 percent of those who are affiliated with a church attended church services at least once a week. The sociologist Pyong Gap Min wrote, "This is a much higher rate than among other Christian groups in the United States. According to national studies of Presbyterians, 78 percent of Korean Presbyterians attend Sunday worship service every week in comparison to 28 percent of white, 34 percent of African American, and 49 percent of Latino Presbyterians."[118] The extraordinary high-level of church participation among Korean immigrants is even more striking when considering that only 2.8 percent of South Korea's population in 1962 considered themselves Protestants.[119] In 1985, less than 15 percent of South Korea's population was affiliated with Protestantism.[120]

The impetus for self-direction that was on display in Korea and Hawaii was also demonstrated in the building of Korean immigrant churches. The way in which Korean immigrants achieved their goals with self-sufficiency surprised denominational leaders in America. E. T. Holland, who, as the New Jersey Conference Program Director for Mission in the United Methodist Church, noted how the Korean Community Church (Leonia, NJ) began and became independent without financial assistance. In 1976, Holland said, "This congregation is unique in that it has been all the way a 'volunteer' project."[121] Holland continued, "To date there has been no conference [or denominational] funding of this congregation."[122]

116. Suh, *Being Buddhist in a Christian World*, 173–74.

117. Min, "Koreans," 185. See also Carnes and Yang, *Asian American Religions*.

118. Min, "Koreans," 185.

119. Park and Cho, "Confucianism and the Korean Family," 119.

120. According to the Korean National Census, 29.2 percent of the South Korean population in 2005 claimed affiliation with Christianity, both Catholics (10.9 percent) and Protestants (18.3 percent) together. In 1995, 26.3 percent (6.6 percent Catholic; 19.7 percent Protestant) and in 1985, 20.7 percent (4.6 percent Catholic; 16.1 percent Protestant) of the population were affiliated with Christianity (Lugo and Grim, "Presidential Election in South Korea").

121. "Profiles of Two Ethnic Minority Churches," 10.

122. "Profiles of Two Ethnic Minority Churches," 10.

Compared to African-Americans, Hispanics, and Caucasians in a sociological survey, Korean Christians had a highest level of church participation. "Four-fifths of Koreans (78 percent) report they attend their congregation's Sunday worship every week, compared with 34 percent of African Americans, 49 percent of Hispanics, and 28 percent of Caucasians."[123] Furthermore the survey also found Koreans spent more time in church activities and contributed more financially to their churches than any other group.[124] In a study of New York Korean Christians, "Eight interviewees (14 percent) said that they attend church every morning [i.e., sunrise services]. . . . Seven respondents reported that they spent 20 or more hours weekly for church activities. They held eldership and/or other important positions, or belonged to a choir in their church, and thus spent a lot of time participating in committee meetings, visiting sick members, cooking in the kitchen, and/or performing other voluntary activities."[125]

In New York City alone, "an astounding 89 percent" of Korean immigrants in a 1986 survey reported attending an ethnic church once or twice a month, "most reporting church attendance once or more a week."[126] According to the *2001 Korean Business Directory of New York*, 633 Korean Christian churches were listed with 20 Buddhist temples in the tri-state region.[127] The *2001 Korean Church Directory of America* reported 3,402 Korean Protestant churches in the United States.[128] Furthermore, the *Directory* revealed that "all 50 states have at least one Korean Protestant church."[129] As the most prominent organization in the Korean community, the Korean ethnic church became, according to Pyong Gap Min, "the most important Korean ethnic organizations in New York as well as in other American cities."[130]

As most of the Korean churches became affiliated with their respective American Protestant denominations, the church leaders in the

123. K. Kim and Kim, "Ethnic Roles," 82.

124. 54 percent of Koreans spent six hours or more at church; 36 percent for African Americans; 39 percent for Hispanics; and 40 percent for Caucasians. In terms of financial donations to their church, 62 percent of Koreans gave $2,000 or more a year; 35 percent of African Americans; 26 percent of Hispanics; and 40 percent of Caucasians (K. Kim and Kim, "Ethnic Roles," 82).

125. Min, "Religion and the Maintenance of Ethnicity," 110.

126. Carnes and Yang, *Asian American Religions*, 48. Studies showed that a "remarkable" 75 percent of Korean immigrants in the US were associated with a Korean American church in the early 1990s (C. Kim, *Bitter Fruit*, 166).

127. Kwon, *Buddhist and Protestant Korean Immigrants*, 7.

128. Kwon, *Buddhist and Protestant Korean Immigrants*, 7.

129. Kwon, *Buddhist and Protestant Korean Immigrants*, 8.

130. Min, "Koreans," 184.

denominations recognized the growth of Korean congregations. For example, Korean churches became the "fastest growing segment" in the United Methodist Church according to James Cowell, the Director of Congregational Development of the United Methodist Church.[131] Cowell stated, "In 1967 there were only seven Korean Methodist churches in this country. Today there are 250 Korean United Methodist churches in this country."[132] In *United Methodism in America*, the author wrote, "The number of Korean United Methodists had been doubling every few years. More than half the United Methodist congregations established since 1981 were Korean, and their success stories became a blueprint to help reverse the denomination's otherwise plummeting membership."[133]

In the 1990s, Kyeyoung Park attended a Korean church service in Queens, NY in which she heard Rev. Ahn preach about the Puritans crossing the Atlantic in order to immigrate to the New World. The Puritans' journey to America was not an accident for it had a divine purpose. Similarly, Korean immigrants, according to the preacher, also have a divine purpose for coming to America.[134] Rev. Ahn and other Korean pastors in America have reinterpreted the importance of Koreans' experience as immigrants and gave it special meaning. A Korean woman who became a Christian in America believes that her immigration to the United States now has "a spiritual purpose."[135] The immigrant life was a very difficult one but the Christian interpretation for Korean immigrants helped redefine their immigrant journey to one having a higher purpose.

RACIAL IDENTITY AND RELIGIOUS ASSIMILATION

Despite its successes, Korean immigrant churches as well as other ethnic churches aroused deep anxiety in mainstream America. From their perspective, the proliferation of ethnic churches evoked a sense of failure in the assimilation of ethnic minorities. At the same time, the presence of ethnic churches demonstrated the loss of power and influence of established denominations over them. For example, in *The Religious History of America*, Edwin Gaustad and Leigh Eric Schmidt noted the "limited" success of "Christianizing and Americanizing" Asian immigrants.[136] Even when Asian

131. H. Kim, *Ten Ideas for Evangelism*, ii.

132. H. Kim, *Ten Ideas for Evangelism*, ii.

133. McEllhenney, *United Methodism in America*, 148–49

134. Park, *Korean American Dream*, 193.

135. Park, *Korean American Dream*, 192.

136. Gaustad and Schmidt, *Religious History of America*, 220.

immigrants became Christians, they "tended to be placed in ethnically restricted churches," a reality that could be "regarded as detrimental to social cohesion and religious destiny."[137]

As Asian American church leaders advocated for their communities, they quickly encountered resistance to the formation of ethnic churches since their mere appearance suggested a blow to their vision of a unified church body. Roy Sano, the first Japanese American bishop in the United Methodist Church,[138] felt the opposition to ethnic churches from the "overwhelming majority of our denomination."[139] Timothy Tseng, an Asian American church historian, noted the indifferent attitude of those in the academic field of American religious history who regarded the study of ethnic churches as unnecessary since they are on the path of "inevitable cultural assimilation."[140]

Someone asked "Why separate churches?" when approached with the vision of diversity of ethnic congregations. One reader scribbled that separate ethnic churches amounted to "ecclesiastical apartheid."[141] A white parishioner in a church survey wrote, "Why can't ethnic minorities join existing organizations and be like whites?"[142] Another who took part in the survey said, "Does not the majority white responses to our survey mean that we want ethnic ministries to lose their distinctiveness, and all of us become one, if not similar or same?"[143]

Many Asian American church leaders voiced their opposition to "integration" or what they regarded as a veiled attempt to erase churches based on ethnicity. Roy Sano said the assimilation effort in the church was "a clear case of 'you become like us, and we will like you.'"[144] The ethnic church in many ways became the last line of defense against assimilationist encroachment and provided a safe haven that affirmed their identity.

137. Gaustad and Schmidt, *Religious History of America*, 220.

138. Roy Isao Sano was elected to the episcopacy in 1984. He served as a bishop for sixteen years before retiring in 2000. He was the bishop of the Denver Episcopal Area from 1984–1992 and of the Los Angeles Area from 1992 to 2000.

139. Sano, *From Every Nation Without Number*, 27.

140. Tseng, "Beyond Orientalism and Assimilation," 61.

141. A reader scribbled those comments on the margins of Roy Sano's *From Every Nation Without Number* on page 26 that described the creation of separate institutions for ethnic people. The copy of Sano's book with the remarks was from the library of Princeton Theological Seminary.

142. Sano, *From Every Nation Without Number*, 29.

143. Sano, *From Every Nation Without Number*, 27.

144. Roy Sano was elected to the United Methodist episcopacy in 1984 and retired in 2000. Sano, *From Every Nation Without Number*, 36.

In 1977, Nancy Jang, a seventeen-year old Korean American in New Jersey, asked "Who am I?" to express the identity crisis that she went through.[145] Jang wrote, "Trying to know myself became a difficult, confusing task."[146] As Nancy Jang and many other Korean American youth experienced, the Korean ethnic church gave them "roots" through the exposure of Korean culture and language and educational programs that nurtured cultural awareness. Jang continued, "The most important thing I have learned in this church is that I am proud to be a Korean and I am proud of my heritage."[147]

The affirmation of ethnic identity in the Korean church enabled a sense of security. A commonly used expression exemplified the unspoken understanding and mutual support in an ethnic church: "I don't have to explain myself to others here."[148] "Only at Korean churches can immigrants meet many fellow immigrants who have gone through the same kinds of problems in their life in America."[149] The former bishop of the United Methodist Church Hae Jong Kim said, "Finding one's identity, or cultural or national identity, is so important for one's well-being . . . because people find their identities in their churches."[150] In 1975, Chan-Hie Kim wrote that the immigrant church provided comfort "in a strange and occasionally hostile society."[151] The Korean ethnic church was a place "where they are fully accepted and respected as persons" and it also offered "not just *a* community but *the* community for the majority of Korean Americans."[152]

It was not long before Korean immigrants realized the complex racialized environment that they entered in the United States. Neither black or white, Koreans operated on the margins of society as an "unmeltable" race. Compounding the stress that they felt as immigrants, they experienced "isolation and alienation" from the dominant society.[153] The Korean American theologian Sang Hyun Lee wrote, "However long I stayed in this country, I

---

145. Jang, "Personal Witness," 6.

146. Jang, "Personal Witness," 6.

147. Jang, "Personal Witness," 6.

148. K. Kim and Kim, "Ethnic Roles," 75.

149. K. Kim and Kim, "Ethnic Roles," 75.

150. H. Kim, "Multicultural Evangelism," 95–96.

151. C. Kim, "Biblical and Theological Basis."

152. C. Kim, "Biblical and Theological Basis."

153. C. Kim, *New Urban Immigrants*, 314. Korean immigrants felt "isolation and alienation from the dominant society . . . because they arrived relatively late, came in relatively small numbers, and were linguistically and racially distinct from the host population" (C. Kim, *New Urban Immigrants*, 314).

seemed to remain a stranger, an alien."[154] A male respondent in a study of New York Korean Christians wrote, "I need to outlet my feelings with fellow Koreans. That is a Korean church."[155] He continued, "When I talk and eat lunch with my friends in my church on Sunday, I feel at home and relaxed. A Korean church is a Korean community." Understanding how important the church has been to him, he added, "I don't know how other Korean immigrants who don't go to a Korean church can survive in this country."[156]

CHURCHES AS SAFE HAVEN

While detractors opposed ethnic churches on the grounds that they stymied their assimilation, Korean American church leaders understood the critical role they played not only in spiritual uplift but also social and mental support. According to the Korean American theologian Chan-Hie Kim, fellowship provided comfort "in a strange and occasionally hostile society."[157] The Korean ethnic church was a place "where they are fully accepted and respected as persons" and it also offered "not just *a* community but *the* community for the majority of Korean Americans."[158] The Korean church functioned as a "pseudo-extended family" and as "a broker between its congregation and the bureaucratic institutions of the larger society."[159]

In the effort to assist Korean immigrants adjust and assimilate into American society, the Korean church offered a wide variety of services, such as English classes, employment counseling, legal center, marriage and family counseling, cultural school, housing service, college prep classes and counseling, nursery school, business networking center, medical clinic, and counseling in immigration law.[160] To meet the needs of their community, Korean church ministers themselves became versed in business, law, and family counseling.[161] "Most of the large [Korean] churches operate 'life

154. Lee, "Pilgrimage and Home," 55.
155. Min, "Religion and the Maintenance of Ethnicity," 110.
156. Min, "Religion and the Maintenance of Ethnicity," 110.
157. C. Kim, "Biblical and Theological Basis."
158. C. Kim, "Biblical and Theological Basis."
159. Kim, *New Urban Immigrants,* 199–207.
160. Kim, *New Urban Immigrants,* 188. Pyong Gap Min listed in Table 4 nine different social services Korean churches provided. Min, "Structures and Social Functions," 1386. Min wrote, "According to my own study conducted in New York, Korean immigrant churches offer a number of services for their members including immigrant orientation, counseling, educational services, job referral, and many other nonmaterial services" (Min, "Introduction," 19).
161. "[Korean-ethnic] churches functioned as community centers and schools,

counseling centers,' which are exclusively addressed to the adjustment problems of Korean immigrants."[162] As the de facto community leaders, ministers also became match-makers, business consultants, and college advisors for the children of immigrants.

Rev. Kim of Namsung Korean Community Church in Queens recalled the myriad of requests he received from immigrants. Their requests range the whole spectrum, from assistance with US immigration laws to interpreting for them. Kim said, "They ask for a place to live. They sometimes ask me to get a job for them. . . . They exchange information among themselves at church, especially those of the same occupation. I have seen kye organizing a few times. Still some ask me to lend a big sum of money, something like $2500 and others ask me to increase their fortune. A few people ask me to find a good man or woman for marriage. Since they are young people, they are also busy with their jobs."[163]

Pyong Gap Min also noted an important difference in the social services provided by Korean and earlier European-ethnic churches. Min wrote, "Korean ethnic churches focus on counseling and educational services for Korean families with marital and juvenile problems, whereas synagogues and Catholic churches seem to have helped earlier European immigrants meet their economic needs, helping to obtain housing and jobs."[164] While Korean American Buddhist temples preserved a traditional Korean identity, Korean ethnic churches in the United States, on the other hand, according to Kyeyoung Park in *The Korean American Dream* (1997) accelerated the acculturation of Korean immigrants through the church's promotion of

---

offering lessons to members in reading, history, and geography. . . . Churches have set up counseling services, in which ministers help newcomers find their way in American society. The churches have also become a prime place for business contacts" (Patterson and Kim, *Koreans in America*, 43).

162. Kim, *New Urban Immigrants*, 201. Pyong Gap Min identified fellowship, maintenance of Korean cultural tradition, social services, and social status and positions as the key social functions of Korean immigrant churches. For a discussion on the specific functions, see Min, "Structures and Social Functions," 1381–90.

163. Kim in Park, *Korean American Dream*, 188.

164. Min, "Structure and Social Function," 1391. Ethnic churches in American religious life provided critical assistance to their people. For example, the African-American church provided many social functions. "The [black] church acts simultaneously as a school, a bank, a benevolent society, a political organization, a party hall, and a spiritual base. As one of the few institutions owned and operated by African Americans, the church is often the center of activity in black communities" (Pattillo-McCoy, "Church Culture," 769). Du Bois said in *The Philadelphia Negro*: "Its family functions are shown by the fact that the church is the center of social life and intercourse; acts as newspaper and intelligence bureau, is the center of amusement—indeed is the world in which the Negro moves and acts" (Du Bois, *Phildelphia Negro*, 201).

Western culture, such as a church choir that wore Western choir gowns and sang classic Western hymns with Western musical instruments playing in the background.[165] Except for the difference in language, the Korean Protestant church services were nearly identical in music, architecture, worship, and liturgy to their American counterpart.

Furthermore, the Korean ethnic church also encouraged the immigrants in the participation of American culture through its athletic events and community activities. In the Korean community, "volleyball, table tennis and fishing are major annual events. Ninety-two percent of the New York Korean churches also hold at least one outdoor service per year, and nearly 70 percent hold two or more such services. . . . Eighty-five percent of Korean churches in New York City also go on at least one retreat per year . . . and 70 percent take two or more retreats per year . . . [retreats include] recreational activities such as swimming, fishing, singing and playing sports and games."[166] The Korean church became "the only place where Korean Americans communally celebrate most of their national holidays, work toward the unification of the divided Koreas, teach Korean languages to their children, and perform other cultural events."[167]

As many Korean immigrants operated small businesses, the Korean church became a partner in nurturing the success of their parishioners' business. The church became a place where Koreans joined together to form "rotating credit clubs (kye)."[168] The church also was a place of network where immigrants recruited employees, discovered new business opportunities,

165. Korean Buddhist temples in America, on the other hand, promoted Korean identity by its emphasis on the preservation of pre-modern Korean traditions and culture. Park wrote, "On 28 May 1985, for example, many Buddhist temples in New York celebrated the 2,529th birthday of Buddha. At the Won'gak Sa, a Korean temple, a lantern parade and the chanting of the Buddhist liturgy were followed by a *kayagum* (Korean zitherlike instrument) concert, a court dance, a Buddhist dance, a *sal'puri* (a dance of exorcism now considered a Korean classical dance), a *p'ansori* concert (folktales sung to drum accompaniment), a folk song concert, and other forms cultivated by folklorists as examples of Korea's indigenous culture. Performances of this type are rare in Korean Christian church functions" (Park, *Korean American Dream*, 187).

166. Min, "Structure and Social Functions," 1383.

167. J. Lee, *Marginality*, 198.

168. Park, *Korean American Dream*, 187. "These clubs have regular meetings where each member pays a fixed or a variable amount of dues. In my interviews with eight ministers in Elmhurst, seven admitted that their church members organized kye at their churches and that members joined kye thorugh networks developed at church. Mr. Choi joined *ponho-kye*, or number kye, at a garment factory where he works. The wife of the owner of a garment factory organized the rotating credit club with variable dues ($755 for Mr. Choi) and a pot of $20,000. She recruited members through her church, where she is deaconess, as well as from her husband's employees."

or found investors to a new business. "Through the church, small business owners meet and discuss capital formation, labor issues, and business information. On occasion, joint ventures are formed. In a few cases, ministers themselves own businesses to supplement small church salaries or become business partners with their members."[169] In many ways, the Korean ethnic church acted as a springboard to the development of civic organizations.

In *Religion and New Immigrants* (2007), the authors determined that the Korean community "developed the highest level of civic organization" among six immigrant groups in the study.[170] The Korean community developed the most number of business and civic associations, social service agencies, and church-related organizations. The church played an integral role in helping immigrants become acculturated to services and organizations in American society as "church leaders were often instrumental in founding the social service agencies."[171]

Korean immigrants founded the Appenzeller Memorial Nairi Korean United Methodist Church in West Paterson, New Jersey and the founding service took place on February 2, 1986. The church was named for Henry G. Appenzeller, the pioneer Methodist missionary in Korea who arrived in Korea nearly a hundred years earlier in 1885. The 'Nairi' part of the name was added to recognize the support of Nairi Methodist Church in Incheon, South Korea—the church that George Heber Jones started and where many of the first passengers of the *SS Gaelic* came from. The name of the immigrant church captures key moments in Korean American church history: the most famous Methodist missionary to Korea and the mother church in Korea that sent the first Koreans to the US.

In the immigrant community, the church became the extended family. The process of moving to the United States entailed the loss of kinship ties that was so important in a Confucian society. Korean immigrants began entering the United States in large numbers from the 1970s. They viewed immigration to the United States as an educational and economic gateway but few understood or knew how to navigate the racialized landscape of America. As Asian immigrants in America, they found themselves

169. Park, *Korean American Dream*, 187.

170. "Of the six immigrant groups we studied, the Korean community has developed the highest level of civic organization" (Foley and Hoge, *Religion and the New Immigrants*, 81).

171. Foley and Hoge, *Religion and the New Immigrants*, 81.

"in-between" the racial hierarchy of American landscape, a situation that exacerbated feelings of isolation and marginalization.

As immigrants become disillusioned with the direction that life in America has taken them, the ethnic church has become a repository of familiar culture that they left behind. Longing, loss, despair, and alienation are a few of the themes that agitate immigrants and the Korean church addressed their particular concerns. Therefore it is not a surprise that Korean immigrant churches offer many more social activities as a way to provide respite from the rigors and harsh realities of immigrant life.

In turn, the Korean ethnic church has become the most important institution for Korean immigrants. Studies of the Korean immigrant community show that more than 80 percent attend church. The high rate of church membership among Korean immigrants gave the church meaning as a kind of sanctuary, as a place where marginalized people can be visible, a place where immigrants learn to navigate through a foreign world, and where others can find the promise of eternal renewal. Becoming a Christian and participating in a Korean church was joining an ethnic network that provided affirmation to cultural sensibilities. Such insights expand our awareness of the multiple points of a complex bi-cultural environment in which Korean immigrants operated.

In addition, the Korean ethnic church shaped their self-understanding by re-interpreting their immigrant experience, away from a purely economic or utilitarian rationale to a religious narrative about a meaningful personal journey. Many immigrants in US history found God in America and Koreans were no exception. In the process of their conversion, Korean immigrants discovered a divine purpose for their lives that they would not have gained if not for venturing abroad. A terracultural rendering of their immigrant experience associated the new birth to not just a spiritual one but also multiple interpretations, including as an inventive, new person living out the American dream.

Bibliography

Adamski, Mary. "A Better Life." *Honolulu Star Bulletin*, January 12, 2003. http://www.archives.starbulletin.com/2003/01/12/news/story3.html.

Adogame, Afe, and Shobana Shankar, eds. *Religion on the Move! New Dynamics of Religious Expansion in a Globalizing World*. Boston: Brill, 2013.

"African Superstition at Bailundu." *Gospel in All Lands* 8 (1887) 115–16.

Ahn, Katherine H. Lee. *Awakening the Hermit Kingdom: Pioneer American Women Missionaries in Korea*. Pasadena, CA: William Carey, 2009.

Allen, Horace N. *Things Korean*. New York: Flemeing Revell, 1908.

Allen, John L., Jr. *The Global War on Christians: Dispatches from the Front Lines of Anti-Christian Persecution*. New York: Image, 2013.

Anderson, Gerald, ed. *Biographical Dictionary of Christian Missions*. Grand Rapids: Eerdmans, 1999.

"Anti-US Protests Grow in Seoul." *BBC News*, December 8, 2002. http://news.bbc.co.uk/2/hi/asia-pacific/2552875.stm.

Appenzeller, Henry G. *The Korea Mission of the Methodist Episcopal Church*. New York: Open Door Commission, 1905.

Armstrong, Charles, ed. *Korean Society: Civil Society, Democracy and the State*. New York: Taylor and Francis, 2007.

———. *The North Korean Revolution, 1945–1950*. Ithaca: Cornell University Press, 2004.

———. *Tyranny of the Weak: North Korea and the World, 1950–1992*. Ithaca, NY: Cornell University Press, 2013.

Avison, O. R. "A Bible Woman's Work." *The Korean Mission Field* 2.11 (1906) 212–13.

Baird, Annie. *Daybreak in Korea: A Tale of Transformation in the Far East*. New York: Fleming R. Revell, 1909.

———. *Inside Views of Mission Life*. Philadelphia, PA: Westminster, 1913.

Baird, Richard. *William Baird of Korea*. Oakland, CA: Baird, 1968.

Baird, William. "Our Mission in Korea." *Woman and Mission* 3.2 (1927) 403–7.

Baker, Don. "Catholic God and Confucian Morality: A Look at the Theology and Ethics of Korea's First Catholics." In *Korean Religions in Relation: Buddhism, Confucianism, Christianity*, edited by Anselm Min, 89–118. Albany, NY: SUNY Press, 2016.

———. "Christianity 'Koreanized.'" In *Nationalism and the Construction of Korean Identity*, edited by Hyung Il Pai and Timothy R. Tangherlini, 108–125. Berkeley, CA: Institute of East Asian Studies, University of California, 1998.

————. "Martyrdom of Paul Yun: Western Religion and Eastern Ritual in Eighteenth-Century Korea." *Transactions of the Royal Asiatic Society, Korea Branch* 54 (1979) 33–58.

————. "Sibling Rivalry in Twentieth-Century Korea: Comparative Growth Rates of Catholic and Protestant Communities." In *Christianity in Korea,* edited by Robert Buswell and Timothy Lee, 283–308. Honolulu: University of Hawaii Press, 2006.

————. "The Transformation of the Catholic Church in Korea: From a Missionary Church to an Indigenous Church." *Journal of Korean Religions* 4.1 (2013) 11–42.

Baker, Frances J. *The Story of the Woman's Foreign Missionary Society of the Methodist Episcopal Church, 1869–1895.* New York: Eaton and Mains, 1898.

Baldwin, S. L. "Taoism." *Heathen Woman's Friend* 19.6 (1887) 170–71.

Barclay, Wade Crawford. *Widening Horizons 1845–1945.* Vol. 3 of *The Methodist Episcopal Church 1845–1939.* New York: Board of Missions of the Methodist Church, 1957.

Barlow, Jane. "Evangelistic Report of Haiju District." In *Korea Woman's Conference of the Methodist Episcopal Church,* 29–30. Seoul: Chang Moon Christian, 1926.

Bays, Daniel, ed. *Christianity in China: From the Eighteenth Century to the Present.* Stanford, CA: Stanford University Press, 1996.

Beaver, Pierce R. *American Protestant Women in the World Mission: A History of the First Feminist Movement in North America.* Grand Rapids: Eerdmans, 1980.

Bell, Matthew. "The Biggest Megachurch on Earth and South Korea's 'Crisis of Evangelism.'" *PRI's The World,* May 1, 2017. www.pri.org/stories/2017-05-01/biggest-megachurch-earth-facing-crisis-evangelism.

Berger, Peter, and Hsin-Huang Michael Hsiao, eds. *In Search of an East Asian Development Model.* New Brunswick, NJ: Transaction, 1988.

Best, Margaret. "Country Bible Classes For Women." *The Korean Mission Field* 9.4 (1913) 102–4.

————. "Course of Study and Rules of Admission of the Pyeng Yang Presbyterian Church Women's Bible Institute." *The Korean Mission Field* 6.6 (1910) 152–54.

————. "The Year at Pyeng Yang." *Woman's Work* 21 (1906) 249–52.

Bevans, Steven, and Katalina Tahaafe-Williams, eds. *Contextual Theology for the Twenty-First Century.* Cambridge, UK: Clark & Co., 2011.

————. *An Introduction to Theology in Global Perspective.* Maryknoll, NY: Orbis, 2009.

————. "What Has Contextual Theology to Offer the Church of the Twenty-First Century?" In *Contextual Theology for the Twenty-First Century,* edited by Steven Bevans and Katalina Tahaafe-Williams, 3–17. Cambridge, UK: Clark & Co., 2011.

Bible Committee of Korea. *Annual Report of the Bible Committee of Korea.* Seoul: YMCA, 1906.

Bishop, Isabella Bird. *Korea and Her Neighbors: A Narrative of Travel, with an Account of the Recent Vicissitudes and Present Position of the Country.* New York: Fleming H. Revell, 1987.

————. "Missionary Spirit and Life." *Gospel in All Lands* 21 (1902) 368–72.

"Bits from Korea Reports." *Woman's Missionary Friend* 46.2 (1914) 54.

Blair, William Newton. "The Care of Babies and Children." *The Korean Mission Field* 14.4 (1918) 79–81.

————. "The Forward Movement in Korea." *The Missionary Review of the World* 44 (1921) 528–32.

————. *Gold in Korea.* Topeka, KS: H. M. Ives & Sons, 1957.

Blair, William Newton, and Bruce Hunt. *The Korean Pentecost and the Sufferings Which Followed*. Carlisle, PA: Banner of Truth, 1977.

Blume, Kenneth. *Historical Dictionary of the US Maritime Industry*. Lanham, MD: Scarecrow, 2012.

Board of Foreign Mission, Methodist Episcopal Church. *Annual Report*. New York: Board of Foreign Mission, 1903.

Board of Foreign Missions of the Presbyterian Church in the USA. *The Fifty-Ninth Annual Report*. New York: Presbyterian Building, 1896.

Bosch, David. *Believing in the Future: Toward a Missiology of Western Culture*. Valley Forge, PA: Trinity, 1995.

———. *Transforming Mission: Paradigm Shifts in Theology of Mission*. Maryknoll, NY: Orbis, 1991.

Bowman, John. *Columbia Chronologies of Asian History and Culture*. New York: Columbia University Press, 2000.

Boyd, Nancy. *Emissaries: The Overseas Work of the American YWCA 1895–1970*. New York: Woman's Press, 1986.

British and Foreign Bible Society. *Reports of the Korea Agency for 1913–1938*. Seoul: Bible House, 1939.

Brown, Arthur J. *Korean Conspiracy Case*. Northfield, MA: Northfield, 1912.

———. *The Mastery of the Far East*. New York: Scribner's Sons, 1919.

———. *New Forces in Old China: An Unwelcome but Inevitable Awakening*. New York: Fleming H. Revell, 1904.

———. *One Hundred Years: A History of the Foreign Missionary Work of the Presbyterian Church in the USA*. New York: Fleming H. Revell, 1936.

———. *Report on a Second Visit to China, Japan and Korea 1909 (with a Discussion of Some Problems of Mission Work)*. New York: Board and the Missions of the Presbyterian Church in the USA, 1909.

———. *Report of a Visitation of the Korea Mission of the Presbyterian Board of Foreign Missions*. New York: Board of Foreign Missions, 1902.

Brudnoy, David. "Japan's Experiment in Korea." *Monumenta Nipponica* 25.1/2 (1970) 155–96.

Buckland, Augustus R. *Women in the Mission Field: Pioneers and Martyrs*. New York: Thomas Whittaker, 1895.

Bunker, Annie E. "As I Found the Korean Women." *Korea Mission Field* 11.1 (1915) 7–9.

Burrows, William, et al., eds. *Understanding World Christianity: The Vision and Work of Andrew F. Walls*. Maryknoll, NY: Orbis, 2011.

Buswell, Robert, and Timothy Lee, eds. *Christianity in Korea*. Honolulu: University of Hawaii Press, 2006.

———. *The Zen Monastic Experience: Buddhist Practice in Contemporary Korea*. Princeton: Princeton University Press, 1993.

Butts, Alice. "Report of Workers' Class of Bible Institute, Pyeng Yang." *The Korea Mission Field* 9.1 (1913) 11.

Buzo, Adrian. *The Guerilla Dynasty: Politics and Leadership in North Korea*. New York: IB Tauris, 1999.

Cable, E. M. "The Bible in Korea." *Gospel in All Lands* 23 (1902) 104–5.

———. "The Longing for Education." *Korea Mission Field* 11.8 (1906) 144–45.

Caldwell, Patricia. *The Puritan Conversion Narrative: The Beginning of American Expression*. New York: Cambridge University Press, 1985.

Carnes, Tony, and Fenggang Yang, eds. *Asian American Religions: The Making and Remaking of Borders and Boundaries*. New York: NYU Press, 2004.

Carpenter, Frank. "The Koreans at Home." *Gospel in All Lands* 20 (1889) 434–41.

Carrier, Herve. *Evangelizing the Culture of Modernity*. Maryknoll, NY: Orbis, 1993.

Carson, D. A., ed. *Biblical Interpretation and the Church: The Problem of Contextualization*. Nashville: Thomas Nelson, 1985.

Cha, Paul. "Unequal Partners, Contested Relations: Protestant Missionaries and Korean Christians, 1884–1907." *Journal of Korean Studies* 17.1 (2012) 5–37.

Chaffin, Anna. "A Macedonian Cry." *Methodist Episcopal Church* (1924) 9–11.

———. "Union Methodist Woman's Bible Training School." In *Fifty Years of Light*, edited by the Woman's Foreign Missionaries Society, 17–20. Seoul: YMCA, 1938.

Chai, Alice. "Integrative Feminist Politics in the Republic of Korea." In *Feminist Nationalism*, edited by Lois West, 169–86. New York: Routledge, 1997.

———. "A Picture Bride from Korea: The Life History of a Korean American Woman in Hawaii." *Bridge: An Asian American Perspective* 6 (1978) 37–42.

Chan, Chung-yan J. "Commands from Heaven: Matteo Ricci's Christianity in the Eyes of Ming Confucian Officials." *Missiology* 31.3 (2003) 269–87.

Chan, Simon. *Grassroots Asian Theology: Thinking the Faith from the Ground Up*. Downers Grove, IL: IVP Academic, 2014.

Chan, Wing Tsit, ed. *Chu Hsi and Neo-Confucianism*. Honolulu: University of Hawaii Press, 1986.

———. *A Sourcebook in Chinese Philosophy*. Princeton: Princeton University Press, 1963.

Chang, Paul Yunski. "Carrying the Torch in the Darkest Hours: The Sociopolitical Origins of Minjung Protestant Movement." In *Christianity in Korea*, edited by Robert Buswell and Timothy Lee, 195–220. Honolulu: University of Hawaii Press, 2006.

Cheon, Samuel. "Biblical Interpretation in Korea." In *Ways of Being, Ways of Reading: Asian American Biblical Interpretation*, edited by Mary Foskett and Jeffrey Kuan, 31–44. St. Louis: Chalice, 2006.

Chilcote, Phil, and Laceye C. Warner, eds. *The Study of Evangelism: Exploring a Missional Practice of the Church*. Grand Rapids: Eerdmans, 2008.

Ching, Julia. *The Religious Thought of Chu Hsi*. New York: Oxford University Press, 2000.

Cho, Eunsik. "Christian Mission Toward Reunification of Korea." *Asia Journal of Theology* 14.2 (2000) 371–98.

Cho, Jeung-Ryeul. "Early Literacy Policy and Practice in Korea." In *The Routledge International Handbook of Early Literacy Education*, edited by Natalia Kuchova, et al., 200–209. New York: Routledge, 2017.

Cho, Kwang. "Human Relations as Expressed in Vernacular Catholic Writings of the Late Chosŏn Dynasty." In *Christianity in Korea*, edited by Robert Buswell and Timothy Lee, 29–37. Honolulu: University of Hawaii Press, 2006.

Cho, Yeon-hyun. "More South Koreans, Particularly the Young, Are Leaving Their Religions." *Hankyoreh*, February 13, 2015. http://english.hani.co.kr/arti/english_ edition/e_national/678355.html.

Ch'oe, Yongho. "Christian Background in the Early Life of Kim Il-Song." *Asian Survey* 26.10 (1986) 1082–91.

————. "History of the Korean Church: A Case Study of Christ United Methodist Church." In *Korean Americans: Past, Present, and Future*, edited by Ilpyong Kim, 38–62. Elizabeth, NJ: Hollym, 2004.

————. "Private Academies and the State in Late Choson Korea." In *Culture and the State in Late Choson Korea*, edited by JaHyun Kim Haboush and Martina Deuchler, 15–45. Cambridge: Harvard University Asia Center, 1999.

Ch'oe, Yongho, et al., eds. *Sources of Korean Tradition: From the Sixteen to the Twentieth Centuries*. New York: Columbia University Press, 2000.

Choi, Hee An. *Korean Women and God: Experiencing God in a Multi-Religious Colonial Context*. Maryknoll, NY: Orbis, 2005.

Choi, Hyaeweol. "An American Concubine in Old Korea: Missionary Discourse on Gender, Race, and Modernity." *Frontiers: A Journal of Women Studies* 25.3 (2004) 134–61.

————. *Gender and Mission Encounters in Korea: New Women, Old Ways*. Berkeley, CA: University of California Press, 2009.

————. "In Search of Hidden Histories, Agency and Global Network: A Response to the Articles on Women and Christianity in East Asia." *Journal of World Christianity* 3.1 (2010) 67–76.

————. Women's Literacy and New Womanhood in Late Choson Korea." *The Asian Journal of Women's Studies* 6.1 (2000) 88–115.

Choi, Hyaeweol, and Margaret Jolly, eds. *Divine Domesticities*. Canberra, AU: Australian National University Press, 2014.

Choi, Jae-Keun. *The Origin of the Roman Catholic Church in Korea: An Examination of Popular and Governmental Responses to Catholic Missions in the Late Chosŏn Dynasty*. Norwalk, CA: Hermit Kingdom, 2006.

Choi, Joon Sik. *Shamanism: Fundamental Belief of Korean*. Seoul: Serving People, 2009.

Choi, Kil Sung. *Understanding of Korean Shamanism*. Seoul: Yejeonsa, 1994.

Choi, Yong Joon (John). "Christian Worldview and the Transformation of Korean Society." In *Sola Scriptura in Asia*, edited by Yongbom Lee and Andrew Talbert, 180–200. Eugene, OR: Pickwick, 2018.

Choy, Bong-youn. *Koreans in America*. Chicago: Nelson Hall, 1979.

"Christian Missions and Social Progress." *The Korean Repository* 5.2 (1898) 64–69.

Chu, Sun Ae. *The History of Presbyterian Women in Korea*. Seoul: Dae Han Presbyterian Church Women's Association, 1978.

Chung, Byung Joon. "A Reflection on the Growth and Decline of the Korean Protestant Church." *International Review of Mission* 103.2 (2014) 319–33.

Chung, Chai-sik. "Confucian Tradition and Nationalist Ideology in Korea." In *South Korea's Minjung Movement: the Culture and Politics of Dissidence*, edited by Kenneth Wells, 61–86. Honolulu: University of Hawaii Press, 1995.

Chung, David. *Syncretism: The Religious Context of Christian Beginnings in Korea*, edited by Kang-nam Oh. Albany, NY: SUNY Press, 2001.

Chung, Edward. *The Korean Neo-Confucianism of Yi T'oegye and Yi Yulgok*. Albany: SUNY Press, 1995.

Chung, Henry. *The Case of Korea*. New York: Fleming Revell, 1921.

Clark, Allen D. *A History of the Church in Korea*. Seoul: Christian Literature Society of Korea, 1971.

Clark, Charles A. "Fifty Years of Missions, Principles and Practice." In *The Fiftieth Anniversary Celebration of the Korea Mission of the Presbyterian Church in the USA,* edited by Harry A. Rhodes and Richard H. Baird. Seoul: n.p., 1934.

———. *The Korean Church and the Nevius Methods.* New York: Fleming H. Revell, 1930.

———. *Religions of Old Korea.* New York: Fleming Revell, 1932.

Clark, Donald N. *Christianity in Modern Korea.* Lanham, MD: University Press of America, 1986.

———. *Culture and Customs of Korea.* Westport, CT: Greenwood, 2000.

———. *Living Dangerously in Korea: The Western Experience 1900–1950.* Norwalk, CT: EastBridge, 2003.

———. "Mothers, Daughters, Biblewomen, and Sisters: An Account of 'Women's Work' in the Korea Mission Field." In *Christianity in Korea,* edited by Robert Buswell and Timothy Lee, 167–94. Honolulu: University of Hawaii Press, 2006.

———. "Protestant Christianity and the State: Religious Organizations As Civil Society." In *Korean Society: Civil Society, Democracy and the State,* edited by Charles Armstrong, 171–90. New York: Taylor and Francis, 2007.

"The Closing Exercises of Pai Chai." *The Korean Repository* 4 (1897) 271–74.

Coen, Roscoe C. "Diagnosing Our Mission Schools: The Revelation of a Questionaire [sic]." *Korea Mission Field* 18.6 (1922) 116.

Conrow, Marion L. "The Korea Woman's Conference of the Methodist Episcopal Church." *Korea Mission Field* 19.8 (1923) 170–73.

Conroy, F. Hilary. *The Japanese Expansion into Hawaii, 1868–1898.* San Francisco: R and E Research Associates, 1973.

Cooper, S. Kate. "The Bible Woman." *The Korea Magazine* 1.1 (1917) 6–10.

———. *Evangelism in Korea.* Nashville: Board of Missions, Methodist Episcopal Church South, 1930.

Copplestone, J. Tremayne. *Twentieth-Century Perspectives (The Methodist Episcopal Church, 1896–1939).* Vol. 4 of *History of Methodist Missions.* New York: Board of Global Ministries, United Methodist Church, 1973.

"Country and People of Alaska." *Gospel in All Lands* 8 (1887) 487–92.

Cram, Rosella H. "Song Do Girls' School." *The Korea Methodist* 1.3 (1905) 26.

Davis, George T. B. "Great Movement in Korea." *Herald of Gospel Liberty* 102 (1910) 824.

———. *Korea for Christ.* London: Christian Workers' Depot, 1910.

de Bary, Wm. Theodore. *East Asian Civilizations: A Dialogue in Five Stages.* Cambridge: Harvard University Press, 1988.

———. *The Message of the Mind in Neo-Confucianism.* New York: Columbia University Press, 1989.

———. *Neo-Confucian Orthodoxy and the Learning of the Mind-and-Heart.* New York: Columbia University Press, 1987.

———. *Sources of East Asian Tradition.* Vol. 2. New York: Columbia University Press, 2008.

———. *The Trouble with Confucianism.* Cambridge, MA: Harvard University Press, 1991.

de Bary, Wm. Theodore, et al., eds. *1600 to 2000.* Vol. 2. of *Sources of Japanese Tradition.* New York: Columbia University Press, 2005.

de Bary, Wm. Theodore, and Irene Bloom, eds. *Principle and Practicality: Essays in Neo-Confucianism and Practical Learning*. New York: Columbia University Press, 1979.

de Bary, Wm. Theodore, and John Chaffee, eds. *Neo-Confucian Education: The Formative Stage*. Berkeley: University of California Press, 1989.

Deuchler, Martina. *The Confucian Transformation of Korea: A Study of Society and Ideology*. Cambridge: Harvard University Press, 1992.

Duus, Peter. *The Abacus and the Sword: The Japanese Penetration of Korea, 1895–1910*. Berkeley: University of California, 1998.

Eckert, Carter, et al., *Korea Old and New: A History*. Seoul: Ilchokak, 1990.

Ecumenical Missionary Conference, 1900. Vol. 2. New York: American Tract Society, 1900.

"Editorial." *The Korean Repository* 4 (1897) 271–78.

"Editorial: The Japanese Cloud in Korea." *The Missionary Review of the World* 35 (1912) 858–59.

"Editorial Notes." *Woman's Work* 21.2 (1906) 29–30.

Edmunds, M. J. "Training Native Nurses." *The Korea Mission Field* 2 (1906) 154–55.

Ellis, William T. "Korea: The Unique Mission." *The Missionary Review of the World* 31.2 (1908) 94–98.

Erdman, Walter C. "Bible Classes and Bible Institutes." *Korea Mission Field* 10.12 (1914) 365–69.

Estey, Ethel. "From Northern Korea." *Woman's Missionary Friend* 42 (1910) 58.

"Experience of a Korean Christian Boy." *Gospel in All Lands* 23 (1902) 129.

Dennett, Tyler. *Americans in Eastern Asia*. New York: MacMillan Co., 1922.

Dennis, James. *Christian Missions and Social Progress*. New York: Fleming Revell, 1906.

Fairbank, John K., et al. *East Asia*. Boston: Houghton Mifflin, 1989.

Fairbanks, Charles Warren. "Korea's Redemption." *Epworth Herald*, December 24, 1910. 1677.

Flemming, Leslie A., ed. *Women's Work for Women: Missionaries and Social Change in Asia*. Boulder, CO: Westview, 1989.

Foley, Michael, and Dean Hoge. *Religion and the New Immigrants: How Faith Communities Form Our Newest Citizens*. New York: Oxford University Press, 2007.

Foote, W. R. "Biblewomen." In *Hundred and Seventh Report of the British and Foreign Bible Society*, 339. London: Bible House, 1911.

———. "A Village Prayer-Meeting." In *Hundred and Sixth Report of the British and Foreign Bible Society*, 355. London: Bible House, 1910.

Foreign Affairs Section, ed. *Thriving Chosen*. Keijo [Seoul]: Taisho Shashin Kogeisho, 1935.

Foskett, Mary, and Jeffrey Kuan, eds. *Ways of Being, Ways of Reading: Asian American Biblical Interpretation*. St. Louis: Chalice, 2006.

Fowler-Willing, Jennie, and Margaret Jones. *The Lure of Korea*. Boston: Woman's Foreign Missionary Society, 1910.

Freston, Paul. *Evangelicals and Politics in Asia, Africa and Latin America*. New York: Cambridge University Press, 2001.

Frey, Lulu. "Opportunities in Korea." *Woman's Missionary Friend* 39 (1907) 286.

———. "Report II—Evangelistic Work of First Church, Seoul." In *Fourth Annual Report of the Korea Woman's Missionary Conference of the Methodist Episcopal Church*, 4. Seoul: Methodist, 1902.

"From Korea to Chosen." *Missionary Review of the World* 39 (1916) 84–85.

"The Fruit of Fidelity." *Missionary Review of the World* 35 (1912) 554.

Gale, James S. "Korea." *Church at Home and Abroad* 17 (1895) 230.

―――. *Korea in Transition*. New York: Young People's Missionary Movement, 1909.

―――, trans. *Korean Folk Stories*. New York: E. P. Dutton, 1913.

―――. "The Korean Mind." *Gospel in All Lands* 23 (1902) 110–11.

―――. *Korean Sketches*. New York: Fleming Revell, 1898.

Gallagher, Robert, and Paul Hertig, eds. *Contemporary Mission Theology*. Maryknoll, NY: Orbis, 2017.

Gaustad, Edwin, and Leigh Eric Schmidt. *The Religious History of America*. New York: HarperCollins, 2004.

"Gensan." In *The Fifty-Ninth Annual Report of the Board of Foreign Missions of the Presbyterian Church in the USA*, 161. New York: Presbyterian Board of Missions, 1896.

Gibbs, Eddie. "Church Response to Culture Since 1985." *Missiology* 35.2 (2007) 157–68.

Gifford, Daniel. *Every-Day Life in Korea: A Collection of Studies and Stories*. Seoul: Institute for Korean Christian History, 1995.

Gilbert, Bill. *Ship of Miracles: 14,000 Lives and One Miraculous Voyage*. Chicago: Triumph, 2000.

Gilmore, George W. *Korea From Its Capital*. New York: Presbyterian Board, 1892.

"Giving at Ewha Haktang." *Woman's Missionary Friend* 48.5 (1916) 168.

Goheen, Michael, ed. *Reading the Bible Missionally*. Grand Rapids: Eerdmans, 2016.

Gonzalez, Justo. *Church History: An Essential Guide*. Nashville: Abingdon, 1996.

―――. "Globalization in the Teaching of Church History." *Theological Education* 29.2 (1993) 49–72.

Government-General of Tyosen. *Annual Report on Administration of Tyosen 1937–1938*. Keijo [Seoul]: Government General Office, 1938.

Grayson, James H. "Dynamic Complementarity: Korean Confucianism and Christianity." In *Religion and the Transformation of Capitalism*, edited by Richard Roberts, 76–85. New York: Routledge, 1995.

―――. *Early Buddhism and Christianity in Korea: A Study in the Emplantation of Religion*. Leiden: E. J. Brill, 1985.

―――. "A Quarter-Millennium of Christianity in Korea." In *Christianity in Korea*, edited by Robert Buswell and Timothy Lee, 7–25. Honolulu: University of Hawaii Press, 2006.

―――. "The Shinto Shrine Conflict and Protestant Martyrs in Korea, 1938–1945." *Missiology* 29.3 (2001) 287–305.

―――. "An Undulating Trajectory: The History of Religious Traditions in Korea." *Irish Journal of Asian Studies* 1.1 (2015) 1–9.

Grenz, Stanley J. *Revisioning Evangelical Theology*. Downers Grove, IL: InterVarsity, 1993.

Griffis, William Elliot. *Corea the Hermit Nation*. New York: Scribner's Sons, 1882.

―――. *Korean Fairy Tales*. New York: Thomas Crowell, 1911.

Gruder, Darrell. *Called to Witness: Doing Missional Theology*. Grand Rapids: Eerdmans, 2016.

Guthapfel, Minerva. "How They Come Into the Kingdom." *Woman's Missionary Friend* 38 (1906) 81–84.

Haboush, JaHyun Kim. *The Confucian Kingship in Korea: Yŏngjo and the Politics of Sagacity*. New York: Columbia University Press, 2001.

———. "The Confucianization of Korean Society." In *The East Asian Region: Confucian Heritage and Its Modern Adaptation,* edited by Gilbert Rozman, 84–110. Princeton: Princeton University Press, 1991

———. "Versions and Subversions: Patriarchy and Polygamy in Korean Narratives." In *Women and Confucian Culture in Premodern China, Korea, and Japan,* edited by Dorothy Ko, et al., 279–303. Berkeley, CA: University of California Press, 2003.

Haboush, JaHyun Kim, and Martina Deuchler, eds. *Culture and the State in Late Chŏson Korea.* Cambridge: Harvard Univ. Asia Center, 2002.

Haga, Kai Yin Allison. "Rising to the Occasion: The Role of American Missionaries and Korean Pastors in Resisting Communism throughout the Korean War." In *Religion and the Cold War: A Global Perspective,* edited by Philip Muehlenbeck, 88–112. Nashville: Vanderbilt University Press, 2012.

Hall, Ernest F. "Education in Korea." *The Missionary Review of the World* 31.2 (1908) 103–6.

Hall, Rosetta S. "Dedication of the New Methodist Church in Korea." *Gospel in All Lands* 19 (1898) 185–86.

———. "Kwang Hya Nyo Won, or 'Woman's Dispensary of Extended Grace,' Pyeng Yang Circuit." In *First Annual Meeting of the Woman's Conference of the Methodist Episcopal Church in Korea,* 15. Seoul: Methodist, 1899.

———. "Report IX—Medical Evangelistic Work for Women, Pyong Yang Circuit." In *Third Annual Report of the Korea Woman's Missionary Conference of the Methodist Episcopal Church,* 21–22. Seoul: Methodist, 1901.

———. *With Stethoscope in Asia: Korea.* McLean, VA: MCL Associate, 1978.

Hall, William J. "A Journey in Korea." *Gospel in All Lands* 13 (1892) 538–39.

Hallock, H. G. C. "A Country Church in Korea." *Gospel in All Lands* 23 (1902) 119–20.

Hammon, Annie. "Crooked Trees." *Woman's Missionary Friend* 44.9 (1911) 306–8.

Hammond, Alice. "Report V.—Evangelistic Work—Mead Memorial Church and South Korea District." In *Fourth Annual Report of the Korea Woman's Missionary Conference of the Methodist Episcopal Church,* 14. Seoul: Methodist, 1902.

Han, Gil-soo, Joy Han, and Andrew Kim. "'Serving Two Masters': Protestant Churches in Korea and Money." *International Journal for the Study of the Christian Church* 9.4 (2009) 333–60.

Harlow, Ralph. "Holy Places—Moslem and Christian." *The Missionary Review of the World* 65.11 (1922) 863–66.

Hartley, Benjamin. *Evangelicals at a Crossroads: Revivalism and Social Reform in Boston, 1860–1910.* Durham, NH: University of New Hampshire Press, 2011.

"Hawaii." *Eighty-Seventh Annual Report of the Missionary Society of the Methodist Episcopal Church, For the Year 1905,* 383–87. New York: Missionary Society of the Methodist Episcopal Church, 1906.

Hayes, Louis B. "The Korean Bible Woman and Her Work." *The Korean Mission Field* 31.7 (1935) 151–53.

Haynes, Irene. "Evangelistic Work Pyeng Yang City and West District." In *Korea Woman's Conference of the Methodist Episcopal Church,* 35. Seoul: YMCA, 1929.

Hazzan, Dave. "Christianity and Korea." *Diplomat,* April 7, 2016. https://thediplomat.com/2016/04/christianity-and-korea.

Hefner, Robert W. "Civil Society: Cultural Possibility of a Modern Ideal." *Society* 35.3 (1998) 16–27.

Hendershot, Heather. "God's Angriest Man: Carl McIntire, Cold War Fundamentalism, and Right-Wing Broadcasting." *American Quarterly* 59.2 (2007) 373–96.

Heo, Uk Heo, and Terence Roehrig. *South Korea's Rise: Economic Development, Power, and Foreign Relations.* New York: Cambridge University Press, 2014.

Hertig, Young Lee. "The Korean Immigrant Church and Naked Public Square." In *Realizing the America of Our Hearts: Theological Voices of Asian Americans,* edited by Matsuoka Fumitaka and Eleazar Fernandez, 131–46. St. Louis: Chalice, 2003.

Hiebert, Paul G. *Anthropological Reflections on Missiological Issues.* Grand Rapids: Baker, 1999.

———. "Critical Contextualization." *Missiology* 12.3 (1984) 287–96.

———. "The Flaw of the Excluded Middle." *Missiology* 10.1 (1982) 35–47.

———. *Transforming Worldviews: An Anthropological Understanding of How People Change.* Grand Rapids: Baker, 2008.

Hiebert, Paul G., et al. *Understanding Folk Religion.* Grand Rapids: Baker, 2000.

Hill, Graham. *Global Church: Reshaping Our Conversations, Renewing Our Mission, Revitalizing Our Churches.* Downers Grove, IL: InterVarsity, 2016.

Hillman, Mary R. "In Journeyings Oft." *Woman's Missionary Friend* 42.2 (1910) 39–41.

Ho, Son Young. "The Search for Ethnic Identity in America: Politics of Korean Nationalism." *Korea Journal* 29.8 (1989) 4–18.

Hong, Isop. "Modern Korean Thought." In *Korea, Its Land, People and Culture of All Ages.* Seoul: Hakwon-sa, 1960.

Hong, Seung Min Hong. "Toward Korean Contextualization: An Evangelical Perspective." *International Bulletin of Mission Research* 41.1 (2017) 18–28.

Hong, Young-gi. "Encounter with Modernity: the 'McDonalization' and 'Charismatization' of Korean Mega-Churches." *International Review of Mission* 92.365 (2003) 239–55.

———. "Nominalism in Korean Protestantism." *Transformation* 16.4 (1999) 135–41.

Hulbert, Homer. *History of Korea.* New York: Hilary, 1962.

———. "Japanese and Missionaries in Korea." *The Missionary Review of the World* 31.3 (1908) 205–9.

———. "The Korean Almanac." *Korean Repository* 2 (1895) 67–73.

Hunt, Everett. "The Legacy of John Livingston Nevius." *International Bulletin of Missionary Research* 15.3 (1991) 120–24.

Hunter, Jane. *The Gospel of Gentility: American Women Missionaries in Turn-of-the-Century China.* New Haven: Yale University Press, 1984.

Huntley, Martha. *Caring, Growing, Changing: A History of the Protestant Mission in Korea.* New York: Friendship, 1984.

———. "Presbyterian Women's Work and Right in the Korea Mission." *American Presbyterians* 65.1 (1987) 37–48.

Hurh, Won Moo, and Kwang Chung Kim. *Korean Immigrants in the United States.* Madison, NJ: Fairleigh Dickinson University Press, 1984.

Hwang, Kyung Moon. *A History of Korea: A Episodic Narrative.* New York: Palgrave MacMillan, 2010.

Hyun, Peter. *Man Sei! The Making of a Korean American.* Honolulu: University of Hawaii Press, 1986.

Im, Hyug Baeg. "The Origins of the *Yushin* Regime: Machiavelli Unveiled." In *The Park Chung Hee Era: The Transformation of South Korea,* edited by Byung-kook Kim and Ezra Vogel, 233–64. Cambridge: Harvard University Press, 2011.

Jackson, H. G. "Methods of Arousing Missionary Interest." *Gospel in All Lands* 20 (1899) 306–9.

Jacobs, Donald. "Contextualization in Mission." In *Toward the Twenty-First Century in Christian Mission*, edited by James Phillips and Robert Coote, 235–39. Grand Rapids: Eerdmans, 1993.

Jang, Nancy. "A Personal Witness." *United Methodist Relay* 22.6 (1977) 6.

Jenkins, Philip. *The Next Christendom.* New York: Oxford University Press, 2002.

Jo, Moon H. *Korean Immigrants and the Challenge of Adjustment.* Westport, CT: Greenwood, 1999.

Johnson, Cameron. "When I Went to Church in Korea." *The Missionary Review of the World* 31.3 (1908) 199–202.

Johnson, Todd M. "Christianity in Global Context: Trends and Statistics." *Pew Forum on Religion & Public Life* (2005). https://www.pewresearch.org/wp-content/uploads/sites/7/2005/05/051805-global-christianity.pdf.

———. "Korean Christianity in the Context of Global Christianity." In *Korean Church, God's Mission, Global Christianity*, edited by Wonsuk Ma and Kyo Seong Ahn, 71–84. Oxford: Regnum, 2015.

Jones, George Heber. *The Bible in Korea: The Transformation of a Nation.* New York: American Bible Society, 1916.

———. "Christian Education in Korea." *Gospel in All Lands* 17 (1896) 559–62.

———. *Korea: Land, People, and Customs.* New York: Eaton and Mains, 1907.

———. "A Korean Class Leader Obeying Christ." *Gospel in All Lands* 23 (1902) 128–29.

———. "The Koreans in Hawaii." *Korea Review* 6.11 (1906) 401–6.

———. "Mission Work on the Chemulpo Circuit, Korea." *Gospel in All Lands* 15 (1894) 413–16.

———. "The People on the Chelmulpo Circuit in Korea." *Gospel in All Lands* 15 (1894) 282–84.

Jones, John P. "Devil Possession in India." *Gospel in All Lands* 8 (1887) 395–96.

———. *The Modern Missionary Challenge.* New York: Fleming Revell, 1910.

Jones, Margaret Bengel. "The Korean Bride." *The Korean Repository* 2 (1895) 55.

———. "Report VII. Evangelistic Work West Korea District." In *Fourth Annual Report of the Korea Woman's Missionary Conference of the Methodist Episcopal Church*, 19. Seoul: Methodist, 1902.

Kalton, Michael. *To Become a Sage: The Ten Diagrams on Sage Learning by Yi T'oegye.* New York: Columbia University Press, 1988.

Kane, Danielle, and Jung Mee Park. "The Puzzle of Korean Christianity: Geopolitical Networks and Religious Conversion in Early-Twentieth-Century East Asia." *American Journal of Sociology* 115.2 (2009) 365–404.

Kane, J. Herbert. *A Concise History of the Christian World Mission: A Panoramic View of Missions from Pentecost to the Present.* Grand Rapids: Baker, 1982.

Kang, Hildi. *Under the Black Umbrella: Voices from Colonial Korea.* Ithaca, NY: Cornell University Press, 2001.

Kang, Jae-eun. *The Land of Scholars: Two Thousand Years of Korean Confucianism.* Paramus, NJ: Homa & Sekey, 2005.

Kang, K. Connie. *Home Was the Land of Morning Calm: A Saga of A Korean-American Family.* Reading, MA: Addison-Wesley, 1995.

Kang, Wi Jo. *Christ and Caesar in Modern Korea: A History of Christianity and Politics.* Albany, NY: SUNY Press, 1997.

————. "Church and State Relations in the Japanese Colonial Period." In *Christianity in Korea,* edited by Robert Buswell and Timothy Lee, 97–115. Honolulu: University of Hawaii Press, 2006.

Kendall, Laurel, and Mark Peterson, eds. *Korean Women: A View from the Inner Room.* New Haven, CT: East Rock, 1983.

Kim, Andrew E. "Christianity, Shamanism, and Modernization in South Korea." *Cross Currents* 50.1/2 (2000) 112–19.

————. "Korean Religious Culture and Its Affinity to Christianity: The Rise of Protestant Christianity in South Korea." *Sociology of Religion* 61.2 (2000) 117–33.

————. "*Minjung* Theology in Contemporary Korea: Liberation Theology and a Reconsideration of Secularization Theory." In *The Role and Meaning of Religion for Korean Society,* edited by Song-Chong Lee, 42–58. Basel: MDPI, 2018.

————. "Political Insecurity, Social Chaos, Religious Void and the Rise of Protestantism in Late-Nineteenth-Century Korea." *Social History* 26.3 (2001) 267–81.

Kim, Bernice B. "The Koreans in Hawaii." *Social Science* 9.4 (1934) 409–413.

Kim, Bok-Lim. *The Asian Americans: Changing Patterns, Changing Needs.* Montclair, NJ: Association of Korean Christian Scholars in North America, 1978.

Kim, Byong-suh. "Modernization and the Explosive Growth and Decline of Korean Protestant Religiosity." In *Christianity in Korea,* edited by Robert Buswell and Timothy Lee, 309–329. Honolulu: University of Hawaii Press, 2007.

Kim, Byoung-kook, and Ezra Vogel, eds. *The Park Chung Hee Era: The Transformation of South Korea.* Cambridge: Harvard University Press, 2011.

Kim, Chan-Hie. "Biblical and Theological Basis of Korean American Ministry." Unpublished Paper for National Consultation on Korean American Ministries. October 9–11, 1975.

Kim, Chang Sik. "Korea's First Ordained Protestant Minister." Translated by W. A. Noble. *Korea Mission Field* 18.5 (1922) 99.

Kim, Chong Bum. "Preaching the Apocalypse in Colonial Korea: The Protestant Millennialism of Kil Sŏn-ju." In *Christianity in Korea,* edited by Robert Buswell and Timothy Lee, 149–66. Honolulu: University of Hawaii Press, 2006.

Kim, Chun-gil. *The History of Korea.* Westport, CT: Greenwood, 2005.

Kim, Claire. *Bitter Fruit.* New Haven: Yale University Press, 2000.

Kim, Dae-jung. *Conscience in Action: The Autobiography of Kim Dae-jung.* Translated by Seung-hee Jeon. New York: Palgrave Macmillan, 2019.

Kim, Hae-Jong. *10 Ideas for Evangelism and Church Growth.* Nashville: Discipleship, 1988.

————. "*Miju Haningyohoiwa Haninsahoi* [Korean immigrant church and Korean society in the US]." *Maeil Shinmun,* January 27, 1983.

————. "Multicultural Evangelism." In *Christ for the World: United Methodist Bishops Speak on Evangelism,* edited by James Logan, 96–109. Nashville: Kingswood, 1996.

————. *The Root and Wings.* Seoul: Voice, 1999.

Kim, Han-Kyo. "The Korean Independence Movement in the United States: Syngman Rhee, An Ch'ang-Ho and Park Yong-Man." In *Korean-Americans: Past, Present, and Future,* edited by Ilpyong Kim, 63–100. Elizabeth, NJ: Hollym, 2004.

Kim, Helen. *Grace Sufficient: The Story of Helen Kim by Herself.* Nashville: Upper Room, 1964.

———. "Methodism and the Development of Korean Womanhood." In *Within the Gate*, edited by Charles A. Sauer, 76–83. Seoul: Korea Methodist News Service, 1934.

Kim, Heung Soo. "Is Christianity a Korean Religion? One Hundred Years of Protestant Churches in Korea." *Evangelical Review of Theology* 30.2 (2006) 162–68.

Kim, Hyung-chan. "The History and Role of the Church in the Korean American Community." In *The Korean Diaspora*, edited by Hyung-chan Kim, 47–64. Santa Barbara: ABC-Clio, 1977.

———, ed. *The Korean Diaspora: Historical and Sociological Studies of Korean Immigration and Assimilation in North America*. Santa Barbara: ABC-Clio, 1977.

Kim, Hyung-chan, and Wayne Patterson, eds. *The Koreans in America, 1882–1974*. New York: Oceana, 1974.

Kim, Ilpyong, ed. *Korean-Americans: Past, Present, and Future*. Elizabeth, NJ: Hollym, 2004.

Kim, Ilsoo. *New Urban Immigrants: The Korean Community in New York*. Princeton: Princeton University Press, 1981.

Kim, In Soo. *History of the Christian Church of Korea*. Seoul: Presbyterian Theological University Press, 1998.

Kim, Jung Han. "Christianity and Korean Culture: The Reasons for the Success of Christianity in Korea." *Exchange* 33.2 (2004) 132–52.

Kim, Kirsteen. "Critical Perspectives on Religions—Especially Christianity—in the Development of South Korea Post-1945." In *The Routledge Handbook of Religions and Global Development*, edited by Emma Tomalin, 250–65. New York: Routledge, 2015.

———. "The Significance of Korean World Mission for Mission Studies." In *Korean Church, God's Mission, Global Christianity*, edited by Wonsuk Ma and Kyo Seong Ahn, 48–56. Oxford, UK: Regnum, 2015.

Kim, Kwang Chung, and Shin Kim. "The Ethnic Roles of Korean Immigrant Churches in the United States." In *Korean Americans and Their Religions: Pilgrims and Missionaries from a Different Shore*, edited by Ho-Youn Kwon, et al., 71–94. State College, PA: Penn State University Press, 2001.

Kim, Lulu Chu. "A Bible Woman on the Hai Ju District." In *Victorious Lives of Early Christians in Korea*, edited by Mattie Wilcox Noble, 51. Seoul: Kyujang, 1985.

Kim, Rebecca Y. *God's New Whiz Kids?: Korean American Evangelicals on Campus*. New York: New York University Press, 2006.

———. "Korean Missionaries: Preaching the Gospel to 'All Nations,' Including the United States." In *Religion on the Move! New Dynamics of Religious Expansion in a Globalizing World*, edited by Afe Adogame and Shobana Shankar, 179–202. Boston: Brill, 2013.

———. *The Spirit Moves West: Korean Missionaries in America*. New York: Oxford University Press, 2015.

Kim, Sadie. "The Story of My Life." In *Victorious Lives of Early Christians in Korea*, edited by Noble Mattie Wilcox, 102–4. Seoul: Kyujang, 1985.

Kim, Sebastian, and Kirsteen Kim. *A History of Korean Christianity*. New York: Cambridge University Press, 2015.

Kim, Simon. *Memory and Honor: Cultural and Generational Ministry with Korean American Communities*. Collegeville, MN: Liturgical, 2010.

Kim, Soo Kyung. "A Study of Bible Women's Impact in the Early Korean Church." MA thesis, Hanshin Graduate School of Theology, 2004.

Kim, Wonil. "Minjung Theology's Biblical Hermeneutics: An Examination of Minjung Theology's Appropriation of the Exodus Account." In *Christianity in Korea,* edited by Robert Buswell and Timothy Lee, 221–37. Honolulu: University of Hawaii Press, 2006.

Kim, Yong-jae. "A Re-evaluation of the Mission Policies of Nevius." In *Korea and Christianity,* edited by Chai-shin Yu, 73–86. Fremont, CA: Asian Humanities, 1996.

Kim-Renaud, Young-Key. *The Korean Alphabet: Its History and Structure.* Honolulu: University of Hawaii Press, 1997.

Kitano, Harry Kitano, and Roger Daniels. *Asian Americans: Emerging Minorities.* Englewood Cliffs, NJ: Prentice Hall, 1988.

Kittridge, J. E. "A Traveler's Impressions of Korean Missions." *The Missionary Review of the World* 31.2 (1908) 110–11.

"Korea." In *Twentieth-Third Annual Report of the Woman's Foreign Missionary Society of the Methodist Episcopal Church.* Boston: J. W. Hamilton, 1892.

"Korea—The Evangelizing Zeal of Koreans." *The Missionary Review of the World* 24 (1911) 393–95.

The Korea Magazine 1.1 (1917).

"Korean Mosaics." *Woman's Missionary Friend* 42 (1910) 308–12.

"A Korean's Own Story of Conversion and Persecution." *Woman's Work for Women* 21 (1906) 258.

Koshiro, Yukiko. *Imperial Eclipse: Japan's Strategic Thinking about Continental Asia Before August 1945.* Ithaca, NY: Cornell University Press, 2013.

Koyama, Kosuke Koyama. "Asian Theology." In *Modern Theologians,* edited by David Ford, 217–34. Vol. 2 of *An Introduction to Christian Theology in the Twentieth Century.* Oxford: Basil Blackwell, 1989.

Kwon, Ho-Youn, et al., eds. *Korean Americans and Their Religions.* State College, PA: Penn State Press, 2001.

Kwon, Insook. "Feminists Navigating the Shoals of Nationalism and Collaboration: The Post-Colonial Korean Debate over How to Remember Kim Hwallan." *Frontiers* 27.1 (2006) 39–66.

Kwon, Okyun. *Buddhist and Protestant Korean Immigrants.* El Paso: LFB, 2003.

Launay, Adrien. *Martyrs Francais et Coreens, 1838–1846.* Paris: Tequis, 1925.

Ledyard, Gari. *The Dutch Come to Korea.* Seoul: Royal Asiatic Society, 1971.

———. "Kollumba Kang Wansuk, an Early Catholic Activist and Martyr." In *Christianity in Korea,* edited by Robert Buswell and Timothy Lee, 38–71. Honolulu: University of Hawaii Press, 2006.

Lee, Albert H. "Tens of Thousands of South Korean Christians Rally to Support US Military, Condemn North Korea." *Christian Post,* January 13, 2003. http://www.christianpost.com/news/tens-of-thousands-of-south-korean-christians-rally-to-support-u-s-military-condemn-north-korea.html.

Lee, Bong. *The Unfinished War: Korea.* New York: Algora, 2003.

Lee, Byeong-cheon, ed. *Developmental Dictatorship and the Park Chung-hee Era.* Translated by Eungsoo Kim and Jaehyun Cho. Paramus, NJ: Homa and Sekey, 2006.

Lee, Dae Suk. "An Effective Internet Ministry Strategy for Church Evangelism Through a Case Study of the Sarang Community Church." DMin diss., Liberty Baptist Theological Seminary, 2010.

Lee, Deborah. "Faith Practices for Racial Healing and Reconciliation." In *Realizing the America of Our Hearts: Theological Voices of Asian Americans*, edited by Matsuoka Fumitaka and Eleazar Fernandez, 147–57. St. Louis: Chalice, 2003.

Lee, Duk Joo Lee. *Stories of Early Christian Women in Korea*. Seoul: Hong Seong Sa, 2007.

Lee, Eojin. *Theology of the Open Table*. Eugene, OR: Resource, 2016.

Lee, Jonathan, et al., eds. *Asian American Religious Cultures*. Santa Barbara, CA: ABC-Clio, 2015.

Lee, Jung Young. *Marginality: The Key to Multicultural Theology*. Minneapolis: Fortress, 1995.

Lee, Ki-baik. *A New History of Korea*. Translated by Edward Wagner. Seoul: Ilchokak, 1984.

Lee, Moonjang, "Identifying an Asian Theology: A Methodological Quest." *Asia Journal of Theology* 6.2 (2009) 256–75.

Lee, Peter, ed. *From the Seventeenth Century to the Modern Period*. Vol. 2 of *Sourcebook of Korean Civilization*. New York: Columbia University Press, 1996.

Lee, Sang Hyun. "Pilgrimage and Home in the Wilderness of Marginality." In *Korean Americans and Their Religions: Pilgrims and Missionaries from a Different Shore*, edited by Ho-Youn Kwon, et al., 55–70. State College, PA: Penn State University Press, 2001.

Lee, Sung Sam. *Methodist and Sinhak Dahaksa*. Seoul: Institute of Book Publishers, 1975.

Lee, Timothy. "Beleaguered Success: Korean Evangelicalism in the Last Decade of the Twentieth Century." In *Christianity in Korea*, edited by Robert Buswell and Timothy Lee, 330–50. Honolulu: University of Hawaii Press, 2006.

———. *Born Again: Evangelicalism in Korea*. Honolulu: University of Hawaii Press, 2010.

———. "A Political Factor in the Rise of Protestantism in Korea: Protestantism and the 1919 March First Movement." *Church History* 69.1 (2000) 116–42.

———. "What Should Christians Do About a Shaman-Progenitor? Evangelicals and Ethnics Nationalism in South Korea." *Church History* 78.1 (2009) 66–98.

Lee, Won Gue. *Crisis and Hope of Korean Churches from the Perspective of Sociology of Religion*. Seoul: KMC, 2010.

Lee, Yohan. "An Analysis of the Christian Prayer Mountain Phenomenon in Korea." PhD diss., Fuller Theological Seminary, 1985.

Lee, Younghoon. "The Holy Spirit Movement: Charismatic Tradition in Korea." In *Korean Church, God's Mission, Global Christianity*, edited by Wonsuk Ma and Kyo Seong Ahn, 57–70. Oxford: Regnum, 2015.

Lew, Young Ick, et al. "A Historical Overview of Korean Perceptions of the United States." *Korea Journal* 44.1 (2004) 109–151.

———. *Korean Perceptions of the United States: A History of Their Origins and Formation*. Seoul: Jimoondang, 2006.

Lewis, Ella A. "A Holocaust of Fetishes." *Korea Mission Field* 2 (1906) 134–35.

Lewis, Hannah. *Deaf Liberation Theology*. Burlington, VT: Ashgate, 2007.

Liem, Channing. *The First Korean American—A Forgotten Hero: Philip Jaisohn.* Philadelphia: Philip Jaisohn Memorial Foundation, 1984.

Linden, Peter. "Chocoletto: A Korean War Orphan joins the Marines." *Korean War Children's Memorial,* April 14, 1953 www.koreanchildren.org/docs/MAG-005. htm.

Logan, James, ed. *Christ for the World: United Methodist Bishops Speak on Evangelism.* Nashville: Kingswood, 1996.

Longden, W. C. "Developments and Value of Mission Work in China." *Gospel in All Lands* 21 (1900) 436–38.

Loomis, Henry. "The Bible and Christianity in Japan." *Gospel in All Lands* 19 (1898) 465.

Lugo, Luis, and Brian Grim. "Presidential Election in South Korea Highlights Influence of Christian Community." *Pew Research Center,* December 12, 2007. http://pewforum.org/docs/?DocID=269.

Ma, Wonsuk. "Three Types of Ancestor Veneration in Asia: An Anthropological Analysis." In *Asian Church and God's Mission,* edited by Wonsuk and Julie C. Ma, 163–80. West Caldwell, NJ: MWM, 2003.

Madsen, Richard. "Religious Renaissance and Taiwan's Middle Class." In *Chinese Religiosities,* edited by Mayfair M. Yang, 295–321. Berkeley: University of California Press, 2008.

"The Man and the Call." *Herald of Gospel Liberty* 102 (1910) 259.

"Manchuria District." In *Minutes of the Korea Annual Conference of the Methodist Episcopal Church,* 243–47. Seoul: Methodist, 1930.

Maskell, Florence. "Work in Korea." *Woman's Missionary Friend* 41.9 (1909) 323.

Matsuo, Takayoshi Matsuo. "The Japanese Protestants in Korea, Part Two: The 1st March Movement and the Japanese Protestants." Translated by S. Takiguchi. *Modern Asian Studies* 13.4 (1979) 581–615.

Matsuoka, Fumitaka, and Eleazar Fernandez, eds. *Realizing the America of Our Hearts: Theological Voices of Asian Americans.* St. Louis: Chalice, 1982.

McEllhenney, John, ed. *United Methodism in America.* Nashville: Abingdon, 1992.

McInturff, Eugenia. "Something About Japanese Idolatry." *Heathen Woman's Friend* 20.4 (1888) 93–94.

"Methodist Missions in Korea." *The Missionary Review of the World* 32 (1909) 140–44.

Miller, Lulu A. "Chelmulpo District." *Korea Woman's Conference of the Methodist Episcopal Church,* 9–10. Seoul: Chang Moon Christian, 1926.

———. "Over Charcoal Fire." *Woman's Missionary Friend* 41.5 (1909) 173.

Millett, Alan. "The Korean People: Missing in Action in the Misunderstood War." In *The Korean War in World History,* edited by William Stueck, 13–60. Lexington, KY: University Press of Kentucky, 2004.

———. *The War for Korea, 1945–1950.* Lawrence, KS: University Press of Kansas, 2005.

Min, Anselm K. "The Division and Reunification of a Nation: Theological Reflections on the Destiny of the Korean People." In *Christianity in Korea,* edited by Robert Buswell and Timothy Lee, 258–82. Honolulu: University of Hawaii Press, 2006.

———, ed. *Korean Religions in Relation: Buddhism, Confucianism, Christianity.* Albany, NY: SUNY Press, 2016

Min, Pyong Gap. "Introduction." In *Religions in Asian America,* edited by Pyong Gap Min and Jung Ha Kim, 1–14. Landham, MD: Altamira, 2002.

———. "Koreans: An 'Institutionally Complete Community' in New York." In *New Immigrants in New York*, edited by Nancy Foner, 173–200. New York: Columbia University Press, 2001.

———. "Religion and the Maintenance of Ethnicity among Immigrants." In *Immigrant Faiths: Transforming Religious Life in America*, edited by Karen Leonard, 99–122. Lanham, MD: Altamira, 2005.

———. "The Structures and Social Functions of Korean Immigrant Churches in the United States." *International Migration Review* 26.4 (1992) 1370–94.

Min, Pyong Gap, and Dae Young Kim. "Intergenerational Transmission of Religion and Culture: Korean Protestants in the US." *Sociology of Religion* 66.3 (2005) 263–82.

Min, Pyong Gap, and Jung Ha Kim, eds. *Religions in Asian America*. Landham, MD: Altamira, 2002.

Miner, George. "Reforms and Christian Education in China." *Gospel in All Lands* 20 (1899) 495–99.

Ministry in Context: The Third Mandate Programme of the Theological Education Fund. Kent, UK: New Life, 1972.

Minutes of the Korea Annual Conference of the Methodist Episcopal Church (23–29 June 1926). Seoul: Methodist, 1926.

Minutes of the Korea Annual Conference of the Methodist Episcopal Church (15–21 June 1927). Seoul: Methodist, 1927.

"Mission Notes." *Gospel in All Lands* 23 (1902) 571–72.

"Missionaries and Politics in Korea." *The Missionary Review of the World* 33 (1910) 220.

Moffett, Alice F. "Like Heaven." *Korea Mission Field* 2.4 (1906) 68–69.

Moffett, Samuel A. "Letter from Dr. Samuel A. Moffett." *The Missionary Review of the World* 31.2 (1908) 102–3.

———. "Native Church in Work of Evangelization (A Paper Read at the World Missionary Conference)." *Union Seminary Magazine* 22.3 (1911) 234–35.

Moffett, Samuel H. *The Christians of Korea*. New York: Friendship, 1962.

———. *A History of Christianity in Asia*. Vol. 2. Maryknoll, NY: Orbis, 2005.

———. "Suh Sang-Yun." In *Biographical Dictionary of Christian Missions*, edited by Gerald Anderson, 651. Grand Rapids: Eerdmans, 1999.

Moll, Rob. "Missions Incredible: South Korea Sends More Missionaries Than Any Country But the US and It Won't be Long Before It's Number One." *Christianity Today* (2006) 28–34.

Montgomery, Helen B. *The Bible and Missions*. West Medford, MA: Central Committee on the United Study of Foreign Missions, 1920.

Moose, J. R. "Mrs. Kim and Mrs. Change." *The Korean Mission Field* 1 (1905) 88–89.

Moreau, Scott. "Contextualization That Is Comprehensive." *Missiology* 34.3 (2006) 325–35.

Morris, Louise O. "Report of Wonju and Kungnung Districts" In *Korea Woman's Conference of the Methodist Episcopal Church*, 76. Seoul: Methodist, 1926.

Mudge, James. "The Debt of Progress to Christianity." *Gospel in All Lands* 19 (1899) 337–41.

Muller, John. *Wearing the Cross in Korea*. Redlands, CA: Muller, 1954.

Mullins, Mark R. "The Empire Strikes Back: Korean Pentecostal Mission to Japan." In *Charismatic Christianity as a Global Culture*, edited by Karla Poewe, 87–102. Columbia, SC: University of South Carolina Press, 1994.

Murabayashi, Duk Hee Lee. *Korean Ministerial Appointments to Hawaii Methodist Churches.* Honolulu: Center for Korean Studies, University of Hawaii Press, 2001.

Myers, Mamie D. *Woman's Missionary Council.* Nashville: Methodist Episcopal Church, South, 1914.

Myers, Ramon, and Mark Pettie, eds. *The Japanese Colonial Empire, 1895–1945.* Princeton: Princeton University Press, 1984.

Neill, Stephen. *A History of Christian Missions.* New York: Penguin, 1975.

Nessan, Craig. *The Vitality of Liberation Theology.* Eugene, OR: Pickwick, 2012.

"New China's Plea for Education." *Woman's Missionary Friend* 43.4 (1911) 135.

Newbigin, Lesslie. *Truth and Authority in Modernity.* Valley Forge, PA: Trinity International, 1996.

———. *A Word in Season: Perspectives on Christian World Missions.* Grand Rapids: Eerdmans, 1994.

Nevius, Helen. "The Nevius Plan." *The Missionary Review of the World* 22.8 (1899) 612–15.

Ninde, W. X., and A.B. Leonard. "Report on Cuba and Porto [sic] Rico." *Gospel in All Lands* 20 (1899) 173–79.

Noble, Mattie Wilcox, ed. *Victorious Lives of Early Christians in Korea.* Seoul: Kyujang, 1985.

Noble, W. Arthur. "Christianity in Korea Today." *The Missionary Review of the World* 44 (1921) 685–90.

———, trans. "The Early Life and Conversion of Tyeng Skil." *Gospel in All Lands* 22 (1901) 208–9.

———. "Korean Decadence." *Korea Mission Field* 11.9 (1906) 176.

Nora, Mary. "Bible Women." In *Hundred and Fifth Report of the British and Foreign Bible Society 1909,* 360. London: Bible House, 1909.

"Notes and Comments." *Korean Repository* 3 (1896) 260.

Oak, Sung-Deuk. "Chinese Protestant Literature and Early Korean Protestantism." In *Christianity in Korea,* edited by Robert Buswell and Timothy Lee, 72–96. Honolulu: University of Hawaii Press, 2006.

———. "Healing and Exorcism: Christian Encounters with Shamanism in Early Modern Korea." *Asian Ethnology* 69.1 (2010) 95–128.

———. *The Making of Korean Christianity.* Waco: Baylor University Press, 2013.

———. "Major Protestant Revivals in Korea, 1903–35." *Studies in World Christianity* 18.3 (2012) 269–90.

———, ed. *Sources of Korean Christianity.* Seoul: Hanguk Gidokkyo Yeonguso, 2004.

"Objects of Intercession." *Woman's Missionary Friend* 48.6 (1916) 209.

Oh, Kang-nam. "The Christian-Buddhist Encounter in Korea." In *Christianity in Korea,* edited by Robert Buswell and Timothy Lee, 371–86. Honolulu: University of Hawaii Press, 2006.

———. "Sagehood and Metanoia: The Confucian-Christian Encounter in Korea." *Journal of the American Academy of Religion* 61.2 (1993) 303–320.

Okihiro, Gary. *Cane Fires: The Anti-Japanese Movement in Hawaii, 1865–1945.* Philadelphia: Temple University Press, 1992.

Ott, Craig, and Harold A. Netland, eds. *Globalizing Theology: Belief and Practice inan Era of World Christianity.* Grand Rapids: Baker, 2006.

———. *The Mission of the Church.* Grand Rapids: Baker, 2016.

"Our Young People." *Woman's Missionary Friend* 44 (1912) 364–65.

"Our Young People." *Woman's Missionary Friend* 45.5 (1913) 170.

"Outlook in Asia." *Gospel in All Lands* 20 (1899) 234.

Pae, Hye K. "The Korean Writing System, *Hangul*, and Word Processing." In *Writing Systems, Reading Processes, and Cross-Linguistic Influence*, edited by Hye K. Pae, 335–52. Amsterdam: John Benjamins Co., 2018.

Page, Melvin, ed. *Colonialism: An International, Social, Cultural, and Political Encyclopedia*. Santa Barbara: ABC-Clio, 2003.

Pai, Margaret K. *The Dreams of Two Yi Min*. Honolulu: University of Hawaii Press, 1988.

Paik, L. George. *The History of Protestant Missions in Korea, 1832–1910*. Seoul: Yonsei University Press, 1929.

Paine, Josephine O. "Ewha Haktang-Seoul." In *Report of Eighth Annual Session of the Korea Woman's Conference of the Methodist Episcopal Church Held at Seoul, June 8–14, 1906*, 5. Seoul: Methodist, 1906.

Pak, Ung Kyu. *Millennialism in the Korean Protestant Church*. New York: Peter Lang, 2005.

Palais, James. *Confucian Statecraft and Korean Institutions: Yu Hyŏngwŏn and the Late Chosŏn Dynasty*. Seattle, WA: University of Washington Press, 1996.

Pang, Morris. "A Korean Immigrant." *Social Forces in Hawaii* 12 (1949) 19–24.

Park, Andrew Sung. "Minjung Theology: A Korean Contextual Theology." *Indian Journal of Theology* 33 (1984) 1–11.

Park, Chung-shin. *Protestantism and Politics in Korea*. Seattle, WA: University of Washington Press, 2003.

Park, Hyunmo. "King Jeongjo's Political Role in the Conflicts between Confucianism and Catholicism in Eighteenth-Century Korea." *The Review of Korean Studies* 7.4 (2004) 205–228.

Park, In-sook, and Lee-Jay Cho. "Confucianism and the Korean Family." *Journal of Comparative Family Studies* 26 (1995) 117–34.

Park, Joon-sik. "Hospitality as Context for Evangelism." *Missiology* 30.3 (2002) 385–95.

———. "Korean Protestant Christianity: A Missiological Reflection." *International Bulletin of Missionary Research* 36.2 (2012) 59–64.

Park, Keun-Won. "Evangelism and Mission in Korea in Ecumenical Perspective." In *From East to West: Essays in Honor of Donald G. Bloesch*, edited by Daniel Adams, 93–106. Lanham, MD: University Press of America, 1997.

Park, Kyeyoung. *The Korean American Dream: Immigrants & Small Business in New York City*. Ithaca, NY: Cornell University Press, 1997.

Park, Timothy. "The Missionary Movement of the Korean Church: A Non-Western Church Mission Model." In *Korean Church, God's Mission, Global Christianity*, edited by Wonsuk Ma and Kyo Seong Ahn, 19–31. Oxford, UK: Regnum, 2015.

Paton, Frank H. L. "A Picture of Korean Christianity." *The Missionary Review of the World* 35 (1912) 615.

Patterson, Wayne. *The Ilse: First Generation of Korean Immigrants in Hawaii, 1903–1973*. Honolulu: University of Hawaii Press, 2000.

———. *The Korean Frontier in America: Immigration to Hawaii, 1896–1910*. Honolulu: University of Hawaii Press, 1988.

Pattillo-McCoy, Mary. "Church Culture as a Strategy of Action in the Black Community." *American Sociological Review* 63 (1998) 767–84.

Paul, Samuel. *The Ubuntu God: Deconstructing a South African Narrative of Oppression*. Eugene, OR: Pickwick, 2009.

Pelley, Patricia. "Colonial Benedictions: Worldly Catholics and Secular Priests in French Indochina." In *Imperialism: Historical and Literary Investigations, 1500–1900*, edited by Balachandra Rajan and Elizabeth Sauer, 163–76. New York: Palgrave MacMillan, 2004.

Peters, Victor W. "What Korean Young People are Thinking." *Korea Mission Field* 28 (1932) 93.

Phan, Peter C. *Being Religious Interreligiously: Asian Perspectives on Interfaith Dialogue*. Maryknoll, NY: Orbis, 2004.

———, ed. *Christianities in Asia*. Malden, MA: Wiley-Blackwell, 2011.

———. "The Dragon and the Eagle: Toward a Vietnamese American Theology." In *Realizing the America of Our Hearts: Theological Voices of Asian Americans*, edited by Matsuoka Fumitaka and Eleazar Fernandez, 158–79. St. Louis: Chalice, 2003.

———. "World Christianity and Christian Mission: Are They Compatible? Insight from the Asian Churches." *International Bulletin of Missionary Research* 32.4 (2008) 193–200.

Phan, Peter C., and Jung Young Lee, eds. *Journeys at the Margin: Toward an Autobiographical Theology in American-Asian Perspective*. Collegeville, MN: Liturgical, 1999.

Pierce, Nellie. "Report IV—Bible Woman's Training School, Evangelistic Work, Mead Memorial Church and South District." In *Minutes of the Korea Annual Conference of the Methodist Episcopal Church*, 10–11. Seoul: Methodist, 1902.

Pierson, Anna. "Korea—The Land of Opportunity—Invest Now, Big Returns!" *The Missionary Review of the World* 24 (1911) 260–74.

Pobee, John. "Political Theology in the African Context." *Africa Theological Journal* 11 (1982) 68–75.

Pollard, Robert T. "American Relations with Korea, 1882–1895." *The Chinese Social and Political Science* 16 (1932) 425–71.

Pratt, Keith, and Richard Rutt. *Korea: A Historical and Cultural Dictionary*. New York: Routledge, 1999.

Preston, J. Fairman. "The Extension Sunday School." *Korea Mission Field* 15.6 (1919) 111–13.

"Profiles of Two Ethnic Minority Churches." *United Methodist Relay* 21.9 (1976) 10.

Pruitt, Keith, et al. *Korea: A Historical and Cultural Dictionary*. New York: Routledge, 1999.

"Pyeng Yang East District." In *Korea Woman's Conference of the Methodist Episcopal Church*, 41. Seoul: Methodist, 1926.

Raboteau, Albert. *Slave Religion*. New York: Oxford University Press, 1978.

Reid, John, et al. *Modern, Postmodern, and Christian*. Carberry, Scotland: Handsel, 1996.

"Reports." In *Minutes of the Korea Annual Conference of the Methodist Episcopal Church, April 21–27, 1915*, 31–55. Seoul: Methodist, 1935.

"Reports of the District Superintendents: Haiju District." In *Minutes of the Korea Annual Conference of the Methodist Episcopal Church, June 15–21, 1927*, 318–19. Seoul: Methodist, 1927.

"Rev. F.H.L. Paton." *Argus*, September 29, 1938. 13.

Reynolds, W. D. "The Contribution of the Bible Societies to the Christianization of Korea." *Korea Mission Field* 12.5 (1916) 126–28.

Rhodes, Harry, ed. *History of the Korea Mission: Presbyterian Church in the USA.* 2 vols. New York: UPC USA, 1964.

Rhodes, Harry, and Richard Baird, eds. *The Fiftieth Anniversary Celebration of the Korea Mission of the Presbyterian Church in the USA.* Seoul: n.p., 1934.

Robert, Dana. *American Women in Mission: A Social History of Their Thought and Practice.* Macon, GA: Mercer University Press, 1996.

———. *Christian Mission.* Malden, MA: Wiley-Blackwell, 2009.

———, ed. *Converting Colonialism: Visions and Realities in Mission History, 1706–1914.* Grand Rapids: Eerdmans, 2008.

Robinson, Michael. *Korea's Twentieth-Century Odyssey.* Honolulu: University of Hawaii Press, 2007.

Robinson, W. T. "Some Experiences of a Missionary in South America." *Gospel in All Lands* 20 (1899) 272–73.

Ross, John. *History of Corea.* London: Elliot Stock, 1891.

Rothweiler, Louisa. "Korea." In *First Annual Meeting of the Woman's Conference of the Methodist Episcopal Church in Korea, Seoul, May 13–19, 1899,* 36–37. Seoul: Methodist, 1899.

Ruiz, Lester Edwin. "The Stranger in Our Midst: Diaspora, Ethics, Transformation." In *Realizing the America of Our Hearts: Theological Voices of Asian Americans,* edited by Matsuoka Fumitaka and Eleazar Fernandez, 217–41. St. Louis: Chalice, 2003.

Ryu, Dae Young. "The Origin and Characteristics of Evangelical Protestantism in Korea at the Turn of the Twentieth Century." *Church History* 77.2 (2008) 371–98.

———. "Understanding Early American Missionaries in Korea (1884–1910): Capitalist Middle-Class Values and the Weber Thesis." *Archives de Sciences Sociales des Religions* 113 (2001) 93–117.

Ryu, Jai P. "Koreans in America: A Demographic Analysis." In *The Korean Diaspora,* edited by Hyung-chan Kim, 205–228. Santa Barbara: ABC-Clio, 1977.

Sanneh, Lamin. *Disciples of All Nations: Pillars of World Christianity.* New York: Oxford University Press, 2007.

———. *Translating the Message: The Missionary Impact on Culture.* Maryknoll, NY: Orbis, 1989.

———. *Whose Religion is Christianity? The Gospel Beyond the West.* Grand Rapids: Eerdmans, 2003.

Sano, Roy. *From Every Nation Without Number: Racial and Ethnic Diversity in United Methodism.* Nashville: Abingdon, 1982.

Scharpff, Hanna. "The Conqueror." *Woman's Missionary Friend* 54 (1922) 401.

Schoppa, R. Keith. *The Columbia Guide to Modern Chinese History.* New York: Columbia University Press, 2000.

Scidmore, George. "Korea's Religious Situation Unique." *Epworth Herald,* December 24, 1910. 1676.

Scranton, Mary F. "Day Schools and Bible." *Korea Mission Field* 2 (1907) 53.

———. "Korea." In *The Hundred and Third Report of the British and Foreign Bible Society 1907,* 394–95. London: Bible House, 1907.

———. "Korea." In *Nineteenth Annual Report of the Woman's Foreign Missionary Society of the Methodist Episcopal Church for the Year 1888,* 47. Boston: J. W. Hamilton, 1888.

———. "Mead Memorial Church and Kyung-keui Do." In *Korea Woman's Conference of the Methodist Episcopal Church*, 26–27. Seoul: Methodist, 1906.

———. "Missionary Work among Women." *The Korean Repository* 5.9 (1898) 313–18.

———. "Sang Dong and Southren [*sic*] Districts." In *Korea Woman's Conference of the Methodist Episcopal Church*, 10–11. Seoul: Methodist, 1907.

———. "Widower Churches." *Woman's Missionary Friend* 41.5 (1909) 167.

Scranton, W. B. "Extracts From Reports at Annual Meeting." *Gospel in All Lands* 23 (1902) 132.

"Self-Sacrifice among Koreans." *The Missionary Review of the World* 35 (1912) 554.

"The Seoul Declaration—Toward an Evangelical Theology for the Third World." *Missiology* 10.4 (1982) 490–94.

"Seoul Station." In *The Eighty-third Annual Report of the Board of Foreign Missions of the Presbyterian Church in the USA*, 193. New York: Presbyterian, 1920.

Seth, Michael. *Education Fever: Society, Politics, and the Pursuit of Schooling in South Korea*. Honolulu: University of Hawaii Press, 2002.

Sharp, C. E. "Under Persecution." *Korea Mission Field* 2.7 (1906) 69.

Shearer, Roy E. *Wildfire: Church Growth in Korea*. Grand Rapids: Eerdmans, 1966.

Shenk, Wilbert, ed. *Enlarging the Story: Perspectives on Writing World Christian History*. Maryknoll, NY: Orbis, 2002.

———. "Mission in Global Perspective." *Mission Focus* 13 (2005) 82–91.

———. "Missionary Encounter with Culture." *International Bulletin of Missionary Research* 15.3 (1991) 104–9.

———. "The Missionary Encounter with Culture Since the Seventeenth Century." In *Appropriate Christianity*, edited by Charles H. Kraft, 38–45. Pasadena, CA: William Carey, 2005.

———. "Recasting Theology of Mission: Impulses from the Non-Western World." *International Bulletin of Missionary Research* (2001) 98–107.

———. *Revisioning Evangelical Theology*. Downers Grove, IL: InterVarsity, 1993.

———. "Rufus Anderson and Henry Venn: A Special Relationship?" *International Bulletin of Missionary Research* 5.4 (1981) 168–72.

———. "Toward a Global Church History." *International Bulletin of Missionary Research* 20.2 (1996) 50–57.

Shin, Gi-wook. *Ethnic Nationalism in Korea*. Stanford: Stanford University Press, 2006.

Sloan, Douglas. *Faith and Knowledge: Mainline Protestantism and American Higher Education*. Louisville: Westminister John Knox, 1994.

Slote, Walter H., and George De Vos, eds. *Confucianism and the Family*. Albany, NY: SUNY Press, 1998.

Smith, Brenda A. "The Story of Paik Salome's Conversion." *Korea Mission Field* 18.2 (1922) 38.

Smith, Mitzi J. "Minjung, the Black Masses, and the Global Imperative: A Womanist Reading of Luke's Soteriological Hermeneutical Circle." In *I Found God in Me: A Womanist Biblical Hermeneutics Reader*, edited by Mitzi Smith, 203–222. Eugene, OR: Cascade, 2015.

Snow, Jennifer. *Protestant Missionaries, Asian Immigrants, and Ideologies of Race in America, 1850–1924*. New York: Routledge, 2007.

Son, Angella. "Crisis of Church Decline in and Revitalization of Korean Churches." *Pastoral Psychology* 67.5 (2018) 569–77.

Song, Young I., and Ailee Moon, eds. *Korean American Women: From Tradition to Modern Feminism*. Westport, CT: Greenwood, 1998.

"South Korean Church Frets as Baptisms Decline, Flocks Grey." *The Union of Catholic Asian News*, April 19, 2018. http://www.ucanews.com/news/south-korean-church-frets-as-baptisms-decline-flocks-grey/82092.

Speer, Robert. "An, the Blind Korean Preacher." *Gospel in All Lands* 23 (1902) 116–17.

———. *Missionary Principles and Practices: A Discussion of Christian Missions, and Some Criticisms upon Them*. New York: Fleming Revell, 1902.

———. *Report on the Mission in Korea of the Presbyterian Board of Foreign Missions*. New York: Board of the Foreign Missions of the Presbyterian Church USA, 1897.

Starr, Florence. "Korea Through a Visitor's Eye." *Woman's Missionary Friend* 44 (1912) 268–71.

"Statistical Summary." In *Minutes of the Korea Annual Conference of the Methodist Episcopal Church, June 15-21, 1927*, 351. Seoul: Methodist, 1927.

Stewart, L. H. "Our Home Missions." *Gospel in All Lands* 20 (1899) 134–35.

"Stirring Letters from Korea." *The Missionary Review of the World* 35.7 (1912) 505–512.

Strawn, Lee Ellen. "Korean Bible Women's Success: Using the 'Anbang' Network and the Religious Authority of the Mudang." *Journal of Korean Religions* 3.1 (2012) 117–49.

———. "Protestant Bible Education for Women: First Steps in Professional Education for Modern Korean Women." *Journal of Korean Religions* 4.1 (2013) 99–121.

Suh, David Kwang-sun. *The Korean Minjung in Christ*. Hong Kong: Christian Conference of Commission on Theological Concerns, 1991.

Suh, Sharon. *Being Buddhist in a Christian World: Gender and Community in a Korean American Temple*. Seattle: University of Washington Press, 2004.

Sunquist, Scott W. *The Unexpected Christian Century: The Reversal and Transformation of Global Christianity, 1900-2000*. Grand Rapids: Baker, 2015.

Swallen, W. L. "Native Bible Women." *The Korean Mission Field* 6.5 (1910) 119.

———. *Sunday School Lessons on the Book of Exodus*. Seoul: Religious Tract Society, 1907.

Switzer, M. "Bible Classes for Women in the Taiku District." *The Korean Mission Field* 15.7 (1919) 150–52.

Taber, Charles. *The World is Too Much With Us: 'Culture' in Modern Protestant Missions*. Macon, GA: Mercer University Press, 1991.

Taft, William Howard. "The Outposts of Civilization." *Epworth Herald*, April 30, 1910. 547–48.

Tai, Hung-chao, ed. *Confucianism and Economic Development: An Oriental Alternative?* Washington, DC: Washington Institute, 1989.

Takaki, Ronald. *From the Land of the Morning Calm: The Korean in America*. New York: Chelsea, 1994.

———. *Pau Hana: Plantation Life and Labor in Hawaii, 1835-1920*. Honolulu: University of Hawaii Press, 1983.

"Tenth Classes." *Woman's Missionary Friend* 41.9 (1909) 318–19.

Tiénou, Tite. "Christian Theology in an Era of World Christianity." In *Globalizing Theology*, edited by Craig Ott and Harold Netland, 37–51. Grand Rapids: Baker, 2006.

Tiénou, Tite, and Paul Hiebert. "Missional Theology." *Missiology* 34.2 (2006) 219–38.

Tipton, Elise. *Society and the State in Interwar Japan*. New York: Routledge, 1997.

"Today's Religious Situation in Korea." In *Encyclopedia of Global Religion,* edited by Mark Juergensmeyer and Wade Clark Roof, 674–75. Washington, DC: Sage, 2012.

Tseng, Timothy. "Beyond Orientalism and Assimilation: the Asian American as Historical Subject." In *Realizing the America of Our Hearts: Theological Voices of Asian Americans,* edited by Matsuoka Fumitaka and Eleazar Fernandez, 55–72. St Louis: Chalice, 2003.

Tucker, Ruth. *From Jerusalem to Irian Jaya: A Biographical History of Christian Missions.* Grand Rapids: Zondervan, 2004.

Underwood, Horace G. *The Call of Korea.* New York: Fleming Revell, 1908.

———. "The Growth of the Church in Korea." *The Missionary Review of the World* 31.2 (1908) 99–101.

———. "Principles of Self-Support in Korea." *Korea Mission Field* 4.6 (1908) 91–94.

Underwood, Lillias H. *Fifteen Years Among the Top-Knots.* New York: American Tract Society, 1904.

———. "Korea and the Gospel." *The Missionary Review of the World* 24 (1911) 695–97.

"Union Bible Class Work in the Seoul, Korea, 1914." *Korea Mission Field* 11.1 (1915) 26.

"Unnecessary Anxiety." *The Korean Repository* 4 (1897) 274–75.

Van Gelder, Craig, and Dwight Zcheile. *The Missional Church in Perspective.* Grand Rapids: Baker, 2011.

Vaughan, John N. "1.6 Million People Now Attend 100 of America's Largest Churches Each Weekend." *ChristianNewsWire,* September 7, 2016. http://www.christiannewswire.com/news/9714778392.html.

Vogel, Ezra. *The Four Little Dragons: The Spread of Industrialization in East Asia.* Cambridge: Harvard University Press, 1991.

Wadman, John W. "Educational Work among Koreans." In *Reports of Public Instruction, December 31, 1910–December 1912.* Honolulu: Department of Public Instruction, 1912.

Wallace, J. H. "Personal Work in Mexico City." *Woman's Missionary Friend* 44.1 (1912) 19.

Walls, Andrew. *The Cross-Cultural Process in Christian History.* Maryknoll, NY: Orbis, 2002.

———. "Eusebius Tries Again." In *Enlarging the Story: Perspectives on Writing World Christian History,* edited by Wilbert Shenk, 1–21. Maryknoll, NY: Orbis, 2002.

———. "The Mission of the Church Today in the Light of Global History." *Word and World* 20.1 (2000) 17–21.

———. *The Missionary Movement in Christian History: Studies in the Transmission of Faith.* Maryknoll, NY: Orbis, 1997.

Wasson, Alfred W. *Church Growth in Korea.* Concord, NH: Rumford, 1934.

Welbon, A. G. "A Yang Ban Lady." *The Korean Mission Field* 11.1 (1915) 6.

"The 'WFMS' in the Lead." *Woman's Missionary Friend* 49 (1917) 286–87.

"What is the Religion of Korea?" *The Church at Home and Abroad* 12 (1892) 135–40.

"What One Christian Endured." *Missionary Review of the World* 35 (1912) 703.

Whiteman, Darrell L. "Anthropology and Mission: The Incarnational Connection." *Missiology* 31.4 (2013) 398–415.

———. "Contextualization: The Theory, the Gap, the Challenge." *International Bulletin of Missionary Research* 21.1 (1997) 2–7.

Wiest, Jean-Paul. "Guébriant, Jean-Baptiste Budes de." In *Biographical Dictionary of Christian Missions*, edited by Gerald Anderson, 268. Grand Rapids: Eerdmans, 1998.

Wittenborn, Allen John, ed. *Further Reflections on Things at Hand: A Reader*. Lanham, MD: University Press of America, 1991.

Woman's Foreign Missionary Society, ed. *Fifty Years of Light*. Prepared by the Missionaries of the Woman's Foreign Missionary Society of the Methodist Episcopal Church in Commemoration of the Completion of Fifty Years of Work in Korea. Seoul: n.p., 1938.

Woman's Missionary Council. *Fourth Annual Report*. Nashville: Methodist Episcopal Church, South, 1914.

Wong, J. Y. *Deadly Dreams: Opium, Imperialism, and the Arrow War (1856–1860) in China*. New York: Cambridge University Press, 1998.

"Words of Remembrance." *Woman's Missionary Friend* 42.1 (1910) 11–13.

Yang, Mayfair, ed. *Chinese Religiosities: Afflictions of Modernity and State Formation*. Berkeley: University of California Press, 2008.

Yang, Migang. "Chogi Chundo Buin Eui Sinang Kwa Hwaldong [The Faith and Activities of Early Bible Women]." *Hanguk Gidokkyo Wa Yeoksa* [Korean Christianity and History] 2 (1992) 91–109.

Yao, Xinzhong. *Wisdom in Early Confucian and Israelite Traditions*. New York: Routledge, 2016.

Yeh, Allen. *Polycentric Missiology: From Everyone to Everywhere*. Downers Grove, IL: InterVarsity Academic, 2016.

Yi, Kwang-soo. "Defects of the Korean Church Today." Translated by Chiho Yun. *Korea Mission Field* 14.12 (1918) 253–56.

Yi, Mahn-yol. "Korean Protestants and the Reunification Movement." In *Christianity in Korea*, edited by Robert Buswell and Timothy Lee, 238–57. Honolulu: University of Hawaii Press, 2006.

Yim, Hyunsu. "Sadly, Churches in South Korea Are Seeing Decline; Survey Reveals Public Views Protestants as 'Selfish, Materialistic.'" *Korea BizWire*, January 1, 2018. http://blackchristiannews.com/2018/01/sadly-churches-in-south-korea-are-seeing-decline-survey-reveals-public-views-protestants-as-selfish-materialistic.

Yim, Louise. *My Forty Year Fight for Korea*. Seoul: Chungang University Press, 1951.

Yoo, David. "Nurturing Religious Nationalism: Korean Americans in Hawaii." In *Practicing Protestants*, edited by Laurie Maffly-Kipp, et al., 100–117. Baltimore: Johns Hopkins University Press, 2006.

Yoo, David, and Ruth Chung, eds. *Religion and Spirituality in Korean America*. Urbana, IL: University of Illinois Press, 2008.

Yoo, Theodore Jun. *The Politics of Gender in Colonial Korea: Education, Labor, and Health, 1910–1945*. Berkeley, CA: University of California Press, 2008.

Yoo, William. *American Missionaries, Korean Protestants, and the Changing Shape of World Christianity, 1884–1965*. New York: Routledge, 2016.

Yoon, Hong-key, ed. *P'ungsu: A Study of Geomancy in Korea*. Albany, NY: SUNY Press, 2017.

Yoon, In-Jin. *On My Own: Korean Businesses and Race Relations in America*. Chicago: University of Chicago Press, 1997.

Yoon, Inshil Choe. "Martyrdom and Social Activism: The Korean Practice of Catholicism." In *Religions of Korea in Practice*, edited by Robert Buswell, 355–375. Princeton: Princeton University Press, 2007.

Yoon, Jung Ran. *History of the Korean Christian Women's Movement 1910–1945*. Seoul: Institute of the History of Christianity in Korea, 2003.

Yu, Chai-Shin, ed. *Korea and Christianity*. Berkeley: Korean Scholar, 1996.

Yu, K. Kale. "American Missionaries and the Korean Independence Movement in the Early Twentieth Century." *International Journal of Korean Studies* 15.2 (2011) 171–87.

———. "Hawaiian Connectionalism: Methodist missionaries, Hawaii Mission and Korean Ethnic Churches." *Methodist History* 50.1 (2011) 3–15.

———. "Korea's Confucian Culture of Learning as Gateway to Christianity: Protestant Missions in Late Nineteenth and Early Twentieth Centuries." *Studies in World Christianity* 22.1 (2016) 37–56.

———. "'Noxious Weed': Persecution in the Development of Korean Christianity." *International Review of Mission* 106.2 (2017) 400–422.

———. "'The Women, the Mothers Mould the Nations': The Christian Home, Korean Women, and WFMS Missionaries." *Methodist History* 55.2 (2017) 47–60.

Yum, K. S. "Book Review: The Korean Church and the Nevius Method." *Korean Student Bulletin* 9.2 (1931) 5.

Yun, Chunbyeong. *Hanguk Gamnikyo Kyohoe Sungchangsa* [History of the Growth of the Korean Methodist Church]. Seoul: Methodist, 1997.

Yun, Yo-jun. "Early History of Korean Immigration to America." In *The Korean Diaspora*, edited by Hyung-chan Kim, 33–46. Santa Barbara: ABC-Clio, 1977.

Yung, Hwa. *Mangoes or Bananas? The Quest for an Authentic Asian Christian Theology*. Maryknoll, NY: Orbis, 2014.

Zaimov, Stoyan. "Joel Osteen's Lakewood Church Ranked America's Largest Megachurch With 52,000 Weekly Attendance." *The Christian Post*, September 8, 2016. https://www.christianpost.com/news/joel-osteens-lakewood-church-ranked-americas-largest-megachurch-with-52k-in-attendance-169279.

Index

·

Made in the USA
Middletown, DE
16 November 2020

24248115R00186